DISTURBINGLY AWFUL MAD

ALSO AVAILABLE FROM MAD BOOKS

Insanely Awesome MAD

Epic MAD

Amazingly Stupid MAD

Extremely Moronic MAD

Totally Useless MAD

Spy vs. Spy Omnibus

MAD About Super Heroes Vol. 2

Spy vs. Spy: The Top Secret Files!

AVAILABLE DIGITALLY WITH THE MAD iPAD APP
(DOWNLOAD APP AT iTUNES)

Do Confidential — The Secret Files of America's First Dog

MAD About Obama: Yes We Can't!

PLUS

Inside MAD — The "Usual Gang of Idiots" Pick Their All-Time Favorite MAD Spoofs (And Tell Why!) (Time Home Entertainment — Available Fall 2013)

MAD's Greatest Artists: Dave Berg (Running Press — Available Fall 2013)

Totally MAD — 60 Years of Humor, Satire, Stupidity and Stupidity (Time Home Entertainment)

Planet Tad (HarperCollins)

MAD's Greatest Artists: Sergio Aragonés (Running Press)

MAD's Greatest Artists: Mort Drucker (Running Press)

The MAD Fold-In Collection 1964-2010 (Chronicle Books)

Spy vs. Spy 2: The Joke and Dagger Files (Watson-Guptill Publications)

MAD About *Star Wars* (Ballantine Books – Del Rey)

MAD Archives Volumes 1, 2, 3 & 4 (DC Comics)

DISTURBINGLY AWFUL MAD

BY
"THE USUAL GANG OF IDIOTS"

MAD
NEW YORK
BOOKS™

MAD BOOKS

William Gaines FOUNDER

John Ficarra VP & EXECUTIVE EDITOR

Charlie Kadau, Joe Raiola SENIOR EDITORS

Dave Croatto EDITOR

Jacob Lambert ASSOCIATE EDITOR

Sam Viviano ART DIRECTOR

Ryan Flanders ASSOCIATE ART DIRECTOR

Doug Thomson ASSISTANT ART DIRECTOR

Lana Limón PRODUCTION ARTIST

CONTRIBUTING WRITERS AND ARTISTS:
"The Usual Gang of Idiots"

ADMINISTRATION

Diane Nelson PRESIDENT

Dan DiDio and Jim Lee CO-PUBLISHERS

Geoff Johns CHIEF CREATIVE OFFICER

John Rood EXECUTIVE VP – SALES, MARKETING AND BUSINESS DEVELOPMENT

Amy Genkins SENIOR VP – BUSINESS AND LEGAL AFFAIRS

Nairi Gardiner SENIOR VP – FINANCE

Jeff Boison VP – PUBLISHING PLANNING

John Cunningham VP – MARKETING

Terri Cunningham VP – EDITORIAL ADMINISTRATION

Anne DePies VP – STRATEGY PLANNING AND REPORTING

Amit Desai SENIOR VP – FRANCHISE MANAGEMENT

Alison Gill SENIOR VP – MANUFACTURING AND OPERATIONS

Bob Harras SENIOR VP – EDITOR-IN-CHIEF, DC COMICS

Jason James VP – INTERACTIVE MARKETING

Hank Kanalz SENIOR VP – VERTIGO & INTEGRATED PUBLISHING

Jay Kogan VP – BUSINESS AND LEGAL AFFAIRS, PUBLISHING

Jack Mahan VP – BUSINESS AFFAIRS, TALENT

Nick Napolitano VP – MANUFACTURING ADMINISTRATION

Rich Palermo VP – BUSINESS AFFAIRS, MEDIA

Sue Pohja VP – BOOK SALES

Courtney Simmons SENIOR VP – PUBLICITY

Bob Wayne SENIOR VP – SALES

Compilation and new material © 2013 by E.C. Publications, Inc. All Rights Reserved.

MAD, Boy's Head Design, and all related indicia are trademarks of E.C. Publications, Inc.

Published by MAD Books. An imprint of E.C. Publications, Inc., 1700 Broadway, New York, NY 10019. A Warner Bros. Entertainment Company.

CARTOON NETWORK and the logo TM & © Cartoon Network.

Printed by RR Donnelley, Salem, VA, USA. 7/5/2013. First Printing. ISBN: 978-1-4012-4190-2

SUSTAINABLE FORESTRY INITIATIVE
Certified Chain of Custody
At Least 20% Certified Forest Content
www.sfiprogram.org
SFI-01042
APPLIES TO TEXT STOCK ONLY

Though Alfred E. Neuman wasn't the first to say "a fool and his money are soon parted," here's your chance to prove the old adage right — subscribe to MAD! Simply call 1-800-4-MADMAG and mention code AWFMDIA. Operators are standing by (the water cooler).

CONTENTS

"Drawn Out Dramas" Throughout By Sergio Aragonés

JOHN CALDWELL'S

OUTRAGEOUSLY STUPID CELL PHONE FEATURES AND ACCESSORIES

Not so long ago, having a cell phone was an amazing, mind-blowing convenience! It was revolutionary...for about a month. Then it got boring — which is why they added cameras, mp3 players, ringtones, text messaging, web browsers and all other kinds of features. And that's great, but now that they're all out of good ideas, we can only look forward to...

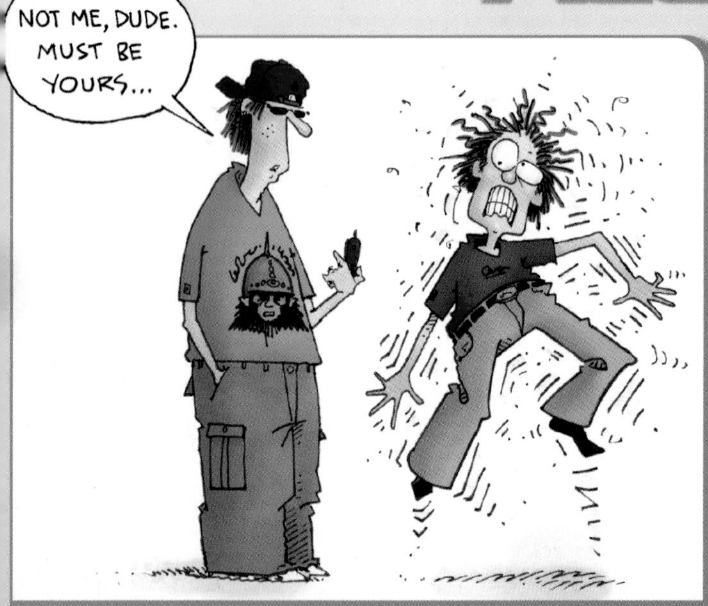
NOT ME, DUDE. MUST BE YOURS...

Jackhammer Ring Mode

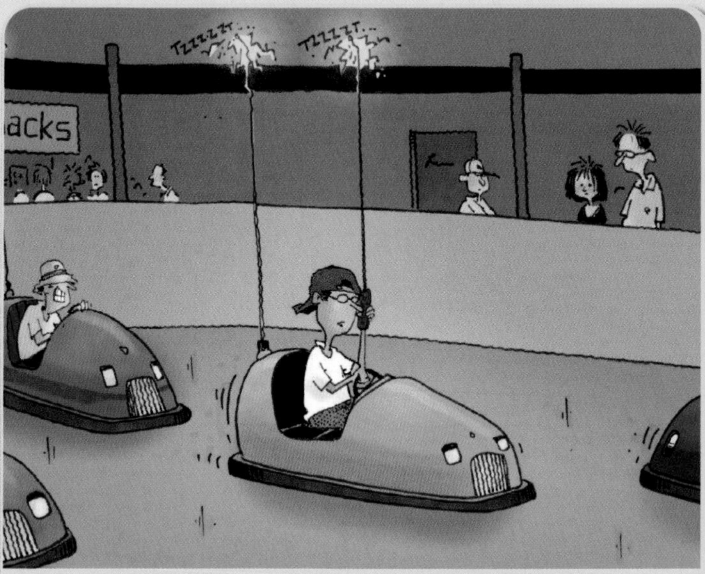

Universal Bumper Car Adaptor

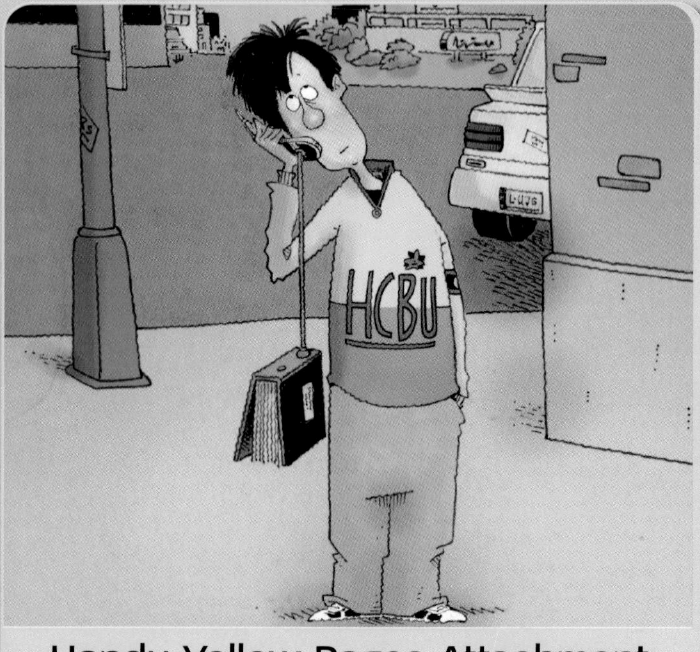
HCBU

Handy Yellow Pages Attachment

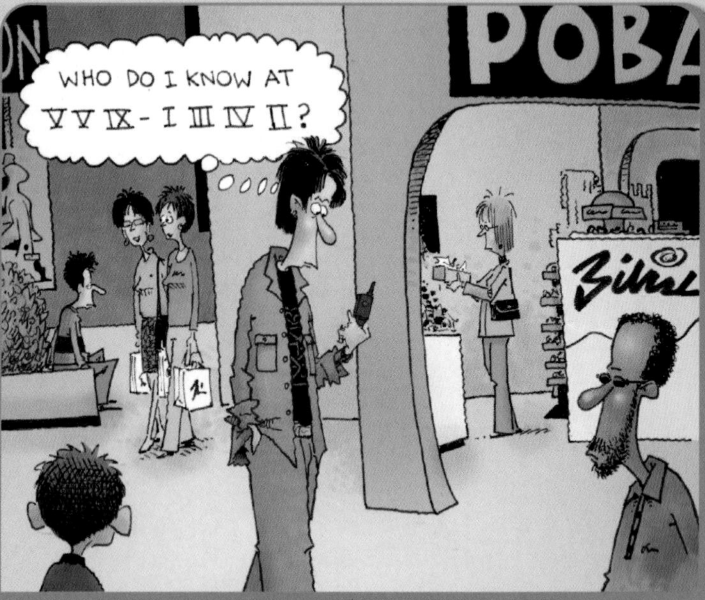
WHO DO I KNOW AT
V V IX - I III IV II?
POBA

Optional Roman Numeral Caller ID

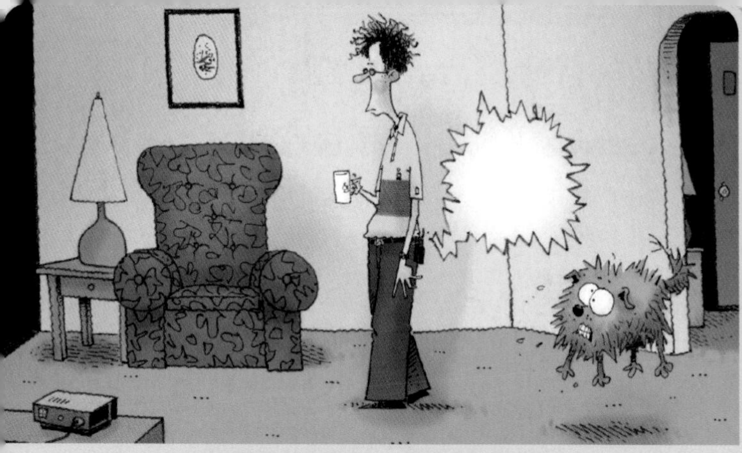

Dogs-Only Ringtone

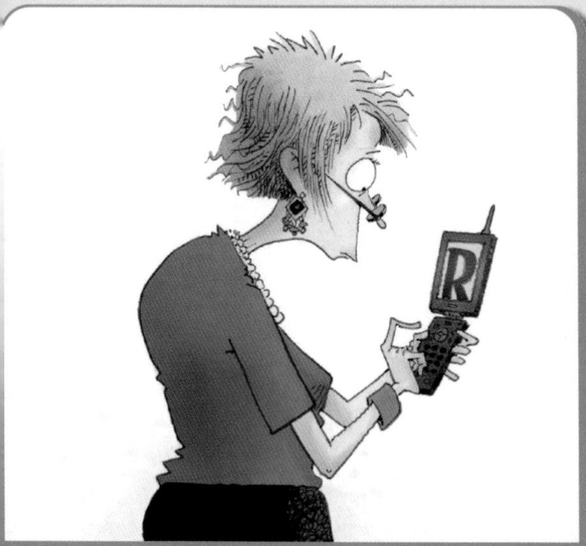

R

Really, Really Large Print Text Messaging

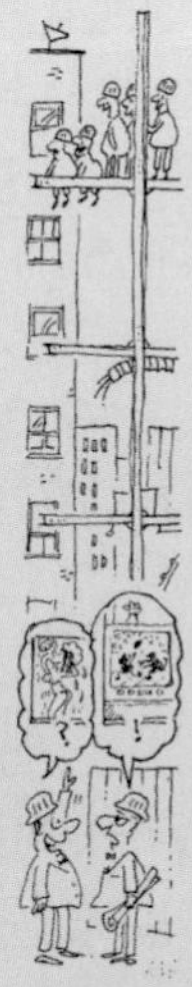

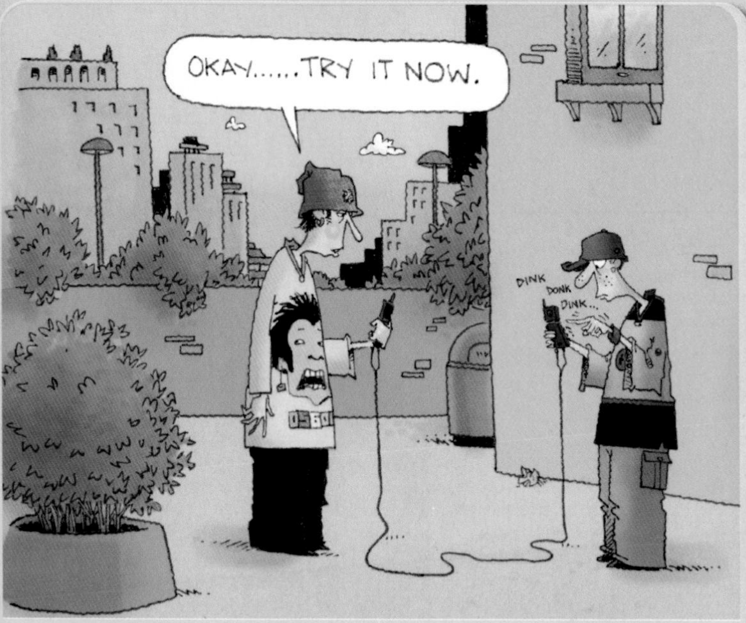

OKAY......TRY IT NOW.
DINK DONK DINK...

12-Ft. Dead Battery Jumper Cables

What if **Alexander Graham Bell** had invented the **cell phone?**

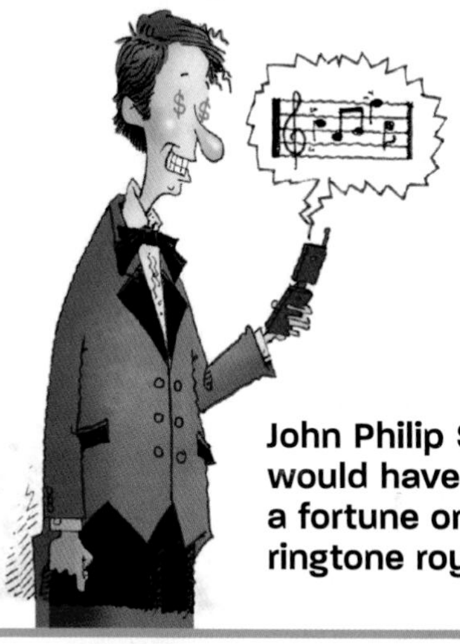

John Philip Sousa would have made a fortune on ringtone royalties.

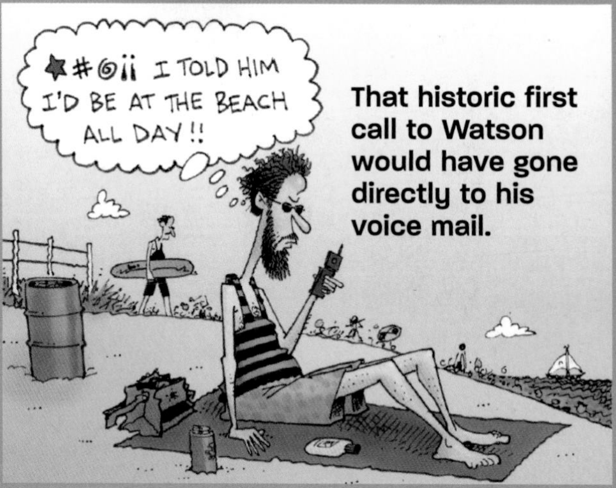

★#@¡¡ I TOLD HIM I'D BE AT THE BEACH ALL DAY!!

That historic first call to Watson would have gone directly to his voice mail.

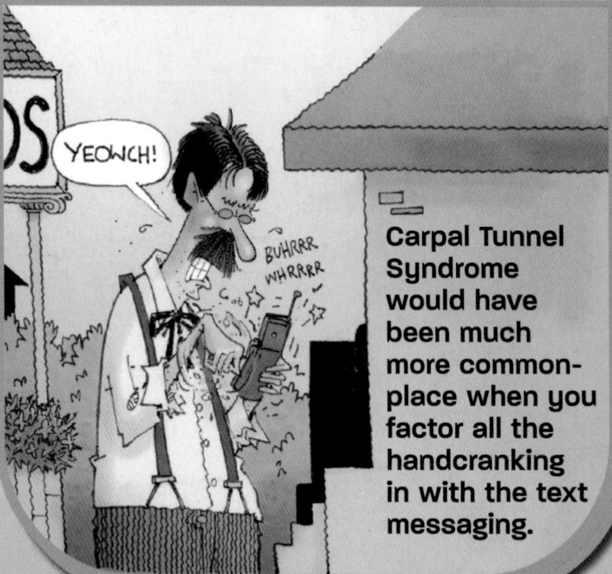

YEOWCH!
BUHRRR WHRRRR

Carpal Tunnel Syndrome would have been much more common-place when you factor all the handcranking in with the text messaging.

WRITER AND ARTIST: JOHN CALDWELL
COLORIST: CARL PETERSON

JEDI KNIGHTMARE DEPT.

There is unrest in the movie theaters. Several thousand multiplexes, under the leadership of George Lucas, are foisting more stiff acting, droid-like dialogue and convoluted plotlines upon a weary and disgusted public. This unfortunate development has made it difficult for the extremely limited number of remaining fans to maintain interest in...

STAR BORES

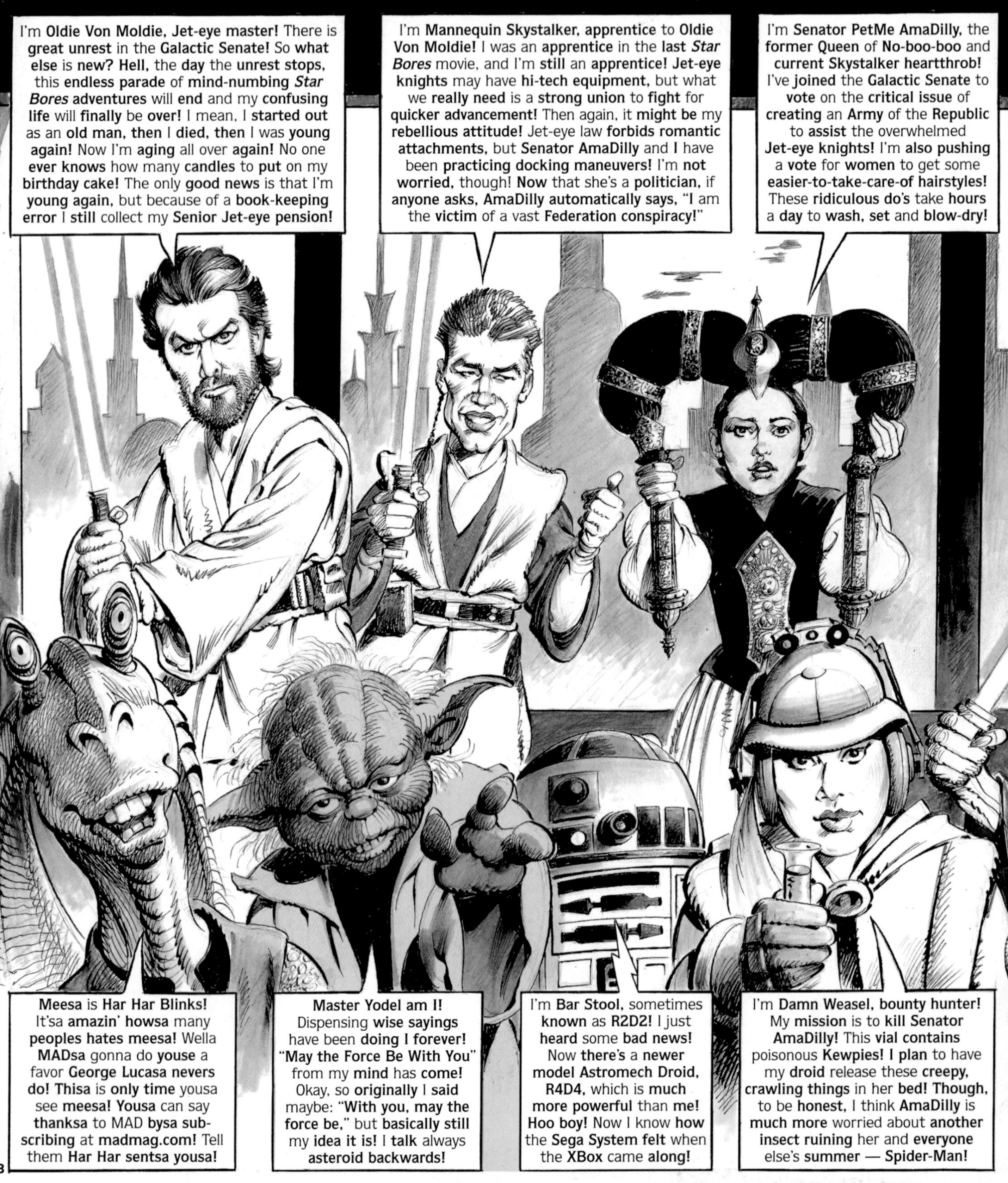

I'm Oldie Von Moldie, Jet-eye master! There is great unrest in the Galactic Senate! So what else is new? Hell, the day the unrest stops, this endless parade of mind-numbing Star Bores adventures will end and my confusing life will finally be over! I mean, I started out as an old man, then I died, then I was young again! Now I'm aging all over again! No one ever knows how many candles to put on my birthday cake! The only good news is that I'm young again, but because of a book-keeping error I still collect my Senior Jet-eye pension!
I'm Mannequin Skystalker, apprentice to Oldie Von Moldie! I was an apprentice in the last Star Bores movie, and I'm still an apprentice! Jet-eye knights may have hi-tech equipment, but what we really need is a strong union to fight for quicker advancement! Then again, it might be my rebellious attitude! Jet-eye law forbids romantic attachments, but Senator AmaDilly and I have been practicing docking maneuvers! I'm not worried, though! Now that she's a politician, if anyone asks, AmaDilly automatically says, "I am the victim of a vast Federation conspiracy!"
I'm Senator PetMe AmaDilly, the former Queen of No-boo-boo and current Skystalker heartthrob! I've joined the Galactic Senate to vote on the critical issue of creating an Army of the Republic to assist the overwhelmed Jet-eye knights! I'm also pushing a vote for women to get some easier-to-take-care-of hairstyles! These ridiculous do's take hours a day to wash, set and blow-dry!
Meesa is Har Har Blinks! It'sa amazin' howsa many peoples hates meesa! Wella MADsa gonna do youse a favor George Lucasa nevers do! Thisa is only time yousa see meesa! Yousa can say thanksa to MAD bysa sub-scribing at madmag.com! Tell them Har Har sentsa yousa!
Master Yodel am I! Dispensing wise sayings have been doing I forever! "May the Force Be With You" from my mind has come! Okay, so originally I said maybe: "With you, may the force be," but basically still my idea it is! I talk always asteroid backwards!
I'm Bar Stool, sometimes known as R2D2! I just heard some bad news! Now there's a newer model Astromech Droid, R4D4, which is much more powerful than me! Hoo boy! Now I know how the Sega System felt when the XBox came along!
I'm Damn Weasel, bounty hunter! My mission is to kill Senator AmaDilly! This vial contains poisonous Kewpies! I plan to have my droid release these creepy, crawling things in her bed! Though, to be honest, I think AmaDilly is much more worried about another insect ruining her and everyone else's summer — Spider-Man!

EPIC LOAD II
ATTACK OF THE CLOWNS

ARTIST: MORT DRUCKER WRITER: DICK DEBARTOLO

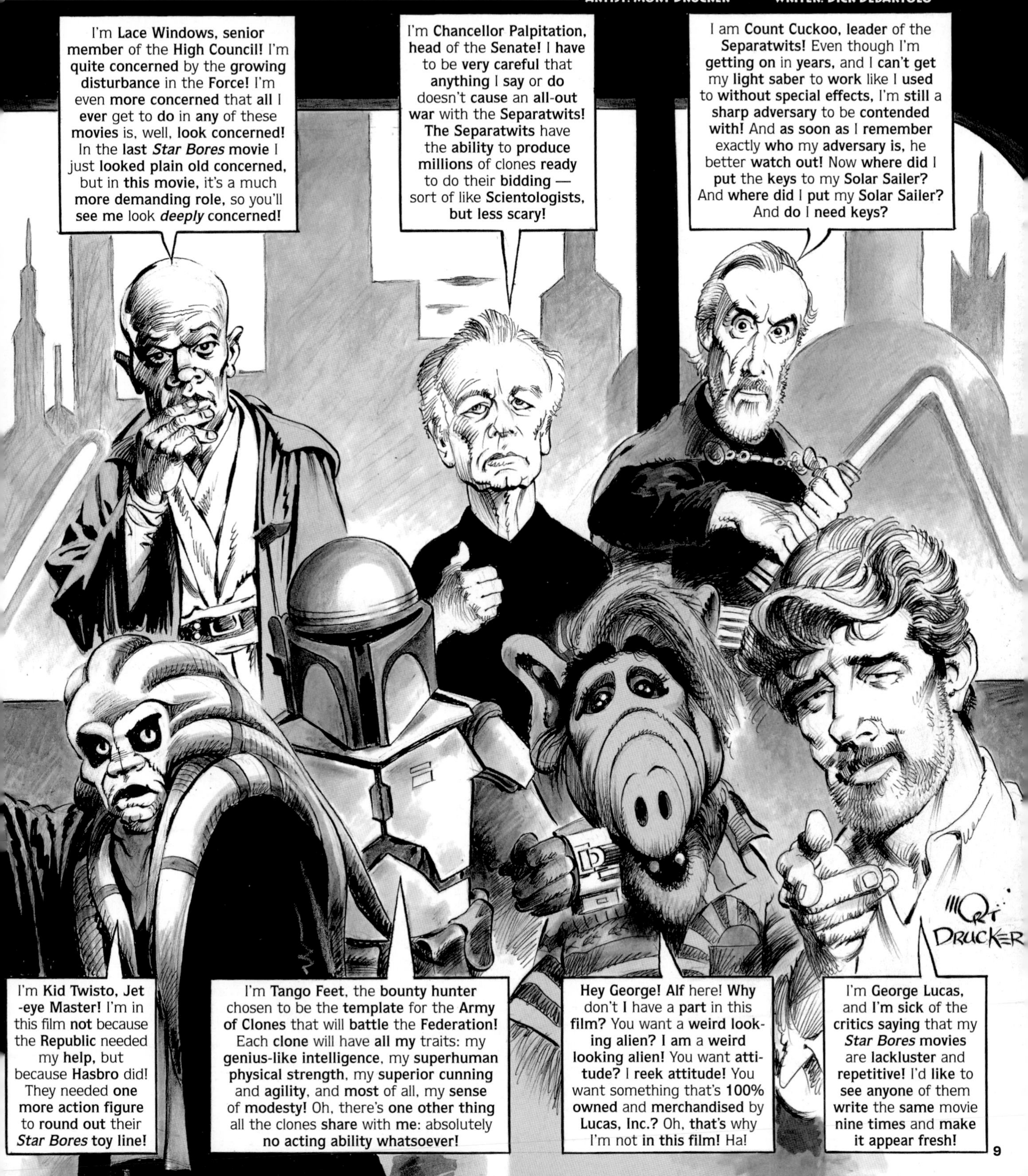

I'm Lace Windows, senior member of the High Council! I'm quite concerned by the growing disturbance in the Force! I'm even more concerned that all I ever get to do in any of these movies is, well, look concerned! In the last Star Bores movie I just looked plain old concerned, but in this movie, it's a much more demanding role, so you'll see me look deeply concerned!
I'm Chancellor Palpitation, head of the Senate! I have to be very careful that anything I say or do doesn't cause an all-out war with the Separatwits! The Separatwits have the ability to produce millions of clones ready to do their bidding — sort of like Scientologists, but less scary!
I am Count Cuckoo, leader of the Separatwits! Even though I'm getting on in years, and I can't get my light saber to work like I used to without special effects, I'm still a sharp adversary to be contended with! And as soon as I remember exactly who my adversary is, he better watch out! Now where did I put the keys to my Solar Sailer? And where did I put my Solar Sailer? And do I need keys?
MORT DRUCKER
I'm Kid Twisto, Jet-eye Master! I'm in this film not because the Republic needed my help, but because Hasbro did! They needed one more action figure to round out their Star Bores toy line!
I'm Tango Feet, the bounty hunter chosen to be the template for the Army of Clones that will battle the Federation! Each clone will have all my traits: my genius-like intelligence, my superhuman physical strength, my superior cunning and agility, and most of all, my sense of modesty! Oh, there's one other thing all the clones share with me: absolutely no acting ability whatsoever!
Hey George! Alf here! Why don't I have a part in this film? You want a weird looking alien? I am a weird looking alien! You want attitude? I reek attitude! You want something that's 100% owned and merchandised by Lucas, Inc.? Oh, that's why I'm not in this film! Ha!
I'm George Lucas, and I'm sick of the critics saying that my Star Bores movies are lackluster and repetitive! I'd like to see anyone of them write the same movie nine times and make it appear fresh!

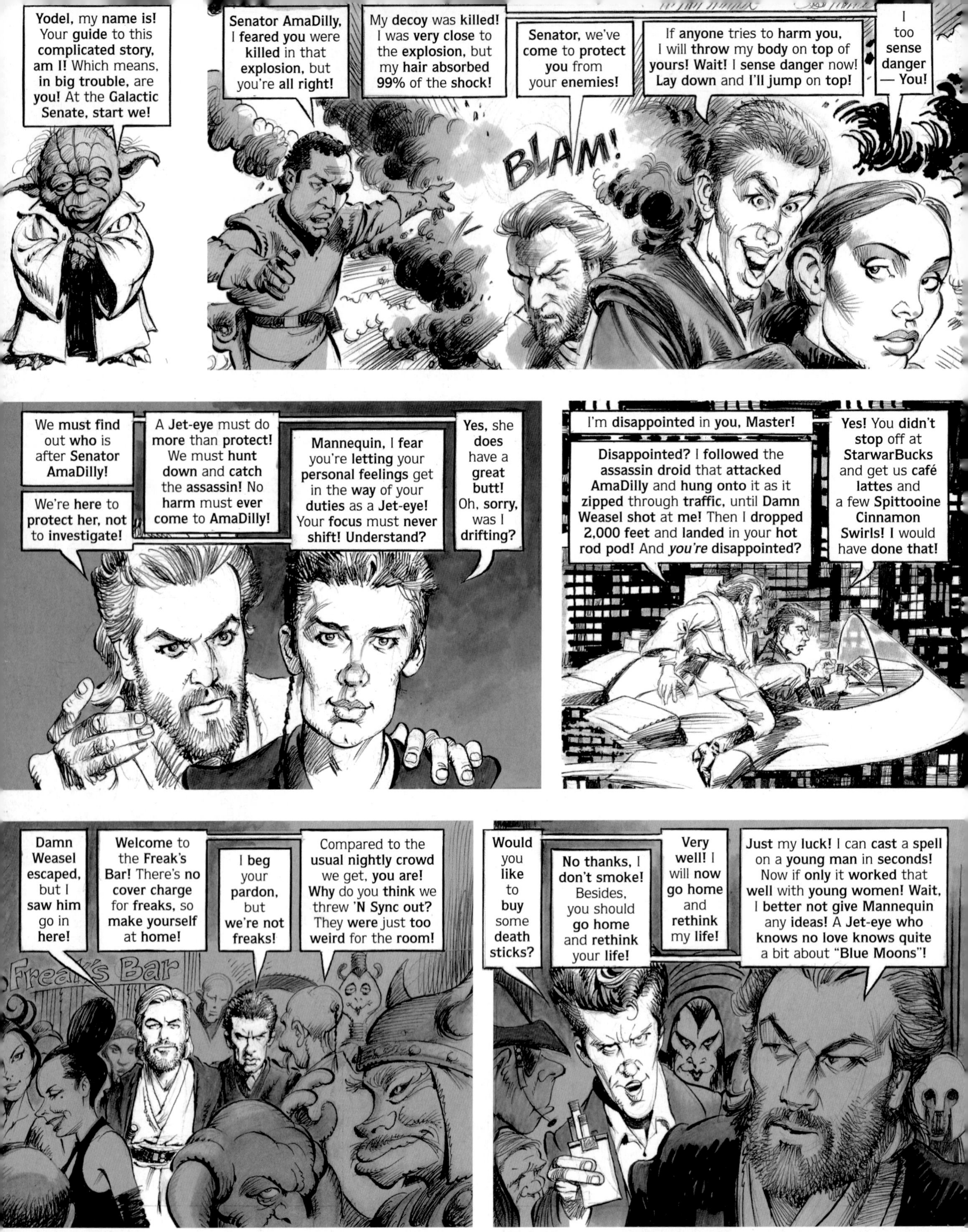
Yodel, my name is! Your guide to this complicated story, am I! Which means, in big trouble, are you! At the Galactic Senate, start we!
Senator AmaDilly, I feared you were killed in that explosion, but you're all right!
My decoy was killed! I was very close to the explosion, but my hair absorbed 99% of the shock!
BLAM!
Senator, we've come to protect you from your enemies!
If anyone tries to harm you, I will throw my body on top of yours! Wait! I sense danger now! Lay down and I'll jump on top!
I too sense danger — You!
We must find out who is after Senator AmaDilly!
We're here to protect her, not to investigate!
A Jet-eye must do more than protect! We must hunt down and catch the assassin! No harm must ever come to AmaDilly!
Mannequin, I fear you're letting your personal feelings get in the way of your duties as a Jet-eye! Your focus must never shift! Understand?
Yes, she does have a great butt! Oh, sorry, was I drifting?
I'm disappointed in you, Master!
Disappointed? I followed the assassin droid that attacked AmaDilly and hung onto it as it zipped through traffic, until Damn Weasel shot at me! Then I dropped 2,000 feet and landed in your hot rod pod! And *you're* disappointed?
Yes! You didn't stop off at StarwarBucks and get us café lattes and a few Spittooine Cinnamon Swirls! I would have done that!
Damn Weasel escaped, but I saw him go in here!
Welcome to the Freak's Bar! There's no cover charge for freaks, so make yourself at home!
I beg your pardon, but we're not freaks!
Compared to the usual nightly crowd we get, you are! Why do you think we threw 'N Sync out? They were just too weird for the room!
Freak's Bar
Would you like to buy some death sticks?
No thanks, I don't smoke! Besides, you should go home and rethink your life!
Very well! I will now go home and rethink my life!
Just my luck! I can cast a spell on a young man in seconds! Now if only it worked that well with young women! Wait, I better not give Mannequin any ideas! A Jet-eye who knows no love knows quite a bit about "Blue Moons"!

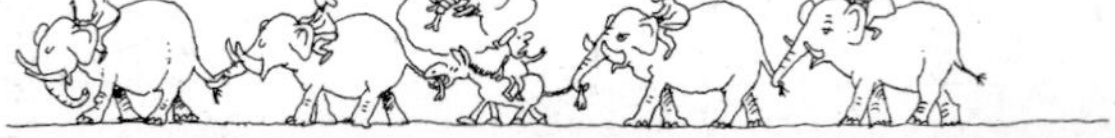

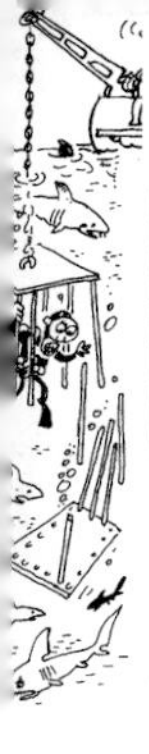

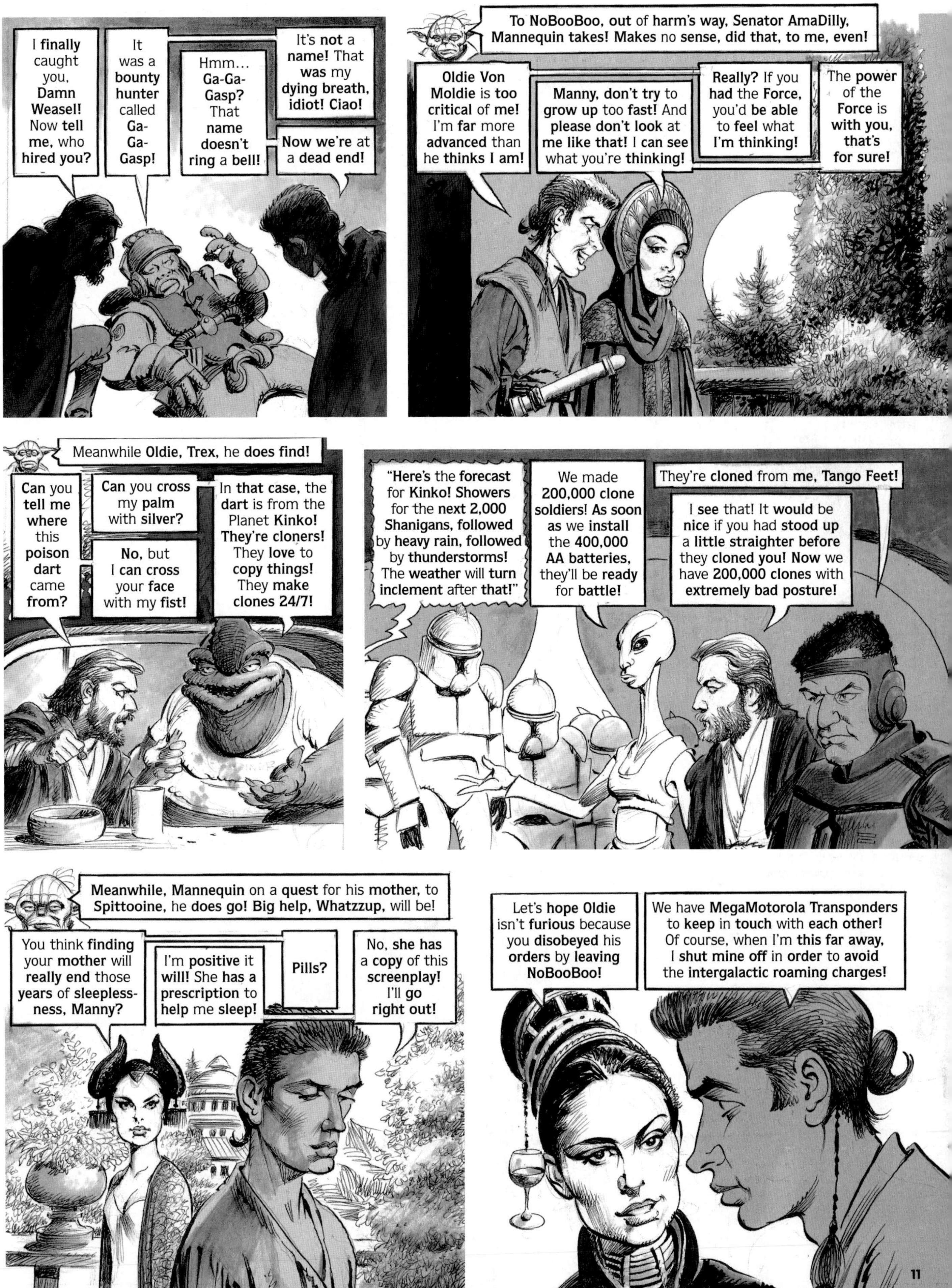

I finally caught you, Damn Weasel! Now tell me, who hired you?
It was a bounty hunter called Ga-Ga-Gasp!
Hmm... Ga-Ga-Gasp? That name doesn't ring a bell!
It's not a name! That was my dying breath, idiot! Ciao!
Now we're at a dead end!
To NoBooBoo, out of harm's way, Senator AmaDilly, Mannequin takes! Makes no sense, did that, to me, even!
Oldie Von Moldie is too critical of me! I'm far more advanced than he thinks I am!
Manny, don't try to grow up too fast! And please don't look at me like that! I can see what you're thinking!
Really? If you had the Force, you'd be able to feel what I'm thinking!
The power of the Force is with you, that's for sure!
Meanwhile Oldie, Trex, he does find!
Can you tell me where this poison dart came from?
Can you cross my palm with silver?
No, but I can cross your face with my fist!
In that case, the dart is from the Planet Kinko! They're cloners! They love to copy things! They make clones 24/7!
"Here's the forecast for Kinko! Showers for the next 2,000 Shanigans, followed by heavy rain, followed by thunderstorms! The weather will turn inclement after that!"
We made 200,000 clone soldiers! As soon as we install the 400,000 AA batteries, they'll be ready for battle!
They're cloned from me, Tango Feet!
I see that! It would be nice if you had stood up a little straighter before they cloned you! Now we have 200,000 clones with extremely bad posture!
Meanwhile, Mannequin on a quest for his mother, to Spittooine, he does go! Big help, Whatzzup, will be!
You think finding your mother will really end those years of sleeplessness, Manny?
I'm positive it will! She has a prescription to help me sleep!
Pills?
No, she has a copy of this screenplay! I'll go right out!
Let's hope Oldie isn't furious because you disobeyed his orders by leaving NoBooBoo!
We have MegaMotorola Transponders to keep in touch with each other! Of course, when I'm this far away, I shut mine off in order to avoid the intergalactic roaming charges!

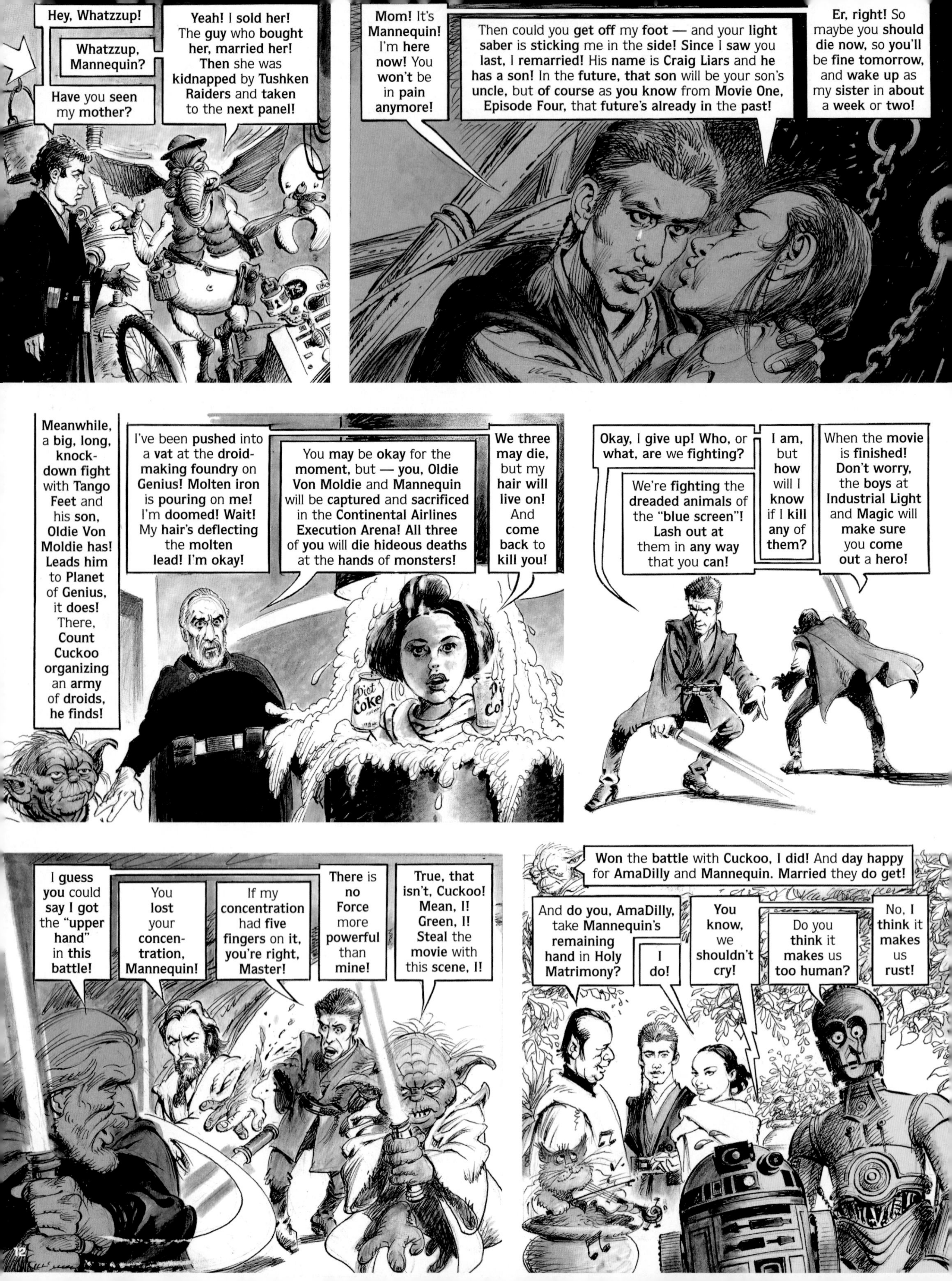

Hey, Whatzzup!
Whatzzup, Mannequin?
Have you seen my mother?
Yeah! I sold her! The guy who bought her, married her! Then she was kidnapped by Tushken Raiders and taken to the next panel!
Mom! It's Mannequin! I'm here now! You won't be in pain anymore!
Then could you get off my foot — and your light saber is sticking me in the side! Since I saw you last, I remarried! His name is Craig Liars and he has a son! In the future, that son will be your son's uncle, but of course as you know from Movie One, Episode Four, that future's already in the past!
Er, right! So maybe you should die now, so you'll be fine tomorrow, and wake up as my sister in about a week or two!
Meanwhile, a big, long, knock-down fight with Tango Feet and his son, Oldie Von Moldie has! Leads him to Planet of Genius, it does! There, Count Cuckoo organizing an army of droids, he finds!
I've been pushed into a vat at the droid-making foundry on Genius! Molten iron is pouring on me! I'm doomed! Wait! My hair's deflecting the molten lead! I'm okay!
You may be okay for the moment, but — you, Oldie Von Moldie and Mannequin will be captured and sacrificed in the Continental Airlines Execution Arena! All three of you will die hideous deaths at the hands of monsters!
We three may die, but my hair will live on! And come back to kill you!
Diet Coke
Okay, I give up! Who, or what, are we fighting?
We're fighting the dreaded animals of the "blue screen"! Lash out at them in any way that you can!
I am, but how will I know if I kill any of them?
When the movie is finished! Don't worry, the boys at Industrial Light and Magic will make sure you come out a hero!
I guess you could say I got the "upper hand" in this battle!
You lost your concentration, Mannequin!
If my concentration had five fingers on it, you're right, Master!
There is no Force more powerful than mine!
True, that isn't, Cuckoo! Mean, I! Green, I! Steal the movie with this scene, I!
Won the battle with Cuckoo, I did! And day happy for AmaDilly and Mannequin. Married they do get!
And do you, AmaDilly, take Mannequin's remaining hand in Holy Matrimony?
I do!
You know, we shouldn't cry!
Do you think it makes us too human?
No, I think it makes us rust!

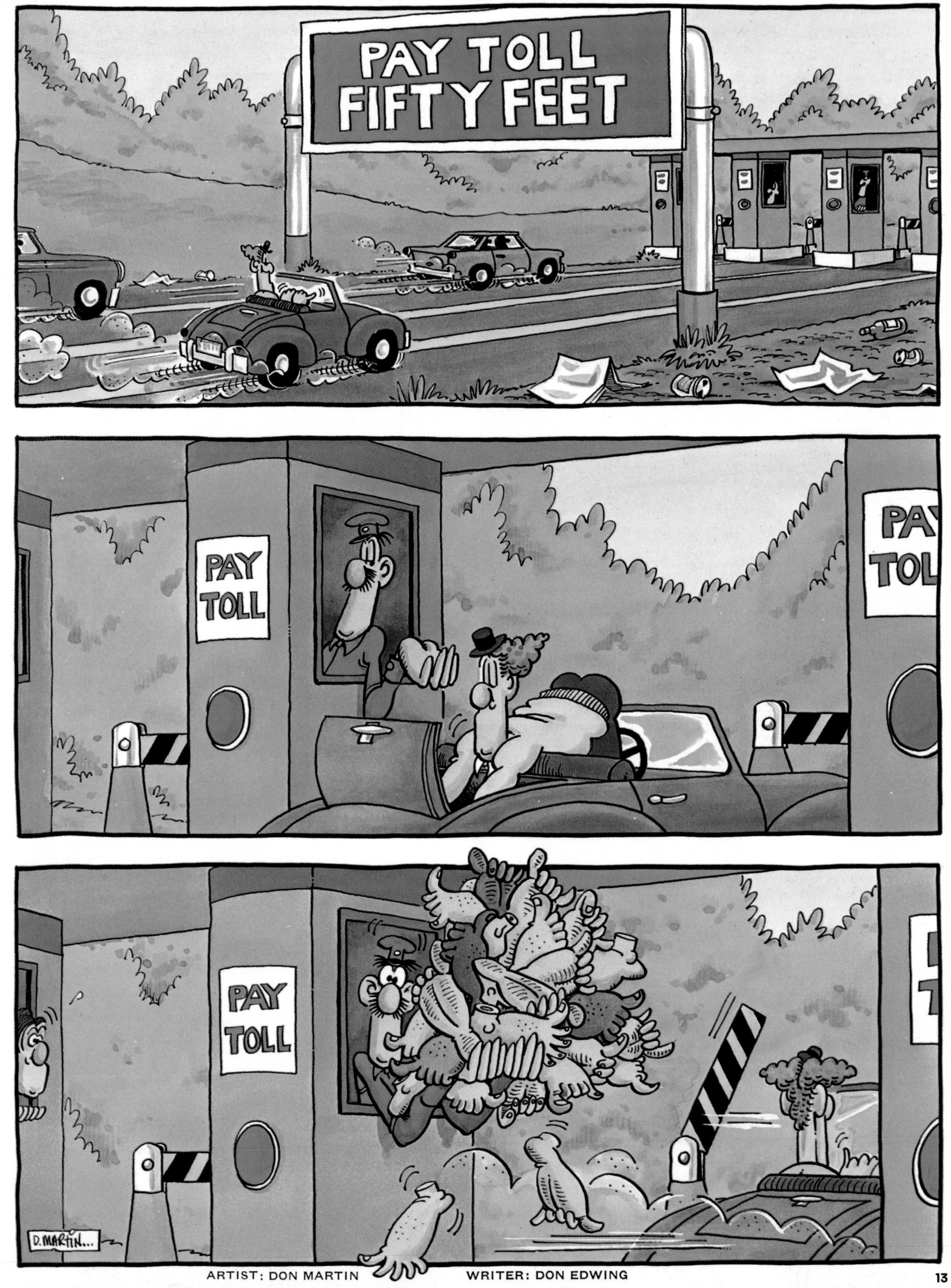
PAY TOLL
FIFTY FEET
PAY TOLL
PAY TOLL
D. MARTIN...

ARTIST: DON MARTIN WRITER: DON EDWING

DO RE ME FA SO LA TEE-HEE DEPT.

A MAD LOOK AT

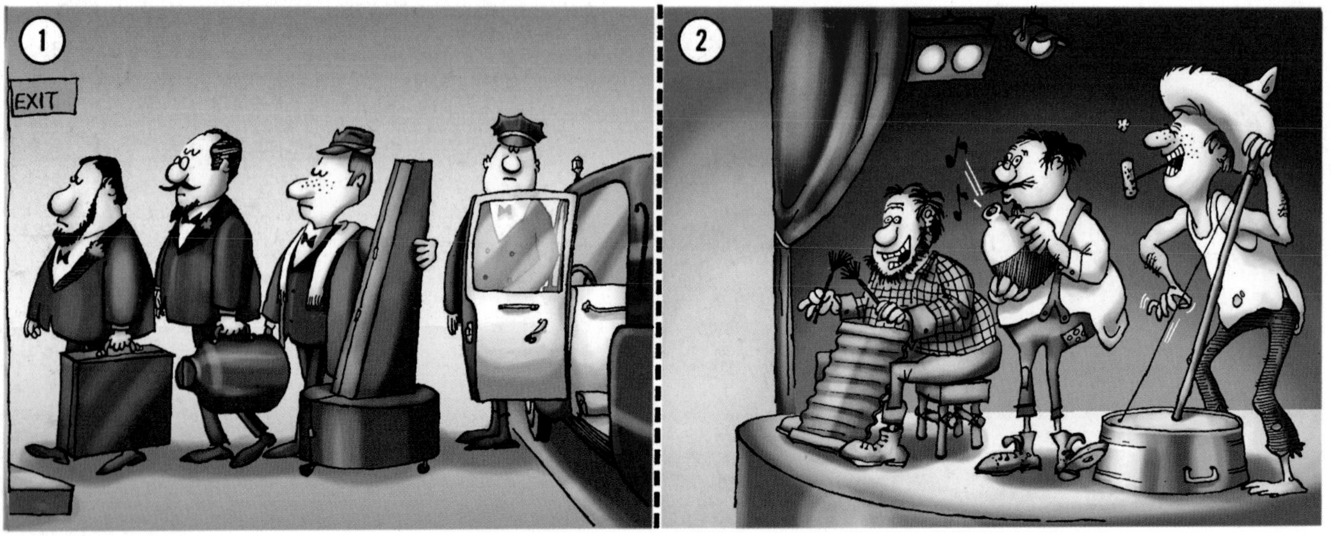
1
EXIT
2

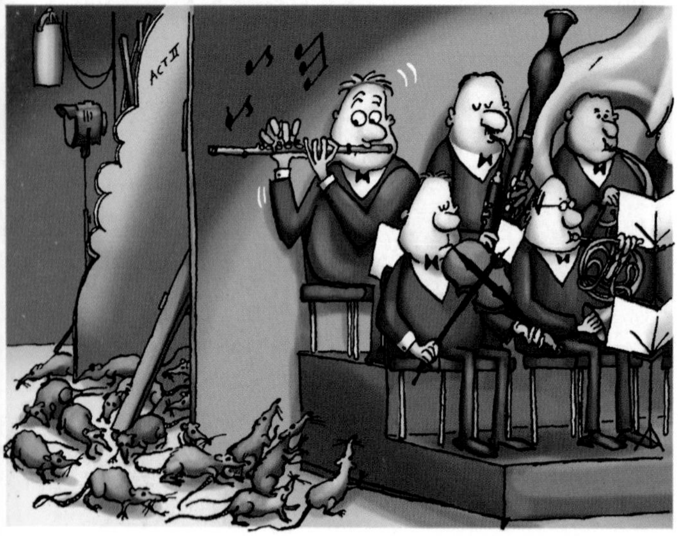
ACT II

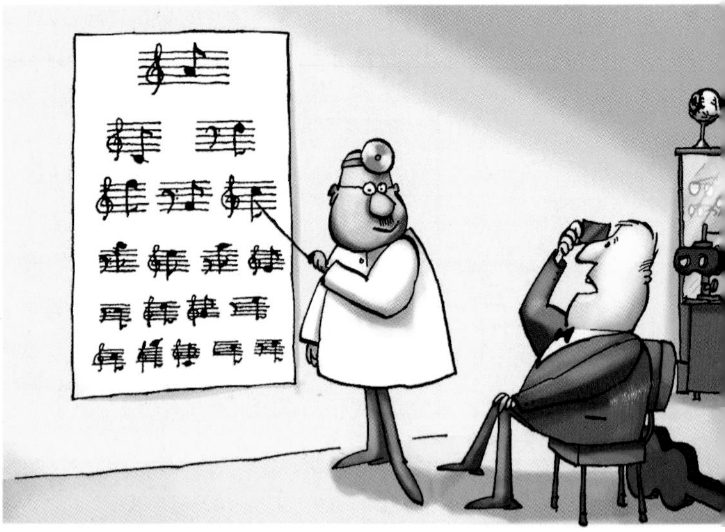

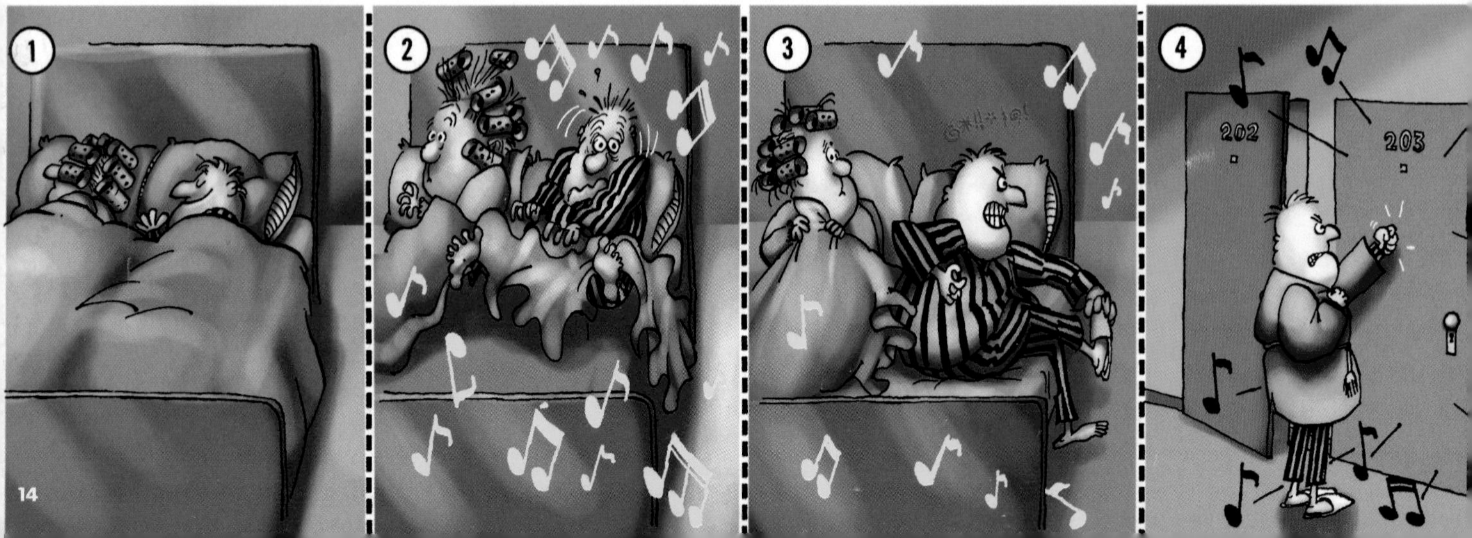
1
2
3
4
202
203

MUSICIANS

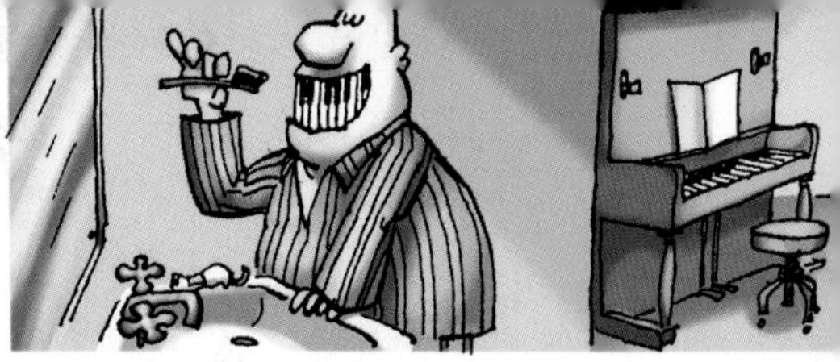

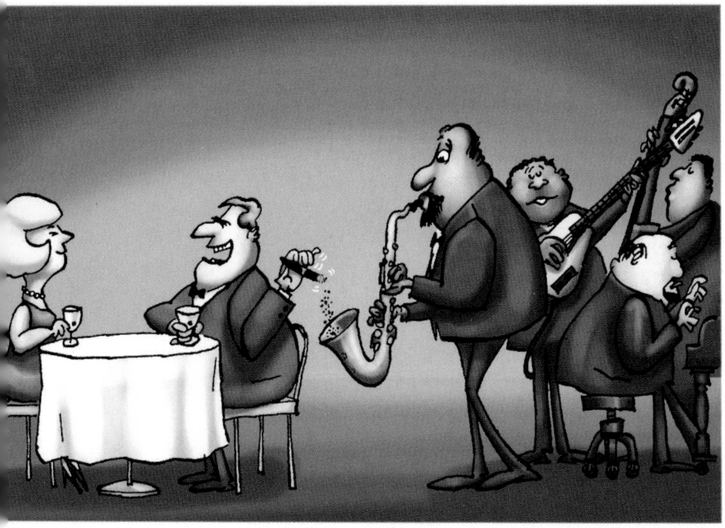

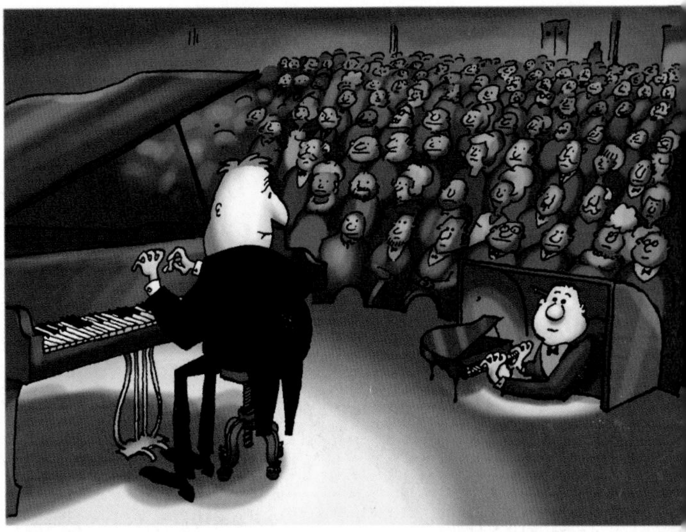

WRITER AND ARTIST: SERGIO ARAGONÉS **COLORIST: CARRIE STRACHAN**

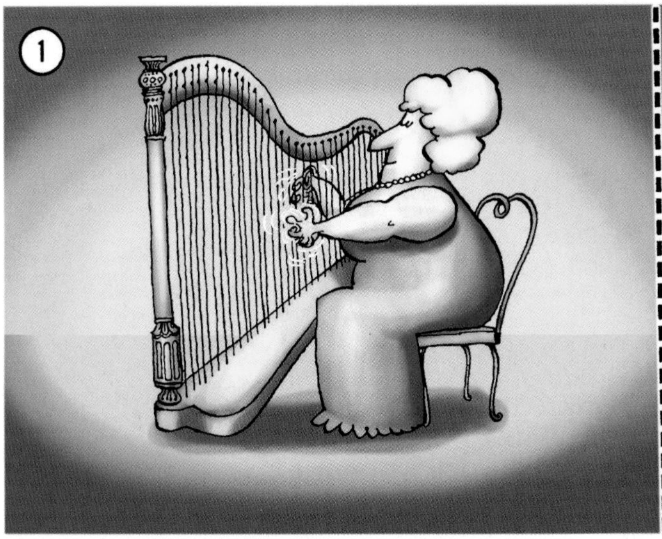
1

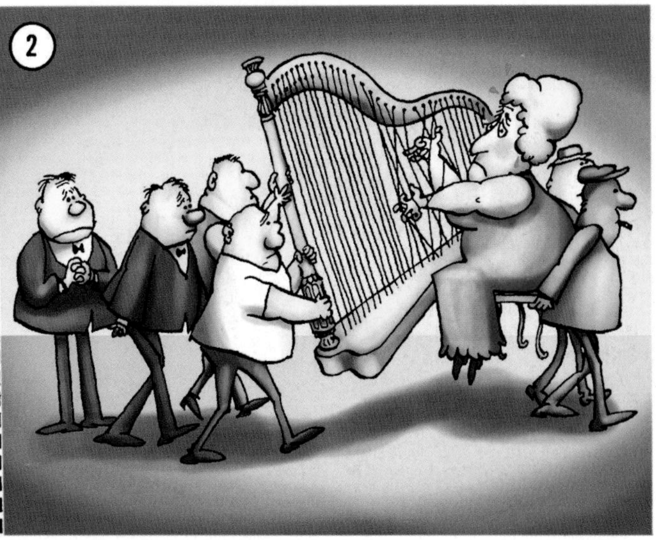
2

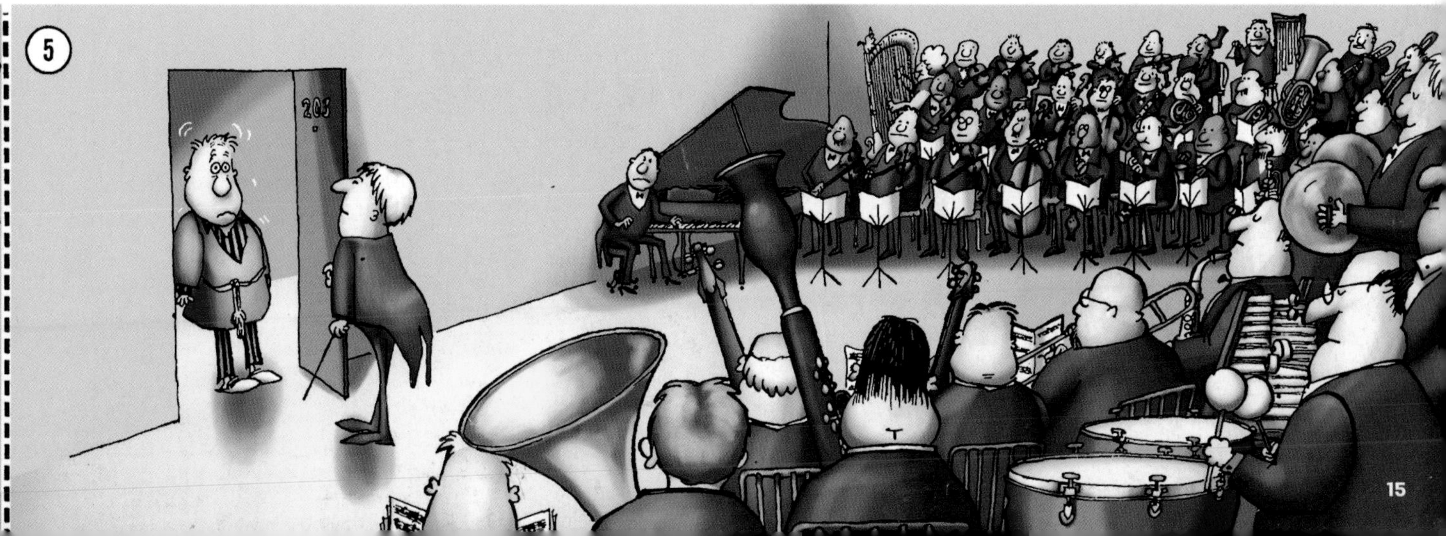
5
205

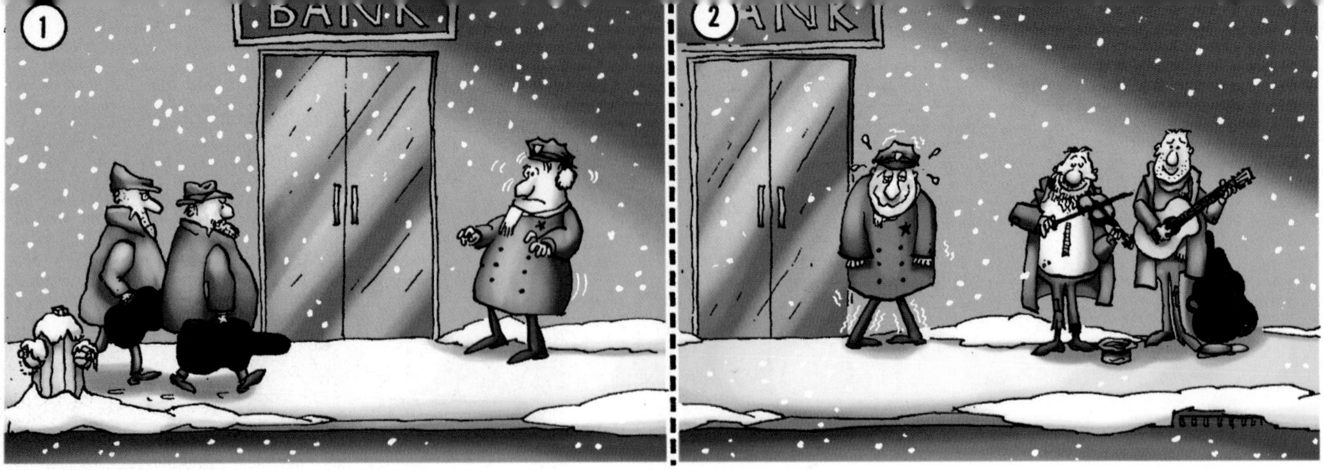
1
BANK
2

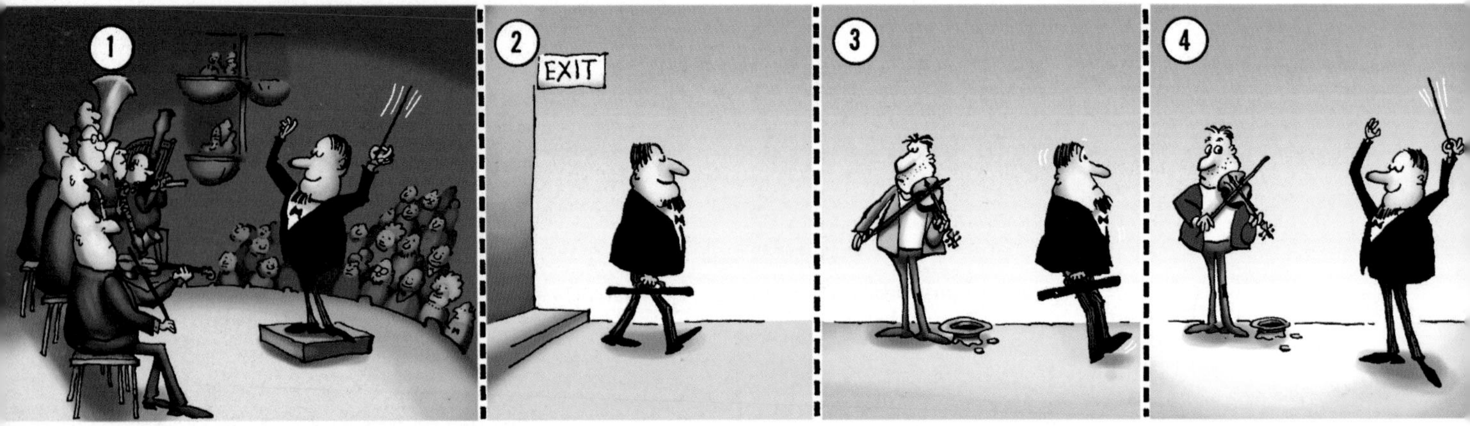
1
2
EXIT
3
4

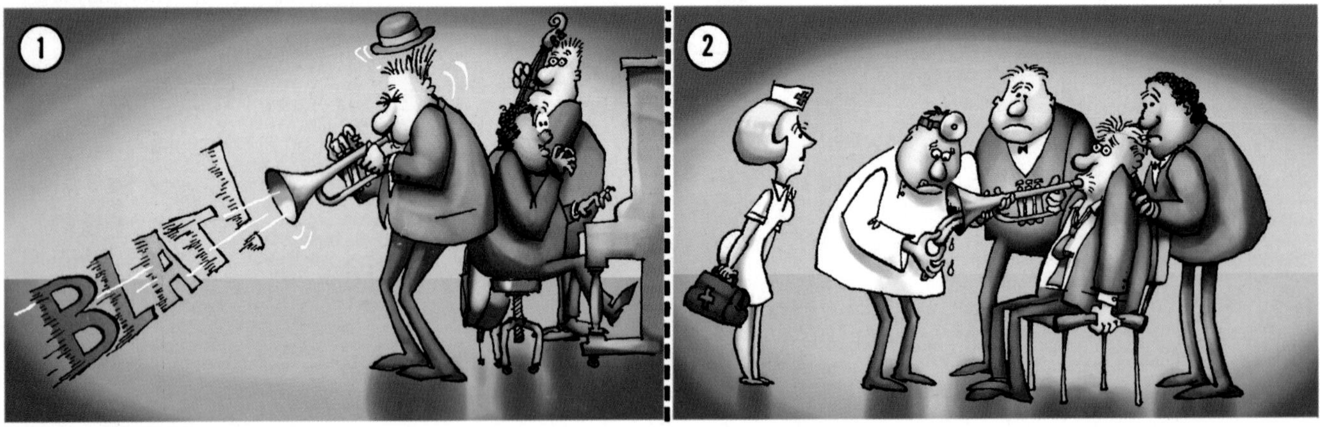
1
BLAT!
2

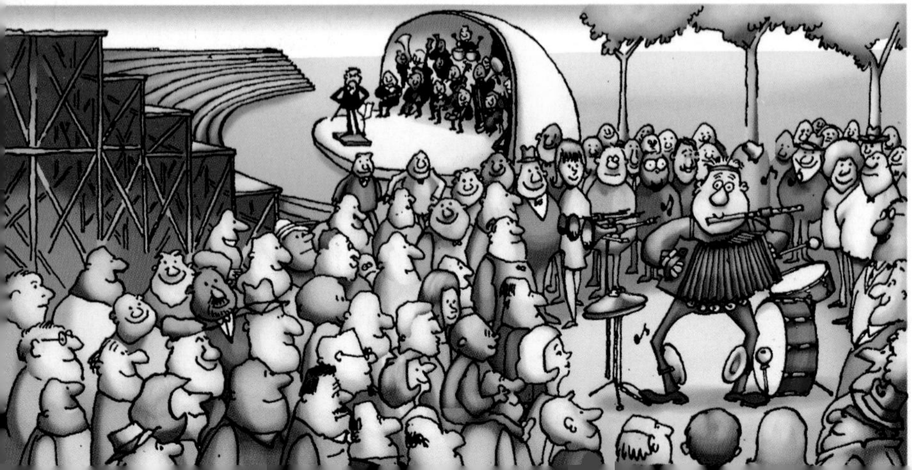

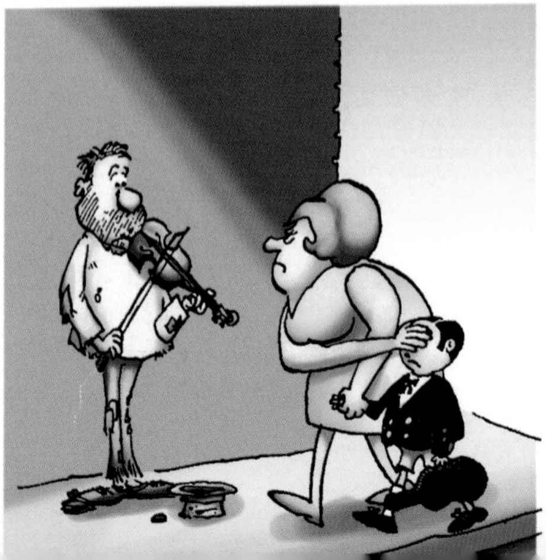

JOKE AND DAGGER DEPT.

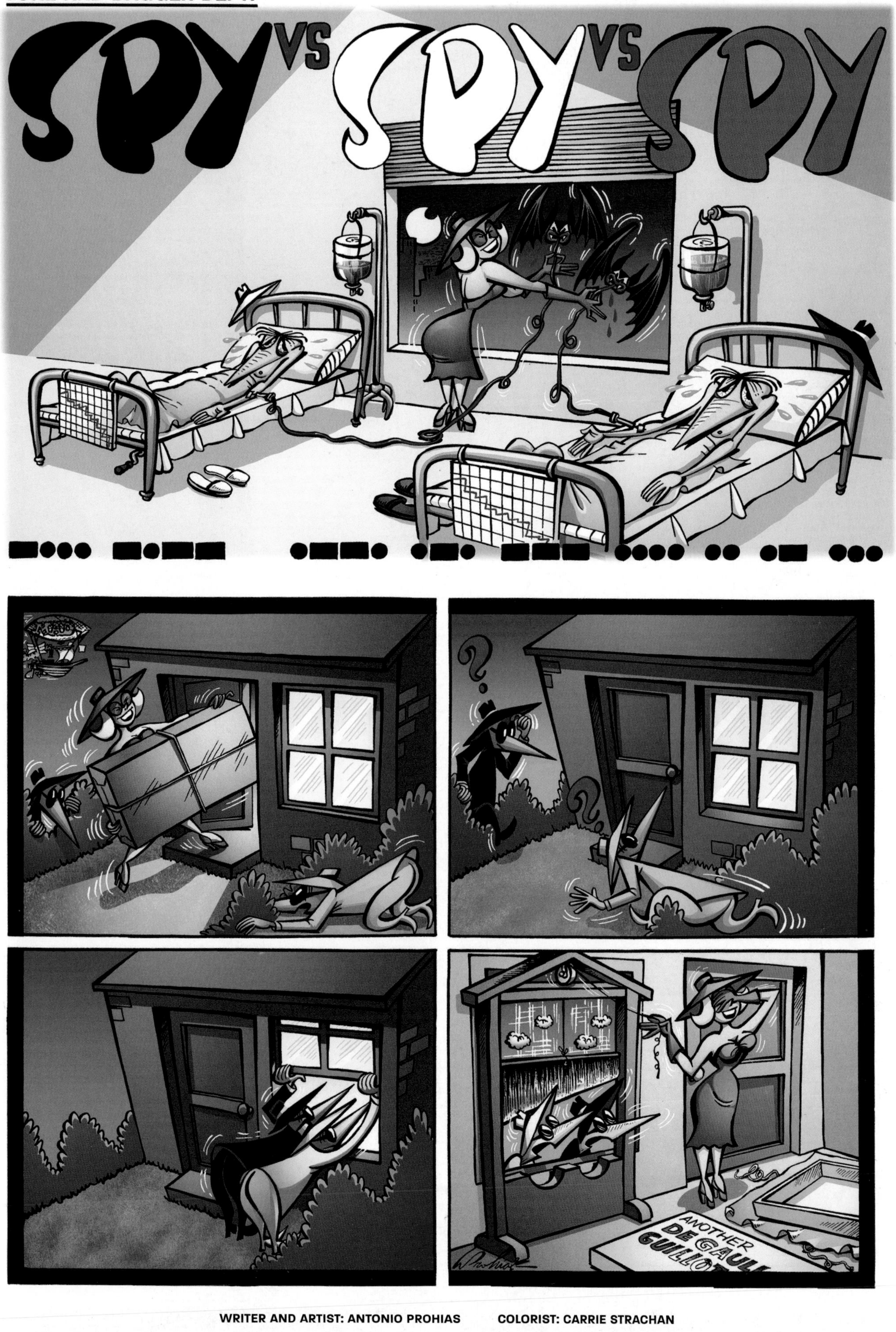
SPY VS SPY VS SPY
ANOTHER
DE GAUL
GUILLOT

WRITER AND ARTIST: ANTONIO PROHIAS COLORIST: CARRIE STRACHAN

MAD's Brain Drool Part One

LITTLE ROGER KAPUTNIK

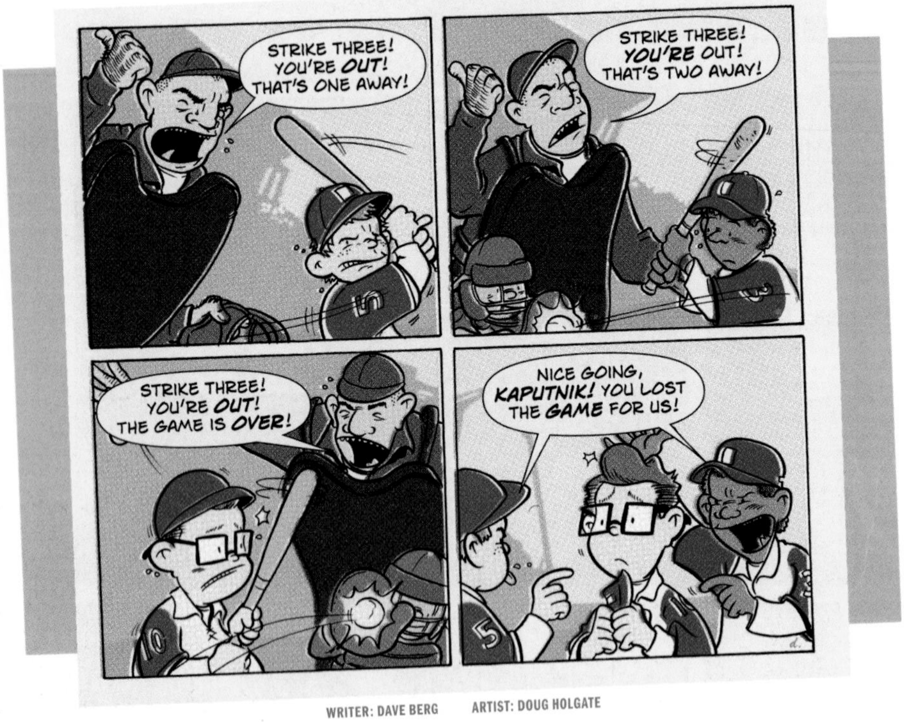
STRIKE THREE! YOU'RE OUT! THAT'S ONE AWAY!
STRIKE THREE! YOU'RE OUT! THAT'S TWO AWAY!
STRIKE THREE! YOU'RE OUT! THE GAME IS OVER!
NICE GOING, KAPUTNIK! YOU LOST THE GAME FOR US!

WRITER: DAVE BERG ARTIST: DOUG HOLGATE

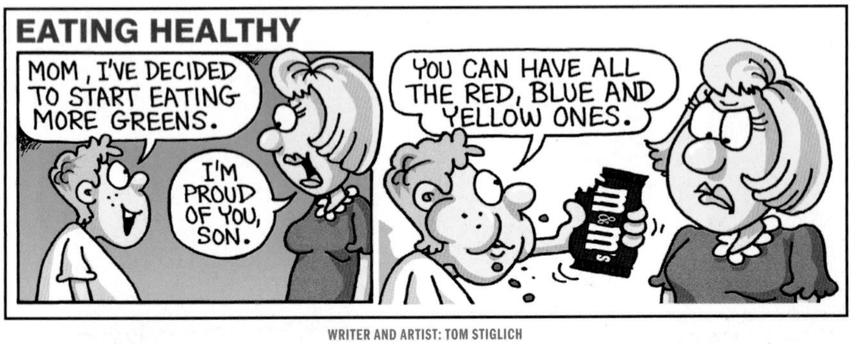
EATING HEALTHY
MOM, I'VE DECIDED TO START EATING MORE GREENS.
I'M PROUD OF YOU, SON.
YOU CAN HAVE ALL THE RED, BLUE AND YELLOW ONES.
m&m's

WRITER AND ARTIST: TOM STIGLICH

AMERICAN IDOL REJECTED THEME WEEKS

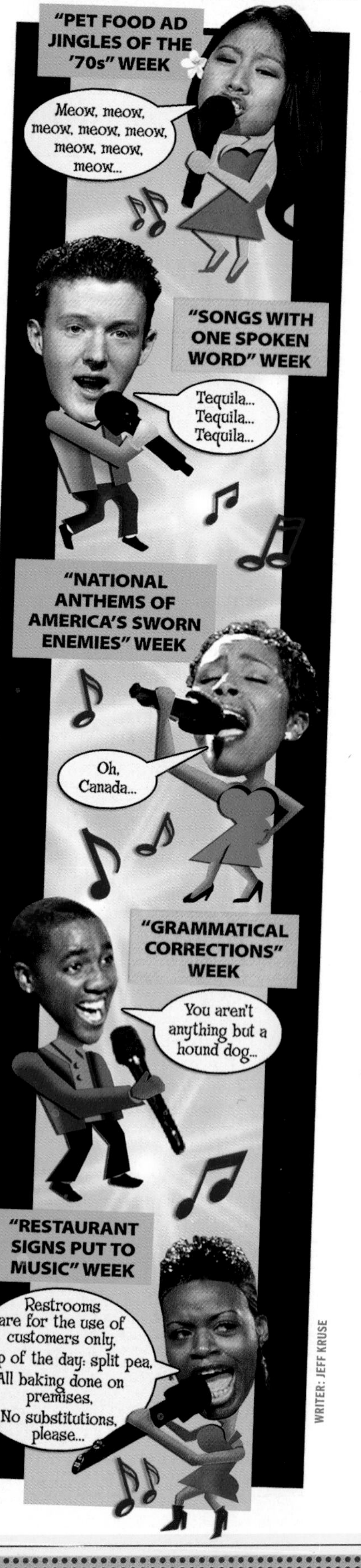
"PET FOOD AD JINGLES OF THE '70s" WEEK
Meow, meow, meow, meow, meow, meow, meow, meow...
"SONGS WITH ONE SPOKEN WORD" WEEK
Tequila... Tequila... Tequila...
"NATIONAL ANTHEMS OF AMERICA'S SWORN ENEMIES" WEEK
Oh, Canada...
"GRAMMATICAL CORRECTIONS" WEEK
You aren't anything but a hound dog...
"RESTAURANT SIGNS PUT TO MUSIC" WEEK
Restrooms are for the use of customers only. Soup of the day: split pea. All baking done on premises. No substitutions, please...

WRITER: JEFF KRUSE

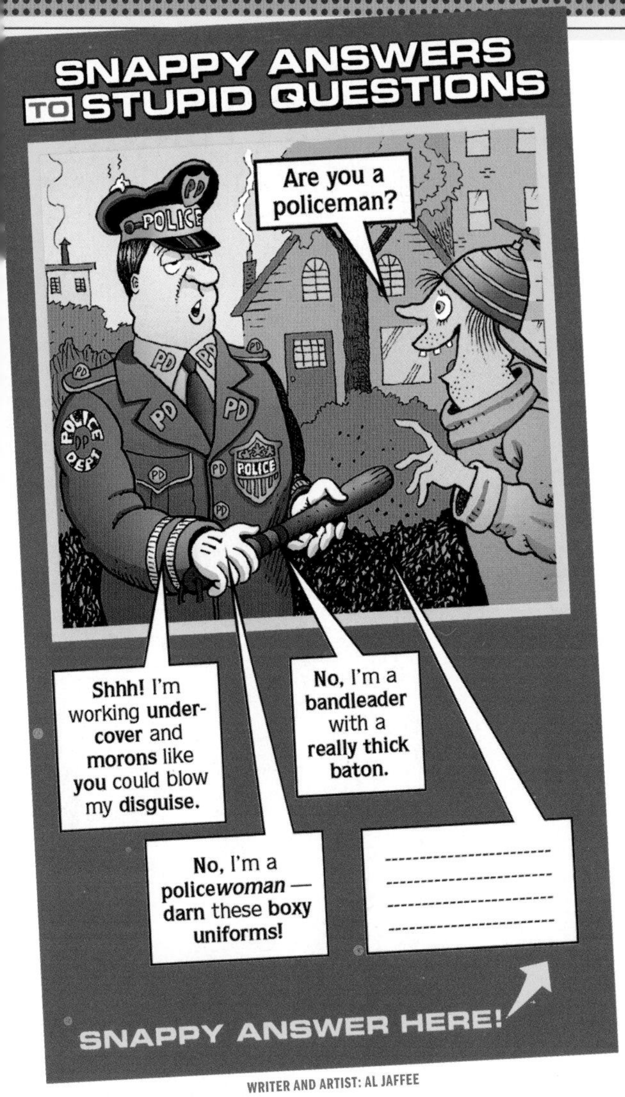
SNAPPY ANSWERS TO STUPID QUESTIONS
POLICE
Are you a policeman?
Shhh! I'm working under-cover and morons like you could blow my disguise.
No, I'm a policewoman — darn these boxy uniforms!
No, I'm a bandleader with a really thick baton.
SNAPPY ANSWER HERE!

WRITER AND ARTIST: AL JAFFEE

MAKE YOUR OWN BEST-SELLING BOOK TITLE

(Choose One From Each Column)

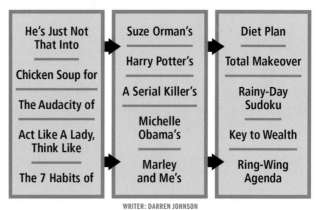

He's Just Not That Into	Suze Orman's	Diet Plan
Chicken Soup for	Harry Potter's	Total Makeover
The Audacity of	A Serial Killer's	Rainy-Day Sudoku
Act Like A Lady, Think Like	Michelle Obama's	Key to Wealth
The 7 Habits of	Marley and Me's	Ring-Wing Agenda

WRITER: DARREN JOHNSON

LELIEVRE AND LET DIE

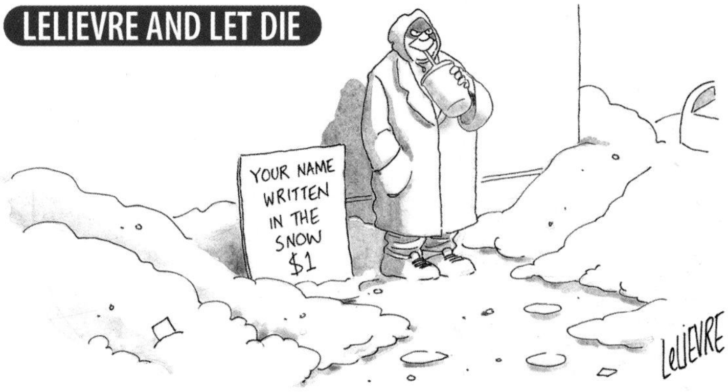
YOUR NAME WRITTEN IN THE SNOW $1
LeLIEVRE

WRITER AND ARTIST: GLEN LE LIEVRE

A SUPER-PLAN OF ACTION

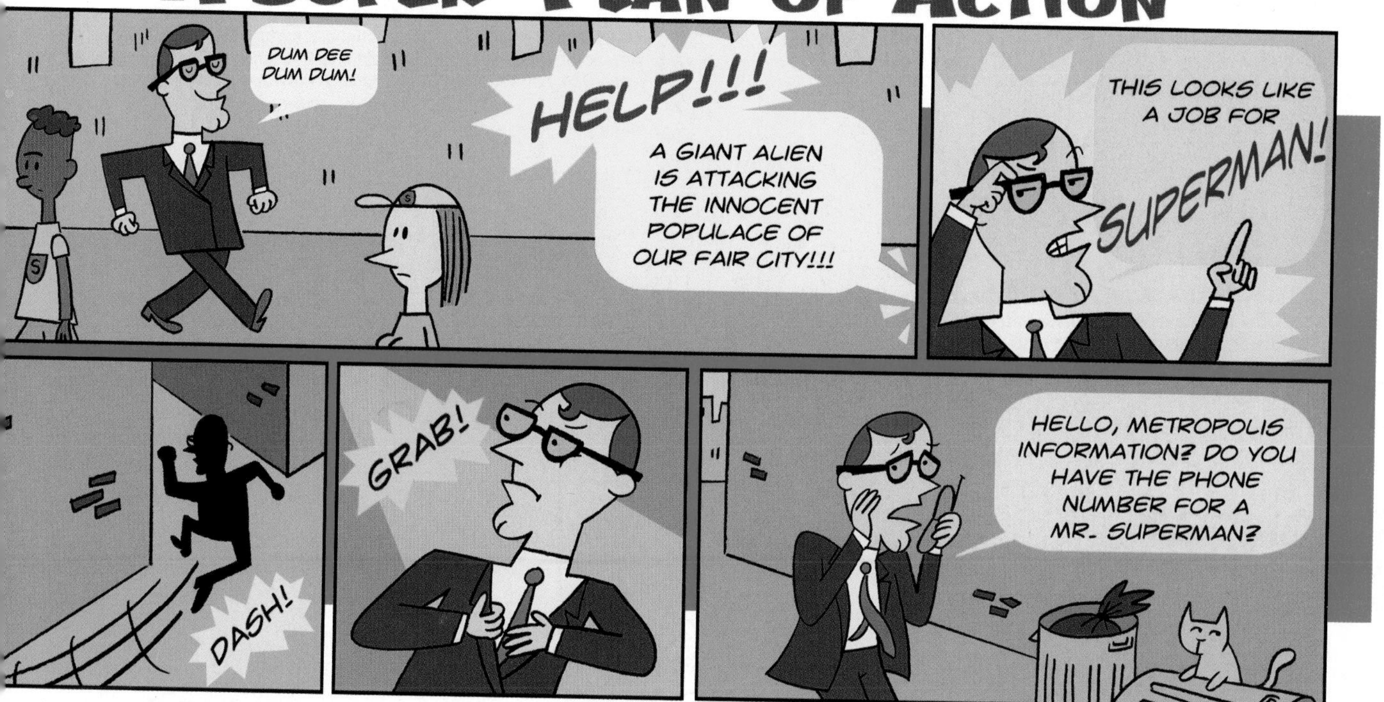
DUM DEE DUM DUM!
HELP!!!
A GIANT ALIEN IS ATTACKING THE INNOCENT POPULACE OF OUR FAIR CITY!!!
THIS LOOKS LIKE A JOB FOR SUPERMAN!
DASH!
GRAB!
HELLO, METROPOLIS INFORMATION? DO YOU HAVE THE PHONE NUMBER FOR A MR. SUPERMAN?

WRITER AND ARTIST: MO WILLEMS

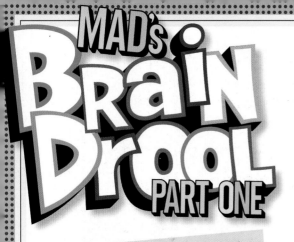

MAD's Brain Drool Part One

THE PUZZLE NOOK

Which of the 4 choices best completes this phrase?

_?_EY IS THE ROOT OF ALL EVIL

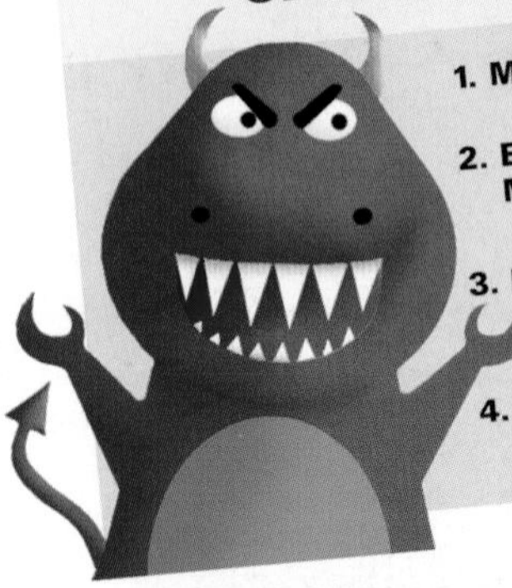

1. MON___
2. EATING MOLDY TURK___
3. DOING THE HOKEY POK___
4. BARN___

WRITER AND ARTIST: PATRICK MERRELL

FAMILY FUNNIES

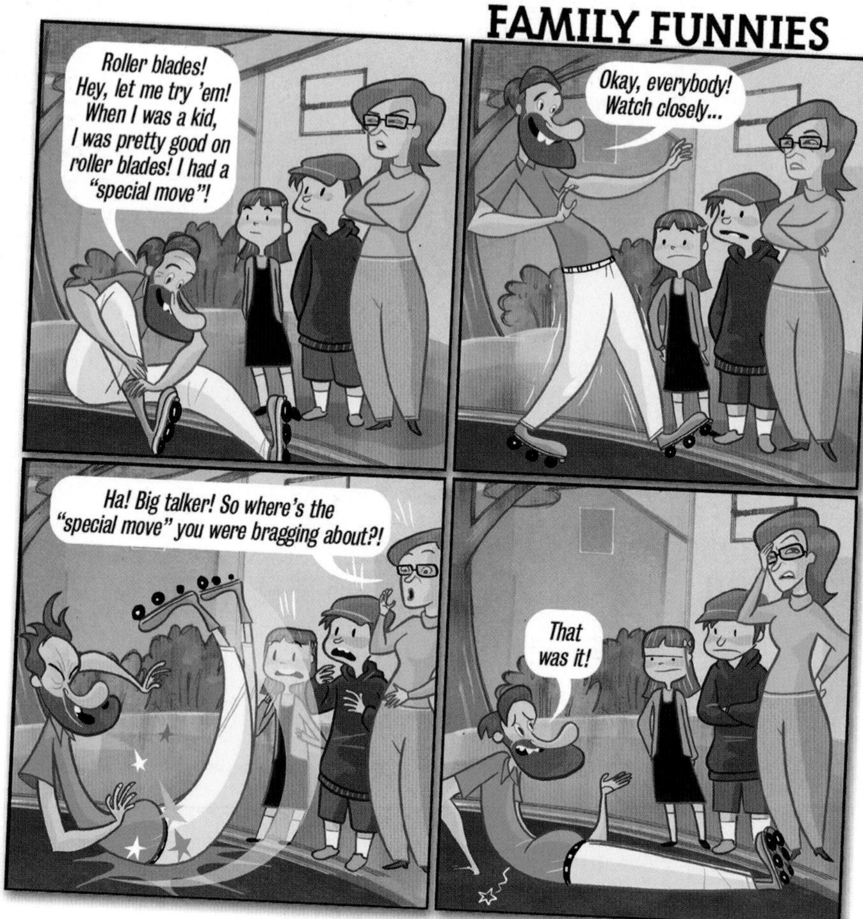

Roller blades! Hey, let me try 'em! When I was a kid, I was pretty good on roller blades! I had a "special move"!
Okay, everybody! Watch closely...
Ha! Big talker! So where's the "special move" you were bragging about?!
That was it!

WRITER: DAVE BERG ARTIST: JOSE GARIBALDI

BITTERMAN

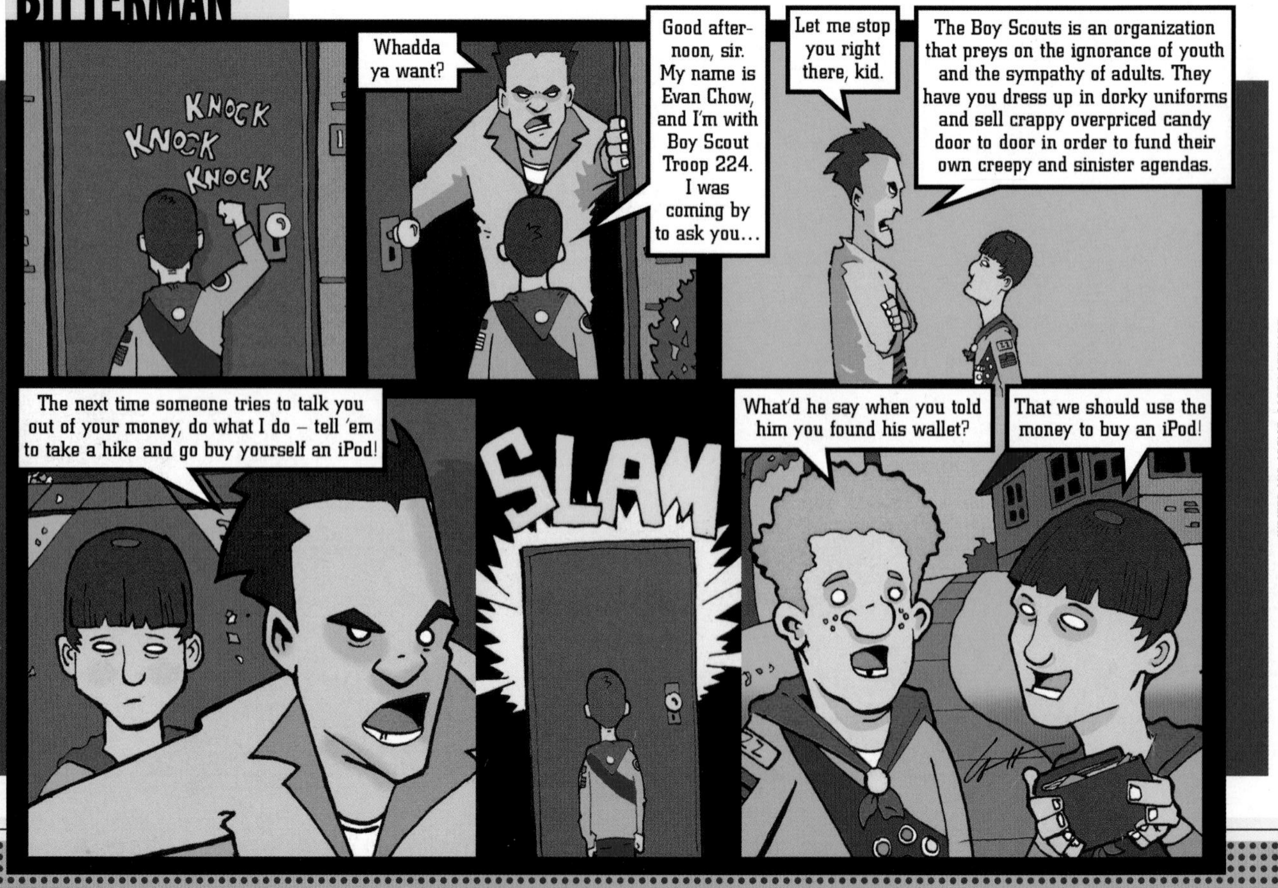

KNOCK KNOCK KNOCK
Whadda ya want?
Good after-noon, sir. My name is Evan Chow, and I'm with Boy Scout Troop 224. I was coming by to ask you...
Let me stop you right there, kid.
The Boy Scouts is an organization that preys on the ignorance of youth and the sympathy of adults. They have you dress up in dorky uniforms and sell crappy overpriced candy door to door in order to fund their own creepy and sinister agendas.
The next time someone tries to talk you out of your money, do what I do – tell 'em to take a hike and go buy yourself an iPod!
SLAM
What'd he say when you told him you found his wallet?
That we should use the money to buy an iPod!

WRITER AND ARTIST: GARTH GERHART

ONE DAY IN METROPOLIS

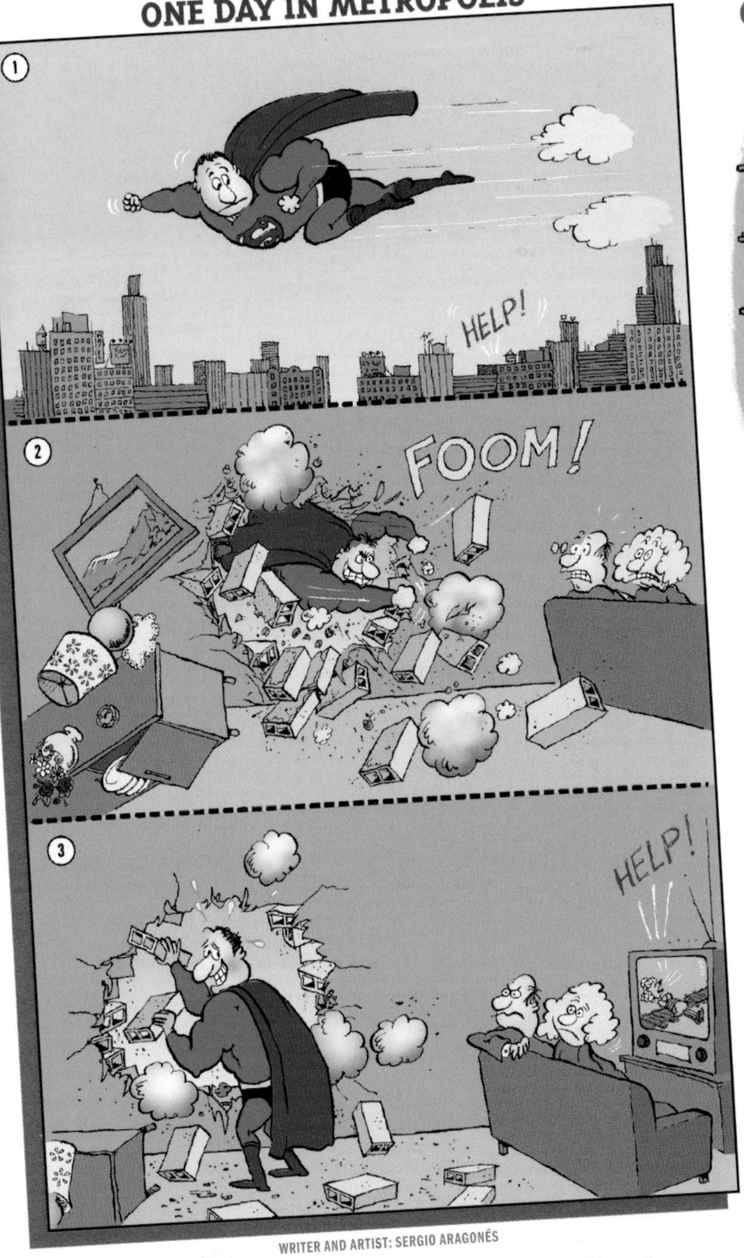
1
HELP!
2
FOOM!
3
HELP!

WRITER AND ARTIST: SERGIO ARAGONÉS

SUTTON FOR PUNISHMENT

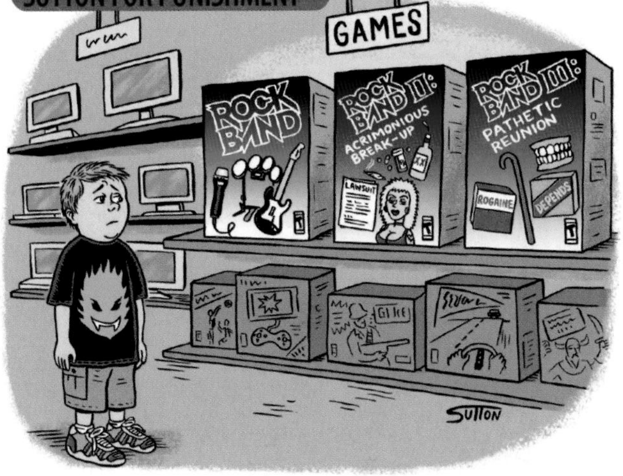
GAMES
ROCK BAND
ROCK BAND II: ACRIMONIOUS BREAK-UP
LAWSUIT
ROCK BAND III: PATHETIC REUNION
ROGAINE
DEPENDS
SUTTON

WRITER AND ARTIST: WARD SUTTON

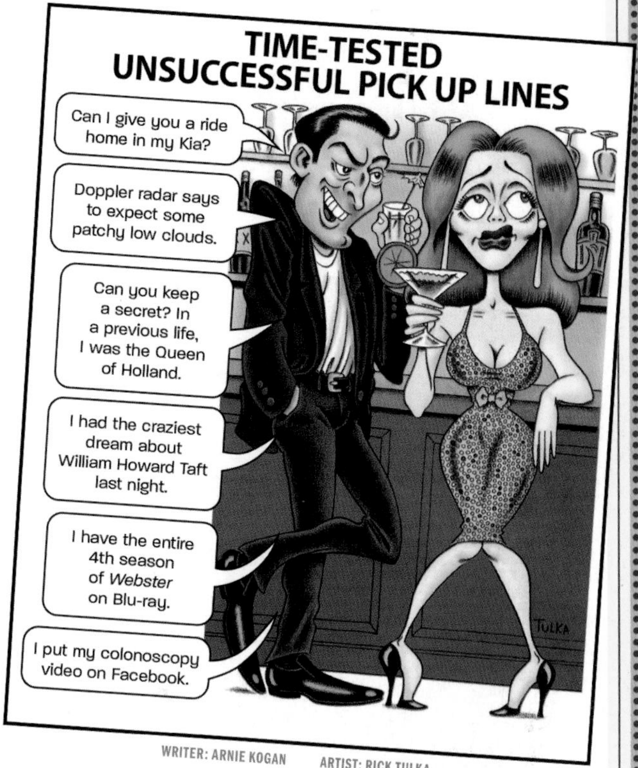
TIME-TESTED UNSUCCESSFUL PICK UP LINES
Can I give you a ride home in my Kia?
Doppler radar says to expect some patchy low clouds.
Can you keep a secret? In a previous life, I was the Queen of Holland.
I had the craziest dream about William Howard Taft last night.
I have the entire 4th season of *Webster* on Blu-ray.
I put my colonoscopy video on Facebook.
TULKA

WRITER: ARNIE KOGAN ARTIST: RICK TULKA

ALFRED

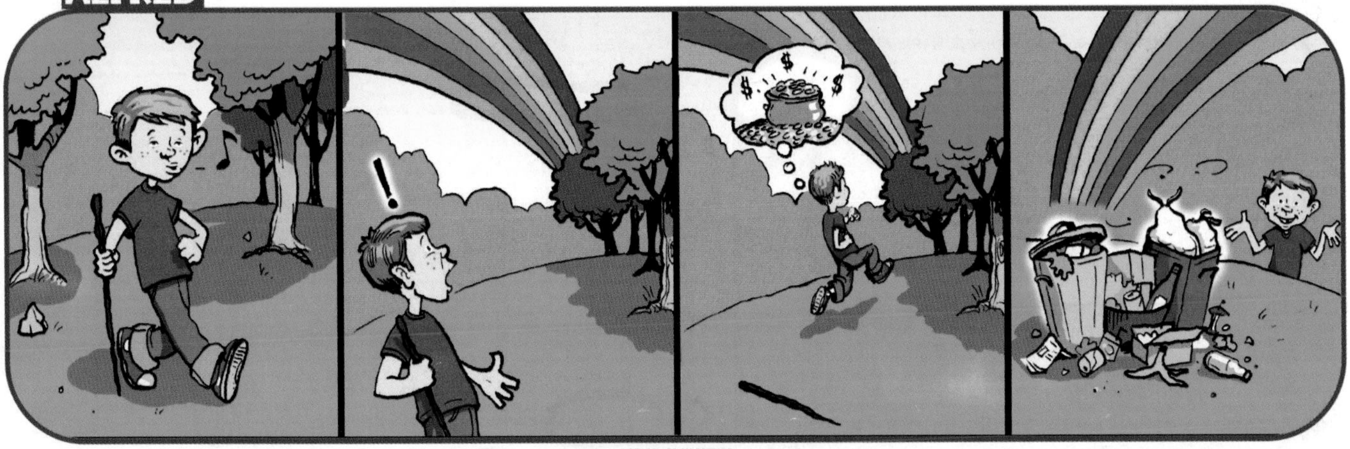
!

ARTIST: CLAY MEYER

What's the worst thing about going to a fast food joint? The long lines? Lousy Food?

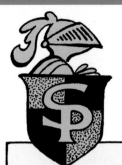

SIR PUFFY'S®

FAMILY RESTAURANTS Serving

COMMUNITY BULLETIN BOARD

PARANOIDS ANONYMOUS will hold its monthly meeting July 24th at 8 PM. All are invited, but since the members wish to maintain their anonymity, they refuse to reveal where the meeting will be held.

THE JASPER HIGH SCHOOL MOTHER'S CLUB is having its monthly mud-wrestling night with the Bunville Ladies Society on July 16th starting at 7:30 PM at Elk's Lodge #59. Bingo to follow.

COMMUNITY BOARD #5 presents an evening of skin rash identification. Refreshments. Victor Lipper Hall, July 9th, 9 PM. Free!!

LITTLE BROTHERS, INC. is a community service organization providing neighborhood bullies and other tough guys with defenseless children to push and order around. Volunteers are desperately needed. Call Mr. Rocco at KL 5-1763.

UNSKILLED MEDICAL VOLUNTEERS, 85 Butt Street, provides second-rate, inadequate and potentially dangerous health services to area residents who can't afford professonal help but make too much to be eligible for Medicare. Also available: Poorly managed day care center. For information phone 171-8898.

SPECIAL OFFER WHILE SUPPLIES LAST

The Toxic Dump Site Collector's Glasses Are Here! Nuclear Waste, Caustic Chemicals and More . . .

All pictured in Full Color on these festive 12-ounce tumblers! FREE with your purchase of a half-gallon size PuffBucket™ Shake. We're adding new dump sites every week.

COLLECT THEM ALL!

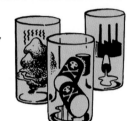

FUN FACTS ABOUT SIR PUFFY'S®

WE'RE PROUD!

Every single one of Sir Puffy's® 912 restaurant managers has completed almost *two years* of high school!

If all the burgers served at Sir Puffy's® in one day were laid from end to end on a highway, it would take over *six hours* to wash, reheat and sell them to unwitting customers!

Sir Puffy's® cups, napkins, styrofoam containers and ketchup packets account for more than 18% of all the litter found in our country's national parks, forests and recreation areas!

A recent FDA report stated that there is only a *casual* connection between our PuffBoat Supreme™ fish fillet sandwiches and arteriosclerosis!

HAVE YOU TRIED SIR PUFFY'S® STUFF ON A STICK™ GOES GREAT WITH OUR GOOP IN A CUP™!

NOW MADE WITH 100% PIG FAT!

WORD GAME

See if you can find the 22 words or phrases that describe things found in Sir Puffy's® kitchen!

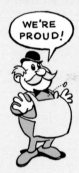

S	L	O	P	N	S	D	R	A	Z	A	H	E	R	I	F
U	N	W	A	L	I	Y	U	D	G	A	E	I	O	C	U
P	S	O	D	F	A	M	A	M	S	I	L	U	T	O	B
D	R	A	I	P	I	N	R	B	S	T	O	G	G	A	M
E	E	A	S	T	R	O	E	E	E	L	E	S	Y	P	Q
I	N	G	R	E	A	S	E	D	V	O	I	N	A	U	U
M	G	I	E	H	T	L	I	F	I	N	B	L	C	R	A
O	I	N	A	O	S	I	O	L	T	S	Z	P	O	H	T
L	E	C	S	M	U	M	V	I	A	J	E	A	R	P	A
D	R	A	E	G	O	E	Q	U	V	S	C	A	U	E	E
B	O	O	G	I	G	T	Z	W	R	H	O	S	S	P	M
I	F	T	L	A	J	D	P	D	E	L	T	Z	T	E	E
P	O	Z	B	W	O	X	I	S	S	R	C	L	I	K	S
A	R	R	G	C	K	R	B	C	E	K	T	M	A	G	R
R	A	V	O	O	T	I	E	J	R	I	O	Y	H	E	O
G	E	R	M	S	F	R	A	A	P	H	Y	E	C	C	H

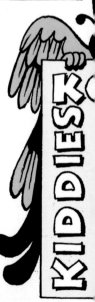

KIDDIES

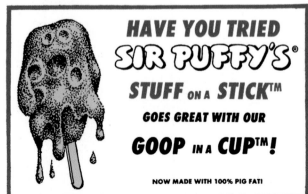

WRITERS: CHARLIE KADAU AND JOE RAIOLA

Good choices! But no, the absolute worst is the shoddy placemat that looks a bit like...

PLACEMAT™

·unville, Cheesetown and surrounding areas

CREW PERSON OF THE MONTH

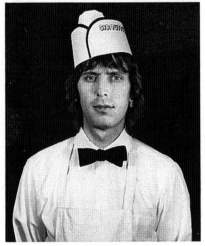

My name is Clarence Shivers. I have been working at Sir Puffy's® for six years. I enjoy earning minimum wage. This is the only job I've ever had. I'm not qualified to do anything else. I'll probably be working here the rest of my miserable life. Have a nice day!

NEW! SIR PUFFY'S® MYSTERY BAG MEAL™

There's no telling what you'll get in one of these plain unmarked bags. That's what makes them fun! Will it be our Deluxe Super-Singed Burger™? A 24-ounce cup of flat, watery cola? Maybe it'll be the stuff our kitchen crew scraped off the grill last night! You won't know for sure until you try it—and even then you may not be certain!

SIR PUFFY'S® MYSTERY BAG MEAL™!
It's perfect for people who love to eat but don't care what!

SAVE 20¢ ON YOUR NEXT PURCHASE OF
REGULAR, JUMBO, MAMMOTH OR NEW MINISCULE

SIR PUFFY'S®
CHICKEN LUMPS ™
available in three great flavors...
VANILLA, PORK and GRAPE
YOU WON'T BELIEVE IT'S CHICKEN!

·RNER

Billy has eaten a Sir Puffy's® 100% sugar caramel and marshmallow topped Apple Inside-Out Tart™ every day for the past two years. See if you can draw a line connecting all the pimples on his face without crossing the line or lifting your pencil from the page!

CAN YOU FIND YOUR WAY TO THE WORD GAME ANSWER?

START

ANSWER TO WORD GAME

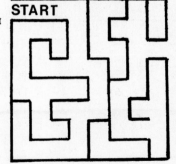

ARTIST: BOB CLARKE

23

Several issues back, we ran an article entitled "The MAD Hate Book", in which we demonstrated to readers how to feel better by blowing off steam about pet hates. The response was more than gratifying. An avalanche of letters poured

THE MAD H

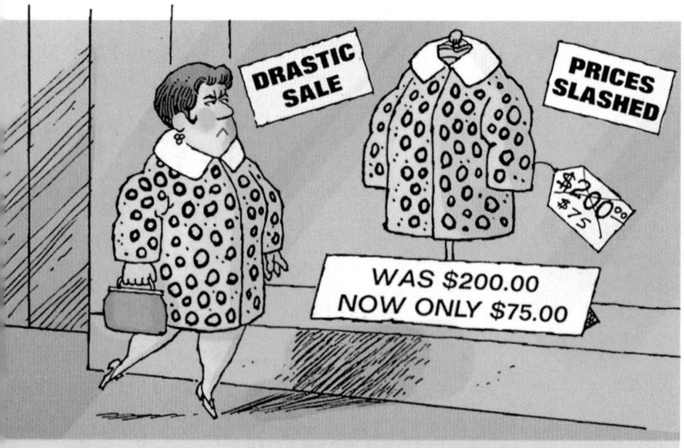
DRASTIC SALE
PRICES SLASHED
$200.00
$75
WAS $200.00
NOW ONLY $75.00

Don't you hate . . . when something goes "On Sale" the day after you bought it!

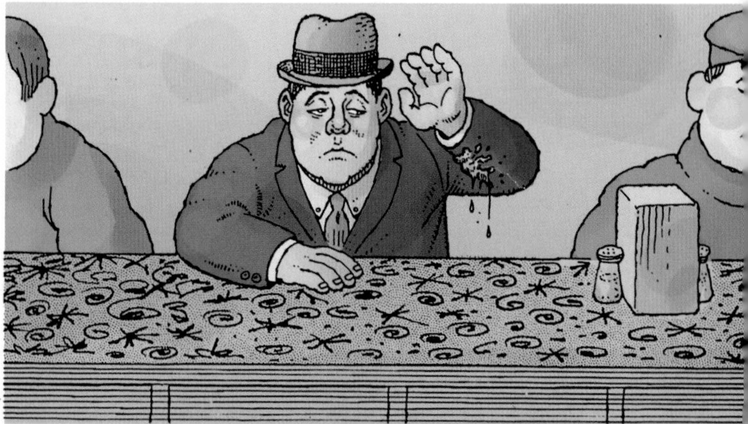

Don't you hate . . . lunch counter-tops with colorful patterns that completely camouflage spilled foods and sauces!

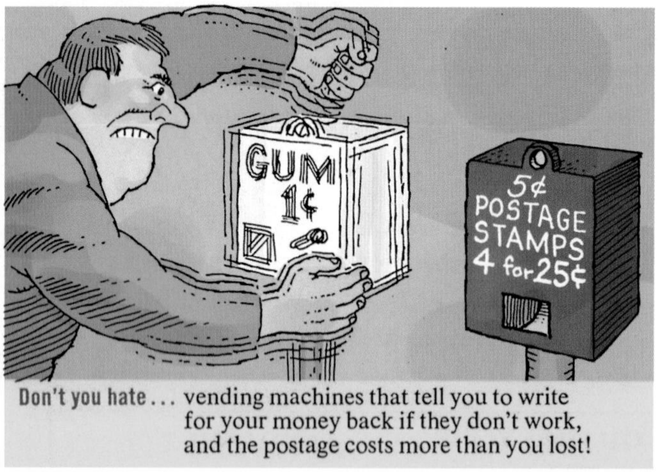
GUM
1¢
5¢
POSTAGE
STAMPS
4 for 25¢

Don't you hate . . . vending machines that tell you to write for your money back if they don't work, and the postage costs more than you lost!

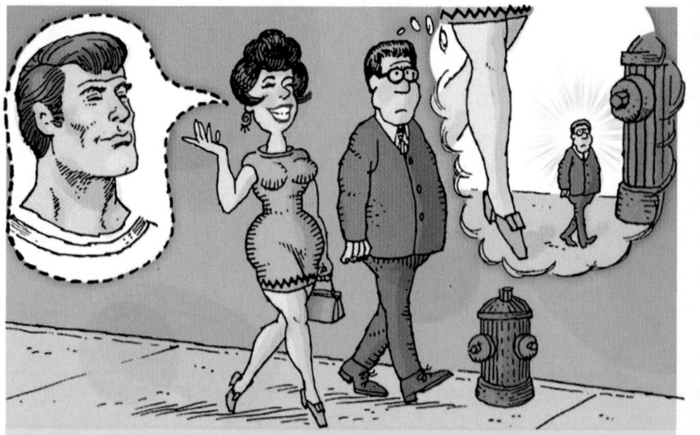

Don't you hate . . . a date who describes the qualities her "ideal man" should have, and none of them fit you!

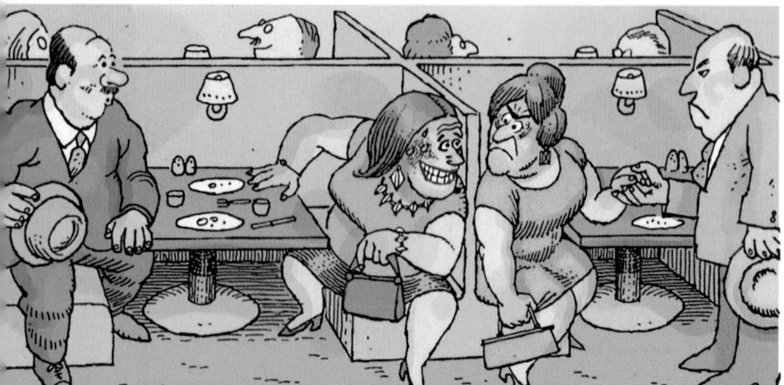

Don't you hate . . . finding out that the person you were tearing apart all through dinner was in the next booth all the time!

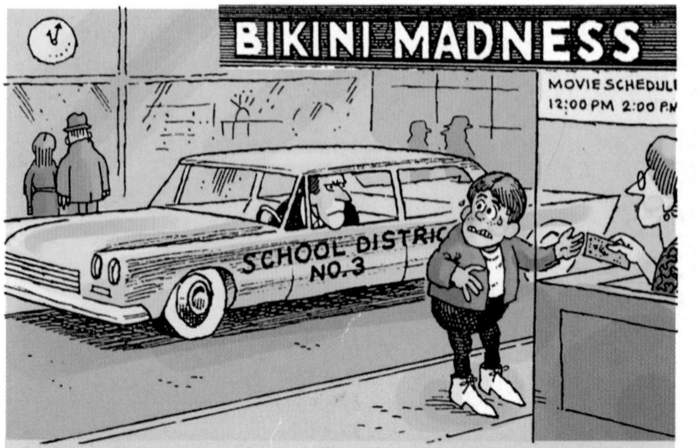
BIKINI MADNESS
12:00 PM 2:00 PM
SCHOOL DISTRIC
NO. 3

Don't you hate . . . meeting a school representative when you're supposed to be home . . . sick!

in from readers blowing off steam about their pet hates—mainly "MAD" and "The MAD Hate Book" article. And so, not to be out-done in the hostility department, here we go again with another more aggravating and exacerbating chapter of . . .

ATE BOOK VOL. II

WRITER AND ARTIST: AL JAFFEE COLORIST: CARL PETERSON

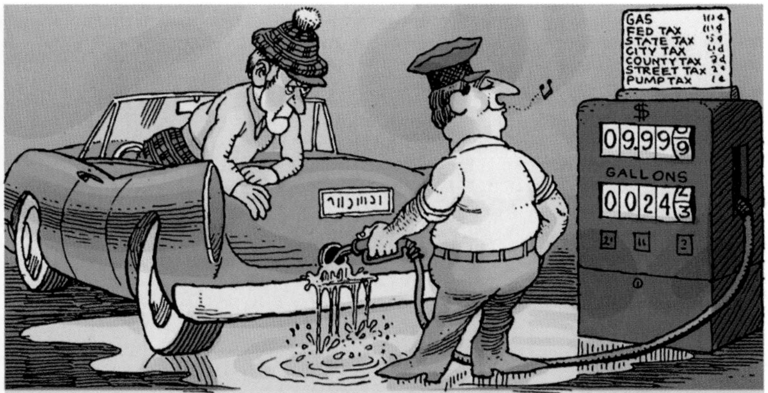
GAS
FED TAX
STATE TAX
CITY TAX
COUNTY TAX
STREET TAX
PUMP TAX
$
GALLONS

Don't you hate . . . gas station attendants who insist on "rounding out" the amount of your purchase so you end up paying for gas that overflowed onto the ground!

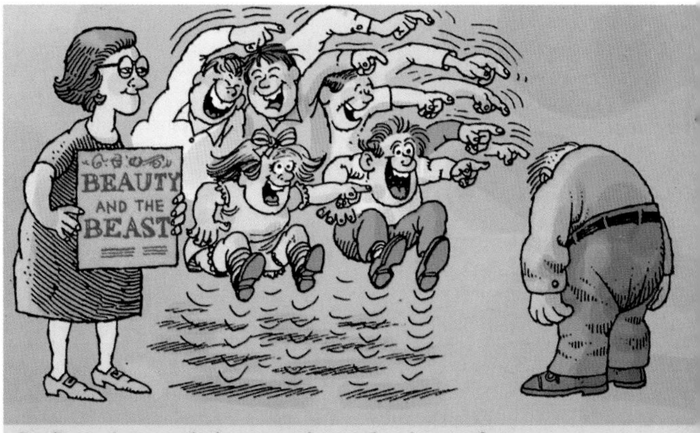
BEAUTY AND THE BEAST

Don't you hate . . . being unanimously chosen for a repulsive role in your school play!

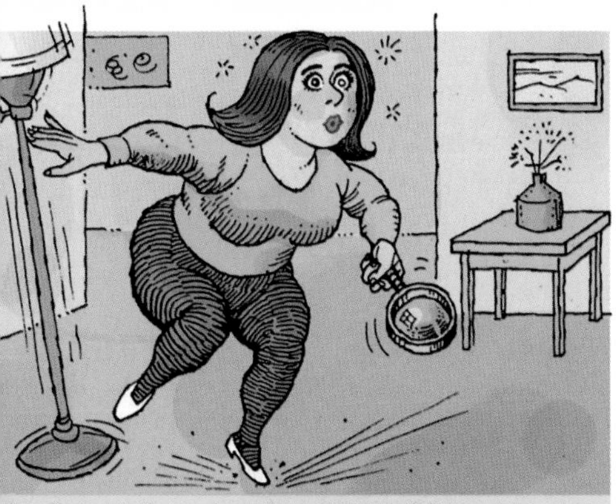

Don't you hate . . . hearing a crunching sound while looking for a lost contact lens!

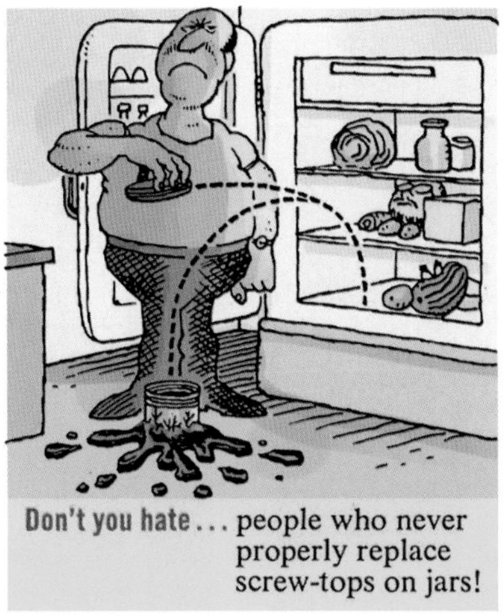

Don't you hate . . . people who never properly replace screw-tops on jars!

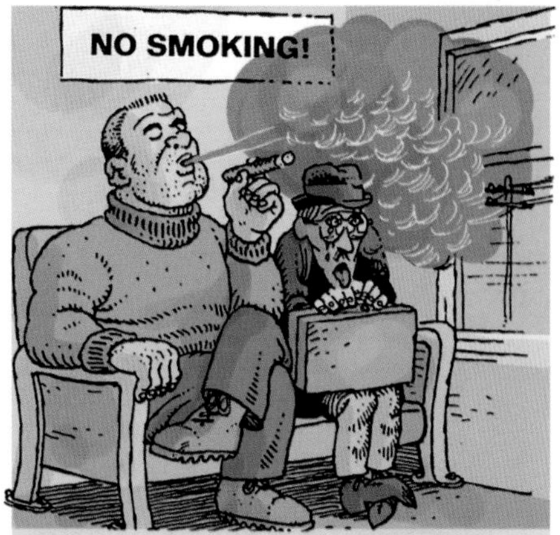
NO SMOKING!

Don't you hate . . . big guys who smoke in "No Smoking" areas!

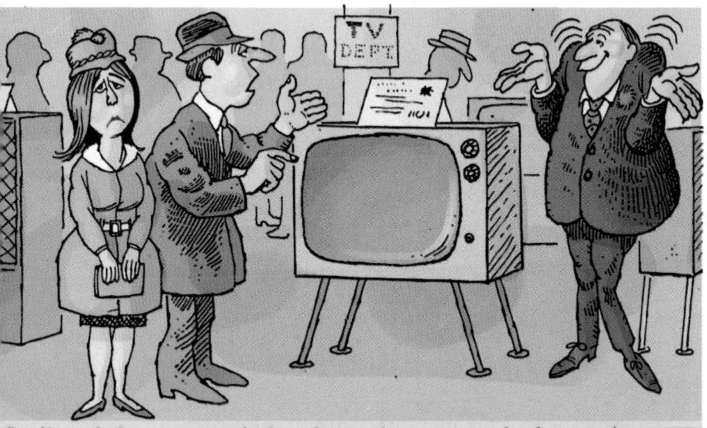
TV DEPT

Don't you hate . . . store clerks who can't answer a single question without first checking with the Manager!

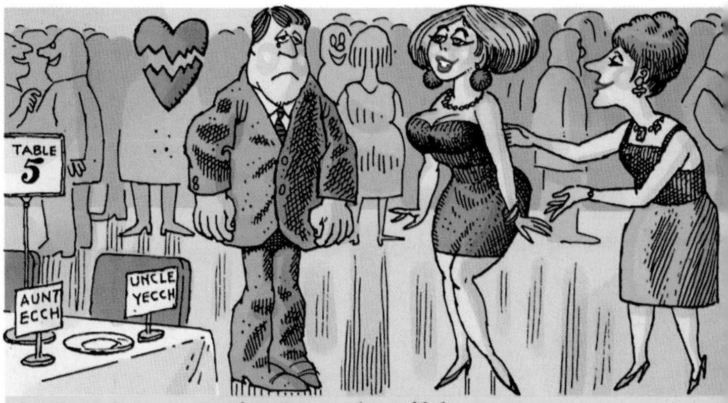
TABLE 5
AUNT ECCH
UNCLE YECCH

Don't you hate . . . meeting a super-beautiful woman at a relative's wedding, and discovering she's a first cousin!

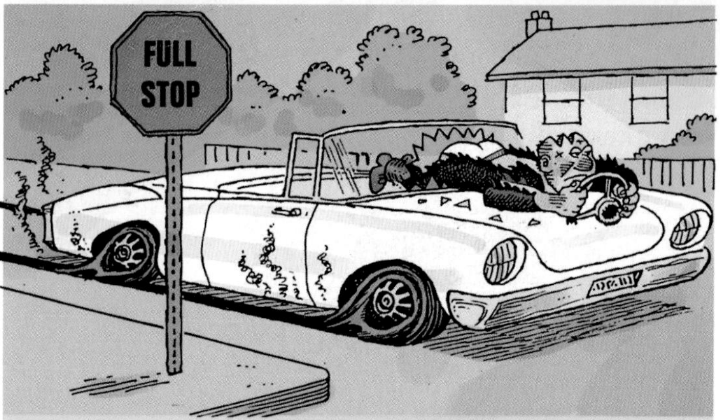
FULL STOP

Don't you hate . . . borrowing a car, and suddenly discovering it has power brakes!

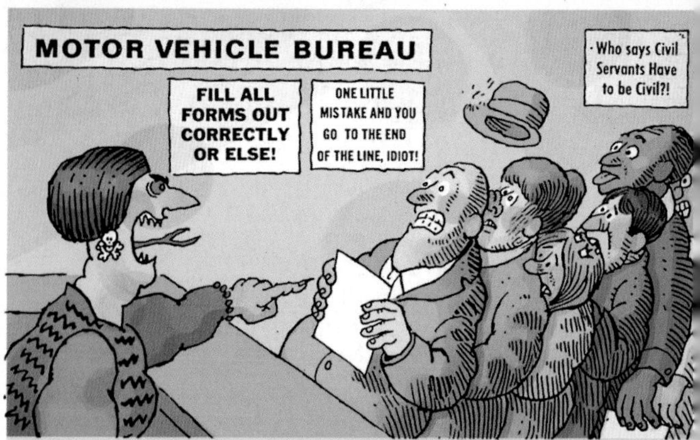
MOTOR VEHICLE BUREAU
FILL ALL FORMS OUT CORRECTLY OR ELSE!
ONE LITTLE MISTAKE AND YOU GO TO THE END OF THE LINE, IDIOT!
Who says Civil Servants Have to be Civil?!

Don't you hate . . . civil servants who know they can't lose their jobs no matter how uncivilly they treat you!

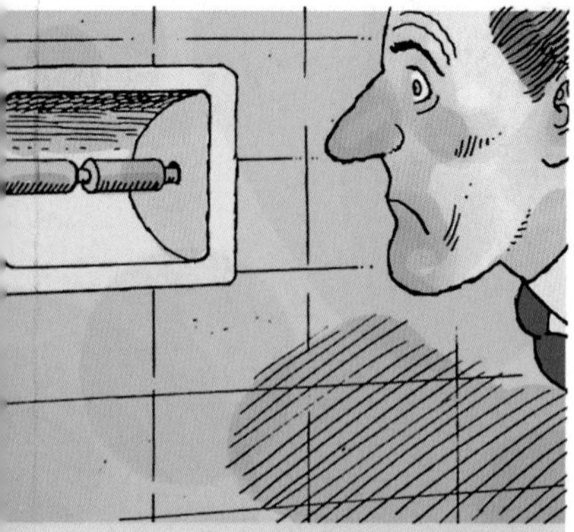

Don't you hate . . . being surprised by an empty tissue dispenser!

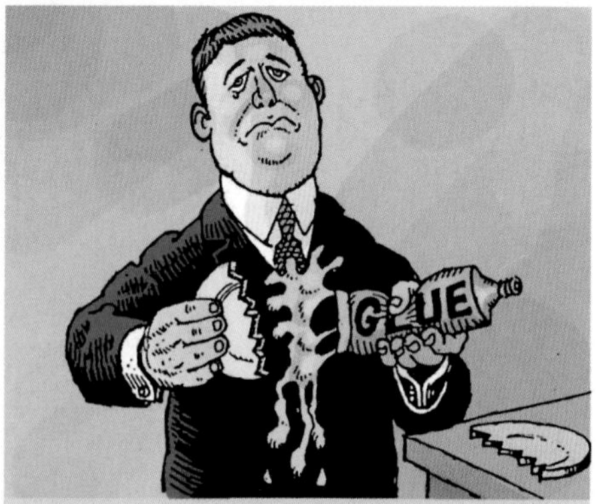

Don't you hate . . . when something ecch-y suddenly comes out of the wrong end of the tube!

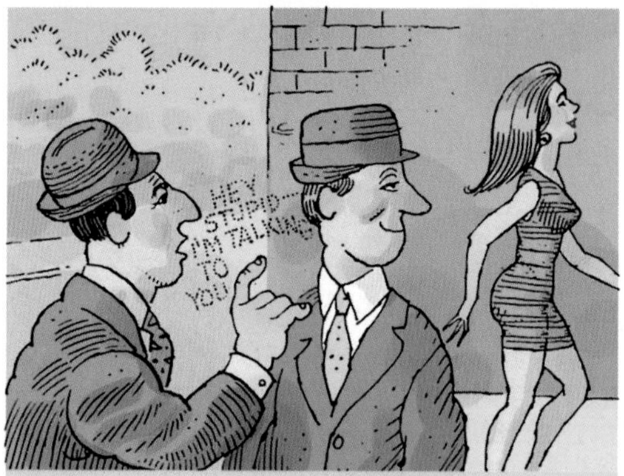
HEY STUPID—I'M TALKING TO YOU

Don't you hate . . . people who ask questions and pay no attention to the answers!

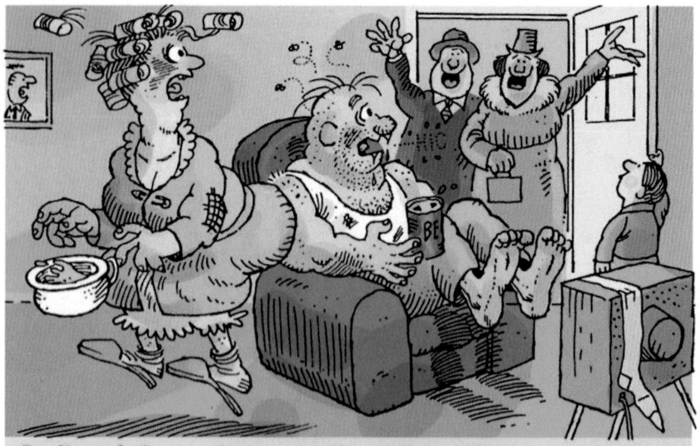

Don't you hate . . . when you tell people to "drop in any time!" . . . and they do!

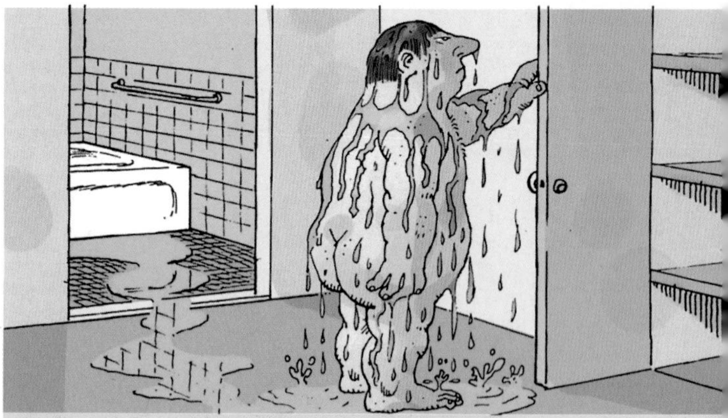

Don't you hate . . . discovering there are no towels after you've just taken a bath!

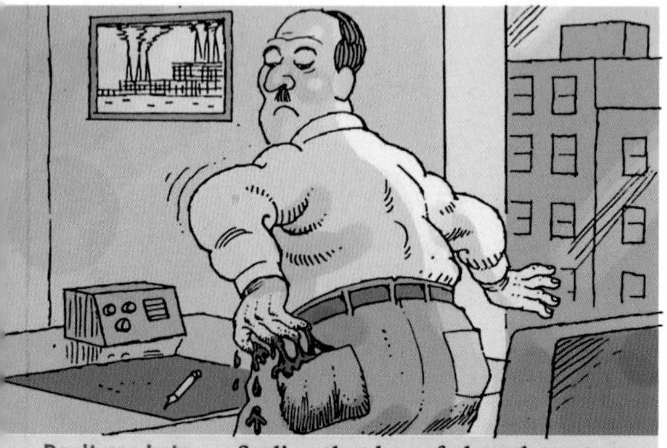

Don't you hate . . . finding that bar of chocolate you stuck into your pocket "for only a moment" eight hours later!

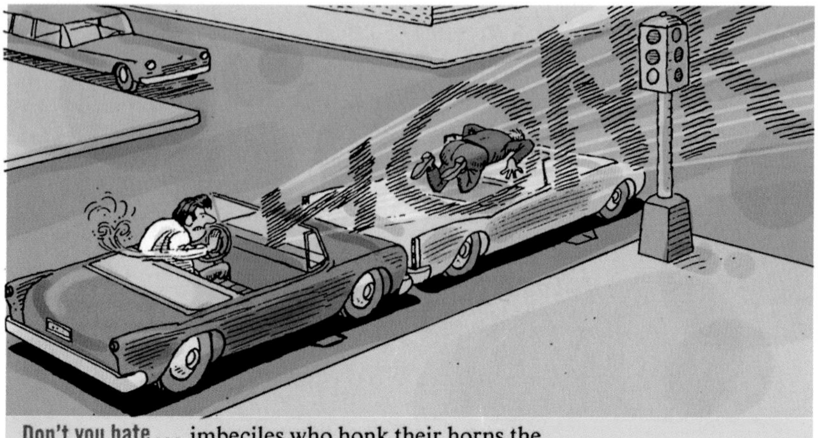
HONK

Don't you hate . . . imbeciles who honk their horns the split second after the light turns green!

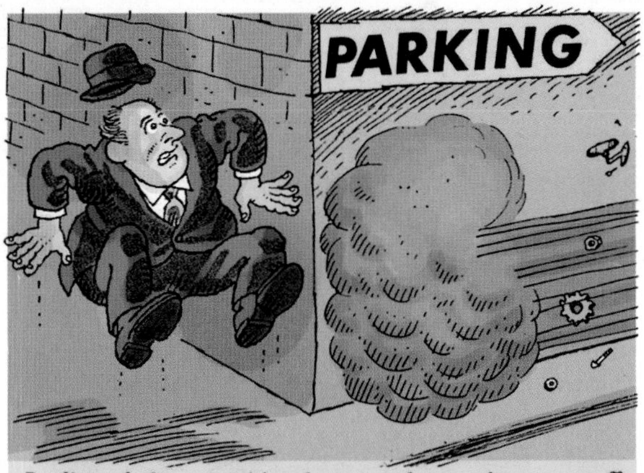
PARKING

Don't you hate . . . parking lot attendants who zoom off in your new car like it was a 727 jet!

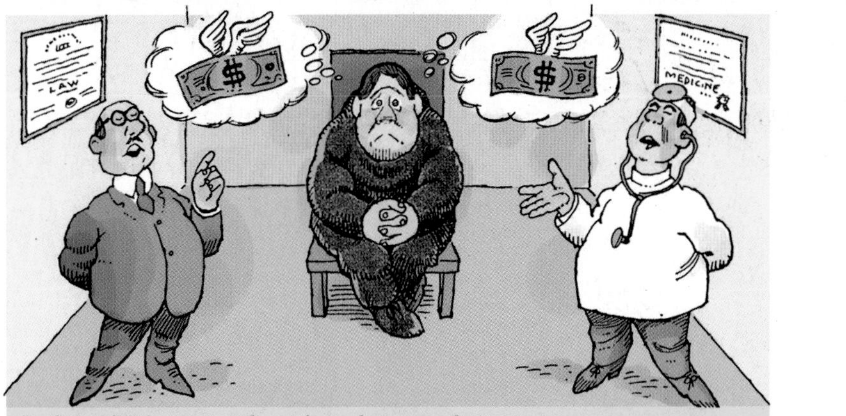
LAW
MEDICINE

Don't you hate . . . never knowing what your doctor or your lawyer's fee will eventually be!

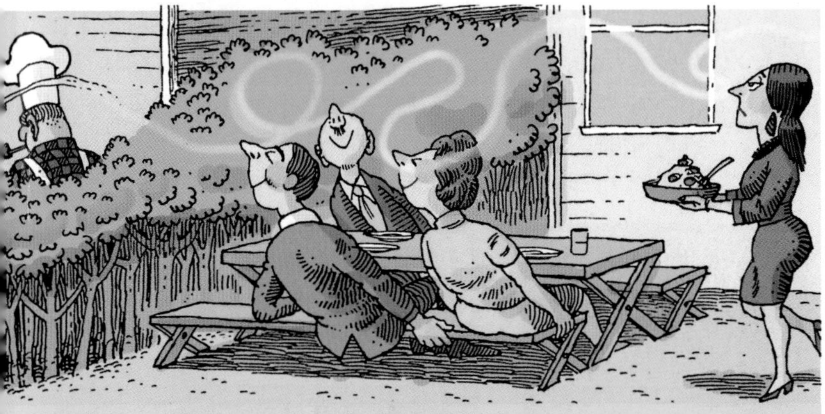

on't you hate . . . neighbors who barbecue steaks when you're downwind serving tuna fish!

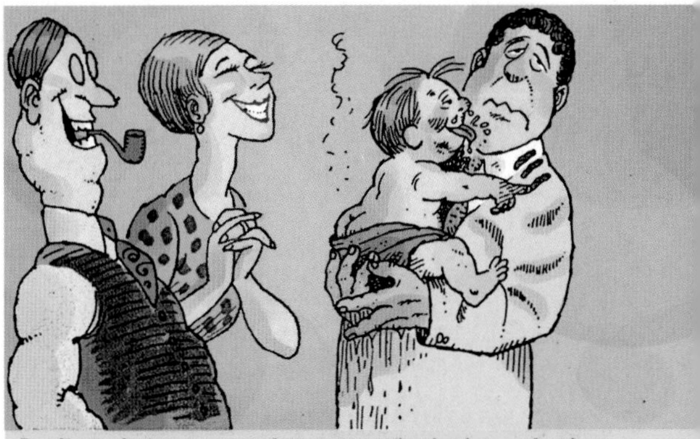

Don't you hate . . . proud parents who insist on letting you enjoy the ecstatic pleasure of holding their brand new baby!

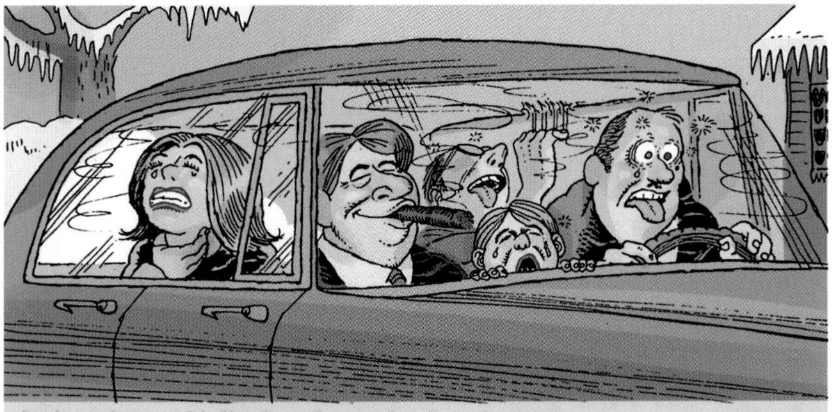

Don't you hate . . . birdbrains who smoke cigars in a car when it's too cold to open a window!

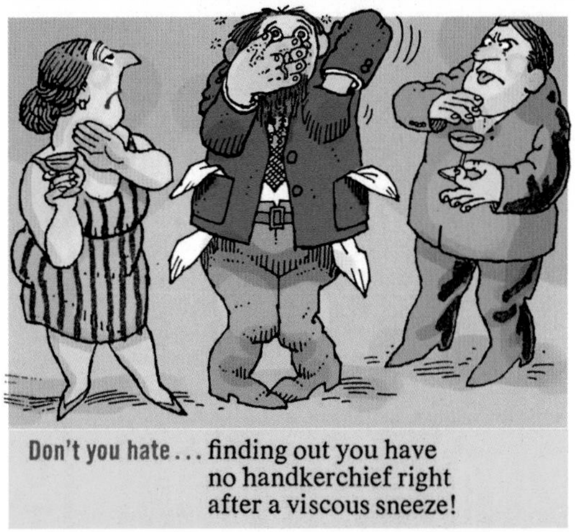

Don't you hate . . . finding out you have no handkerchief right after a viscous sneeze!

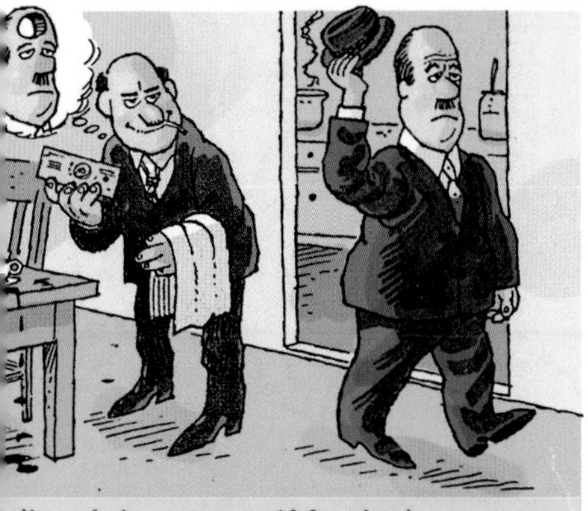

n't you hate . . . yourself for tipping when you know darn well the service was terrible!

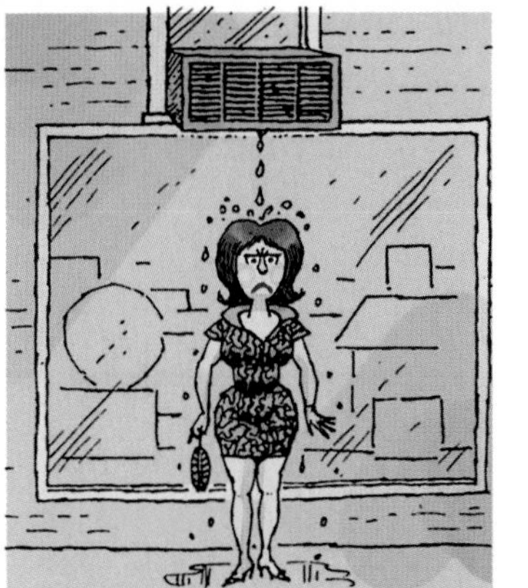

Don't you hate . . . dripping window air-conditioners!

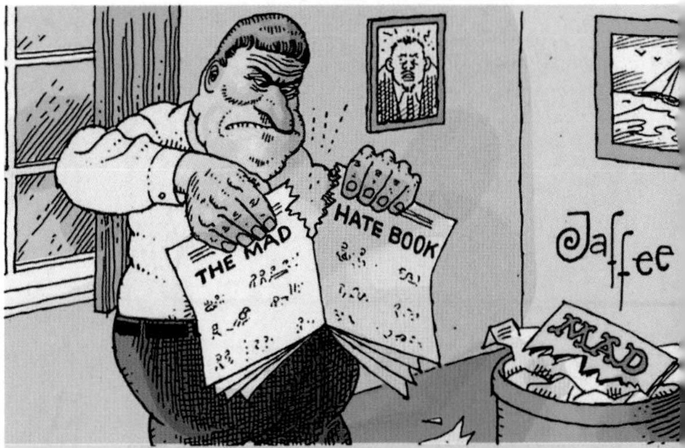
THE MAD
HATE BOOK
Jaffee
MAD

Don't you hate . . . magazines that print sequels to articles that never should have been run in the first place!

THE DWAYNE CHRONICLES

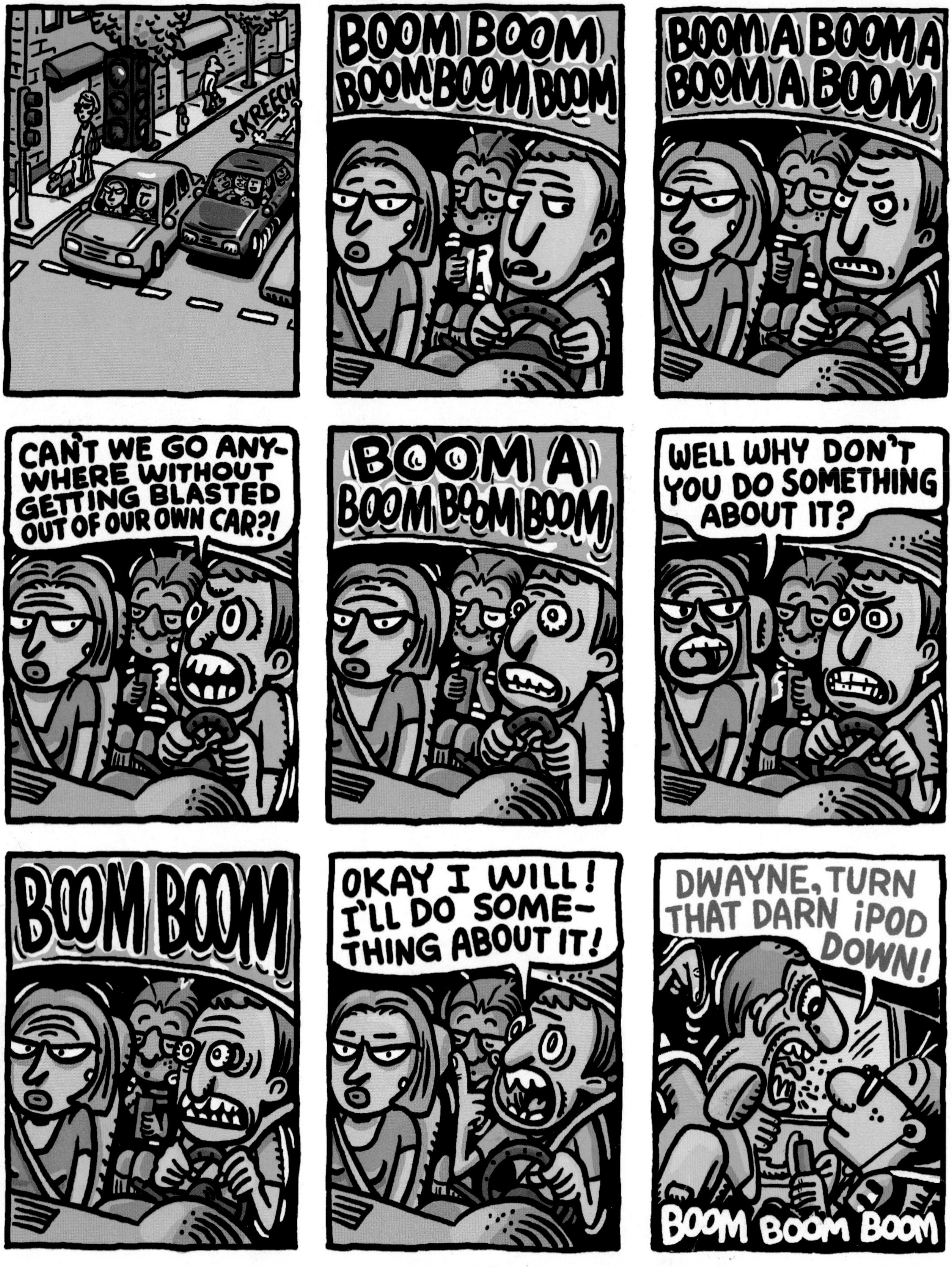
SKREECH
BOOM BOOM BOOM BOOM BOOM
BOOM A BOOM A BOOM A BOOM
CAN'T WE GO ANYWHERE WITHOUT GETTING BLASTED OUT OF OUR OWN CAR?!
BOOM A BOOM BOOM BOOM
WELL WHY DON'T YOU DO SOMETHING ABOUT IT?
BOOM BOOM
OKAY I WILL! I'LL DO SOMETHING ABOUT IT!
DWAYNE, TURN THAT DARN iPOD DOWN!
BOOM BOOM BOOM

WRITER AND ARTIST: ERIC SCOTT

If you're planning on visiting one of our national parks, you better hurry before the oil companies begin drilling for oil under each and every rock like they were Jed Clampett on a Saturday night bender. But at least for now these great natural wonder treasures are here for you to enjoy and us to make fun of. Here's...

A MAD PEEK BEHIND THE SCENES AT A NATIONAL PARK

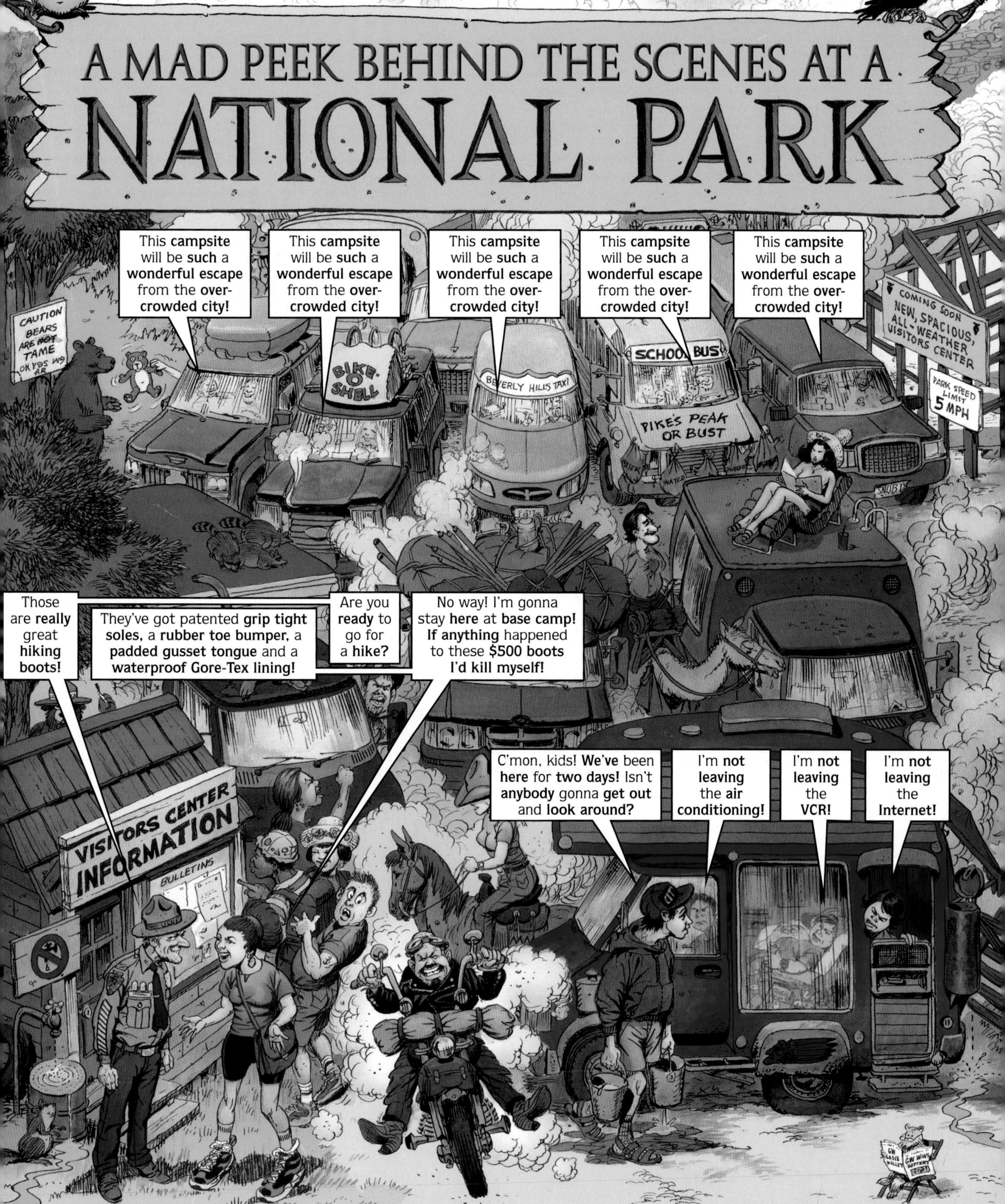
CAUTION BEARS ARE ~~NOT~~ TAME
This campsite will be such a wonderful escape from the over-crowded city!
This campsite will be such a wonderful escape from the over-crowded city!
This campsite will be such a wonderful escape from the over-crowded city!
This campsite will be such a wonderful escape from the over-crowded city!
This campsite will be such a wonderful escape from the over-crowded city!
COMING SOON NEW, SPACIOUS, ALL-WEATHER VISITORS CENTER
PARK SPEED LIMIT 5 MPH
BIKE-O-SHELL
BEVERLY HILLS TAXI
SCHOOL BUS
PIKE'S PEAK OR BUST
Those are really great hiking boots!
They've got patented grip tight soles, a rubber toe bumper, a padded gusset tongue and a waterproof Gore-Tex lining!
Are you ready to go for a hike?
No way! I'm gonna stay here at base camp! If anything happened to these $500 boots I'd kill myself!
VISITORS CENTER INFORMATION
BULLETINS
C'mon, kids! We've been here for two days! Isn't anybody gonna get out and look around?
I'm not leaving the air conditioning!
I'm not leaving the VCR!
I'm not leaving the Internet!

ARTIST: GEORGE WOODBRIDGE WRITER: AMY GILLETT COLORIST: DIGITAL CHAMELEON

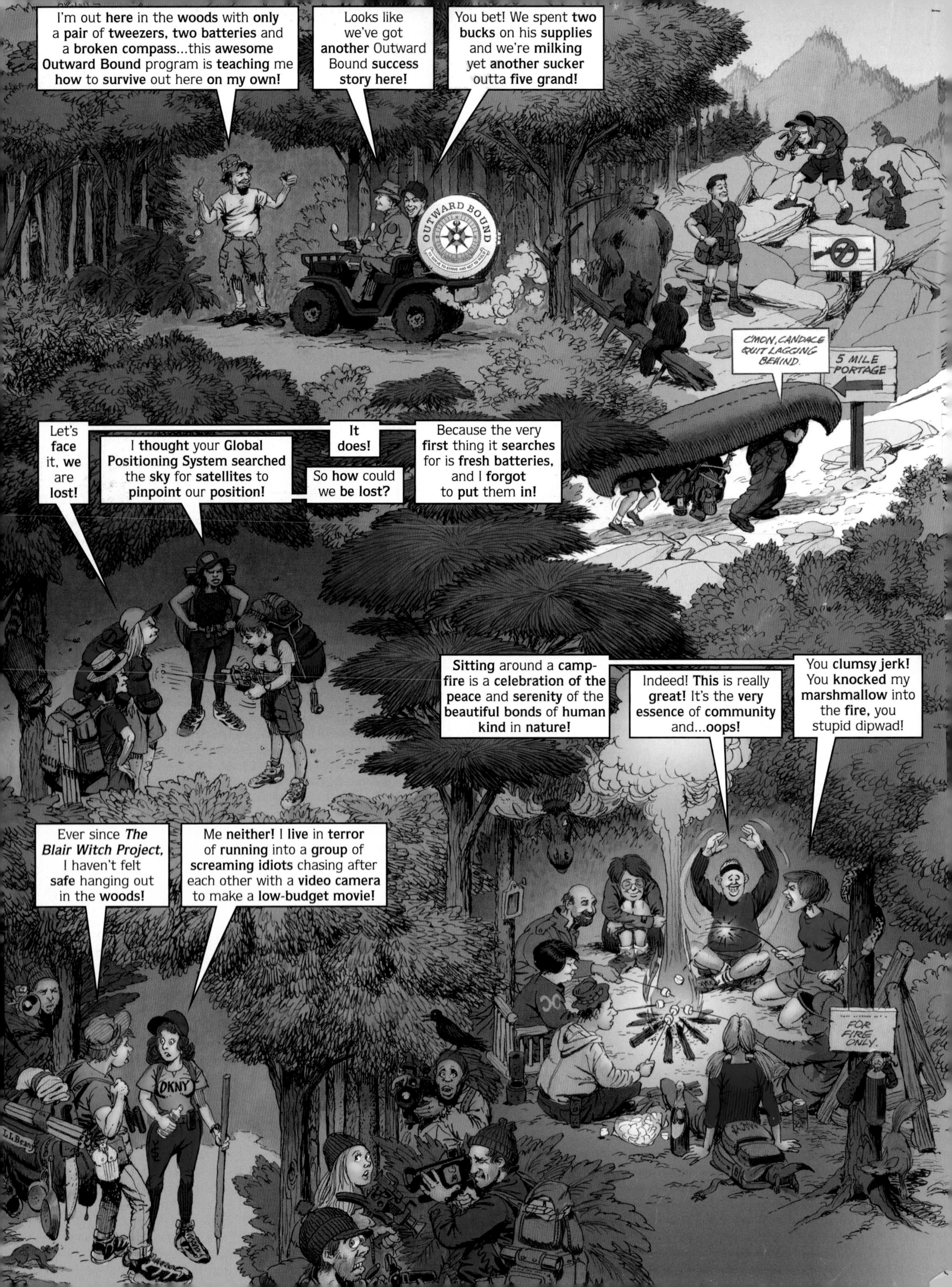
I'm out **here** in the **woods** with **only** a **pair** of **tweezers, two batteries** and a **broken compass**...this **awesome Outward Bound** program is **teaching** me **how** to **survive** out here **on my own!**
Looks like we've got **another** Outward Bound **success story here!**
You bet! We spent **two bucks** on his **supplies** and we're **milking** yet **another sucker** outta **five grand!**
OUTWARD BOUND
C'MON, CANDACE QUIT LAGGING BEHIND.
5 MILE PORTAGE
Let's **face** it, **we** are **lost!**
I **thought** your **Global Positioning System searched** the **sky** for **satellites** to **pinpoint** our **position!**
So **how** could we **be lost?**
It does!
Because the very **first** thing it **searches** for is **fresh batteries,** and I **forgot** to **put** them **in!**
Sitting around a **camp-fire** is a **celebration of the peace** and **serenity** of the **beautiful bonds** of **human kind** in **nature!**
Indeed! **This** is really **great!** It's the **very essence** of **community** and...**oops!**
You **clumsy jerk!** You **knocked** my **marshmallow** into the **fire,** you stupid dipwad!
Ever since ***The Blair Witch Project,*** I haven't felt **safe** hanging out in the **woods!**
Me **neither!** I **live** in **terror** of **running** into a **group** of **screaming idiots** chasing after each other with a **video camera** to make a **low-budget movie!**
FOR FIRE ONLY.
DKNY
L.L.Bean

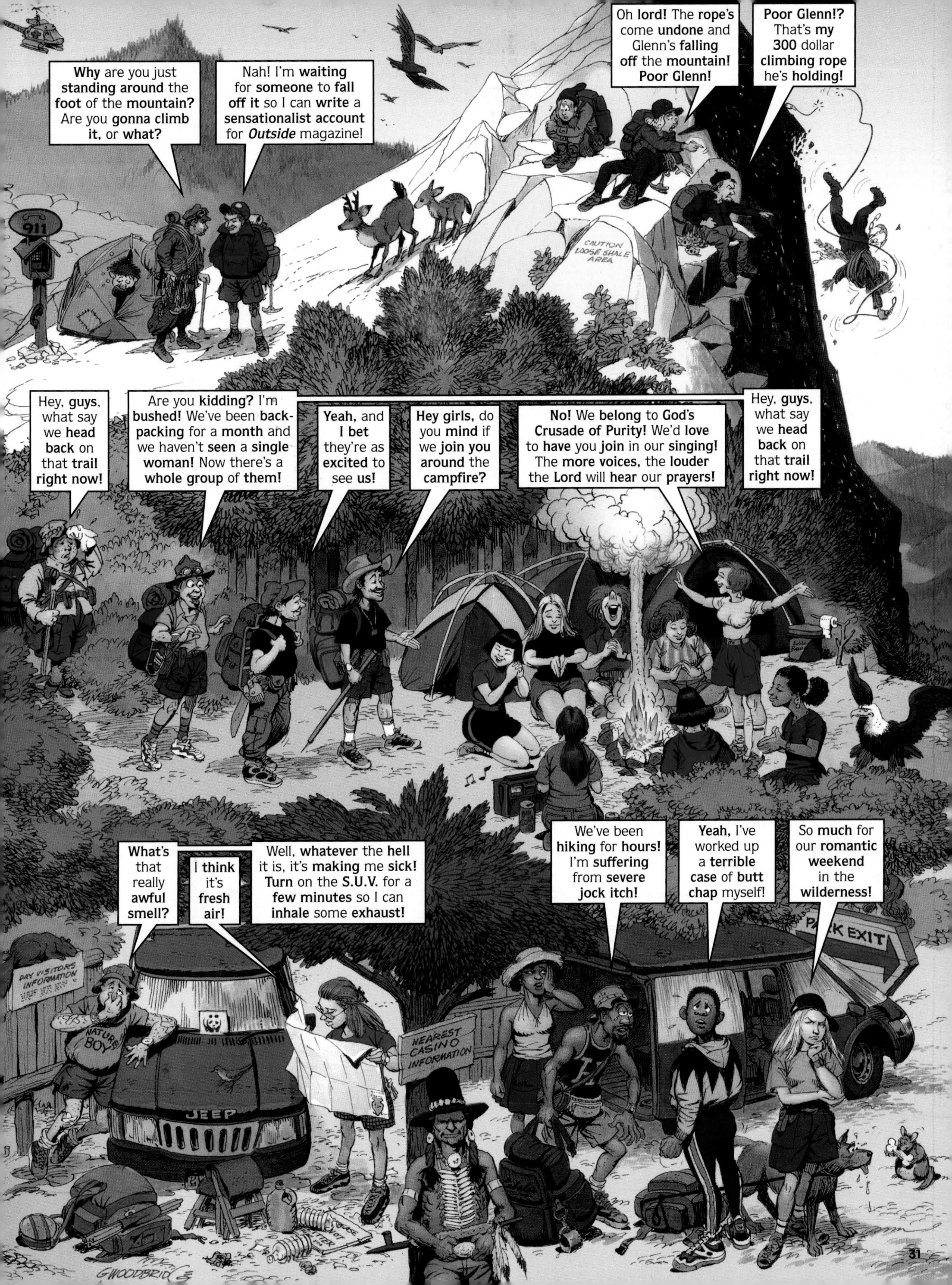

Why are you just standing around the foot of the mountain? Are you gonna climb it, or what?
Nah! I'm waiting for someone to fall off it so I can write a sensationalist account for *Outside* magazine!
Oh lord! The rope's come undone and Glenn's falling off the mountain! Poor Glenn!
Poor Glenn!? That's my 300 dollar climbing rope he's holding!
911
CAUTION LOOSE SHALE AREA
Hey, guys, what say we head back on that trail right now!
Are you kidding? I'm bushed! We've been back-packing for a month and we haven't seen a single woman! Now there's a whole group of them!
Yeah, and I bet they're as excited to see us!
Hey girls, do you mind if we join you around the campfire?
No! We belong to God's Crusade of Purity! We'd love to have you join in our singing! The more voices, the louder the Lord will hear our prayers!
Hey, guys, what say we head back on that trail right now!
What's that really awful smell?
I think it's fresh air!
Well, whatever the hell it is, it's making me sick! Turn on the S.U.V. for a few minutes so I can inhale some exhaust!
We've been hiking for hours! I'm suffering from severe jock itch!
Yeah, I've worked up a terrible case of butt chap myself!
So much for our romantic weekend in the wilderness!
DAY VISITORS INFORMATION
NATURE BOY
JEEP
NEAREST CASINO INFORMATION
PARK EXIT
G WOODBRIDGE

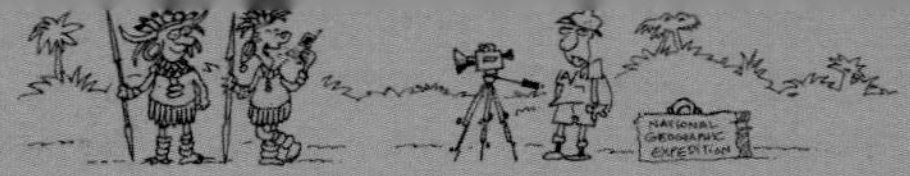

Planet TAD!!!!!

http://www.galaxyo'blogs.com/planettad

Search

Planet TAD!!!!!

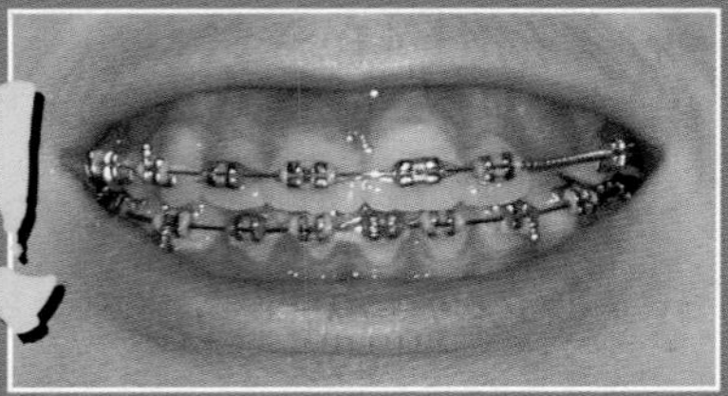

[**About Me**]

[**Name**|Tad]
[**Grade**|Nine]
[**Briefcase I Would Choose on "Deal or No Deal":** |Six]

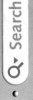

[1 June|**03:43pm**]

[**mood**| so depressed]

Ugh. I'm in so much trouble, my stomach hurts. My friend Kevin let me borrow his dad's digital camera, and before I could even use it, I kind of put it in my bookbag and threw it into a corner. Now, it's broken, and it's going to cost $300 to get it fixed. I spend every day avoiding Kevin at school, and every evening grabbing the phone whenever it rings, in case the guy who looks like David Spade from the camera store calls, so my parents don't find out what I did. I'm so stressed, I've been having the dry heaves.

Then again, I also had the school cafeteria chili dogs for lunch. That might also have something to do with it.

[2 June|**01:02pm**]

[**mood**| frustrated]

I gathered together all my money today, and went through all the sofa cushions in the house, twice. You know, just in case someone had dropped 1,200 quarters in there lately. Nobody had. In total, I have $37. That's $263 less than I need. I'm too embarrassed to ask my mom and dad, which means I need to figure out a way to get that much money, and fast. There is one option, but it's too scary to even think about.

[3 June|**07:39pm**]

[**mood**| trying to distract myself]

I'm not entirely sure why Commissioner Gordon decided the best way to summon Batman was the Bat-Signal. Like, what if the skies are clear, and the signal doesn't show up? Or what if Batman's indoors — like, at a movie or something — and he doesn't see it for a few hours? Seems to me like the way to go would've been a Bat-Text Messager.

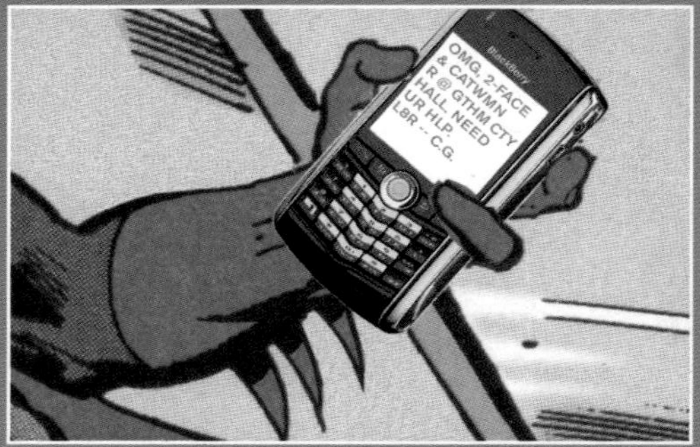
BlackBerry
OMG, 2-FACE & CATWMN R @ GTHM CTY HALL. NEED UR HLP. L8R -- C.G.

[4 June|**03:11pm**]

Kevin finally cornered me at lunch and asked me where his dad's camera was. I lied and told him I'd left it at home. He said to be sure to bring it in by Wednesday, because his dad was looking for it over the weekend.

So I had no choice: I borrowed money from my kid sister Sophie. She's kept every penny anyone ever gave her — all her allowance, all her birthday checks from Grandma, even her money from the Tooth Fairy. I asked her if I could borrow the money, and pay her back with my summer job money. She told me she'd loan me the $263, but only if I paid her back $375 by July 20. Also, she told me that I might owe her more money, if something called the "prime lending rate" goes up.

Sophie is the scariest 9-year-old in the universe.

[4 June|07:38pm]

I don't know why they call them EYEglasses. Where else would you put your glasses? It's not like there are earglasses and noseglasses to get them confused with.

NOSEGLASSES?

EARGLASSES?

[5 June|4:42pm]

[**mood**|  baffled]

So, we've been assigned 1984 in Mrs. Bernard's English class, and we've been reading it for a few weeks now, and only during today's class did Doug Spivak raise his hand and say, "Hey, wait a minute: This didn't really happen in 1984, did it?"

Doug isn't the sharpest knife in the drawer. In fact, he's more like a spoon or something.

[6 June|03:17pm]

[**mood**| relieved]

Well, I went to the store last night, and David Spade had fixed the camera. I paid him the money, then today I gave the camera back to Kevin. It's going to take forever for me to pay back Sophie, but at least everything's over.

[7 June|08:22pm]

I think it might be fun if, in addition to helper monkeys for the disabled, there were also hinderer monkeys, for the non-disabled. They'd just live in your house and thwart you — like, put stuff in your way, or hide your keys on a high shelf. It'd make life more interesting.

[8 June|05:39pm]

[**mood**|  cranky]

NOW THAT'S WHAT I CALL *THE ABSENCE OF BAGPIPES!*

Today there was an assembly at school. Our vice-principal plays the bagpipes, so he and some of his other bagpiping friends put on a concert for us. It was awful. But I did realize something: I don't think there's a more beautiful sound in the whole world than the silence right after someone has stopped playing the bagpipes. If you could make an album just out of that silence, you'd sell millions of copies.

[11 June|04:12pm]

[**mood**| depressed yet again]

So, Kevin came up to me at lunch today and said, "Hey, what did you do to my dad's camera?" I almost puked up my ravioli, but instead I just said, "Nothing. I didn't do anything." Then he said, "Are you sure?" And I said, "Yeah." And that's when he told me that the weirdest thing had happened. His dad told him he'd dropped the camera a few weeks ago, and it had stopped working. That's why he'd been looking for it — to take it in for repairs — but now it was working fine again. Kevin shrugged and said, "Funny, huh?"

Yeah. It's funny. It's freaking hilarious.

WRITER: TIM CARVELL   ARTIST: BRIAN DURNIAK

THE COURAGEOUS COIL'S CRUSADE

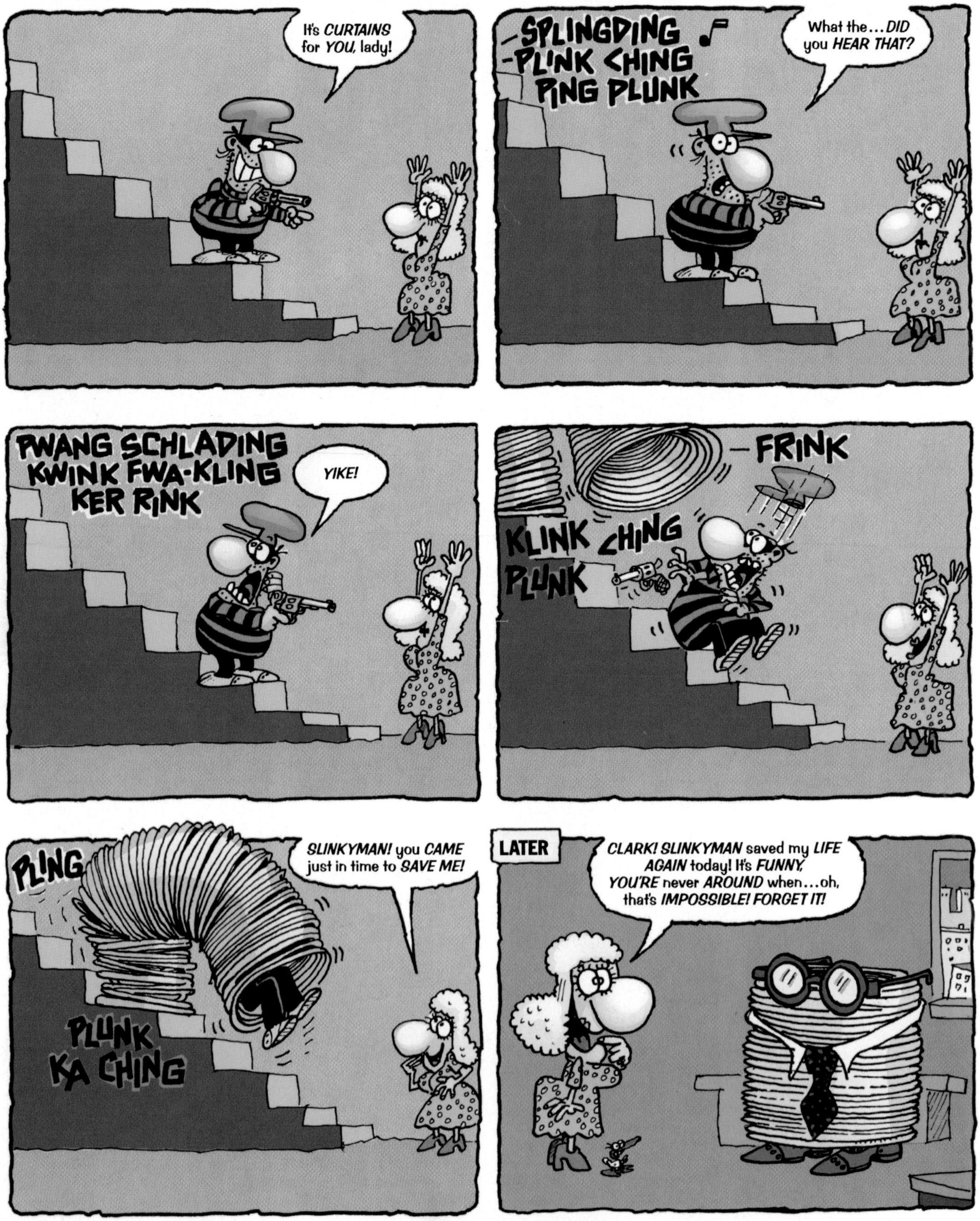
It's CURTAINS for YOU, lady!
-SPLINGDING -PLINK CHING PING PLUNK
What the...DID you HEAR THAT?
PWANG SCHLADING KWINK FWA-KLING KER RINK
YIKE!
-FRINK
KLINK CHING PLUNK
PLING
PLUNK KA CHING
SLINKYMAN! you CAME just in time to SAVE ME!
LATER
CLARK! SLINKYMAN saved my LIFE AGAIN today! It's FUNNY, YOU'RE never AROUND when...oh, that's IMPOSSIBLE! FORGET IT!

ARTIST AND WRITER: DUCK EDWING

THE SHODDIER IMAGE

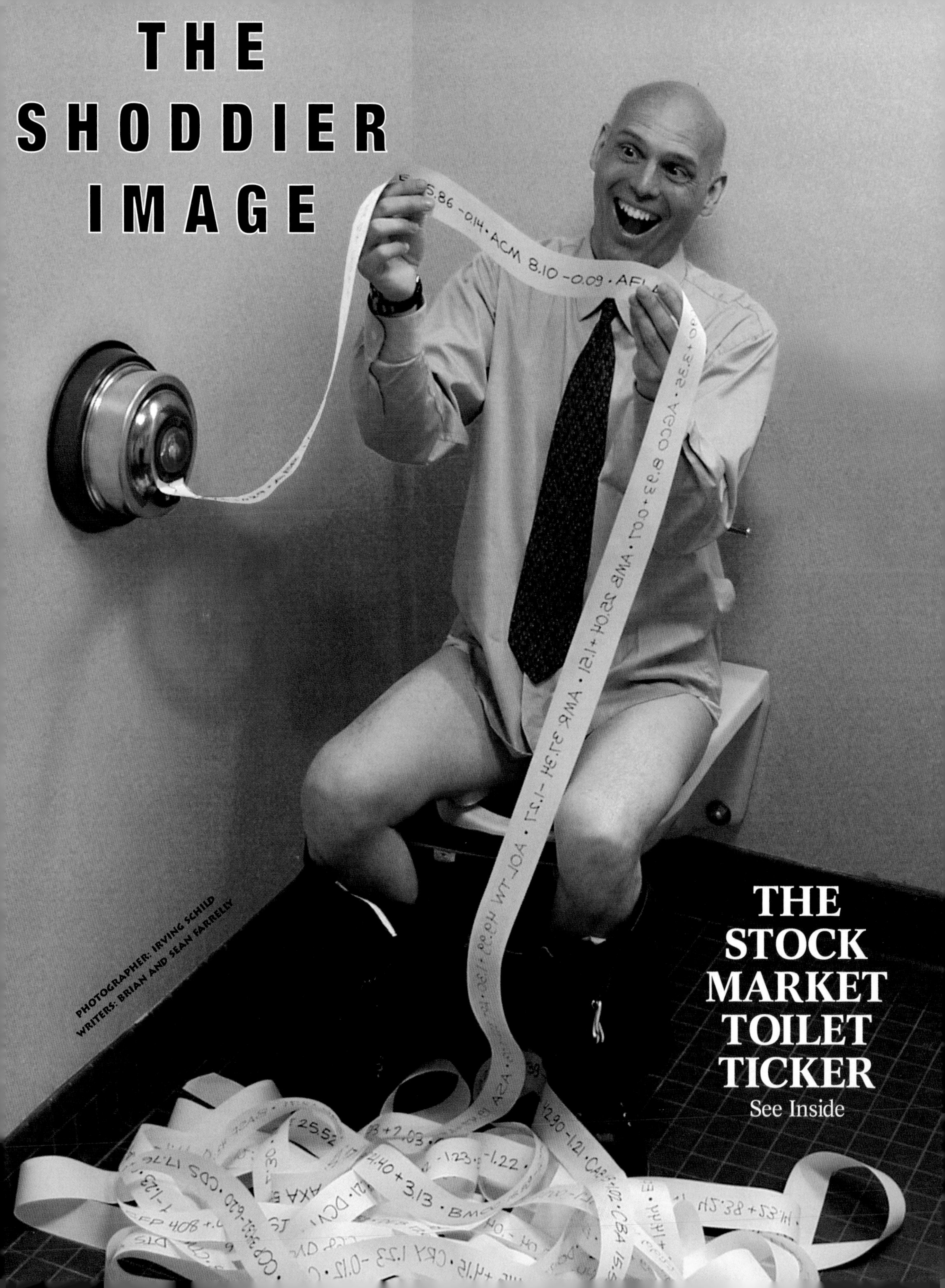
ACM 8.10 -0.09 • AFL
AMR 37.34 -1.27
AOL WT 49.99

PHOTOGRAPHER: IRVING SCHILD
WRITERS: BRIAN AND SEAN FARRELLY

THE STOCK MARKET TOILET TICKER

See Inside

THE SHODDIER IMAGE

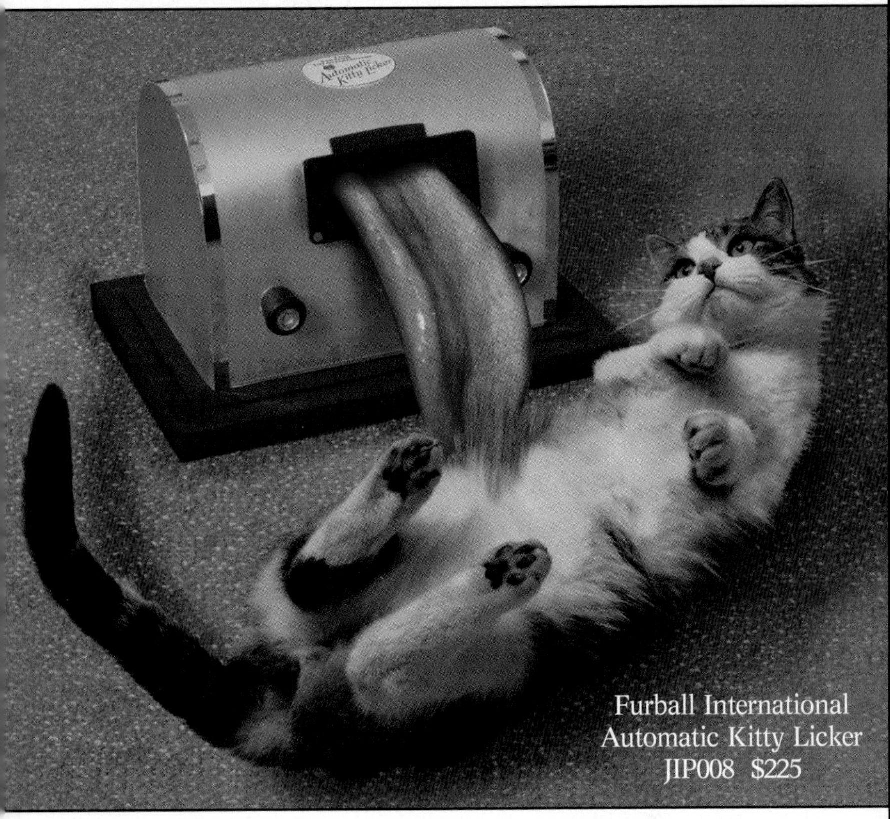
Automatic Kitty Licker

Furball International
Automatic Kitty Licker
JIP008 $225

Give your cat's tongue a much-needed rest with Furball International's Automatic Kitty Licker.

Specially created for elderly or just plain lazy felines who have given up on personal grooming! This amazing device actually licks your cat clean so it has more time for eating, sleeping and clawing your upholstery to shreds. The Kitty Licker's computerized auto-licking tongue is realistically textured to simulate the sandpapery feel of a cat's tongue while using three layers of micro-bristles to wash it free of dirt, dander and excess hair. It also reduces hairballs and provides a more hygienic cleaning than the usual feline "spit bath." The only way to get your cat cleaner is to lick it yourself!

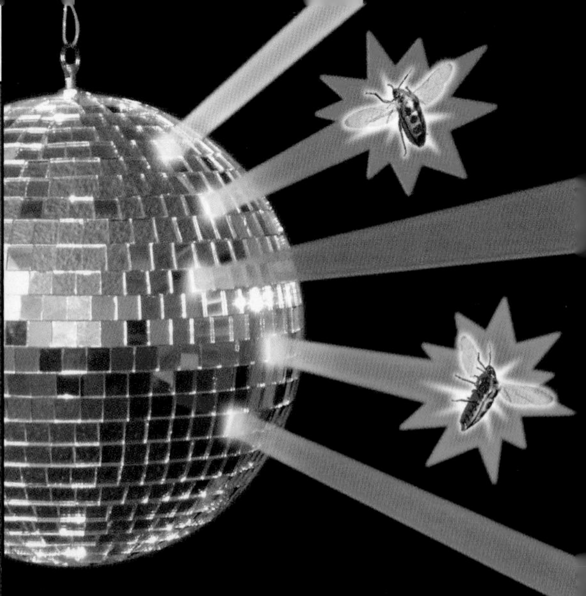

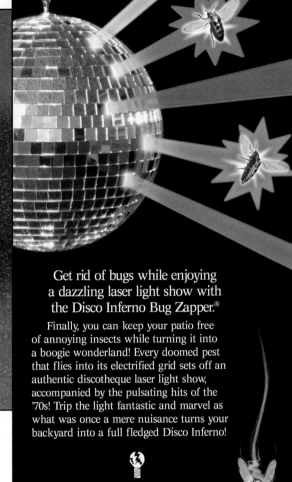

Get rid of bugs while enjoying a dazzling laser light show with the Disco Inferno Bug Zapper.®

Finally, you can keep your patio free of annoying insects while turning it into a boogie wonderland! Every doomed pest that flies into its electrified grid sets off an authentic discotheque laser light show, accompanied by the pulsating hits of the '70s! Trip the light fantastic and marvel as what was once a mere nuisance turns your backyard into a full fledged Disco Inferno!

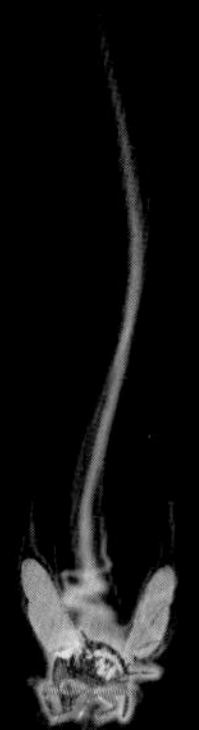

INVENTED HERE.
SO YOU KNOW IT'S SHODDY.

Disco Inferno Bug Zapper®
JIP709 $550

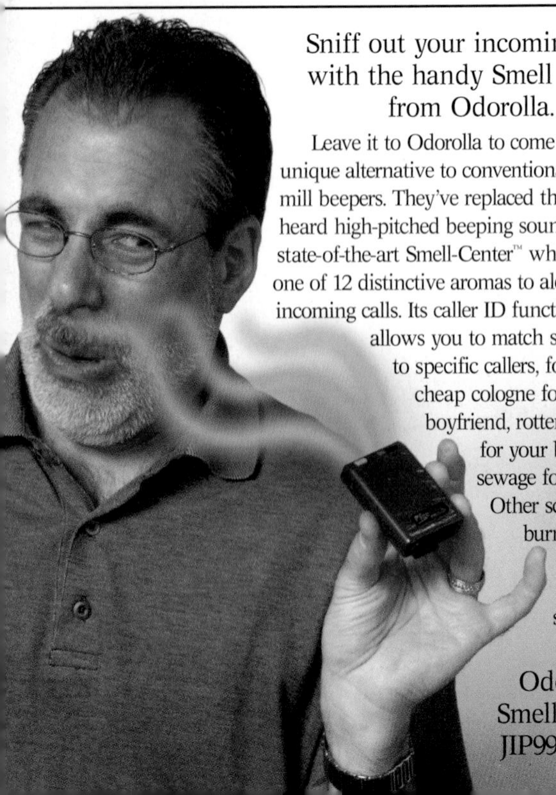

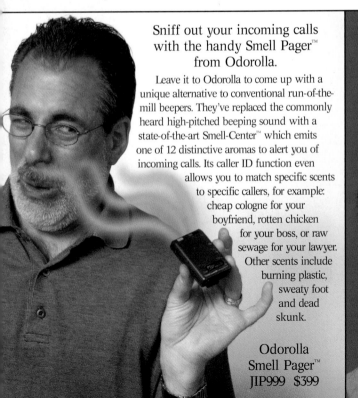

Sniff out your incoming calls with the handy Smell Pager™ from Odorolla.

Leave it to Odorolla to come up with a unique alternative to conventional run-of-the-mill beepers. They've replaced the commonly heard high-pitched beeping sound with a state-of-the-art Smell-Center™ which emits one of 12 distinctive aromas to alert you of incoming calls. Its caller ID function even allows you to match specific scents to specific callers, for example: cheap cologne for your boyfriend, rotten chicken for your boss, or raw sewage for your lawyer. Other scents include burning plastic, sweaty foot and dead skunk.

Odorolla
Smell Pager™
JIP999 $399

Sensational home theater for your eyeballs!

Fool your boss or teacher into thinking you're deep in thought when you're actually watching your favorite TV show with the revolutionary Soony Cornea-Man™, the micro-television that fits directly onto your eyes like a contact lens! Channels can be switched easily by blinking and you can watch two shows at the same time by having different channels play on each pupil. Available with Dolby Surround Sound Ear Implants or close-captioned subtitles for the hearing impaired. (Please note: Reception may vary during head colds.)

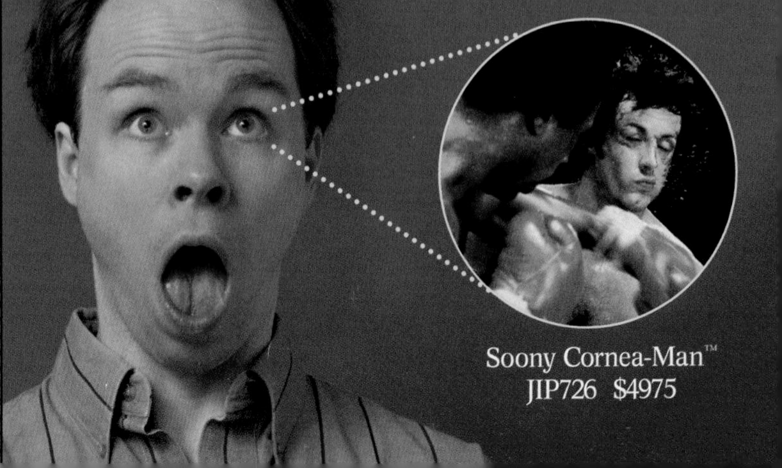

Soony Cornea-Man™
JIP726 $4975

Use laser power to carve your next holiday bird!

Shoddier Image Design's Ultra-Laser Turkey Carver® is the super-convenient, high-tech carving knife for the 21st Century! This essential kitchen tool is gentle enough to remove grandpa's cataracts, yet powerful enough to whack off a turkey drumstick! Its high-intensity, precision beam can also be turned down, making it an ideal laser pointer for your vacation slide show presentations after dinner. (Special attachment for trimming ear and nose hairs sold separately.)

Ultra-Laser Turkey Carver®
JIP434 $995

INVENTED HERE.
SO YOU KNOW IT'S SHODDY.

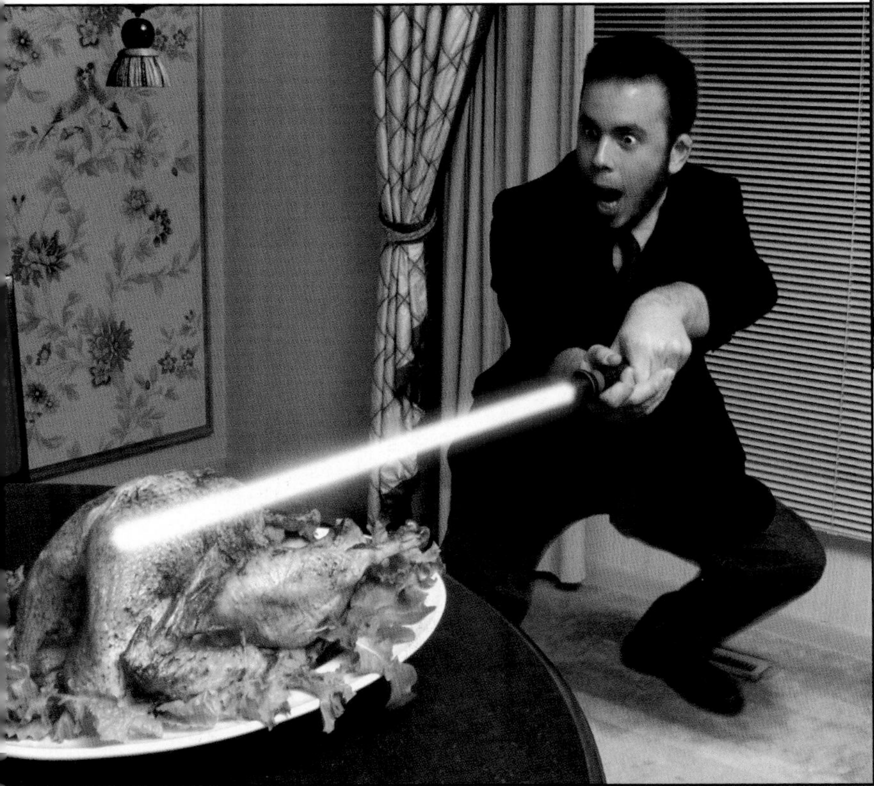

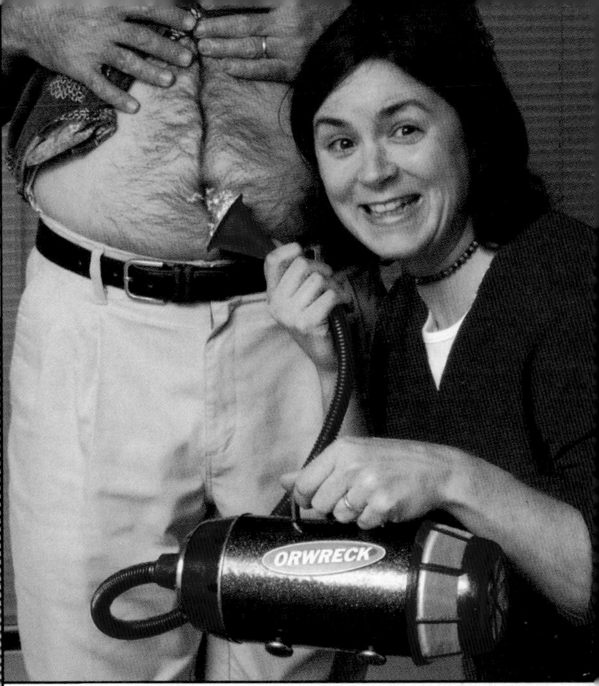
ORWRECK

Get rid of navel lint with your own personal mini-vacuum!

Clean out that embarrassing belly button lint in an instant with the new Orwreck Belly Button Vac!™ Its high-torque, 110V motor generates enough power to remove even the most stubborn pieces of dirt, string or food crumbs. Comes with both "innie" and "outie" turbo suction attachments. (Note: Manufacturer not responsible for injuries caused by sucking spleen or parts of small intestine through navel.)

Orwreck Belly Button Vac™
JIP627 $1175

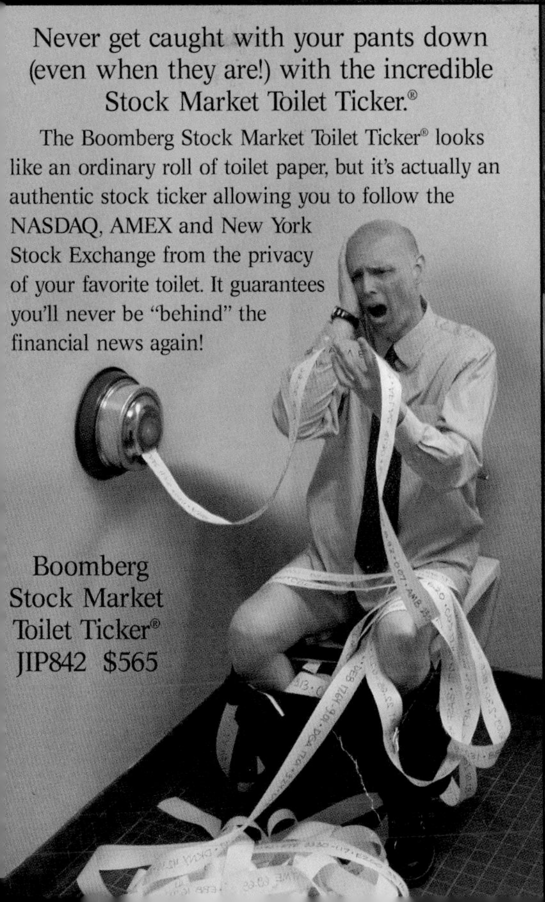

Never get caught with your pants down (even when they are!) with the incredible Stock Market Toilet Ticker.®

The Boomberg Stock Market Toilet Ticker® looks like an ordinary roll of toilet paper, but it's actually an authentic stock ticker allowing you to follow the NASDAQ, AMEX and New York Stock Exchange from the privacy of your favorite toilet. It guarantees you'll never be "behind" the financial news again!

Boomberg Stock Market Toilet Ticker®
JIP842 $565

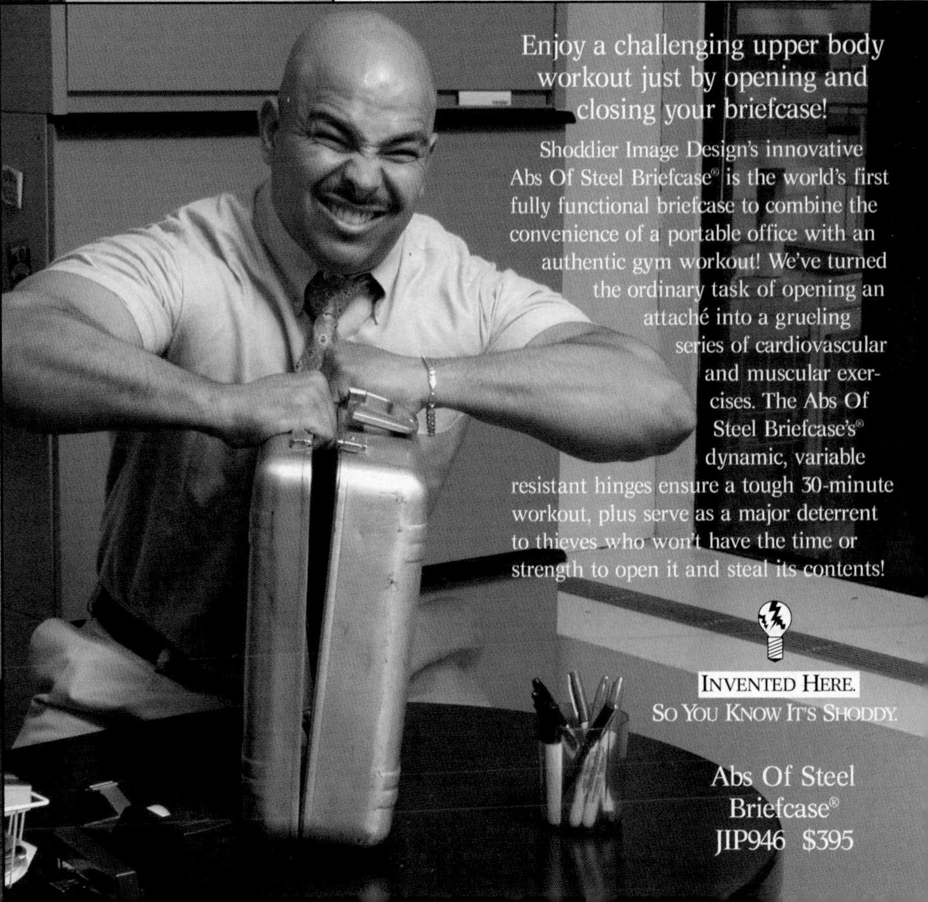

Enjoy a challenging upper body workout just by opening and closing your briefcase!

Shoddier Image Design's innovative Abs Of Steel Briefcase® is the world's first fully functional briefcase to combine the convenience of a portable office with an authentic gym workout! We've turned the ordinary task of opening an attaché into a grueling series of cardiovascular and muscular exercises. The Abs Of Steel Briefcase's® dynamic, variable resistant hinges ensure a tough 30-minute workout, plus serve as a major deterrent to thieves who won't have the time or strength to open it and steal its contents!

INVENTED HERE.
SO YOU KNOW IT'S SHODDY.

Abs Of Steel Briefcase®
JIP946 $395

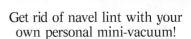

THE SHODDIER IMAGE

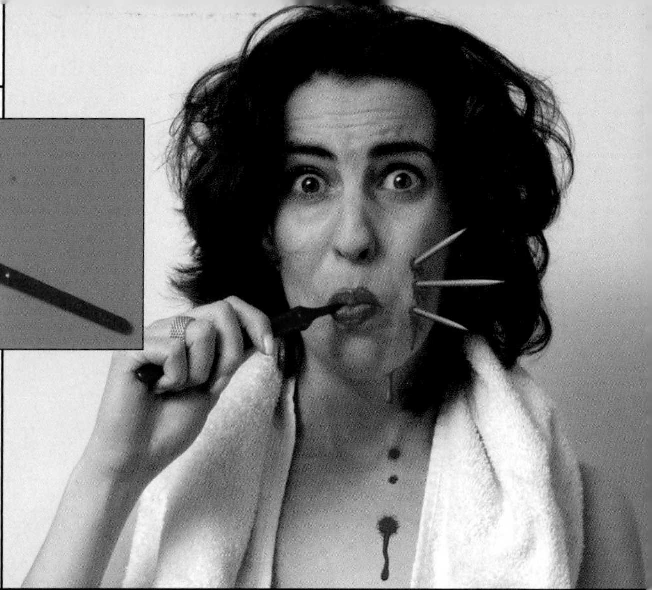

Miniature metal spikes prevent others from using the ingenious Personal Security Toothbrush.™

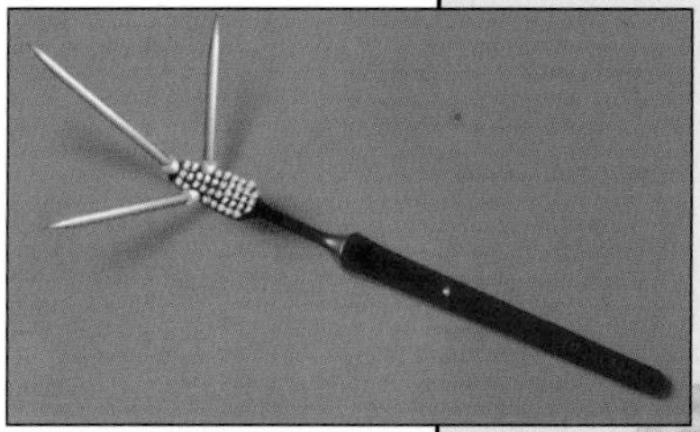

Oral Security Systems' state-of-the-art electric toothbrush provides you with total dental protection and complete peace of mind. Auto sensors recognize your fingerprints and allow you to use its high-tech contour bristles to remove plaque and polish teeth. But if someone else tries to use it, razor-sharp stainless steel spikes are suddenly released cutting through the offender's mouth and teaching them a lesson in oral hygiene they won't soon forget!

Oral Security Systems
Personal Security Toothbrush™
JIP667 $475

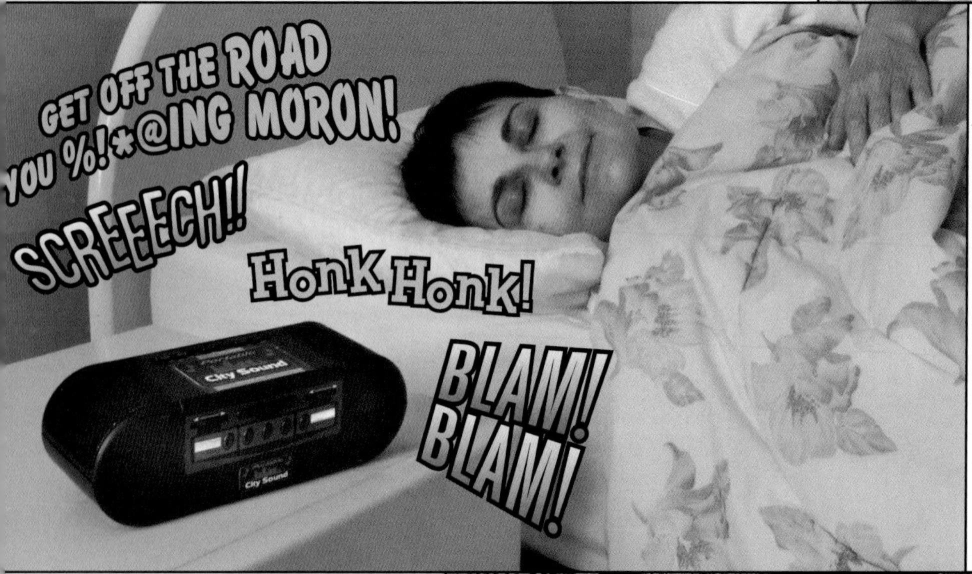
GET OFF THE ROAD
YOU %!*@ING MORON!
SCREEECH!!
HonK HonK!
BLAM! BLAM!
City Sound
City Sound

Fall asleep and wake up to the harrowing sounds of the city.

These days, nearly everyone sells machines that play soothing sounds of rain, ocean waves and babbling brooks to help you get some shut-eye. But suppose you're actually at the beach or camped near a mountain stream, yet unable to fall asleep because you miss the familiar sounds of the big city? Well, just flip on the new Portable City Sound™ and relax to a violent cacophony of actual urban noise! Choose from 12 realistic settings, including: IRT express train, blaring rush hour horns, random gunshots, non-stop jack-hammer and ranting, deranged street person.

Portable City Sound®
JIP893 $695

Now you can effectively hide from your boss and co-workers while on the job!

Created exclusively for Shoddier Image by legendary fashion designer Gianni Gnocchi, this Italian tailored, three-piece Camouflage Suit is constructed of 30% rayon and 70% chameleon skin, so that it automatically changes to blend into any office setting. Now you can instantly assume the color and properties of the copy machine, washroom sink or common office furniture! Excellent for eavesdropping on upper management.

INVENTED HERE.
SO YOU KNOW IT'S SHODDY.

Gianni Gnocchi Camouflage Suit
JIP911 $650

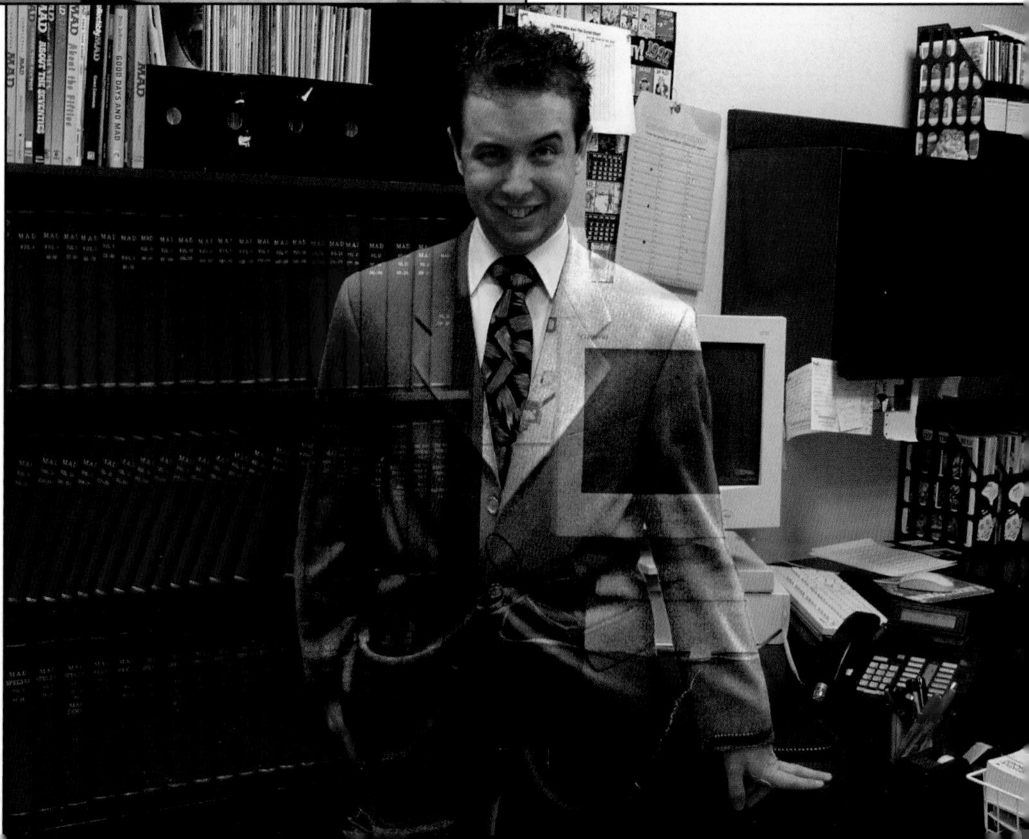

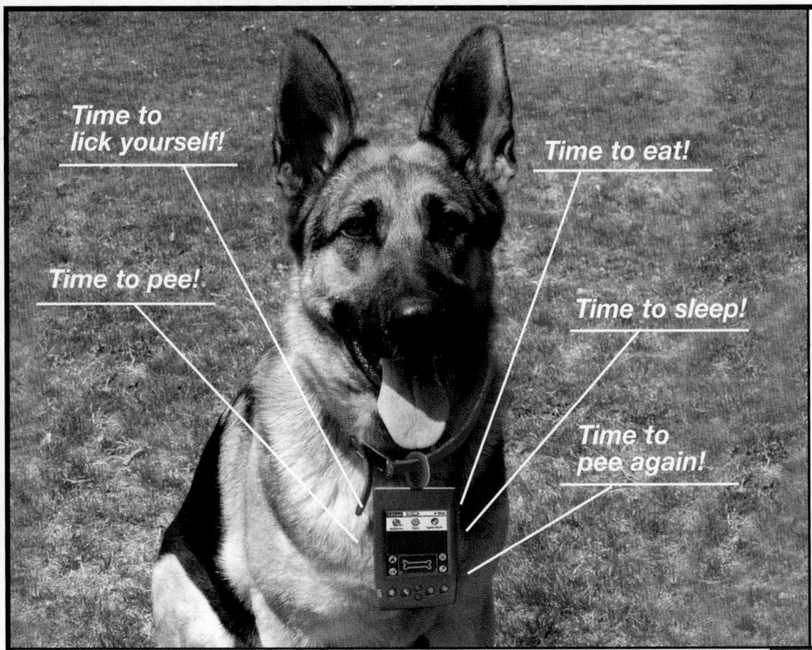
Time to lick yourself!
Time to eat!
Time to pee!
Time to sleep!
Time to pee again!

Let your dog plan his day with the amazing 3Com Paw Pilot.™

You're not the only one with a jam-packed itinerary. Your favorite canine has a busy schedule and a long list of things to do as well. And now, thanks to 3Com and Shoddier Image Design, little Fido will never miss an appointment! This beautiful compact planner attaches easily to flea collars and includes a calculator, digital alarm clock, 200-year calendar (in dog years) and a multi-function touch pad specially designed to be compatible with a dog's paw.

INVENTED HERE.
SO YOU KNOW IT'S SHODDY.

3Com Paw Pilot™
JIP671 $749

World's most powerful cell phone/razor.

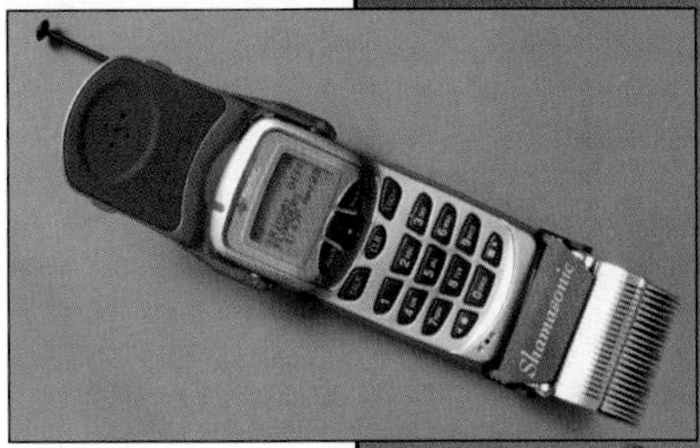
Shamasonic

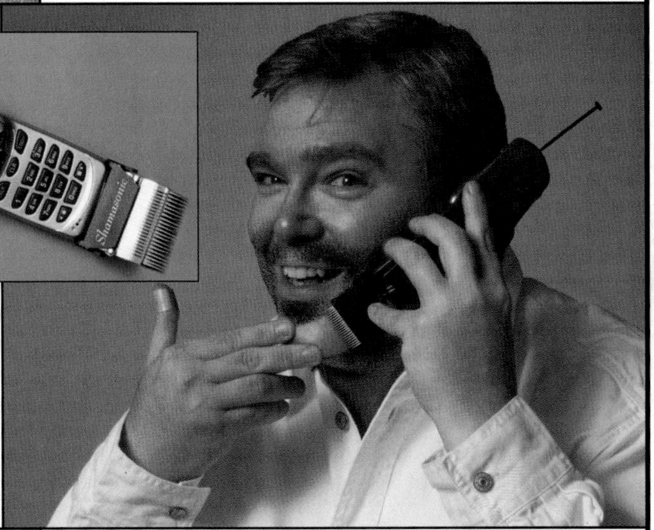

Shamasonic created this one-of-a-kind cellular device for the successful businessman on the go. The handsome design features a twin-blade, battery-powered razor built right into the mouthpiece, assuring an ultra-close shave even while you're wheeling and dealing on the phone. Its whisper-quiet silencer allows you to chat for hours without the other party ever knowing that you're also trimming that unwanted 5 o'clock shadow. Or, simply get rid of unwanted callers by turning off the silencer, claim you can't hear them because of "all that buzzing on their phone line" and hang up! (Available for ladies: the Cell Phone/Leg and Lip Waxer.)

Shamasonic Cell Phone/Razor
JIP893 $650

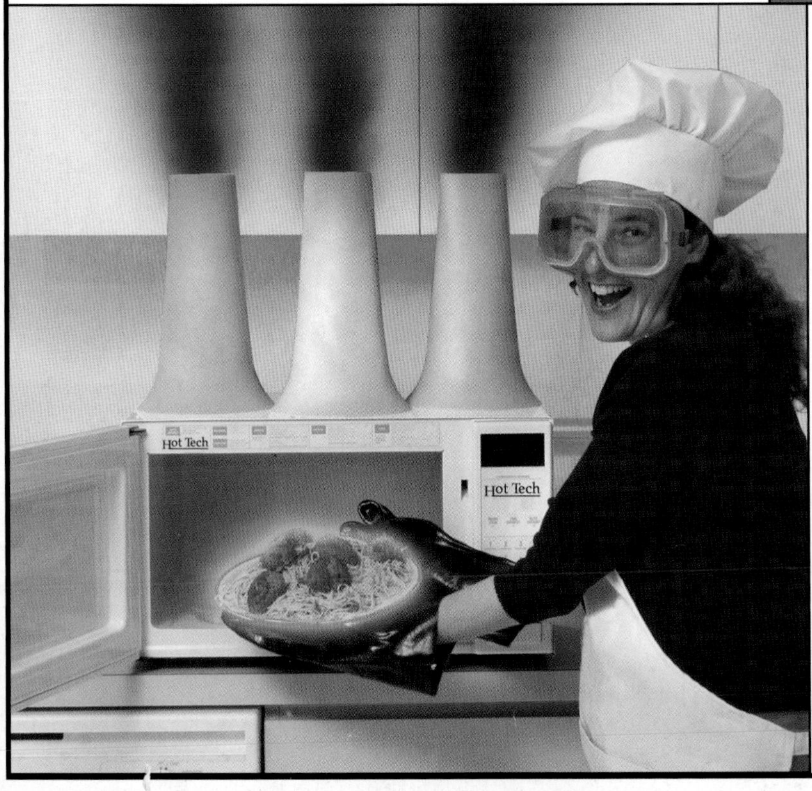
Hot Tech
Hot Tech

Hot Tech's Hyper-FusionWave Oven™ roasts a suckling pig in 9.3 seconds!

Leave it to Hot Tech and Shoddier Image to put the latest military advances in nuclear fusion to work in your kitchen! Their Hyper-FusionWave Oven™ is to the microwave what the microwave was to the gas oven! Cook a jumbo tub of popcorn in .14 seconds, a hearty plate of spaghettini classico in 2.6 seconds, or a full goose with all the trimmings in just 8.2 seconds! Comes fully equipped with safety glasses, matching lead oven mitts and a "Kiss The Cook" lead apron.

INVENTED HERE.
SO YOU KNOW IT'S SHODDY.

Hot Tech Hyper-FusionWave Oven™
JIP643 $3,095

SERGE-IN GENERAL DEPT.

A MAD LOOK AT

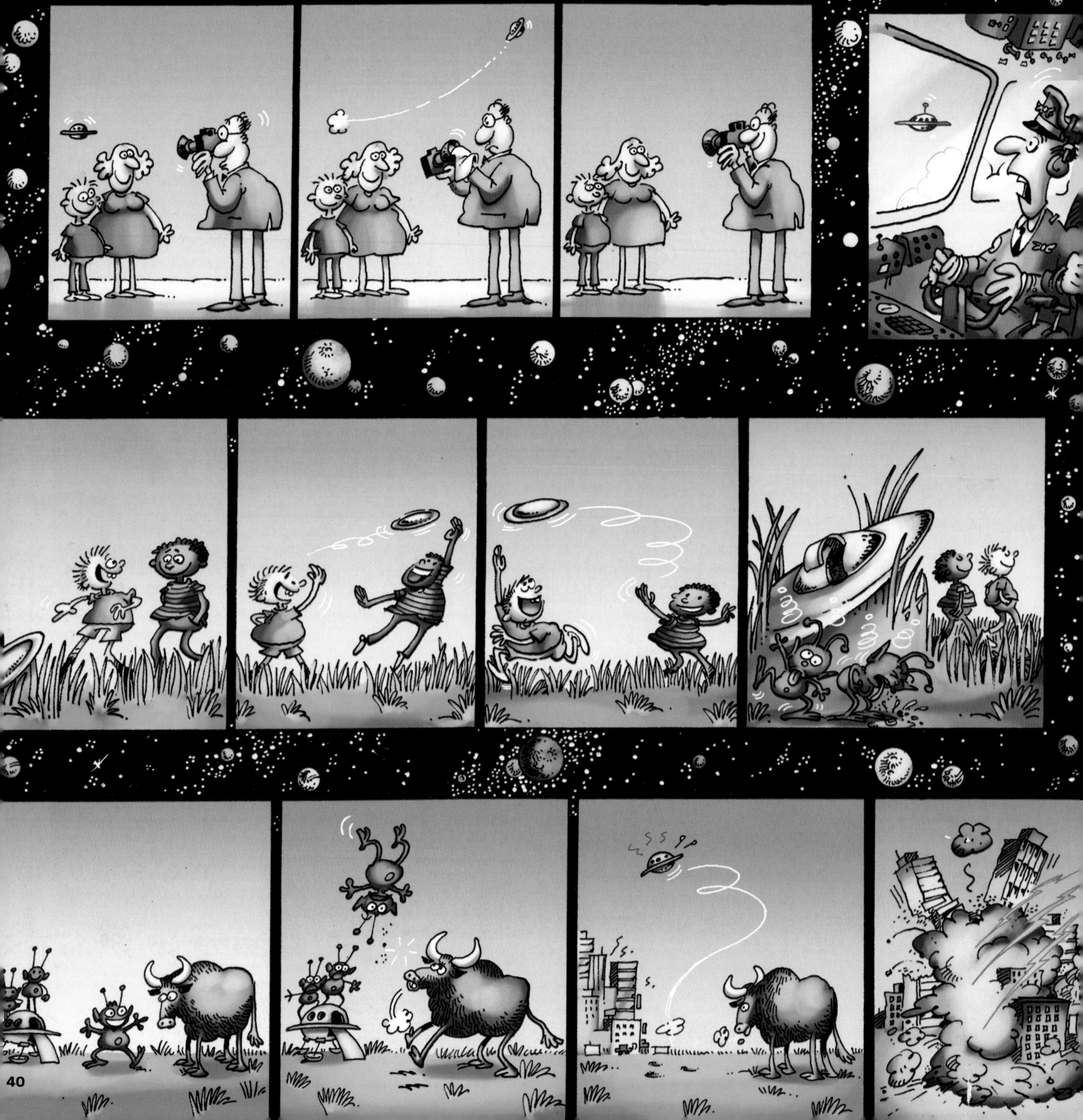

U.F.O.s

WRITER AND ARTIST: SERGIO A
COLORIST: CARRIE STRAC

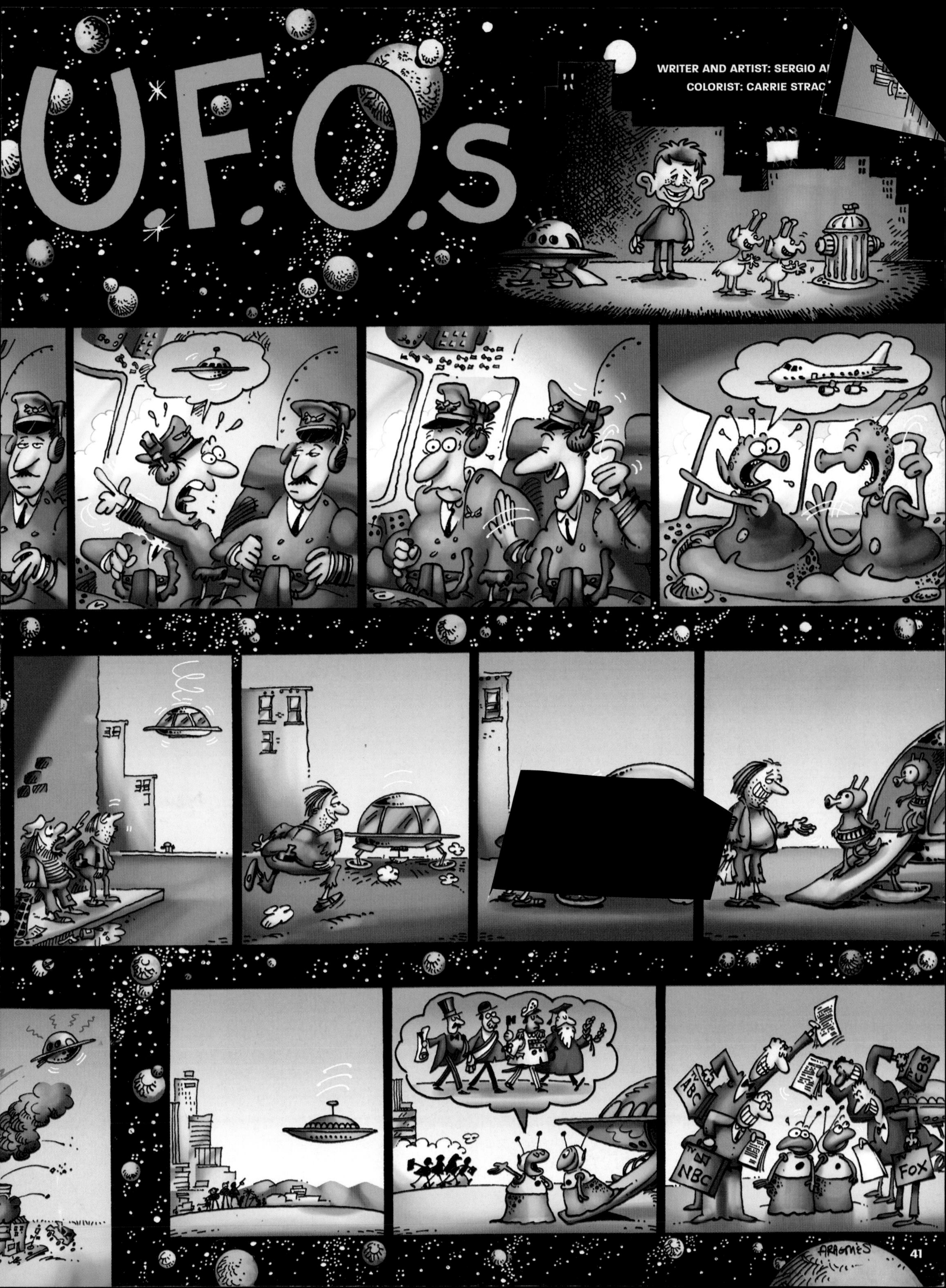

ABC
CBS
NBC
FOX
ARAGONES

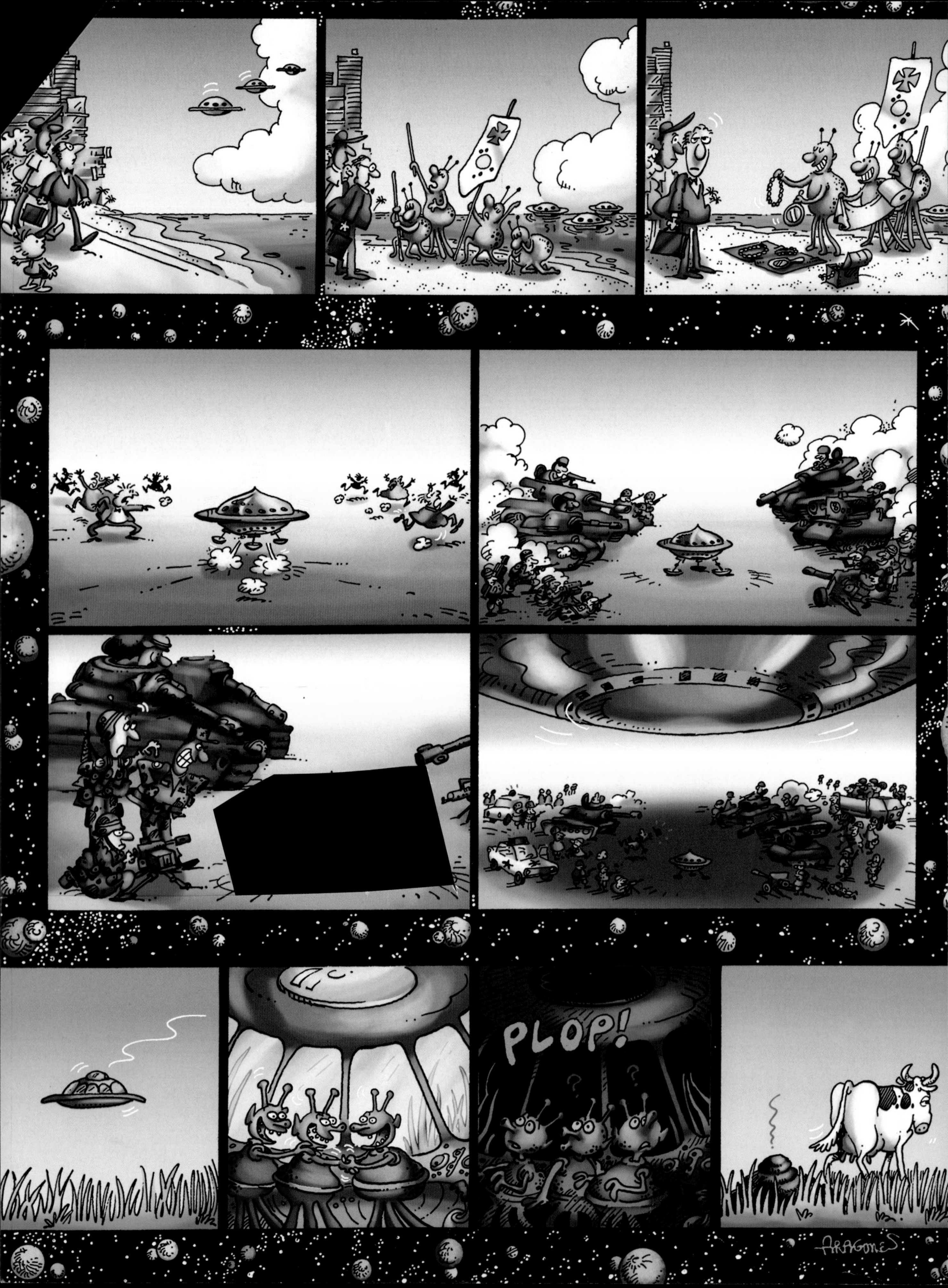
PLOP!
ARAGONES

JOKE AND DAGGER DEPT.

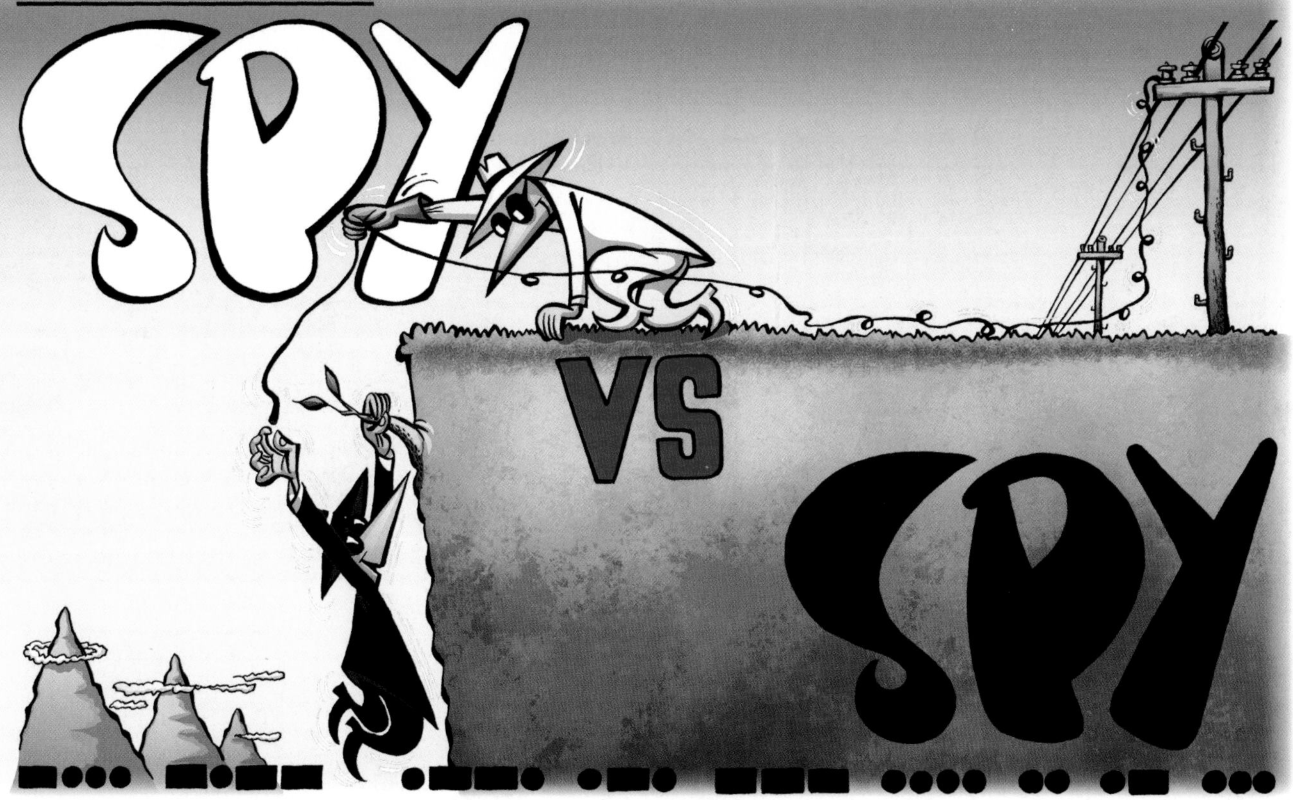
SPY
VS
SPY

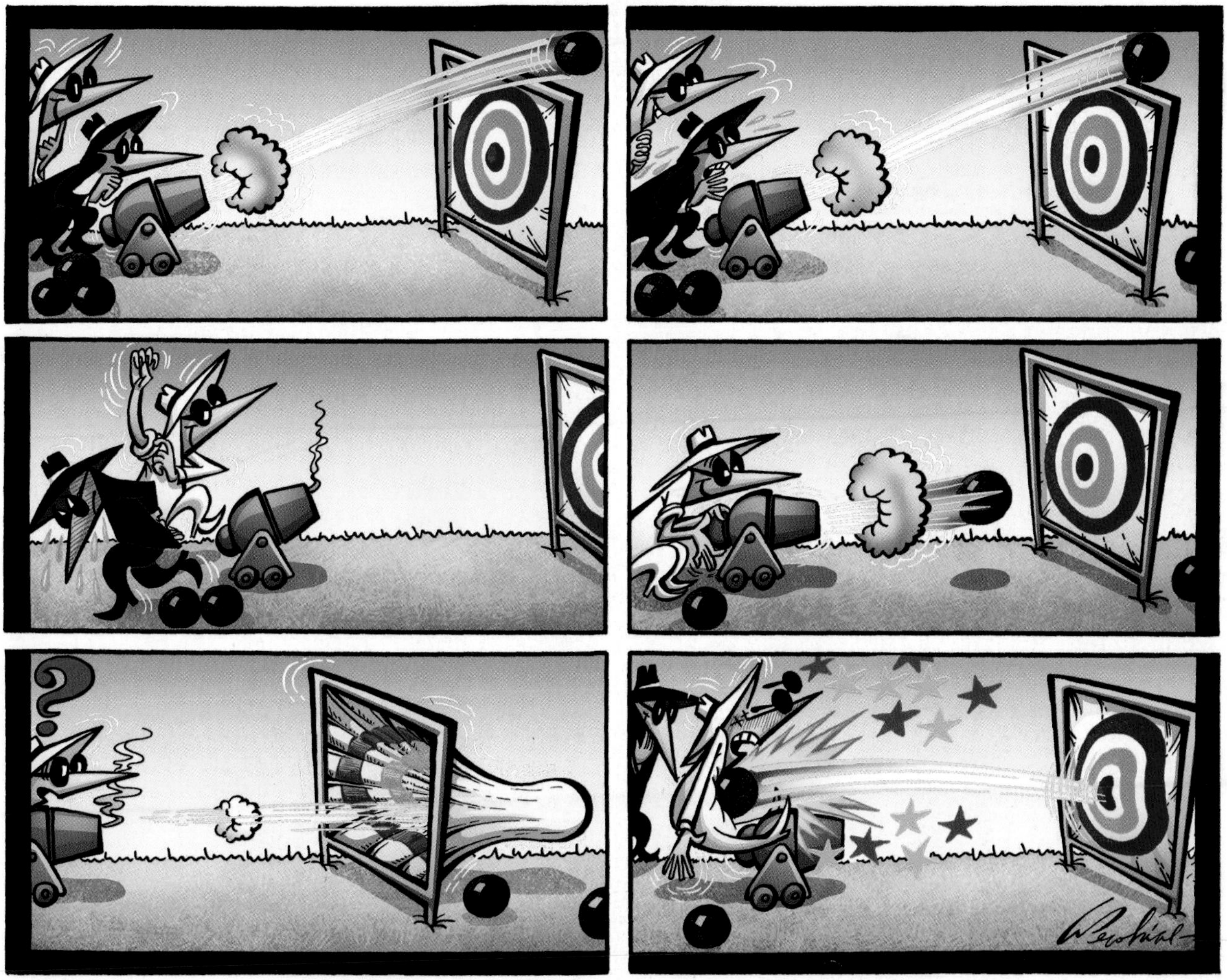

INSECT ASIDES DEPT.

The Bold . . . The Brave . . . The Easily Squished . .

MAD SALUTES
Unsung Heroes of the Bug Wars

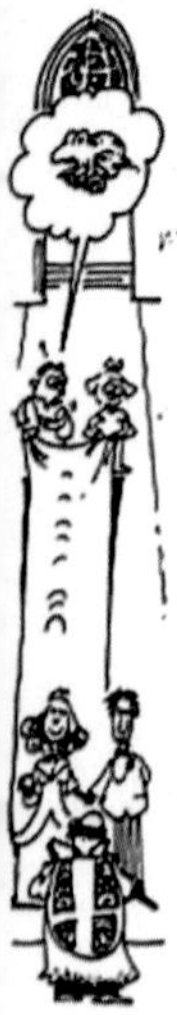

ARTIST AND WRITER: PAUL PETER PORGES

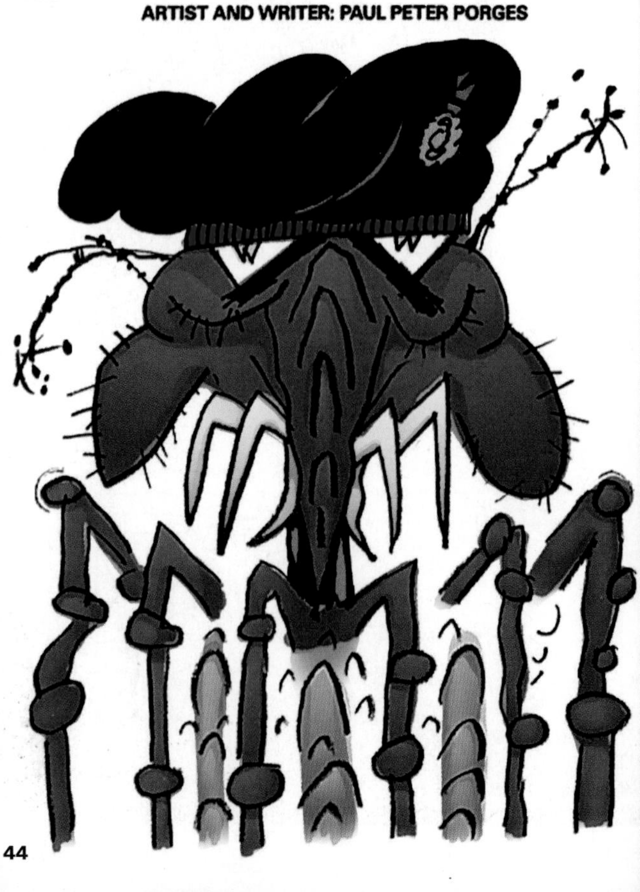

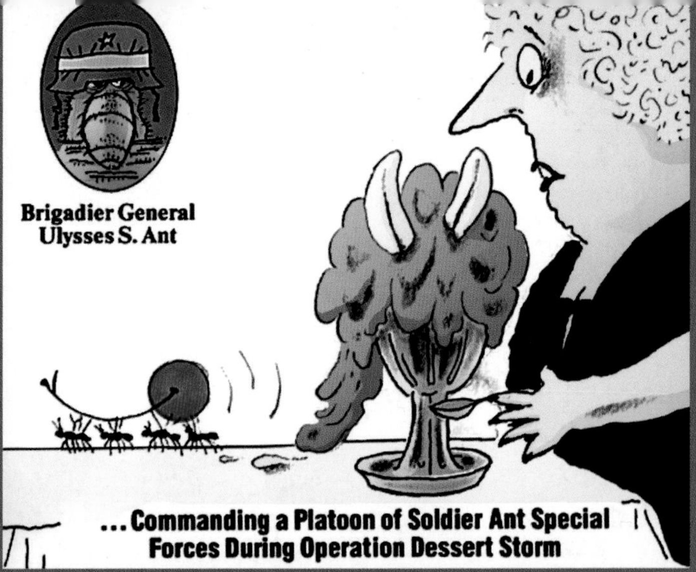
Brigadier General
Ulysses S. Ant

. . . Commanding a Platoon of Soldier Ant Special Forces During Operation Dessert Storm

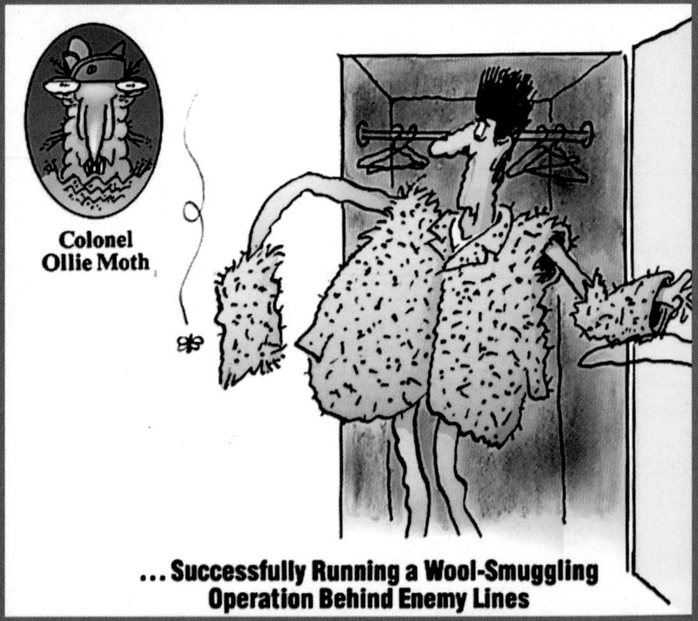
Colonel
Ollie Moth

. . . Successfully Running a Wool-Smuggling Operation Behind Enemy Lines

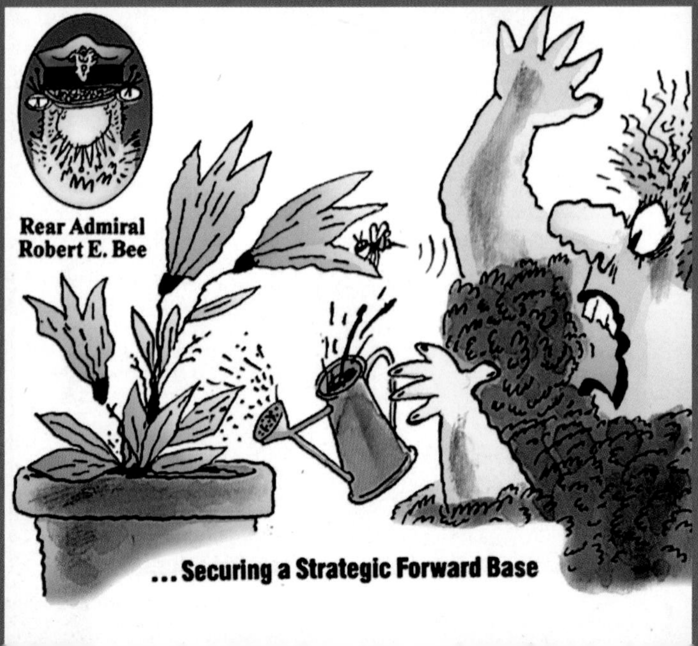
Rear Admiral
Robert E. Bee

. . . Securing a Strategic Forward Base

Air Recon Specialist Dwight D. Flysenhower

... Celebrating an Emergency Evacuation of a Landing Field with a Victory Roll

General William Pestmoreland

... Surveying Effects of a Recent Sabotage Operation by his Royal Corps of Engineers

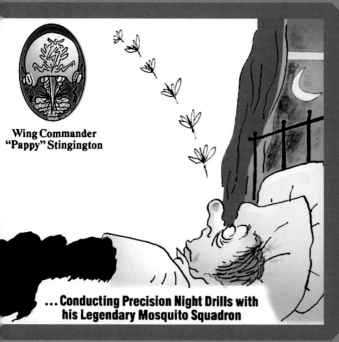

Wing Commander "Pappy" Stingington

... Conducting Precision Night Drills with his Legendary Mosquito Squadron

Commander Tick Cheney

... Triumphantly Invading Primary and Secondary Targets with his Paratrooper Commandos

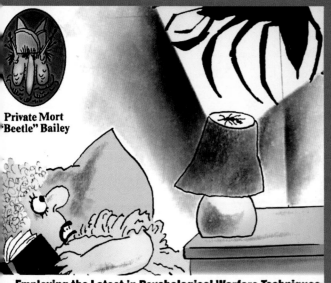

Private Mort "Beetle" Bailey

.. Employing the Latest in Psychological Warfare Techniques

4-Star General "Stormin' Norman" Roachkopf

... Leading his Roach Rangers in a Pre-Dawn Pre-Emptive Strike

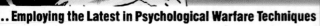

DON'T LET THE BID BUG BITE DEPT.

monkeYbaY

Buy | Sell | MymonkeyBay | Community | Help

All Categories | Search

Categories | Express | Stores

Home > monkeyBay Stores > Gorilla4Sale

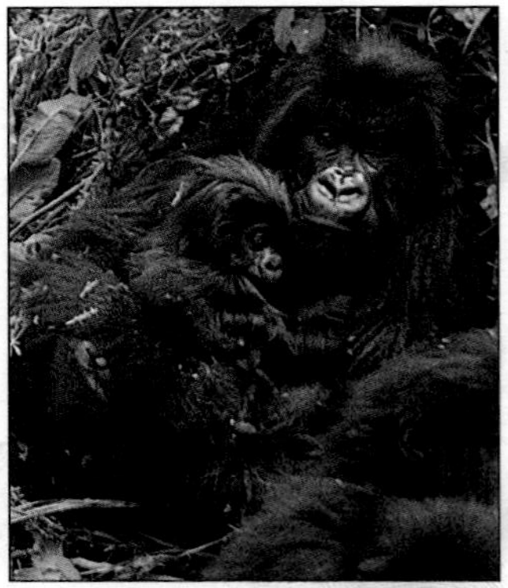

Proud mama with
Jason, April 1999
They grow up SO Fast!!!!!

GORILLA4SALE

Maintained by: Gorilla4Sale (358)

Thank you for visiting my Monkeybay store!!!! I am a stay-at-home (as much as our roving troop allows, LOL!!!) mom of two who emigrated from my natal group two years ago due to an instinctual fear of inbreeding. My new, secondary group consists of six other females, nine newborns (but given the high rate of infanticide in our species who knows what tomorrow will bring, j/k!!!) and our dominant alpha male who recently ran off with my two boys, Jason and Justin (currently serving in a small all-male group until they reach adulthood, at which point I assume at least one will return and challenge his father to take his place). I started selling on monkeyBay three years ago when a friend from a neighboring troop found an elephant tusk and sold it for $11,000!!!! I started off auctioning bamboo shoots but have "branched" out into whatever I can find. In my spare time I enjoy grooming, scrapbooking, grazing on herbs, stems and roots, and collecting vintage Bakelite costume jewelry!!!! I love all the new friends I've made on monkeyBay!!!!!!

List View | Picture Gallery

Item Title

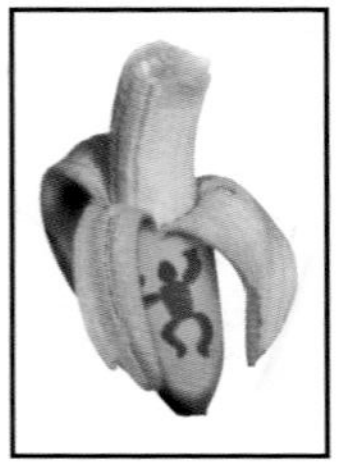

MIRACLE Image of King Kong On Banana Peel!!!! MUST SEE to BELIEVE!!!

Amazing Manifestation of Great Ape on Quickly Ripening Tropical Fruit

I could not believe my eyes when I reached for a banana the other day and took one bite before noticing what is CLEARLY the image of the great Kong himself, formed by a grouping of six overlapping brown spots on this obviously blessed piece of fruit. Word has spread to nearby troops and dozens of believers…(see more)

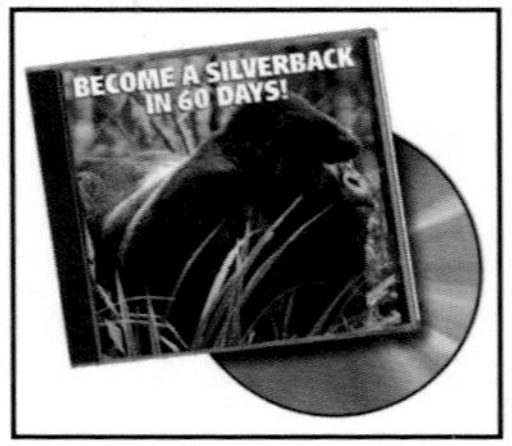
BECOME A SILVERBACK IN 60 DAYS!

Pills and Supplements Don't Work! Turn Into a Silverback in 60 Days – Or Your Money Back!

Complete Self-Hypnosis Course On CD

Forget all the touchy-feely myths you've heard. The truth is, celebratory grunts and beating your chest will only go so far in impressing us females. When all is said and done, having a back of thick, lush silver hair DOES matter. And studies have shown that you won't get it with any pharmaceuticals currently on the market…(see more)

Latest Feedback

Gorilla4Sale (358)

(+) Auction ended during my estrus cycle and I was not able to send payment for a week – seller was wonderful & patient!

SHANK OF HAIR YANKED FROM DIAN FOSSEY'S HEAD CIRCA 1975 WITH PHOTO PROVENANCE (Item #190167536222)

Buyer: MonkeysAunt (245)

(+) Excellent customer! Paid fast! All bidders should be so friendly! A+!!!

SMALL LOT OF ITEMS THROWN IN CAGE BY ZOO VISITORS (INCL. 2 SHINY ITEMS!!!)
(Item #1156733345902)

Seller: MightyJoeMiddleAge (4620)

(−) Item arrived damaged! Eep! Eeeeep! Seller OVERCHARGES for shipping! EEEP! EEEEP!

20 SCRAP-BOOKING SCISSORS IN HANDY CAROUSEL – NEVER USED!
(Item #190167299732)

Buyer: PrehensileUtensils (1344)

Response by Gorilla4Sale: SCREEEEEEEEECH! Shipping costs are listed in auction description!!! EEEEP! EEEEEEEP! ROOOAR! Do NOT bid on my auctions again! Oo-Oo-Oo! SHRIEEEEEEK!!!

Solid Granite Edible Root-Mashing Rock

Refurbished – All Parts 100% Guaranteed!

Smart buyers know to go with refurbished items to save lots of $$$ over their brand-new counterparts. And there's no need to worry since all parts are 100% guaranteed. Here is a solid granite rock, weighing approximately 9 lbs, which is ideal for mashing edible roots into a soft, palatable paste. Equally versatile as a weapon in territorial disputes, this rock, worn smooth…(see more)

NATIONAL GEOGRAPHIC
VERVET MONKEYS
OF THE SERENGETI

Nat'l Geographic Magazine 1965: Vervet Monkeys of the Serengeti

Perfect for Genealogy Buffs!

Here's a very old issue of National Geographic with an 18-page article about Vervet monkeys. May be of value to any Vervet monkeys tracing their family history, as it features nearly a dozen photos of at least six colonies in sub-Saharan Africa, and includes text by Louis Leakey who named the one who stole his watch…(see more)

Complete Living Room Ensemble

Redecorating: Must $ELL!!!!!

We're redecorating and will have NO room for this delightful branch/tire ensemble once the new tree comes. Six-foot tall oak is secured in 67-quart, cement-filled tub – will not tip over. Uniroyal whitewall tire off '73 Plymouth Duster contains some kibble, desiccated grapes, dried leaves and fresh excrement. Happy to leave as-is for high bidder! Perfect for single orangutan, chimp couple or large colony of spider monkeys…(see more)

SAVANNAH
BUTT ROUGE
ALL-NATURALS

Butt Rouge

Get Your Big Red Baboon Butt Its Reddest!

Savanna All-Naturals Butt Rouge blends powdered clay, dried and pulverized crimson scarabs, and Barbary striped grass mouse blood to get your ischial callosities – AKA your big swollen butt-pads – their absolute reddest. Just dab on for a bright red, youthful butt! Allergen and fragrance-free, but really, like that matters because it's going on your butt and you're a baboon...(see more)

Please Note:
You must email me before bidding if you have more than 10 negative feedbacks or if you have been rejected/abandoned by your troop or breeding colony.

Payment Methods Accepted:
ApePal, Cashier's Checks, Money Orders, Tender Young Plant Shoots, Thistles (in season), some Tree Bark (email for list)

Bid with Confidence:
All items for sale come from an ebola-free home!

Scroll down to see some other auctions I think are cool…

WRITER: SCOTT "SCAMPERS" MAIKO

monkeYbaY

Buy | Sell | MymonkeyBay | Community | Help

GORILLA4SALE

Maintained by: Gorilla4Sale (358)

SOME OTHER AUCTIONS I THINK ARE COOL!

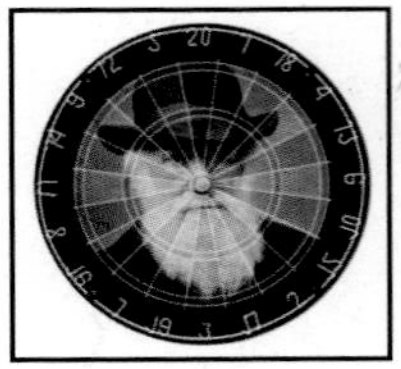

Seller: Barrel Of Us (239)
High Bidder: DKjr (79)
Current Bid: $4.77

Charles Darwin Dartboard
Relieve Your Aggression Without Biting Off Someone's Nose!

Featuring an ominous image of the notorious naturalist who set back monkey/human relations untold years with his irresponsible, backward, crack-pot theories (which were largely debunked in a 1968 film starring human Charlton Heston), this sturdy dartboard made of compressed paper comes with six dangerously pointy metal-tipped darts and is also available in a non-porous, plastic, wipe clean version (with suction cup darts) for those who might be inclined to fling their poo at it instead. (See my other auctions). The Creation Museum's website charges three times more than my Grab-It-Now price!

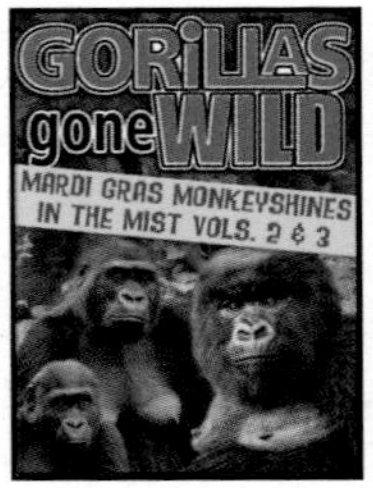
GORILLAS gone WILD
MARDI GRAS MONKEYSHINES IN THE MIST VOLS. 2 & 3

Seller: OrganGrinder (27)
High Bidder: DamnDirtyApe (117)
Current Bid: $16.68

Gorillas Gone Wild: Mardis Gras Monkeyshines In the Mist Vol. 2&3
Not Bootlegs! Original DVDs in Original Packaging!

They sent me these two copies by accident and only billed me for one set so I am selling them on here! Sealed and never opened! These are not bootlegs they are the real things! Uncensored footage of gorillas – gorilla-on-gorilla grooming action – bedding down for the night – getting totally wild!

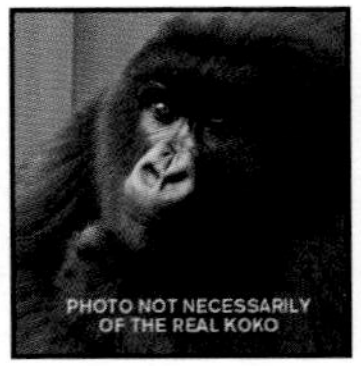
PHOTO NOT NECESSARILY OF THE REAL KOKO

Seller: KnuckleWalker (12)
No Bids Yet Place Bid
Opening Bid: $275.00

Ten-Minute Phone Call with Koko!!!!
Charity Auction with Proceeds to Benefit the Ape-A-Wish Foundation

Here is a unique experience that the winner will remember the rest of his or her life: The chance to communicate with Koko, the world-famous "talking" lowland gorilla. Following auction, confirmation of payment and thorough background check, winning bidder will be contacted by Koko's representatives to set up a time mutually convenient for auction winner and Koko. At the appointed time, winning bidder will receive an actual phone call from Koko!!!! What will you ask her? The sky's the limit!!!

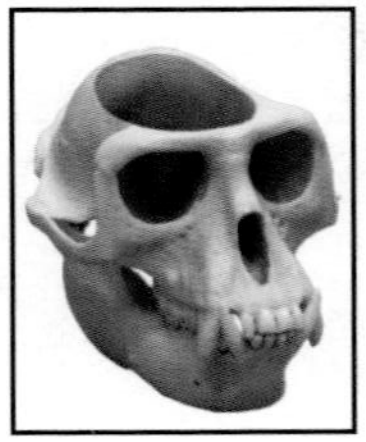

Seller: PoachedImportsInc
(No longer a registered user)
No Bids Yet
Opening Bid: $47.95

Authentic Monkey Skull Ashtray!!! COOL!!!!! Wow!!! Actual cleaned and bleached skull!

Here's a wonderful conversation piece that earns a place in any smoker's home as a fully functional ashtray! We've taken the skull of a Rhesus monkey and carefully sliced off the top third of the cranium. Three recessed notches have been cut into the resulting brim so you can rest your cigarette between drags. Generous brain cavity holds dozens of butts and plenty of ashes. Hinged jaw handily flips open when it's time to empty. This auction is for the Rhesus monkey skull you see pictured, but we do take custom orders for similar ashtrays from the head bones of spider monkeys, chimps, and orangutans (see our About Me page here).

AUCTION CANCELLED
Due to Violation of MonkeyBay Policies

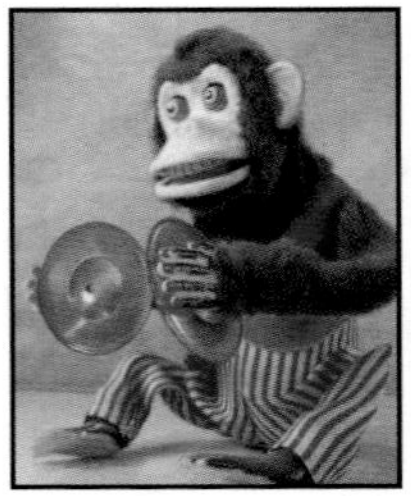

Seller: Gleek Is Blue (905)
High Bidder: MonkeySeeMonkeyBid (2351)
Current Bid: $68.74

Vintage Monkey Banging Cymbals Wind-Up Toy!!!! Amazing Historic & Iconic Item Perfect for A Serious Collector of Monkeyana

Here is a vintage 1930s tin wind-up toy of a monkey banging two cymbals together. The monkey features celluloid face, hands and feet, fake fur covered arms and a flocked head. Also he is wearing a vest made of a velvet-like material and simple cotton pants, though there looks like some moth damage to the seat. It is otherwise in excellent condition and works fine when wound up, he clangs cymbals together and eyes roll and mouth opens and closes. BEFORE YOU EMAIL TO COMPLAIN: I am selling this as a historical artifact. It is the product of a bygone era that like it or not is part of our heritage. It is NOT offensive when viewed in the correct context so please do NOT email to complain or try to get my auction pulled!!!!

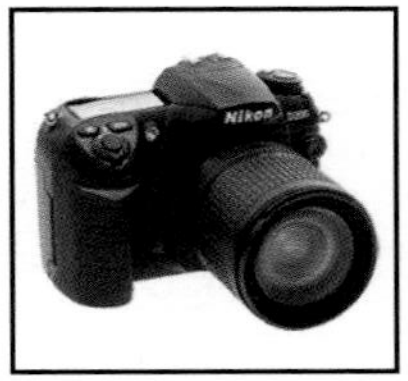

Seller: ChimpsAhoy (4629)
High Bidder: MonkeyTown (36)
Opening Bid: $252.66

Nikon D200 10.2 Megapixel! Grabbed When Tourist Got Too Close To Cage

Here is a near-mint condition Nikon D200 that retails for $799+. Camera is in excellent condition! It looks like it was used only a few times before previous owner got too close to enclosure and I grabbed it and didn't let go. Given by wife to previous owner for birthday last week according to subsequent screaming match with unsympathetic zoo staffer. Camera likely still under warranty, but I do not know for sure. Only flaw is the neck strap broke when violently yanked from visitor. Easily replaced, actual camera works fine. Possibly amusing photos on memory card, as camera was snapping images during tug of war. Reason to sell: No computer to download images to (unless some other jackass visits the zoo carrying one).

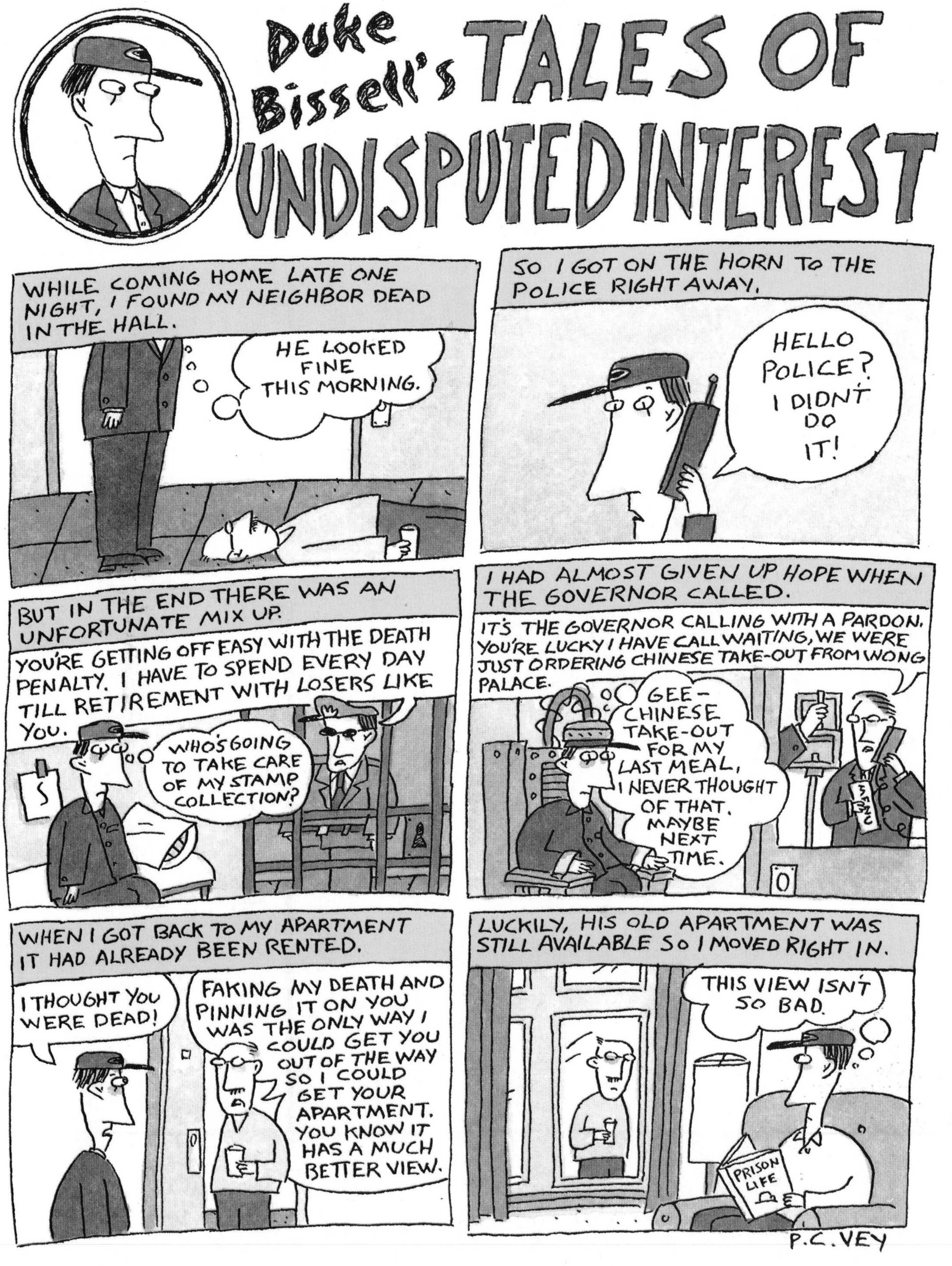

Duke Bissell's TALES OF UNDISPUTED INTEREST
WHILE COMING HOME LATE ONE NIGHT, I FOUND MY NEIGHBOR DEAD IN THE HALL.
HE LOOKED FINE THIS MORNING.
SO I GOT ON THE HORN TO THE POLICE RIGHT AWAY.
HELLO POLICE? I DIDN'T DO IT!
BUT IN THE END THERE WAS AN UNFORTUNATE MIX UP.
YOU'RE GETTING OFF EASY WITH THE DEATH PENALTY. I HAVE TO SPEND EVERY DAY TILL RETIREMENT WITH LOSERS LIKE YOU.
WHO'S GOING TO TAKE CARE OF MY STAMP COLLECTION?
I HAD ALMOST GIVEN UP HOPE WHEN THE GOVERNOR CALLED.
IT'S THE GOVERNOR CALLING WITH A PARDON. YOU'RE LUCKY I HAVE CALL WAITING, WE WERE JUST ORDERING CHINESE TAKE-OUT FROM WONG PALACE.
GEE—CHINESE TAKE-OUT FOR MY LAST MEAL, I NEVER THOUGHT OF THAT. MAYBE NEXT TIME.
MENU
WHEN I GOT BACK TO MY APARTMENT IT HAD ALREADY BEEN RENTED.
I THOUGHT YOU WERE DEAD!
FAKING MY DEATH AND PINNING IT ON YOU WAS THE ONLY WAY I COULD GET YOU OUT OF THE WAY SO I COULD GET YOUR APARTMENT. YOU KNOW IT HAS A MUCH BETTER VIEW.
LUCKILY, HIS OLD APARTMENT WAS STILL AVAILABLE SO I MOVED RIGHT IN.
THIS VIEW ISN'T SO BAD.
PRISON LIFE
P.C. VEY

A POKE IN THE EISNER DEPT.

It's those goofy mouse-ear hats! It's Donald Duck on skis! It's those same monotonous TV commercials over and over again! Our response?

WRITER: CHARLIE KADAU ARTIST: TOM BUNK COLORIST: CARRIE STRACHAN

Here's Mad's Reasons NOT to Visit Disney World This Year!

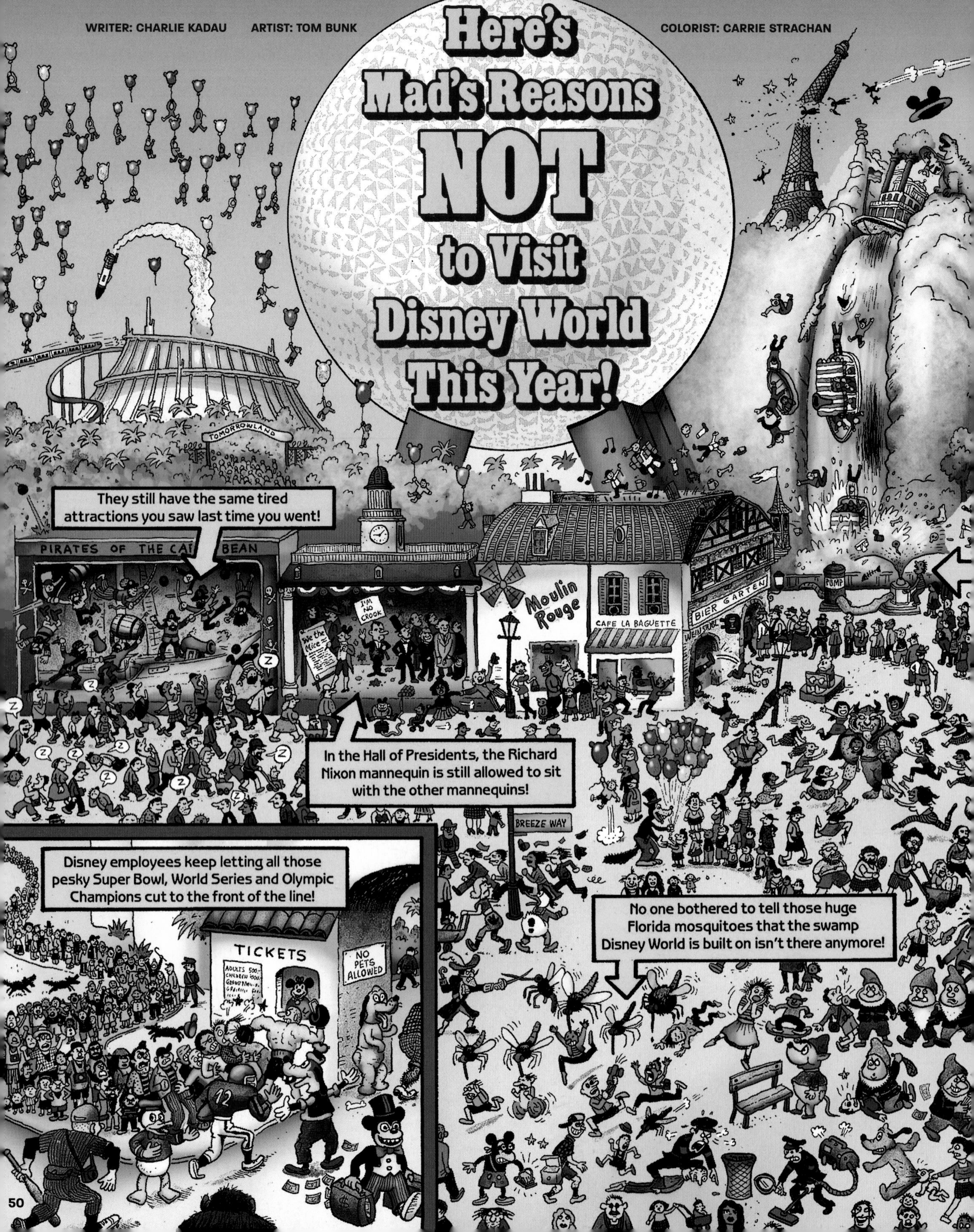
TOMORROWLAND
They still have the same tired attractions you saw last time you went!
PIRATES OF THE CA BEAN
I'M NO CROOK
We the Mice
Moulin Rouge
CAFE LA BAGUETTE
BIER GARTEN
WEINSTUBE
PUMP
In the Hall of Presidents, the Richard Nixon mannequin is still allowed to sit with the other mannequins!
BREEZE WAY
Disney employees keep letting all those pesky Super Bowl, World Series and Olympic Champions cut to the front of the line!
TICKETS
NO PETS ALLOWED
No one bothered to tell those huge Florida mosquitoes that the swamp Disney World is built on isn't there anymore!

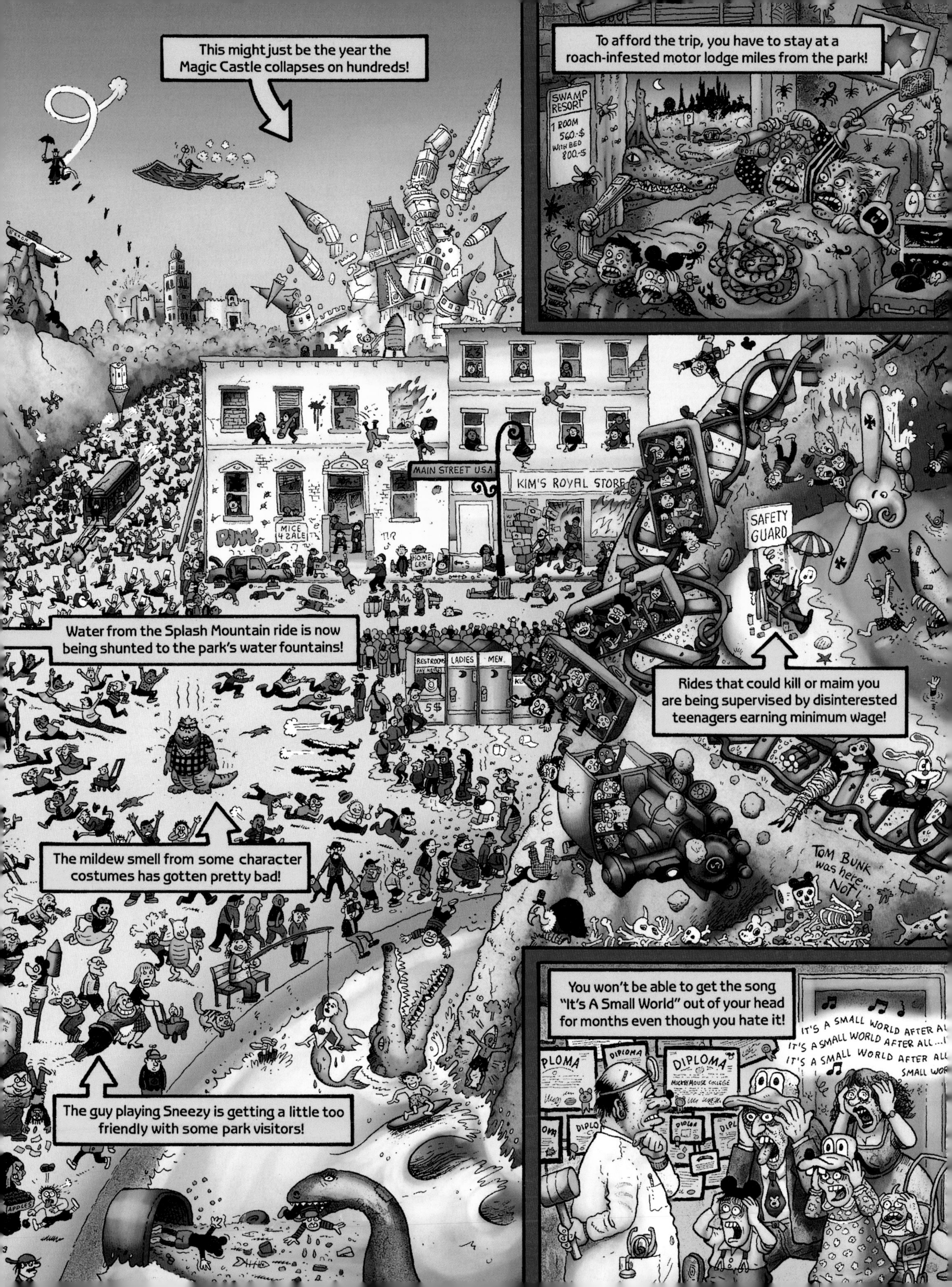
This might just be the year the Magic Castle collapses on hundreds!
To afford the trip, you have to stay at a roach-infested motor lodge miles from the park!
SWAMP RESORT
1 ROOM 560.-$
WITH BED 800.-$
MAIN STREET U.S.A.
KIM'S ROYAL STORE
MICE 4 SALE
HOME LESS
SAFETY GUARD
Water from the Splash Mountain ride is now being shunted to the park's water fountains!
RESTROOMS
LADIES
MEN
5$
Rides that could kill or maim you are being supervised by disinterested teenagers earning minimum wage!
The mildew smell from some character costumes has gotten pretty bad!
TOM BUNK was here... NOT!
You won't be able to get the song "It's A Small World" out of your head for months even though you hate it!
IT'S A SMALL WORLD AFTER AL
IT'S A SMALL WORLD AFTER ALL...
IT'S A SMALL WORLD AFTER AL
SMALL WO
DIPLOMA
MICKEY MOUSE COLLEGE
The guy playing Sneezy is getting a little too friendly with some park visitors!
APPLES

What's in a name?  Zoo-

 SH🔺RK

P🦔RCUPINE

TU🦃KEY

 B   S

G

PIC

🐌 Snail

RAFFE

DAC━━━━━━SHUND

Tòons

HOOT OWL

rabbit

SEAL

KAN G a ROO

ORM

BAT

Sion

M.USE

C⊙W

WRITER AND ARTIST: MAX BRANDEL

Spring. The time of year when your parents begin their annual ritual of telling you how hard they work all year to make money so they can send you away to camp for the summer and give you the life they never had. Of course, it's all a big fat lie. They're sending you away to camp because you make them crazy and they're hoping to get a week or two of peace and quiet with you out of their hair. The only thing you can hope for is that dear mom and dad spent at least five minutes researching where they're shipping you off to and didn't just book you into the first swamphole that came along. Knowing your parents, that's probably way too much to hope for! Anyway, goodbye, good luck, and don't forget to pack some MADs for kindling. Here's...

THINGS YOU NEVER WANT TO READ ABOUT THE SUMMER CAMP YOU'RE BEING SENT TO

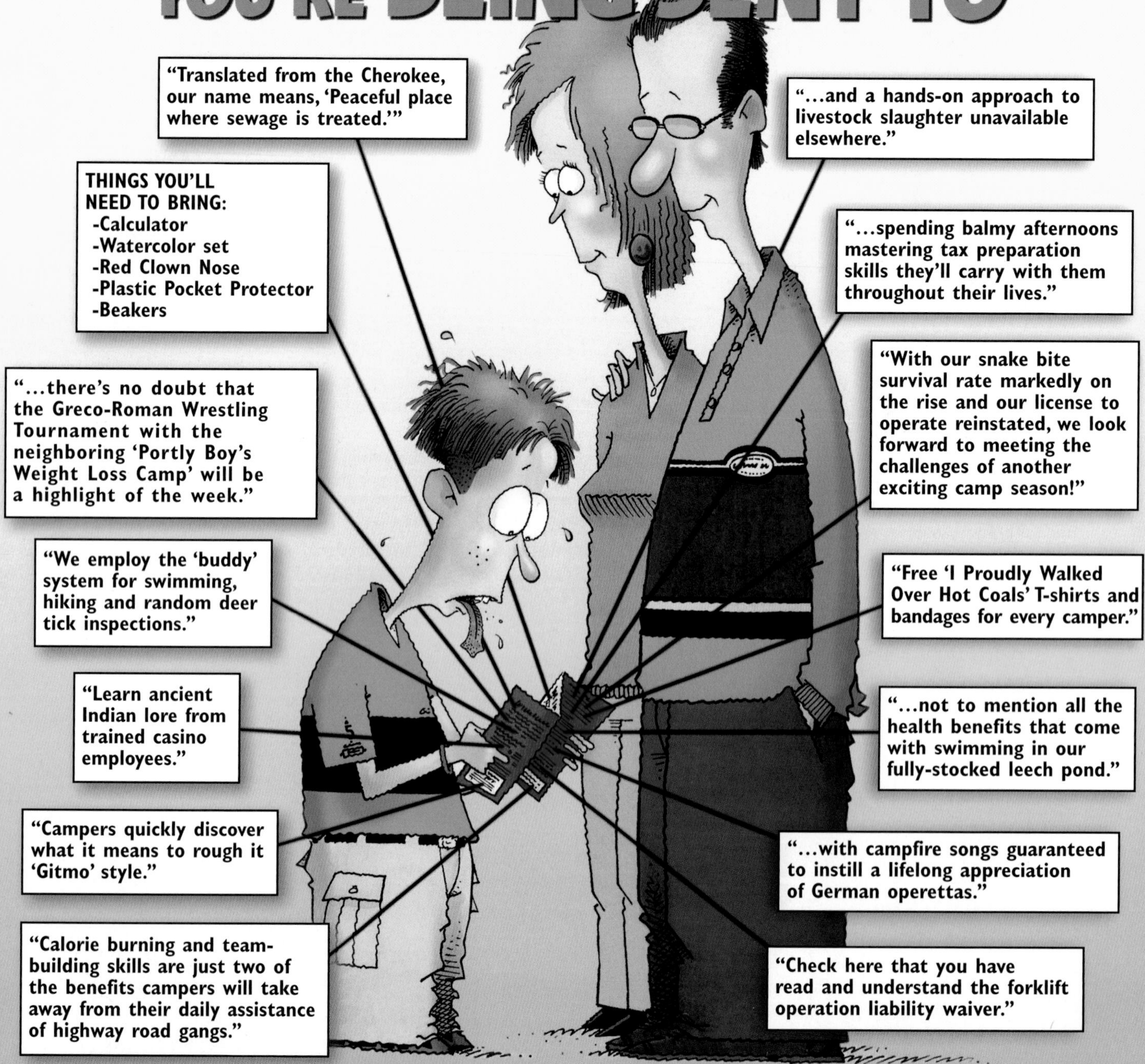
"Translated from the Cherokee, our name means, 'Peaceful place where sewage is treated.'"
"...and a hands-on approach to livestock slaughter unavailable elsewhere."
THINGS YOU'LL NEED TO BRING: -Calculator -Watercolor set -Red Clown Nose -Plastic Pocket Protector -Beakers
"...spending balmy afternoons mastering tax preparation skills they'll carry with them throughout their lives."
"...there's no doubt that the Greco-Roman Wrestling Tournament with the neighboring 'Portly Boy's Weight Loss Camp' will be a highlight of the week."
"With our snake bite survival rate markedly on the rise and our license to operate reinstated, we look forward to meeting the challenges of another exciting camp season!"
"We employ the 'buddy' system for swimming, hiking and random deer tick inspections."
"Free 'I Proudly Walked Over Hot Coals' T-shirts and bandages for every camper."
"Learn ancient Indian lore from trained casino employees."
"...not to mention all the health benefits that come with swimming in our fully-stocked leech pond."
"Campers quickly discover what it means to rough it 'Gitmo' style."
"...with campfire songs guaranteed to instill a lifelong appreciation of German operettas."
"Calorie burning and team-building skills are just two of the benefits campers will take away from their daily assistance of highway road gangs."
"Check here that you have read and understand the forklift operation liability waiver."

WRITER AND ARTIST: JOHN CALDWELL COLORIST: CARL PETERSON

DON MARTIN DEPT.

THE ACCIDENT

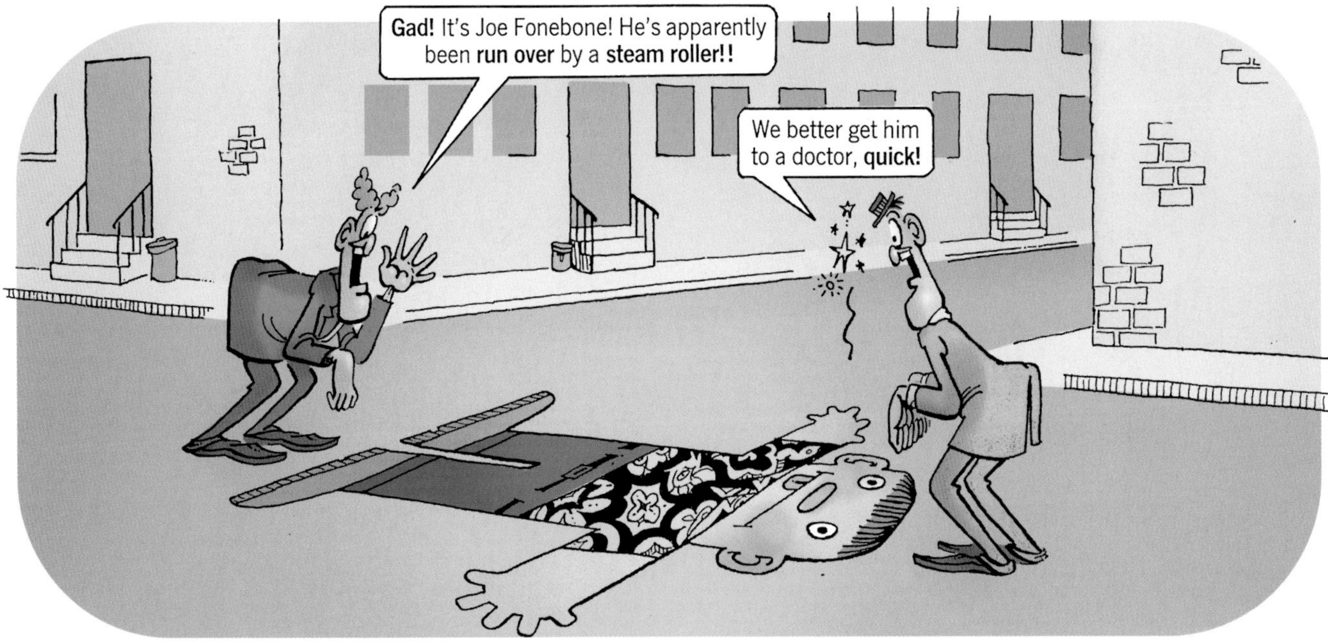
Gad! It's Joe Fonebone! He's apparently been run over by a steam roller!!
We better get him to a doctor, quick!

WRITER AND ARTIST: DON MARTIN COLORIST: CARL PETERSON

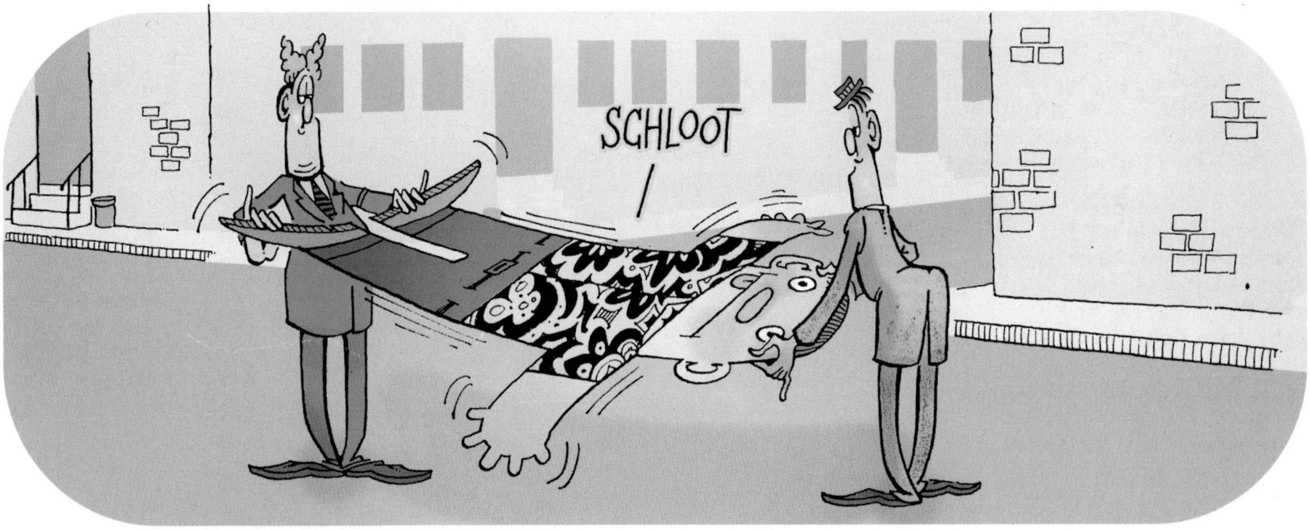
SCHLOOT

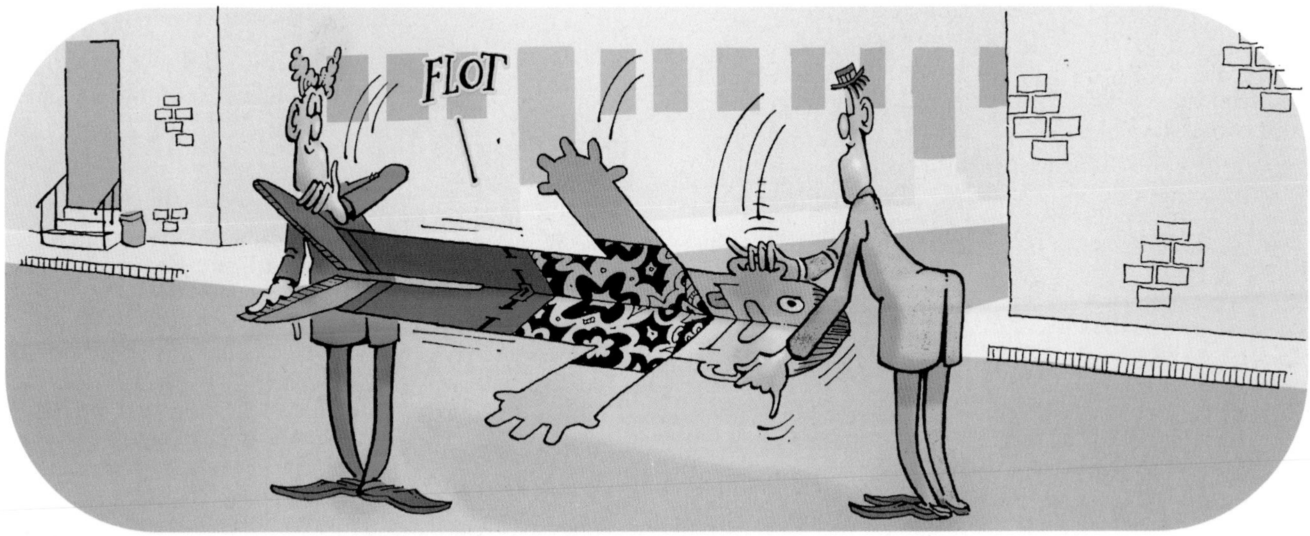
FLOT

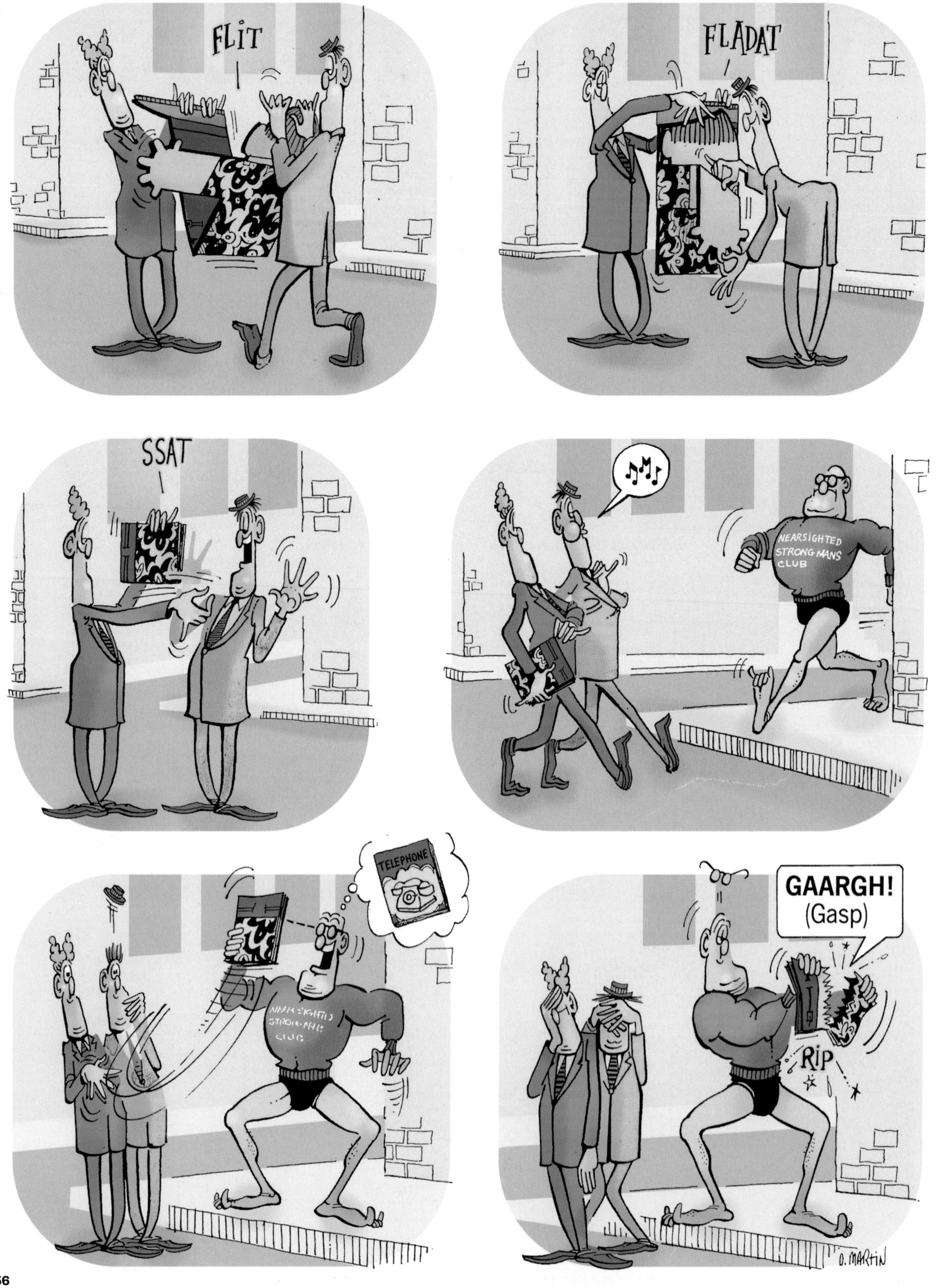
FLIT
FLADAT
SSAT
NEARSIGHTED STRONG MANS CLUB
TELEPHONE
GAARGH! (Gasp)
RIP
O. MARTIN

JOKE AND DAGGER DEPT.

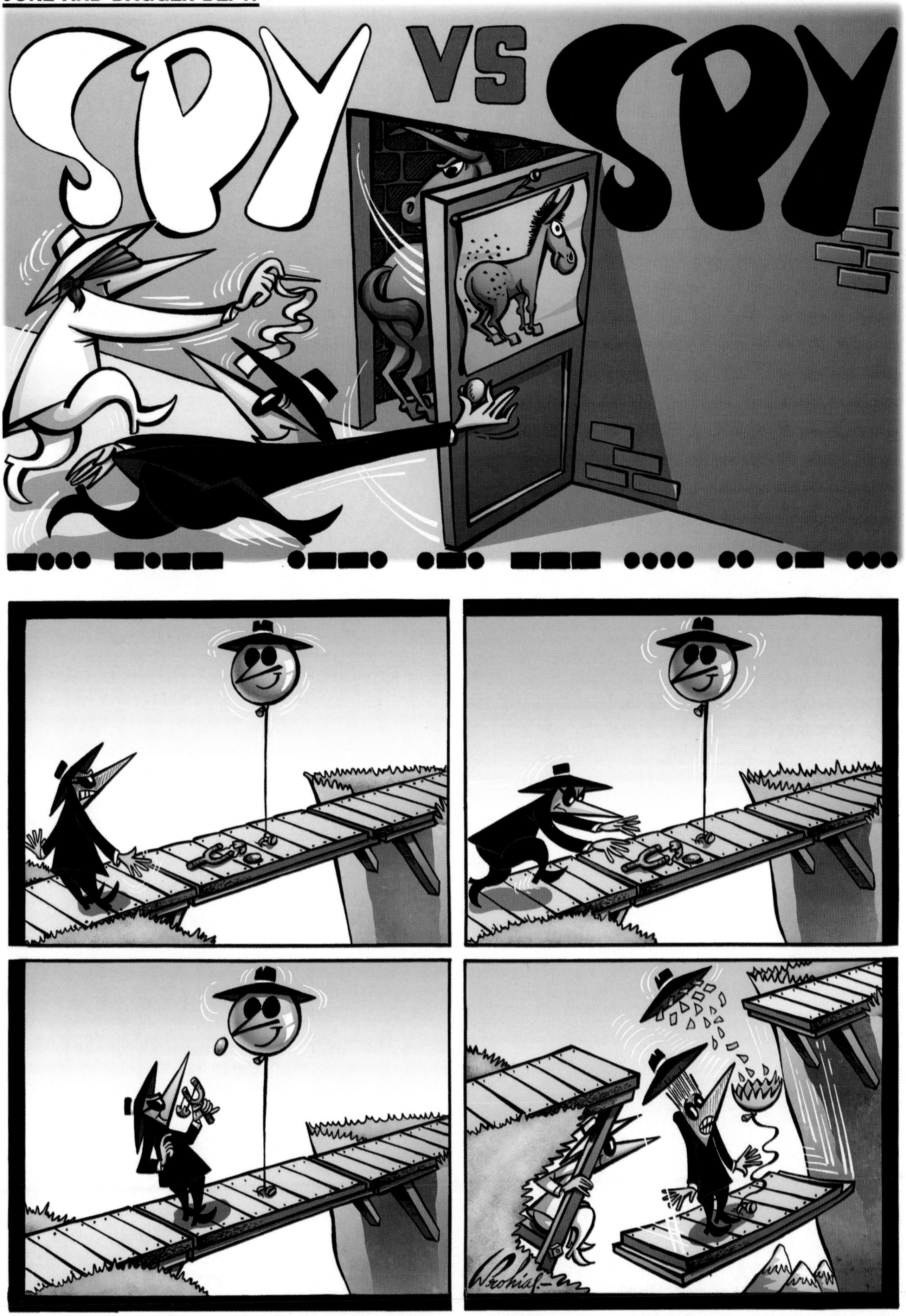
SPY VS SPY

WRITER AND ARTIST: ANTONIO PROHIAS COLORIST: CARRIE STRACHAN

GOT A MONKEY ON YOUR BACK? CAN'T COME OUT OF YOUR SHELL? THERE'S SOMEONE WHO CAN HELP...

From the Case Files of Wanda Goldstein Flenkman: Animal Psychologist

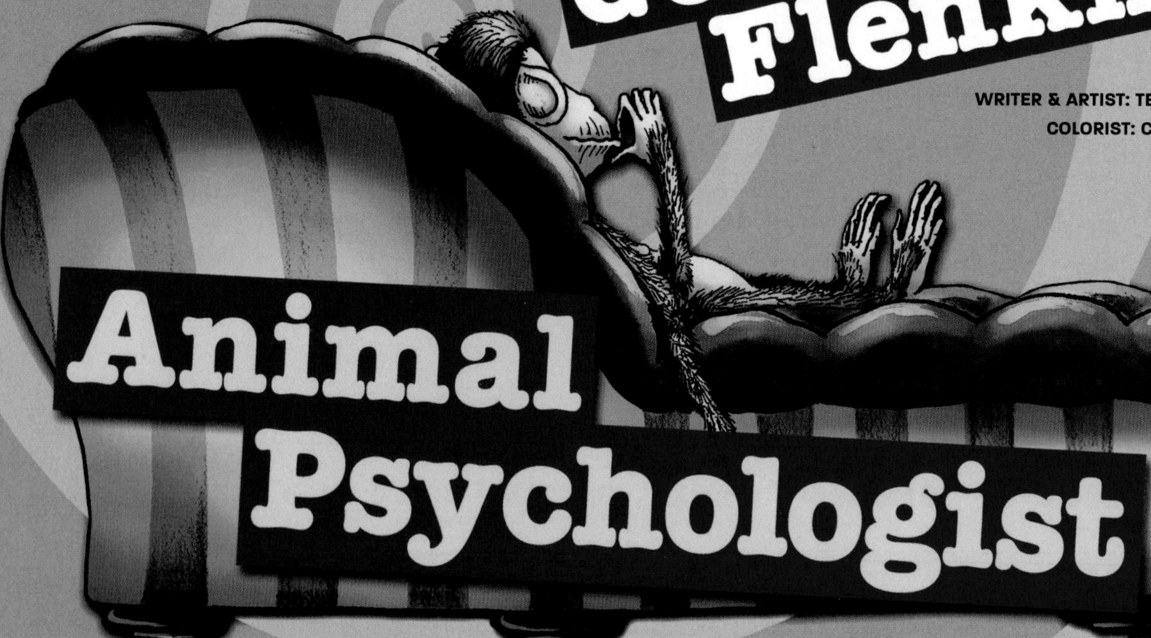

WRITER & ARTIST: TERESA BURNS PARKHURST
COLORIST: CARRIE STRACHAN

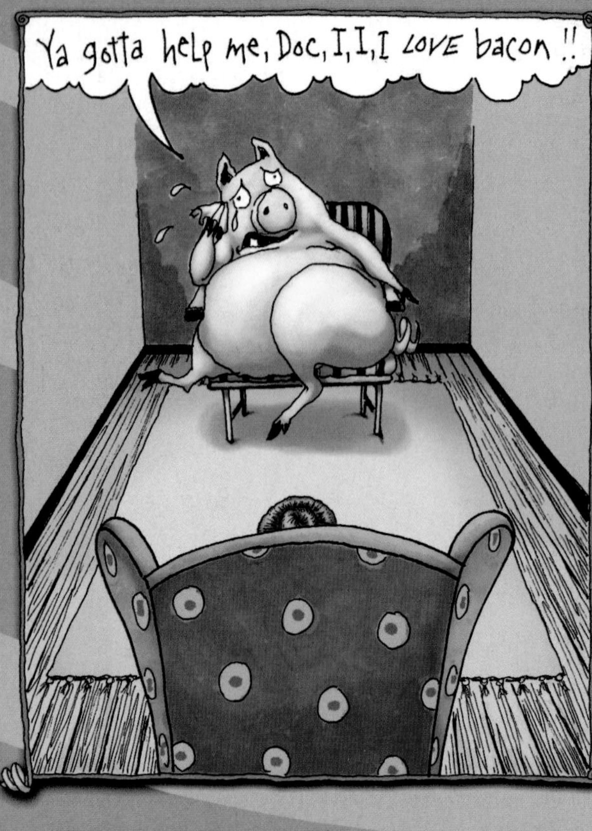
Ya gotta help me, Doc, I, I, I LOVE bacon!!

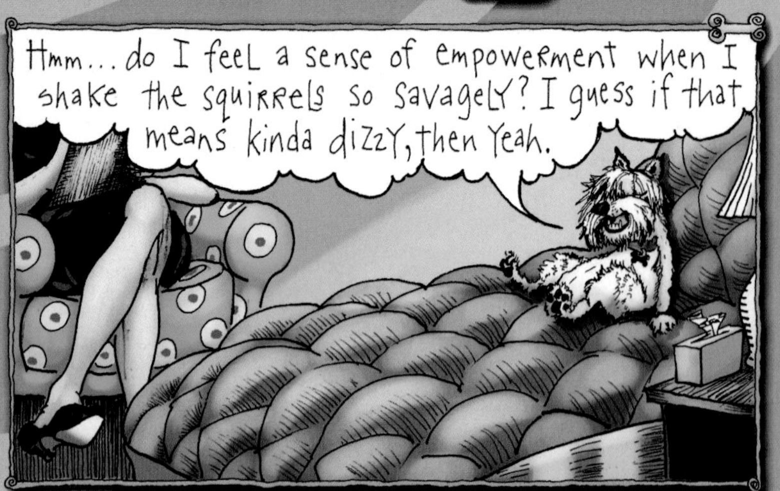
Hmm... do I feel a sense of empowerment when I shake the squirrels so savagely? I guess if that means kinda dizzy, then yeah.

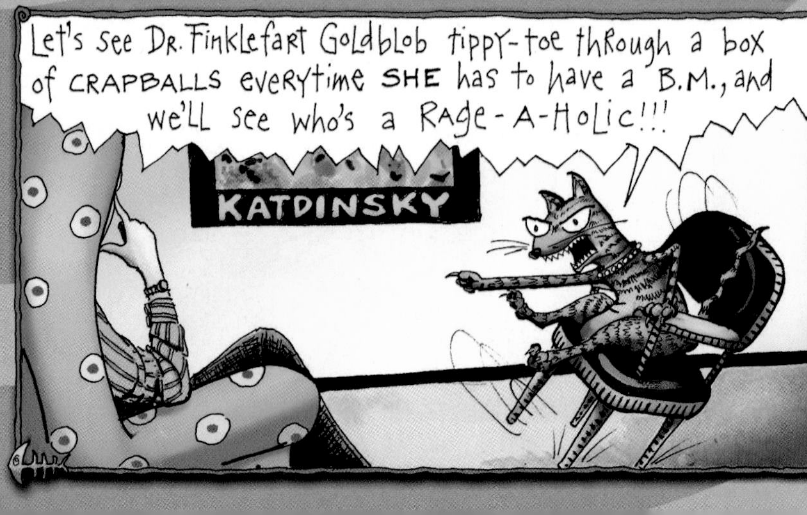
Let's see Dr. Finklefart Goldblob tippy-toe through a box of CRAPBALLS everytime SHE has to have a B.M., and we'll see who's a Rage-A-Holic!!!
KATDINSKY

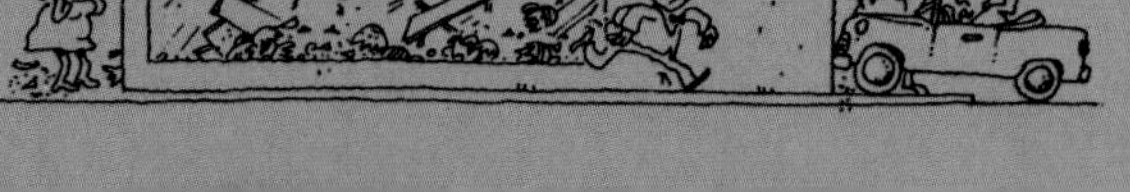
ANTIQUE GLASS

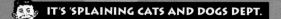

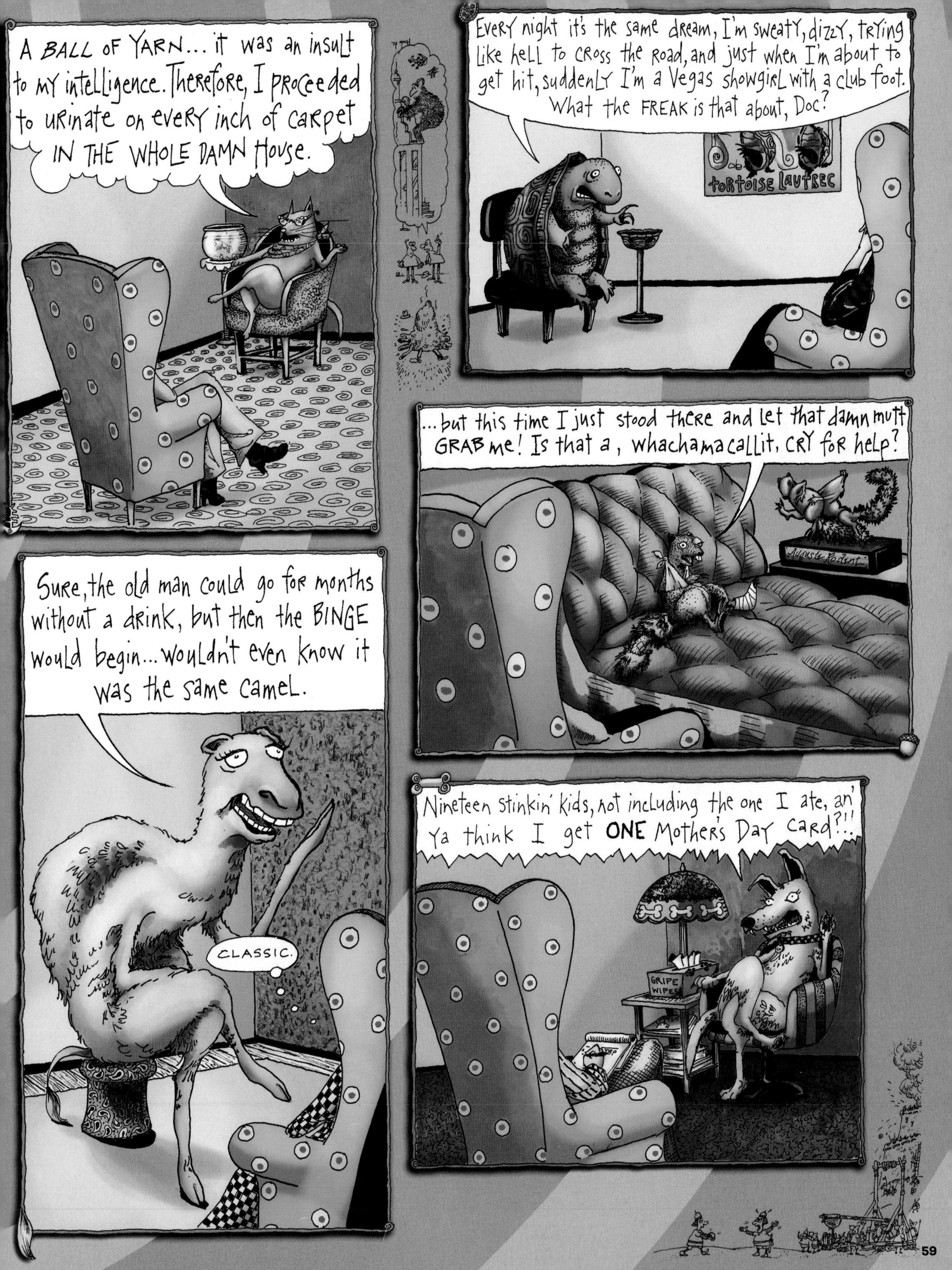
A BALL OF YARN... it was an insult to my intelligence. Therefore, I proceeded to urinate on every inch of carpet IN THE WHOLE DAMN House.
Every night it's the same dream, I'm sweaty, dizzy, trying like hell to cross the road, and just when I'm about to get hit, suddenly I'm a Vegas showgirl with a club foot. What the FREAK is that about, Doc?
tortoise Lautrec
...but this time I just stood there and let that damn mutt GRAB me! Is that a, whachamacallit, cry for help?
Auguste Rodent
Sure, the old man could go for months without a drink, but then the BINGE would begin... wouldn't even know it was the same camel.
CLASSIC.
Nineteen stinkin' kids, not including the one I ate, an' Ya think I get **ONE** Mother's Day card?!!
GRIPE WIPES

LUNA-SEE DEPT.

THE WEREWOLF

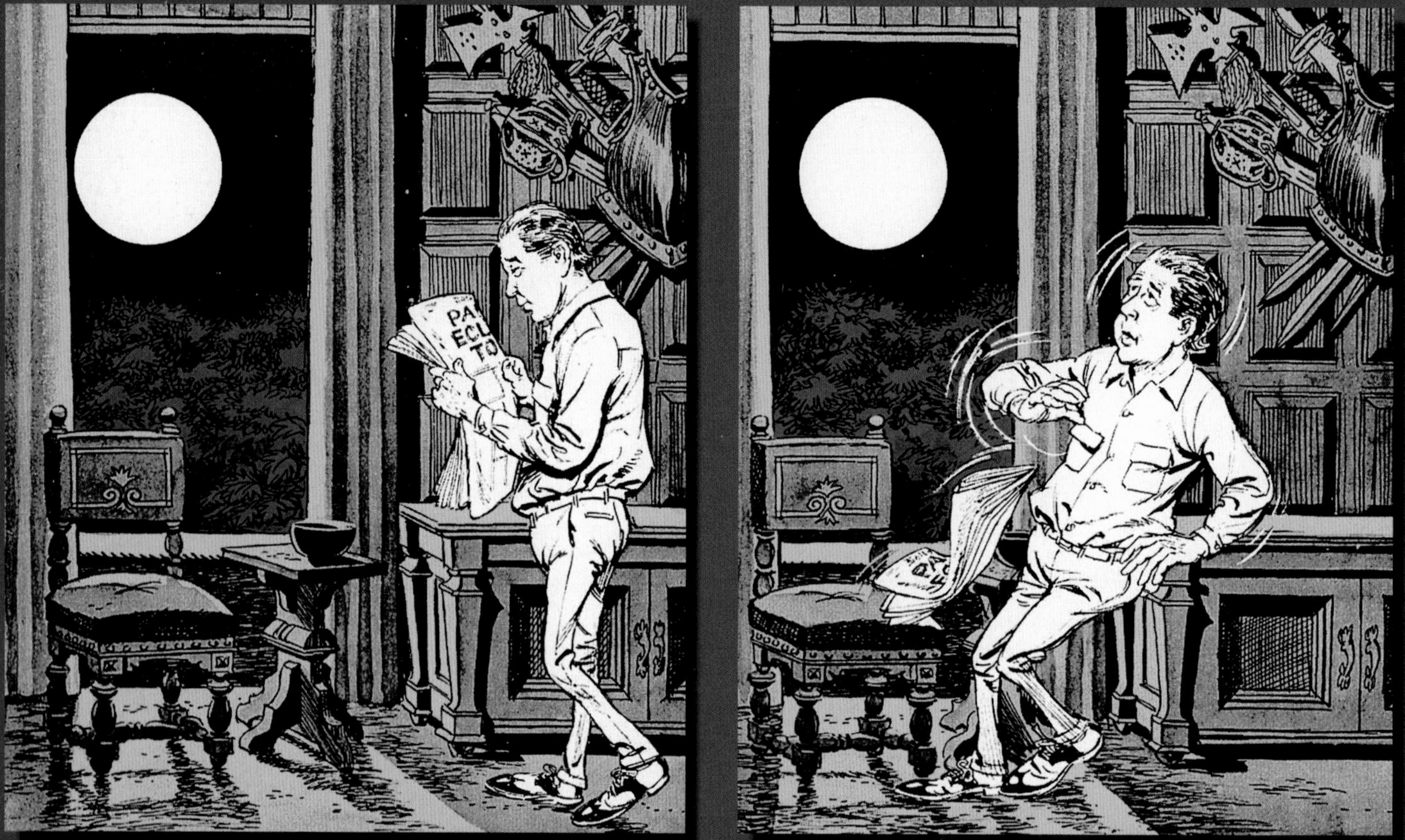

WRITER: SEMI ARTIST: GEORGE WOODBRIDGE

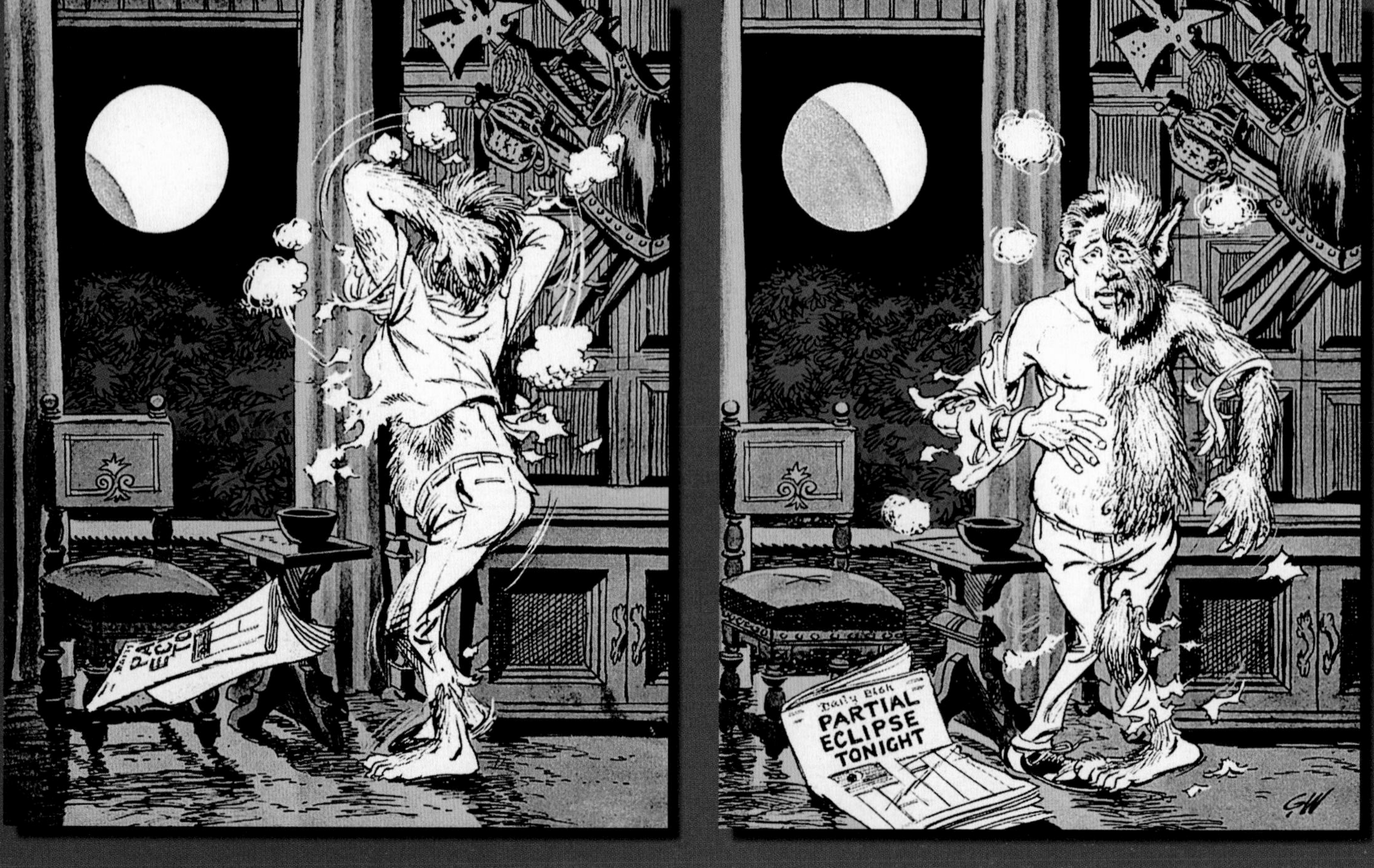
PARTIAL ECLIPSE TONIGHT

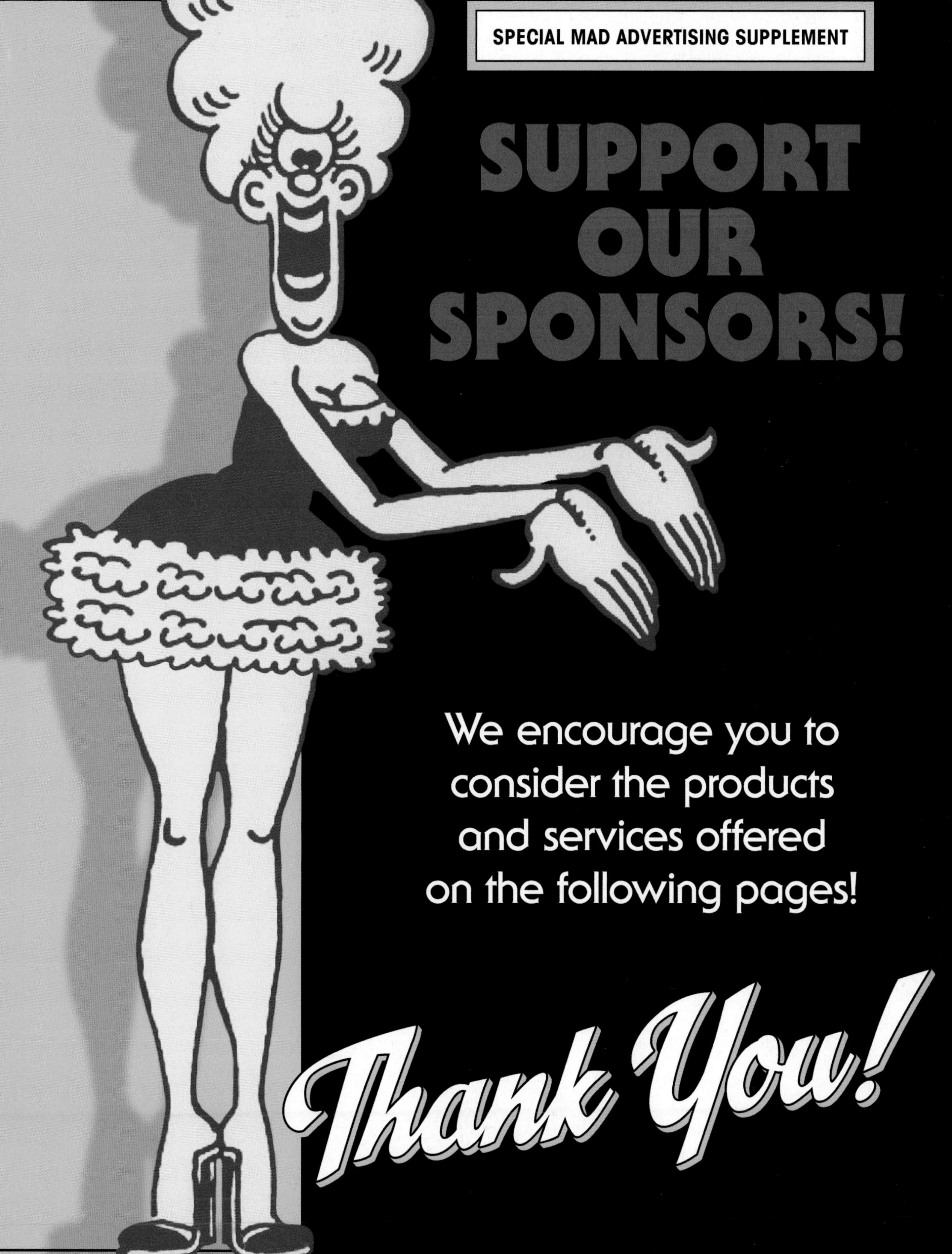
SPECIAL MAD ADVERTISING SUPPLEMENT
SUPPORT OUR SPONSORS!
We encourage you to consider the products and services offered on the following pages!
Thank You!

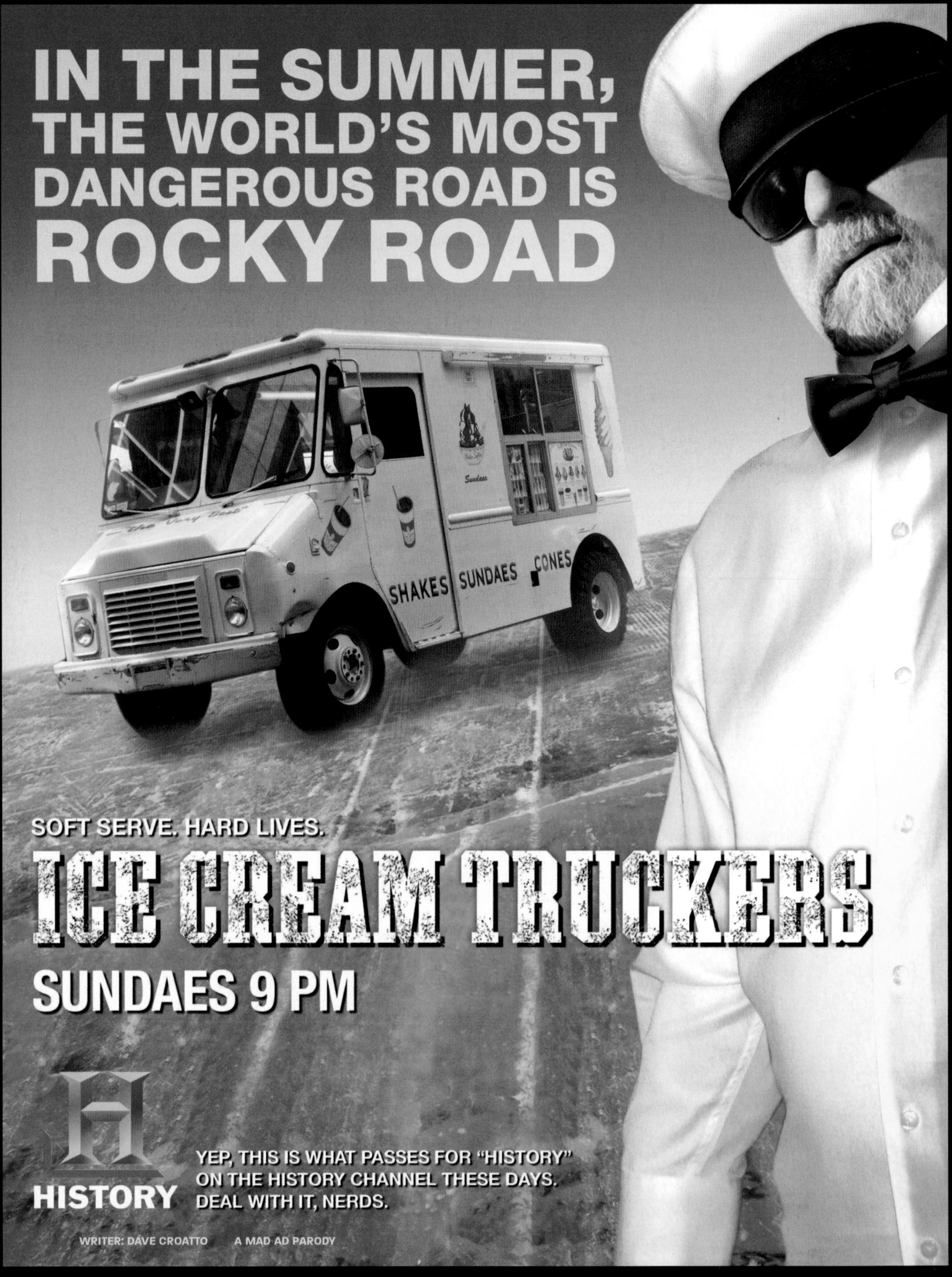
IN THE SUMMER,
THE WORLD'S MOST
DANGEROUS ROAD IS
ROCKY ROAD
SHAKES
SUNDAES
CONES
SOFT SERVE. HARD LIVES.
ICE CREAM TRUCKERS
SUNDAES 9 PM
HISTORY
YEP, THIS IS WHAT PASSES FOR "HISTORY"
ON THE HISTORY CHANNEL THESE DAYS.
DEAL WITH IT, NERDS.
WRITER: DAVE CROATTO
A MAD AD PARODY

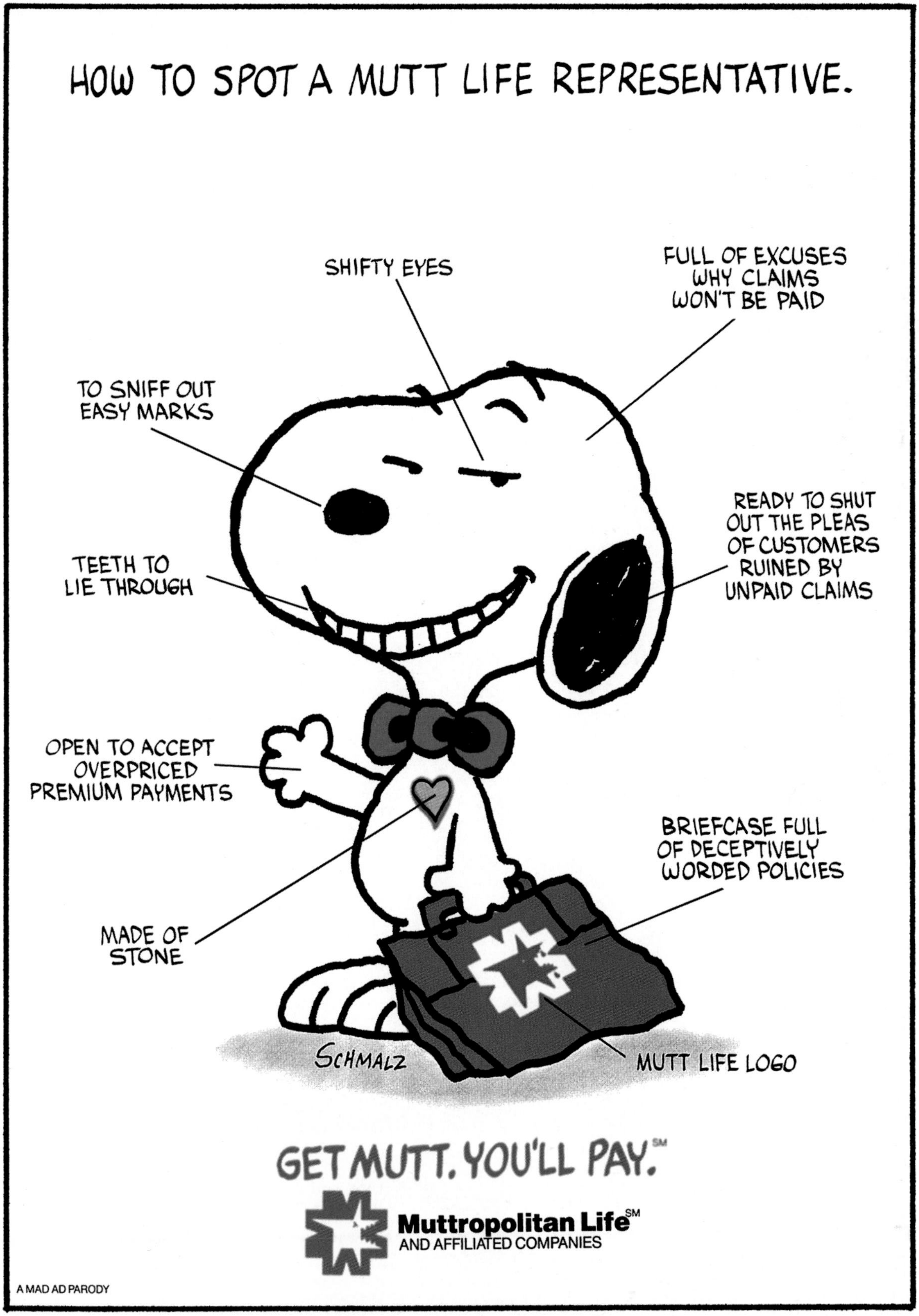
HOW TO SPOT A MUTT LIFE REPRESENTATIVE.
SHIFTY EYES
FULL OF EXCUSES WHY CLAIMS WON'T BE PAID
TO SNIFF OUT EASY MARKS
READY TO SHUT OUT THE PLEAS OF CUSTOMERS RUINED BY UNPAID CLAIMS
TEETH TO LIE THROUGH
OPEN TO ACCEPT OVERPRICED PREMIUM PAYMENTS
BRIEFCASE FULL OF DECEPTIVELY WORDED POLICIES
MADE OF STONE
SCHMALZ
MUTT LIFE LOGO
GET MUTT. YOU'LL PAY.SM
Muttropolitan LifeSM
AND AFFILIATED COMPANIES
A MAD AD PARODY

WRITER: CHARLIE KADAU ARTIST: ANGELO TORRES

Dead Lobster

For the Sea Crude Lover In You

Surf's up
on new
catastrophic
seafood
creations!

Come Celebrate Our Gulf Coast Disaster Deals!

America's favorite greasy, discount seafood restaurant just got a little greasier, and a whole lot cheaper!
How can we bring you these irresistible entrées at such a low cost? It's all thanks to BP — Bargain Pricing!
At Dead Lobster, our seafood is so plentiful, it's literally washing up on shore! Hurry in today! It's gonna be a BLOWOUT!

New Orleans Blackened Seafood Jumble-aya!

A Creole-inspired blend of scallops, crab, sea turtle, and whatever else might be in there. Sautéed in the same oil they were dripping in when we caught them!

Only $12.99!

Battered & Bruised Shrimp

Get this home-style dish while you still can! Because, Gulf shrimp this big and non-deformed won't be around much longer. Served with garlic potatoes as thoroughly smashed as the surrounding wetlands!

Only $8.99!

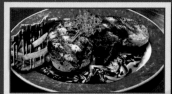

Grilled Blackfin Tuna

Formerly Bluefin Tuna, this succulent dish will have you shouting "Grill, Baby, Grill!" The irresistible flavor explodes in your mouth like an oil rig that lacked any government oversight! Try pairing it with our new, refreshing Texas Tea!

Only $9.99!

Try these Signature Sides!

Plumin' Onion.........$5.99
Jalapeño Tar Balls...$2.25
Potato Leak Soup....$1.99

All entrées come with a wilted marsh grass salad covered in oil and vinegar and MORE oil!

A MAD AD PARODY

WRITER: ANDY ROSS

PHOTOGRAPHY: IRVING SCHILD

You won't find better seafood! Seriously, you won't...it's all dead.

THE CONTINUING ADVENTURES OF WILLY NILLY

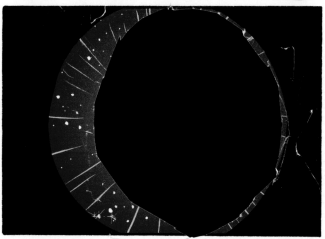

WRITER: NATE NEAL   ARTIST: JACOB CHABOT

BERG'S-EYE VIEW DEPT.

THE LIGHTER SIDE OF SWIMM

Hi, Mrs. De Salv[redacted]
Is Bobby ho[redacted]
Hi, Bobby! Whatchya wanna do today?
It must be nice to have your own pool, you lucky stiff!
Yeah, it's nice. But it's also a lot of work!
I've got to test the water a couple of times a day by taking a sample, pouring in a chemical, and matching the color . . .
. . . and I've got to add chlorine and some other stuff that gets rid of algae . . .
Yeah, but think of all the FUN, you lucky stiff!
Oh, it's fun. But I've got to skim the water to remove the leaves and bugs! And I've got to clean out the filter by backwashing it!
I even have a special vacuum for cleaning the bottom of the pool!
Let's see—what did the swimming instructor say about diving? "Hands together over head . . ."
"Take a slight spring on the board . . . keep the legs straight and the toes together . . ."
"Enter the water with a slightly arched back—" Okay! I think I got it! Now . . . here goes . . .

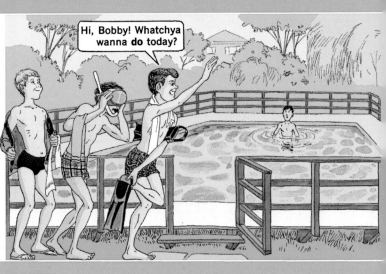

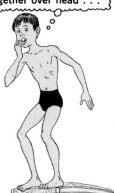

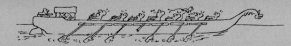

ARTIST & WRITER: DAVE BERG

BRRR! This water is **ice cold!** I'll have to slip in gradually and get used to it—a little at a time!

Don't be **ridiculous!** Le'me show you how to **do it!**

SLASH!

See? You've got to get yourself wet **all at once!**

C'mon! Now **YOU** try it!

Wh-What F-F-FOR?! Y-You've already t-t-taken c-c-care of th-that little m-matter!

C'mon! Let's take a **swim** in your pool, you **lucky stiff!**

No, thanks!

Why not?

I'm **too stiff!**

Listen, I **distinctly told you** that I want a reservation at a motel that has a **pool!** If you **can't** get me one with a pool, then I'll just have to get me **another travel agent!**

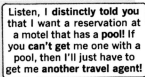

Frankly, I don't understand **why** you insisted on a motel with a **pool** when you don't even **swim!**

Boy, his is un!

Hey, **Kid!** What's the fun of wearing a **face mask** in a swimming pool?

You can **see** everything so clear!

Oh, yeah? Le'me borrow your mask so I can see what you're talking about?

You're right, kid! Those are the **CLEAREST** tiles, Bobby Pins, **hunks of hair** and **lost Band-Aids** I've **EVER SEEN!**

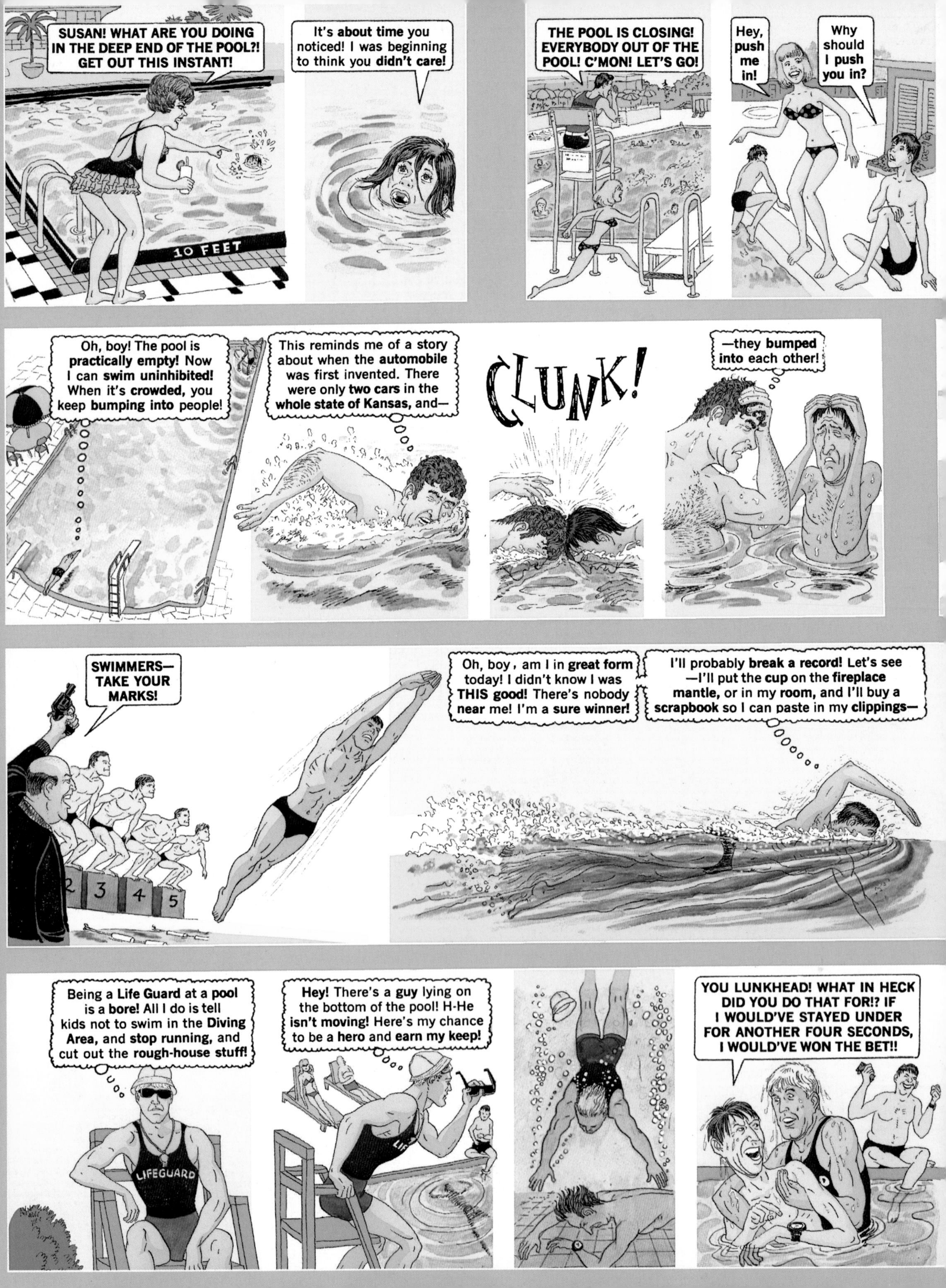

SUSAN! WHAT ARE YOU DOING IN THE DEEP END OF THE POOL?! GET OUT THIS INSTANT!
10 FEET
It's about time you noticed! I was beginning to think you didn't care!
THE POOL IS CLOSING! EVERYBODY OUT OF THE POOL! C'MON! LET'S GO!
Hey, push me in!
Why should I push you in?
Oh, boy! The pool is practically empty! Now I can swim uninhibited! When it's crowded, you keep bumping into people!
This reminds me of a story about when the automobile was first invented. There were only two cars in the whole state of Kansas, and—
CLUNK!
—they bumped into each other!
SWIMMERS— TAKE YOUR MARKS!
2 3 4 5
Oh, boy, am I in great form today! I didn't know I was THIS good! There's nobody near me! I'm a sure winner!
I'll probably break a record! Let's see —I'll put the cup on the fireplace mantle, or in my room, and I'll buy a scrapbook so I can paste in my clippings—
Being a Life Guard at a pool is a bore! All I do is tell kids not to swim in the Diving Area, and stop running, and cut out the rough-house stuff!
LIFEGUARD
Hey! There's a guy lying on the bottom of the pool! H-He isn't moving! Here's my chance to be a hero and earn my keep!
YOU LUNKHEAD! WHAT IN HECK DID YOU DO THAT FOR!? IF I WOULD'VE STAYED UNDER FOR ANOTHER FOUR SECONDS, I WOULD'VE WON THE BET!!

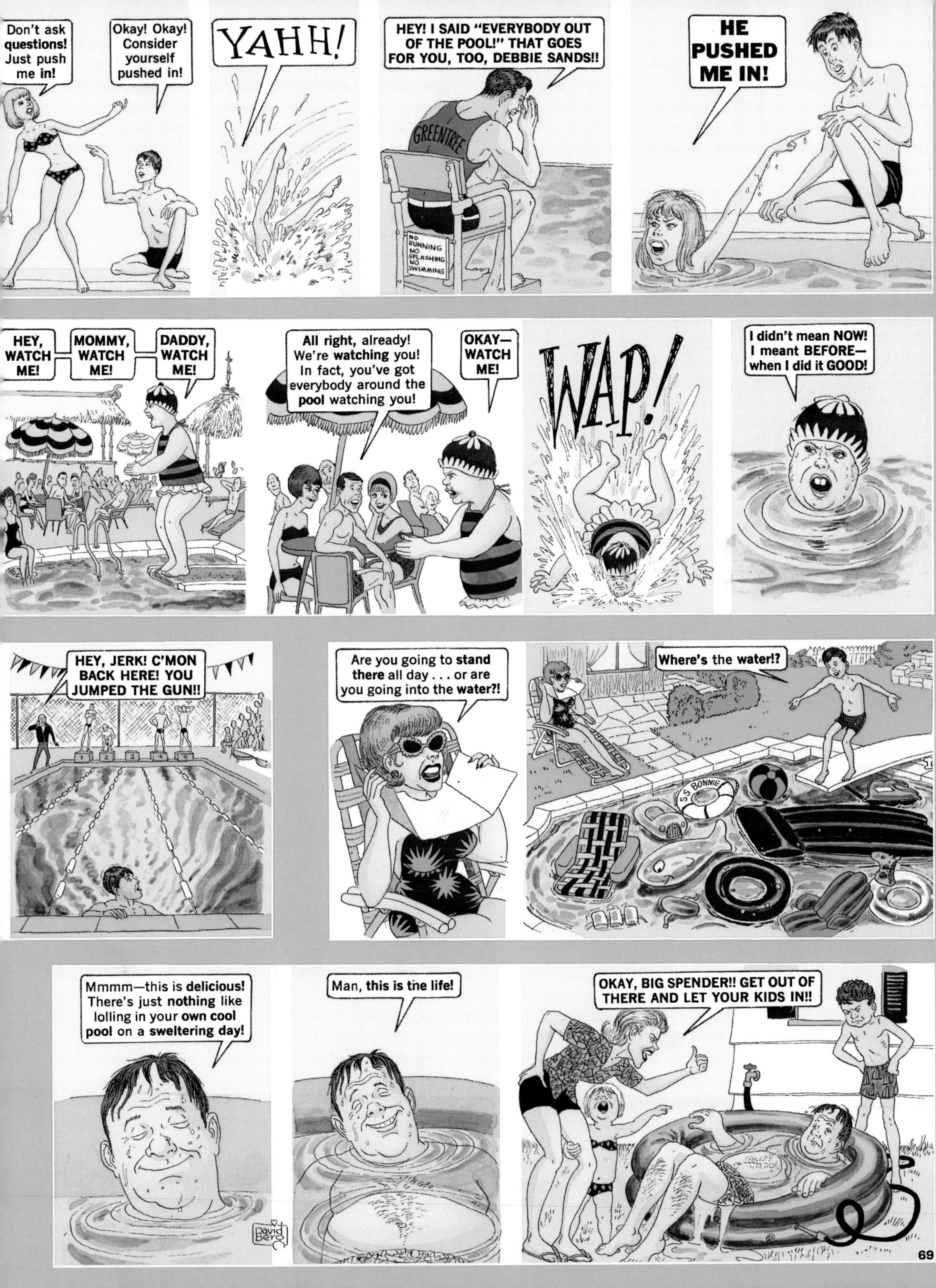
Don't ask questions! Just push me in!
Okay! Okay! Consider yourself pushed in!
YAHH!
HEY! I SAID "EVERYBODY OUT OF THE POOL!" THAT GOES FOR YOU, TOO, DEBBIE SANDS!!
GREENTREE
NO RUNNING NO SPLASHING NO SWIMMING
HE PUSHED ME IN!
HEY, WATCH ME!
MOMMY, WATCH ME!
DADDY, WATCH ME!
All right, already! We're watching you! In fact, you've got everybody around the pool watching you!
OKAY—WATCH ME!
WAP!
I didn't mean NOW! I meant BEFORE—when I did it GOOD!
HEY, JERK! C'MON BACK HERE! YOU JUMPED THE GUN!!
Are you going to stand there all day . . . or are you going into the water?!
Where's the water!?
SS BONNIE
Mmmm—this is delicious! There's just nothing like lolling in your own cool pool on a sweltering day!
David Berg
Man, this is the life!
OKAY, BIG SPENDER!! GET OUT OF THERE AND LET YOUR KIDS IN!!

VENDING MACHINE FU

THE JAMMED COIN RETURN CRESCENT KICK

THE COLD COFFEE FLYING DOUBLE STOMP

WRITER AND ARTIST: TOM CHENEY
COLORIST: CARRIE STRACHAN

THE STALE CUPCAKE GOUGE AND PEEL

THE NO-SHOW CUP REVERSE ELBOW JAB

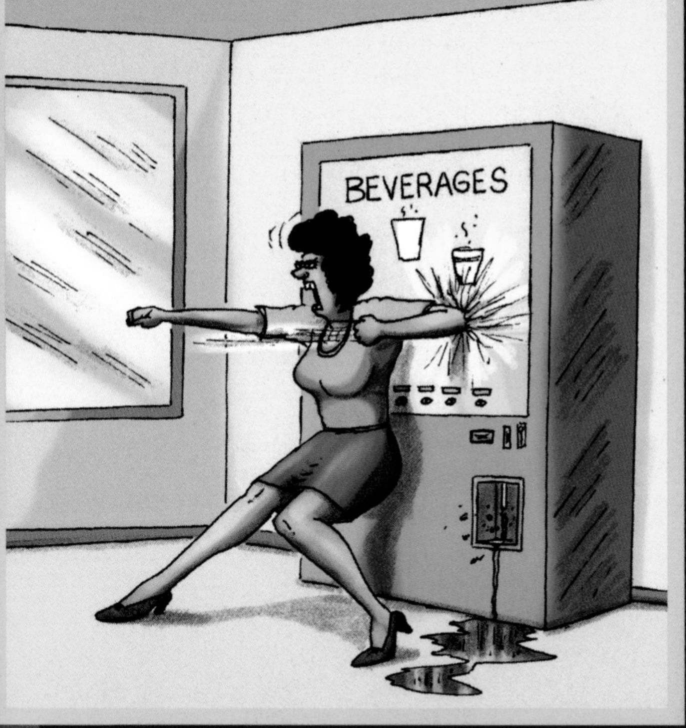
BEVERAGES

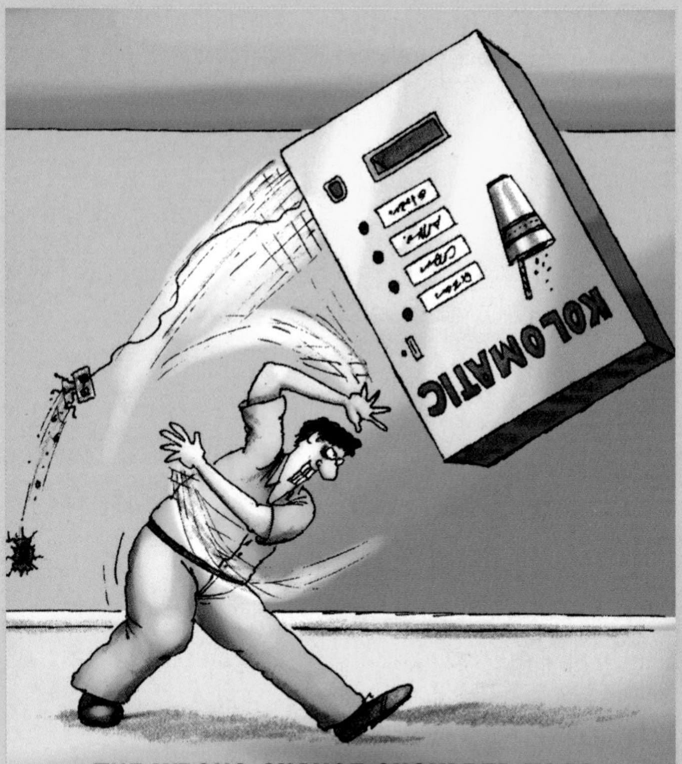
KOLOMATIC

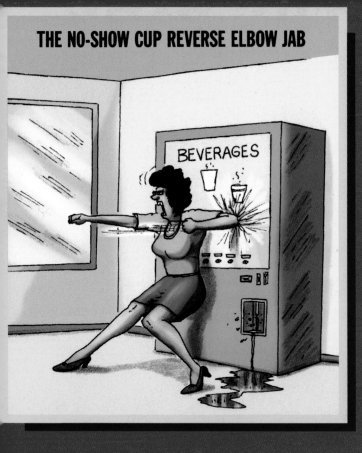

THE WRONG CHANGE SHOULDER TOSS

THE WRONG ITEM HEAD BUTT

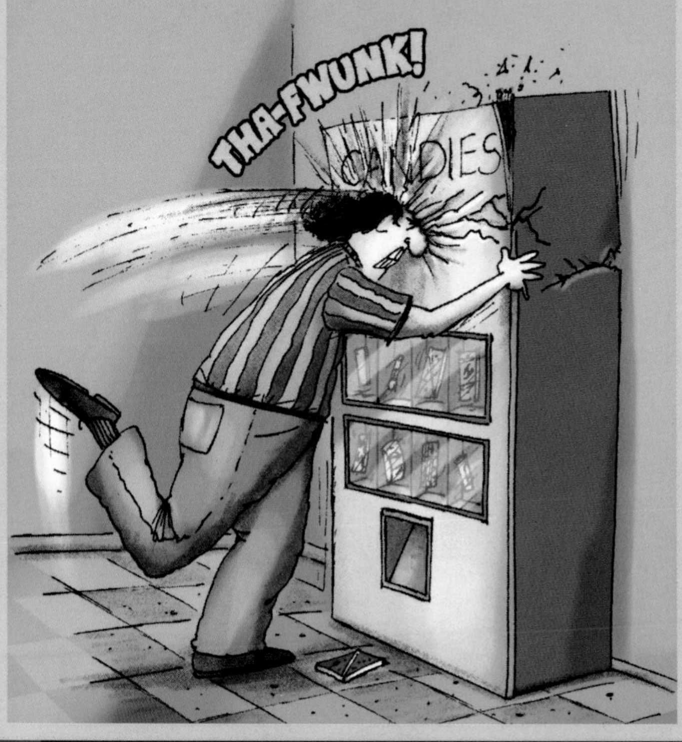
THA-FWUNK!

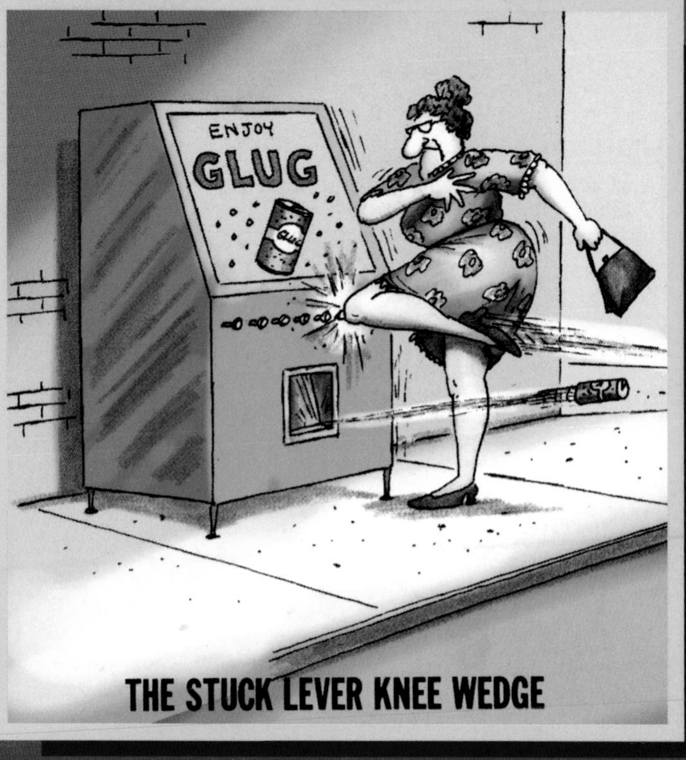
ENJOY
GLUG

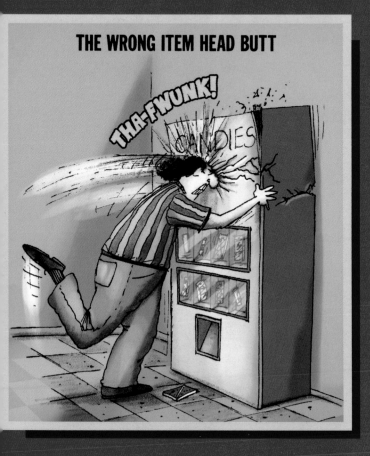

THE STUCK LEVER KNEE WEDGE

ONE DAY IN THE PARK

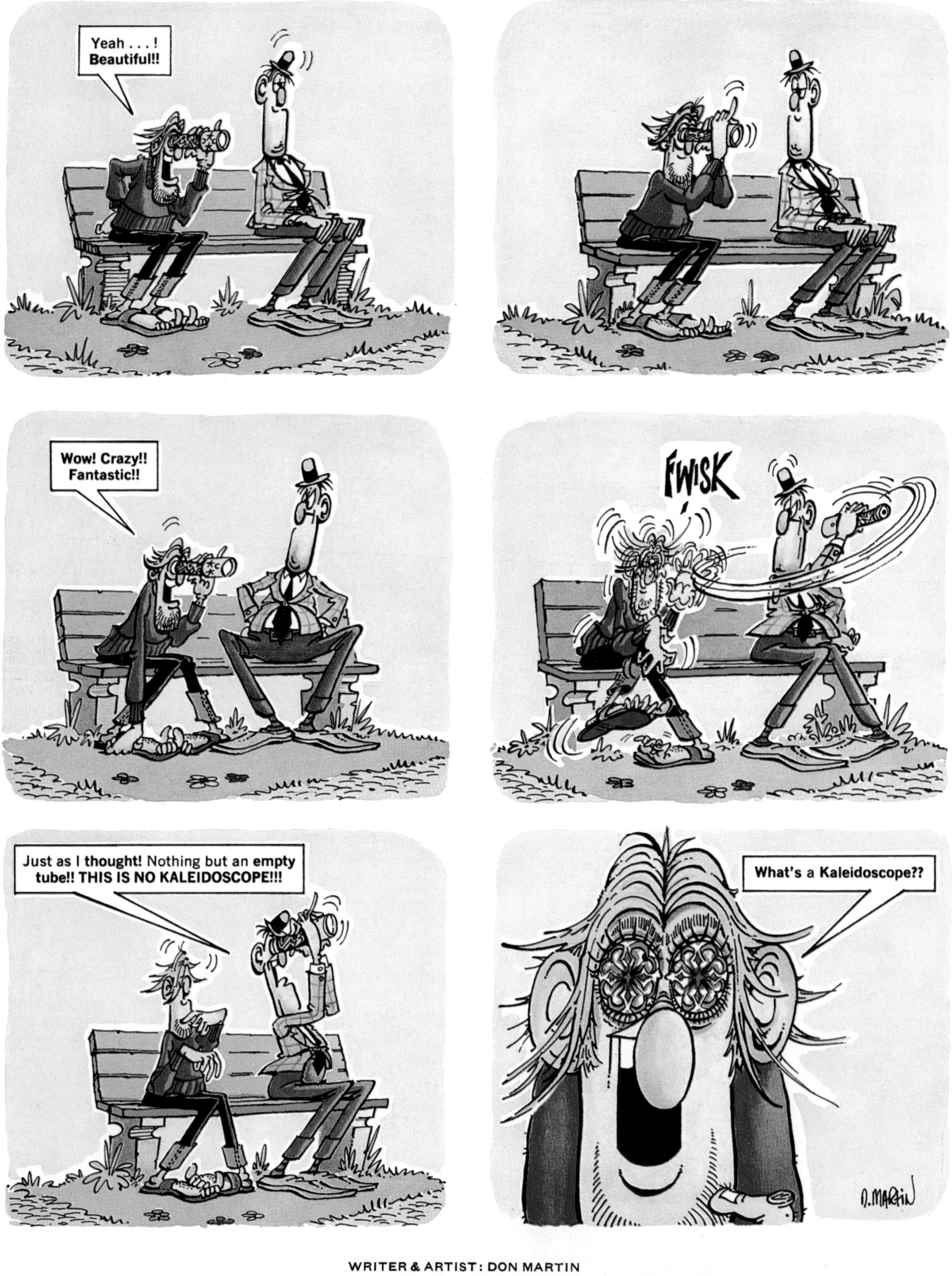

Yeah . . . ! Beautiful!!
Wow! Crazy!! Fantastic!!
FWISK
Just as I thought! Nothing but an empty tube!! THIS IS NO KALEIDOSCOPE!!!
What's a Kaleidoscope??
D. MARTIN

WRITER & ARTIST: DON MARTIN

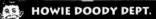

HOWIE DOODY DEPT.

Welcome to the TV phenomenon that's sweeping the world! It's the highest-rated show in its time period in over 35 third-world countries that feature only one channel of television broadcasting! So far, nearly a quarter of a billion dollars in prize money has been offered!! But thanks to the sneaky way they keep switching those "money cases" around, they've only given away .002% of that amount! The entire one-hour show consists of s-l-o-w-l-y and painfully opening 26 cases. So judge for yourself. Is this TV show...

DULL OR NOT DULL?

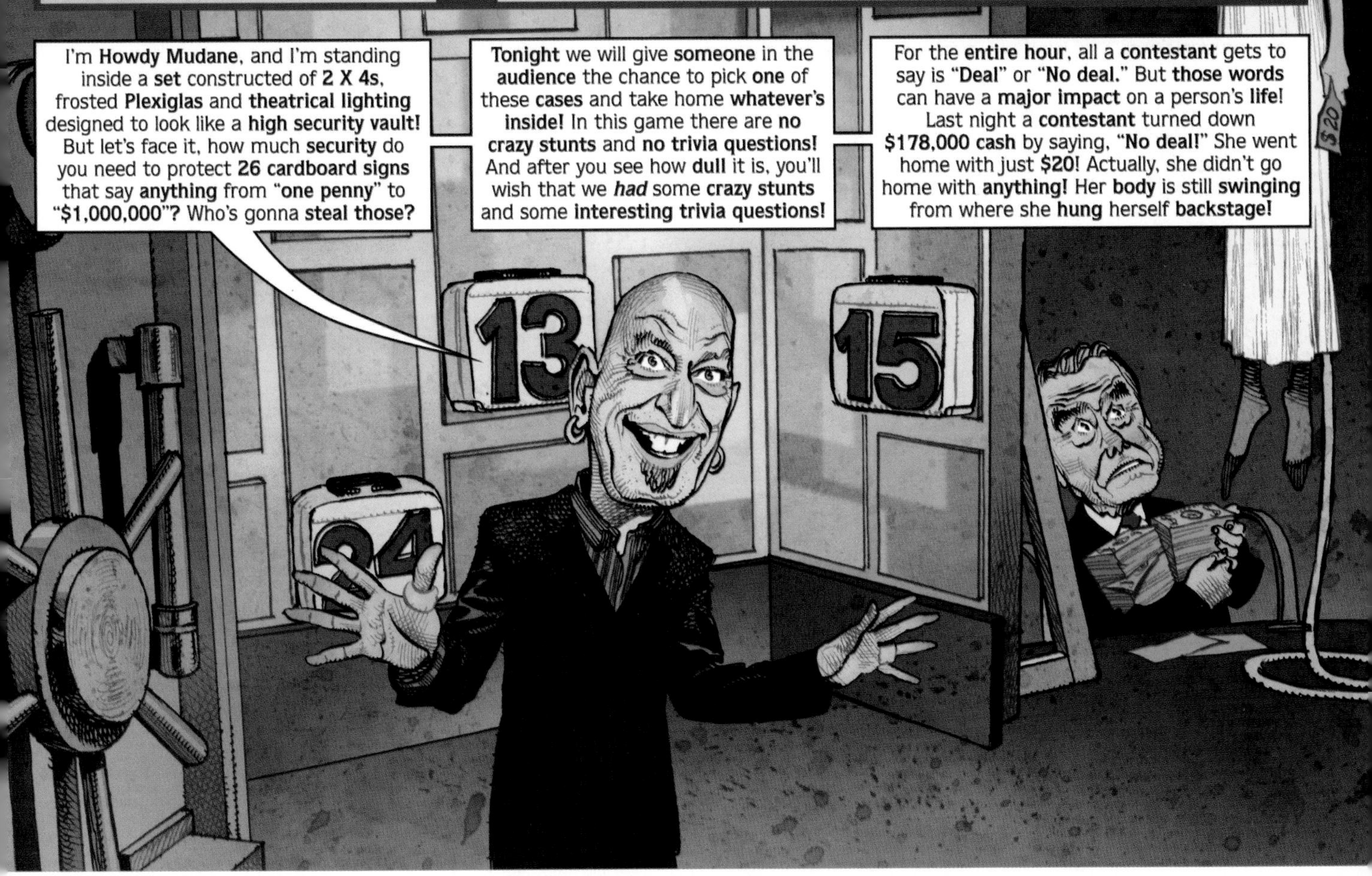

I'm **Howdy Mudane**, and I'm standing inside a **set** constructed of **2 X 4s**, frosted **Plexiglas** and **theatrical lighting** designed to look like a **high security vault!** But let's face it, how much **security** do you need to protect **26 cardboard signs** that say **anything** from "**one penny**" to "**$1,000,000**"? Who's gonna **steal those?**
Tonight we will give **someone** in the **audience** the chance to pick **one** of these **cases** and take home **whatever's inside!** In this game there are **no crazy stunts** and **no trivia questions!** And after you see how **dull** it is, you'll wish that we ***had*** some **crazy stunts** and some **interesting trivia questions!**
For the **entire hour**, all a **contestant** gets to say is "**Deal**" or "**No deal.**" But **those words** can have a **major impact** on a person's **life!** Last night a **contestant** turned down **$178,000 cash** by saying, "**No deal!**" She went home with just **$20!** Actually, she didn't go home with **anything!** Her **body** is still **swinging** from where she **hung** herself **backstage!**
13
15

WRITER: DICK DEBARTOLO ARTIST: HERMANN MEJIA

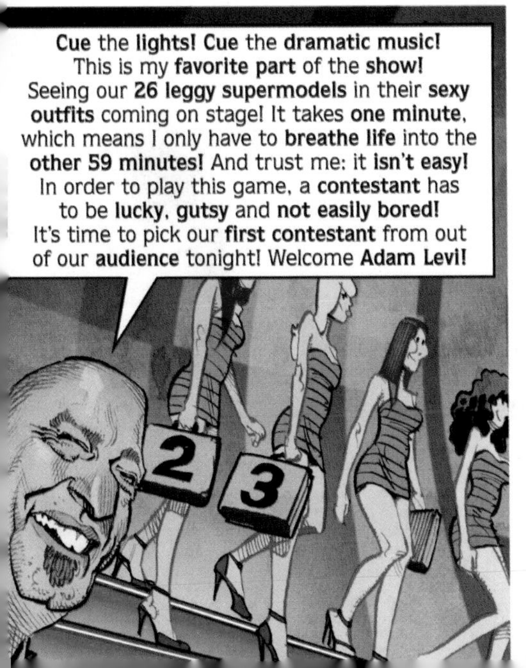

Cue the **lights! Cue** the **dramatic music!** This is my **favorite part** of the **show!** Seeing our **26 leggy supermodels** in their **sexy outfits** coming on stage! It takes **one minute**, which means I only have to **breathe life** into the **other 59 minutes!** And trust me: it **isn't easy!** In order to play this game, a **contestant** has to be **lucky**, **gutsy** and **not easily bored!** It's time to pick our **first contestant** from out of our **audience** tonight! Welcome **Adam Levi!**
2
3

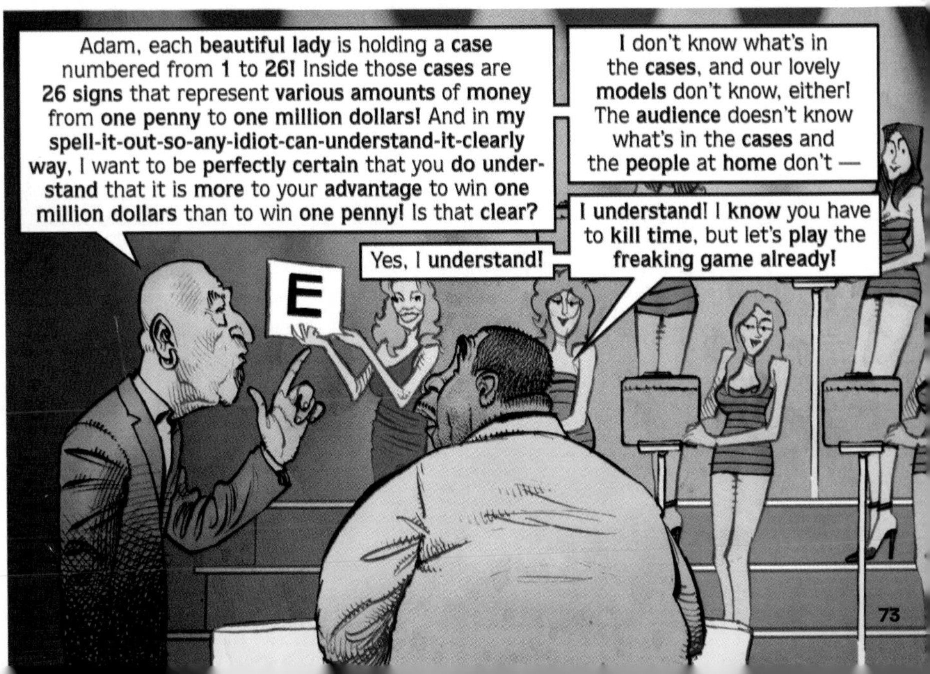

Adam, each **beautiful lady** is holding a **case** numbered from **1** to **26!** Inside those **cases** are **26 signs** that represent **various amounts of money** from **one penny** to **one million dollars!** And in **my spell-it-out-so-any-idiot-can-understand-it-clearly way**, I want to be **perfectly certain** that you **do understand** that it is **more** to your **advantage** to win **one million dollars** than to win **one penny!** Is that **clear?**
Yes, I **understand!**
I don't know what's in the **cases**, and our lovely **models** don't know, either! The **audience** doesn't know what's in the **cases** and the **people** at **home** don't —
I understand! I **know** you have to **kill time**, but let's **play** the **freaking game already!**
E

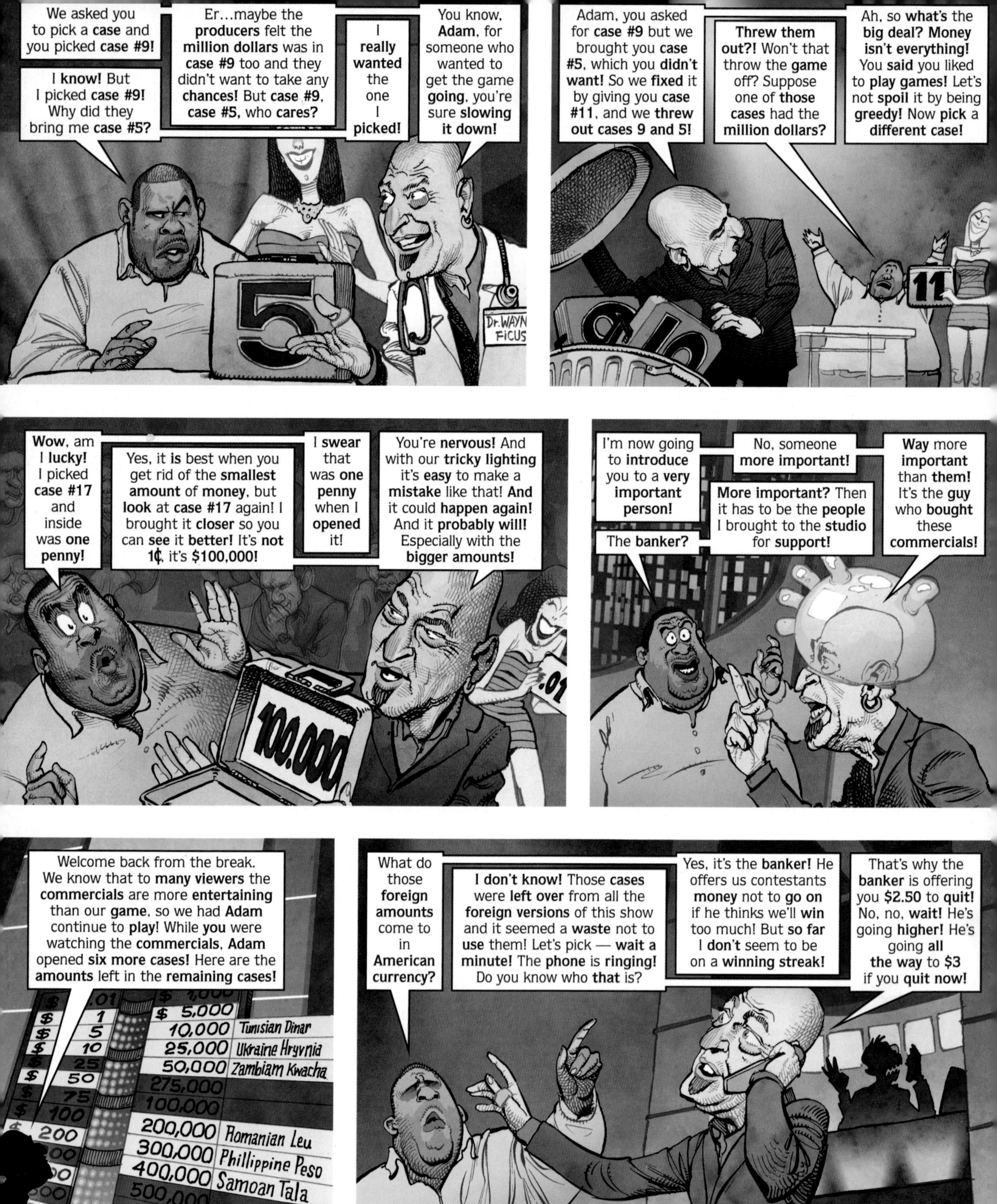
We asked you to pick a case and you picked case #9!
I know! But I picked case #9! Why did they bring me case #5?
Er…maybe the producers felt the million dollars was in case #9 too and they didn't want to take any chances! But case #9, case #5, who cares?
I really wanted the one I picked!
You know, Adam, for someone who wanted to get the game going, you're sure slowing it down!
Dr. WAYNE FICUS
5
Adam, you asked for case #9 but we brought you case #5, which you didn't want! So we fixed it by giving you case #11, and we threw out cases 9 and 5!
Threw them out?! Won't that throw the game off? Suppose one of those cases had the million dollars?
Ah, so what's the big deal? Money isn't everything! You said you liked to play games! Let's not spoil it by being greedy! Now pick a different case!
11
Wow, am I lucky! I picked case #17 and inside was one penny!
Yes, it is best when you get rid of the smallest amount of money, but look at case #17 again! I brought it closer so you can see it better! It's not 1¢, it's $100,000!
I swear that was one penny when I opened it!
You're nervous! And with our tricky lighting it's easy to make a mistake like that! And it could happen again! And it probably will! Especially with the bigger amounts!
100,000
.01
I'm now going to introduce you to a very important person!
The banker?
No, someone more important!
More important? Then it has to be the people I brought to the studio for support!
Way more important than them! It's the guy who bought these commercials!
Welcome back from the break. We know that to many viewers the commercials are more entertaining than our game, so we had Adam continue to play! While you were watching the commercials, Adam opened six more cases! Here are the amounts left in the remaining cases!
$ .01
$ 1
$ 5
$ 10
$ 25
$ 50
$ 75
$ 100
$ 200
$ 5,000
10,000 Tunisian Dinar
25,000 Ukraine Hryvnia
50,000 Zambiam Kwacha
275,000
100,000
200,000 Romanian Leu
300,000 Phillippine Peso
400,000 Samoan Tala
500,000
750,000
$ 1,000,000
What do those foreign amounts come to in American currency?
I don't know! Those cases were left over from all the foreign versions of this show and it seemed a waste not to use them! Let's pick — wait a minute! The phone is ringing! Do you know who that is?
Yes, it's the banker! He offers us contestants money not to go on if he thinks we'll win too much! But so far I don't seem to be on a winning streak!
That's why the banker is offering you $2.50 to quit! No, no, wait! He's going higher! He's going all the way to $3 if you quit now!

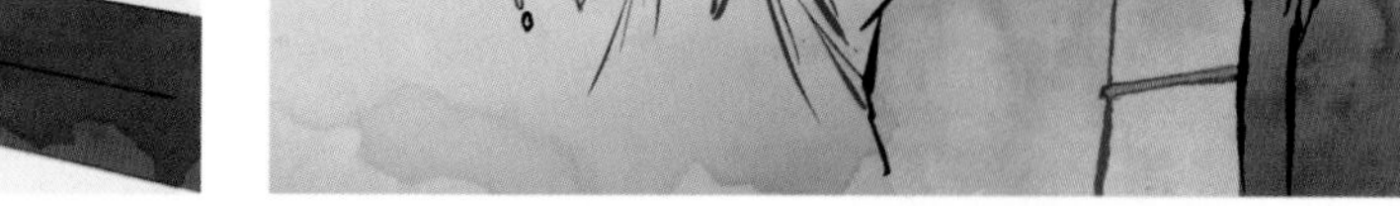

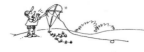

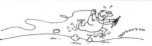

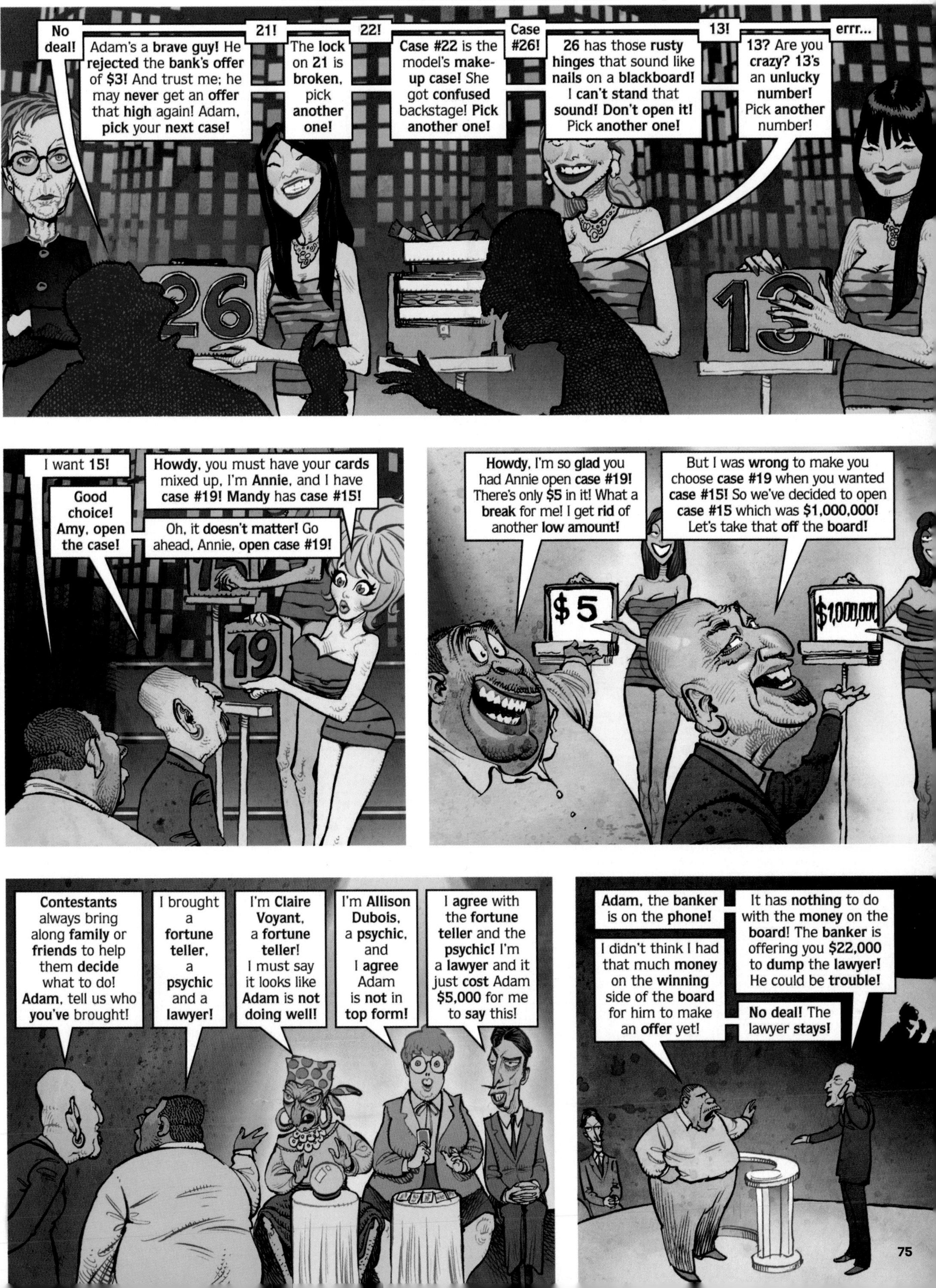
No deal!
Adam's a brave guy! He rejected the bank's offer of $3! And trust me; he may never get an offer that high again! Adam, pick your next case!
21!
The lock on 21 is broken, pick another one!
22!
Case #22 is the model's make-up case! She got confused backstage! Pick another one!
Case #26!
26 has those rusty hinges that sound like nails on a blackboard! I can't stand that sound! Don't open it! Pick another one!
13!
13? Are you crazy? 13's an unlucky number! Pick another number!
errr...
26
13
I want 15!
Good choice! Amy, open the case!
Howdy, you must have your cards mixed up, I'm Annie, and I have case #19! Mandy has case #15!
Oh, it doesn't matter! Go ahead, Annie, open case #19!
19
Howdy, I'm so glad you had Annie open case #19! There's only $5 in it! What a break for me! I get rid of another low amount!
But I was wrong to make you choose case #19 when you wanted case #15! So we've decided to open case #15 which was $1,000,000! Let's take that off the board!
$5
$1,000,000
Contestants always bring along family or friends to help them decide what to do! Adam, tell us who you've brought!
I brought a fortune teller, a psychic and a lawyer!
I'm Claire Voyant, a fortune teller! I must say it looks like Adam is not doing well!
I'm Allison Dubois, a psychic, and I agree Adam is not in top form!
I agree with the fortune teller and the psychic! I'm a lawyer and it just cost Adam $5,000 for me to say this!
Adam, the banker is on the phone!
I didn't think I had that much money on the winning side of the board for him to make an offer yet!
It has nothing to do with the money on the board! The banker is offering you $22,000 to dump the lawyer! He could be trouble!
No deal! The lawyer stays!

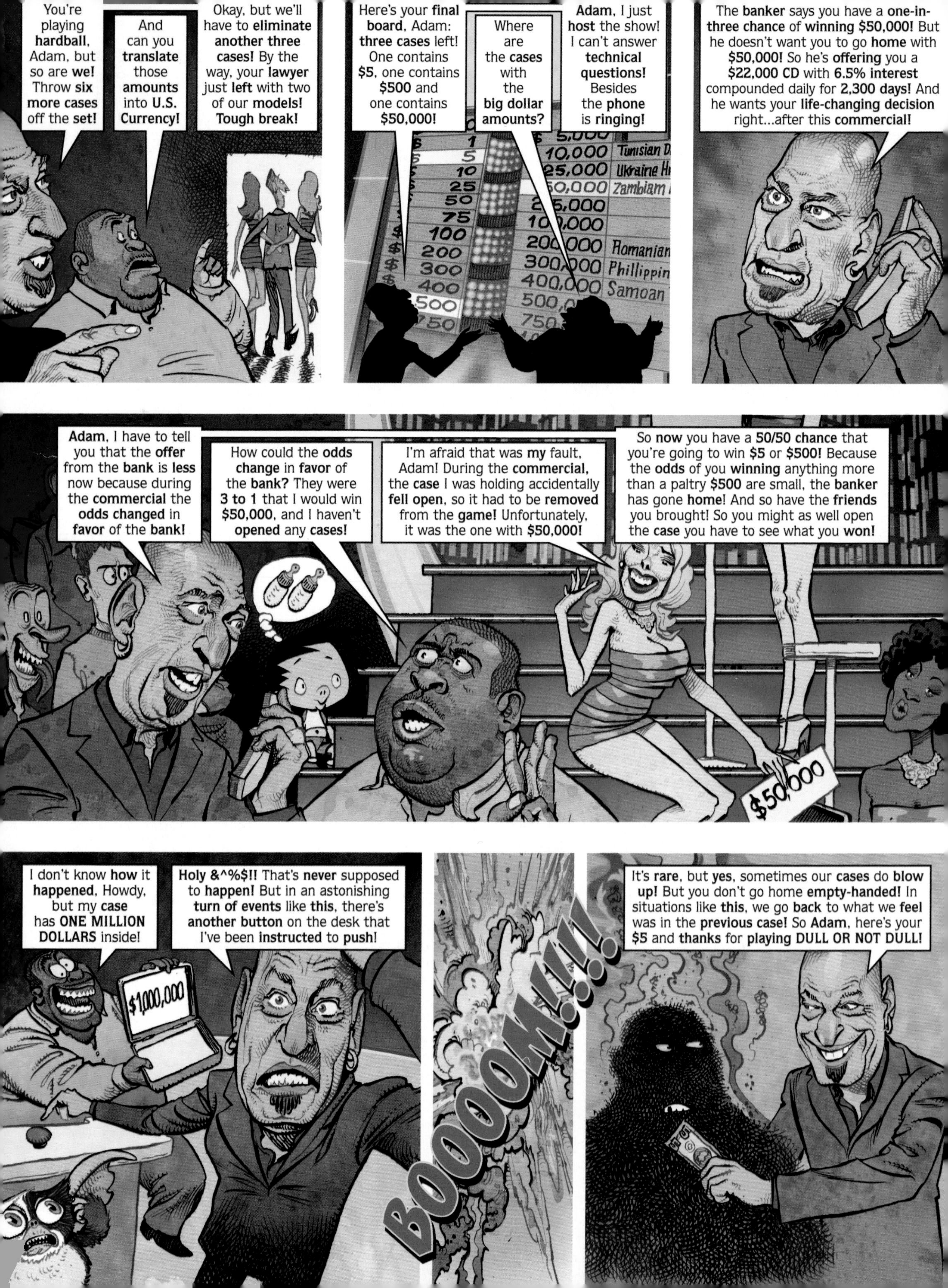
You're playing **hardball**, Adam, but so are **we!** Throw **six more cases** off the **set!**
And can you **translate** those **amounts** into **U.S. Currency!**
Okay, but we'll have to **eliminate another three cases!** By the way, your **lawyer** just **left** with two of our **models! Tough break!**
Here's your **final board**, Adam: **three cases** left! One contains **$5**, one contains **$500** and one contains **$50,000!**
Where are the **cases** with the **big dollar amounts?**
Adam, I just **host** the show! I can't answer **technical questions!** Besides the **phone** is **ringing!**
Romanian
Samoan
The **banker** says you have a **one-in-three chance** of **winning $50,000!** But he doesn't want you to go **home** with **$50,000!** So he's **offering** you a **$22,000 CD** with **6.5% interest** compounded daily for **2,300 days!** And he wants your **life-changing decision** right...after this **commercial!**
Adam, I have to tell you that the **offer** from the **bank** is **less** now because during the **commercial** the **odds changed** in **favor** of the **bank!**
How could the **odds change** in **favor** of the **bank?** They were **3 to 1** that I would win **$50,000**, and I haven't **opened** any **cases!**
I'm afraid that was **my** fault, Adam! During the **commercial**, the **case** I was holding accidentally **fell open**, so it had to be **removed** from the **game!** Unfortunately, it was the one with **$50,000!**
So **now** you have a **50/50 chance** that you're going to win **$5** or **$500!** Because the **odds** of you **winning** anything more than a paltry **$500** are small, the **banker** has gone **home!** And so have the **friends** you brought! So you might as well open the **case** you have to see what you **won!**
$50,000
I don't know **how** it **happened**, Howdy, but my **case** has **ONE MILLION DOLLARS** inside!
$1,000,000
Holy &^%$!! That's **never** supposed to **happen!** But in an astonishing **turn of events** like **this**, there's **another button** on the desk that I've been **instructed** to **push!**
BOOOOM!!!!!
It's **rare**, but **yes**, sometimes our **cases** do **blow up!** But you don't go home **empty-handed!** In situations like **this**, we go **back** to what we **feel** was in the **previous case!** So Adam, here's your **$5** and **thanks** for **playing DULL OR NOT DULL!**

JOKE AND DAGGER DEPT.

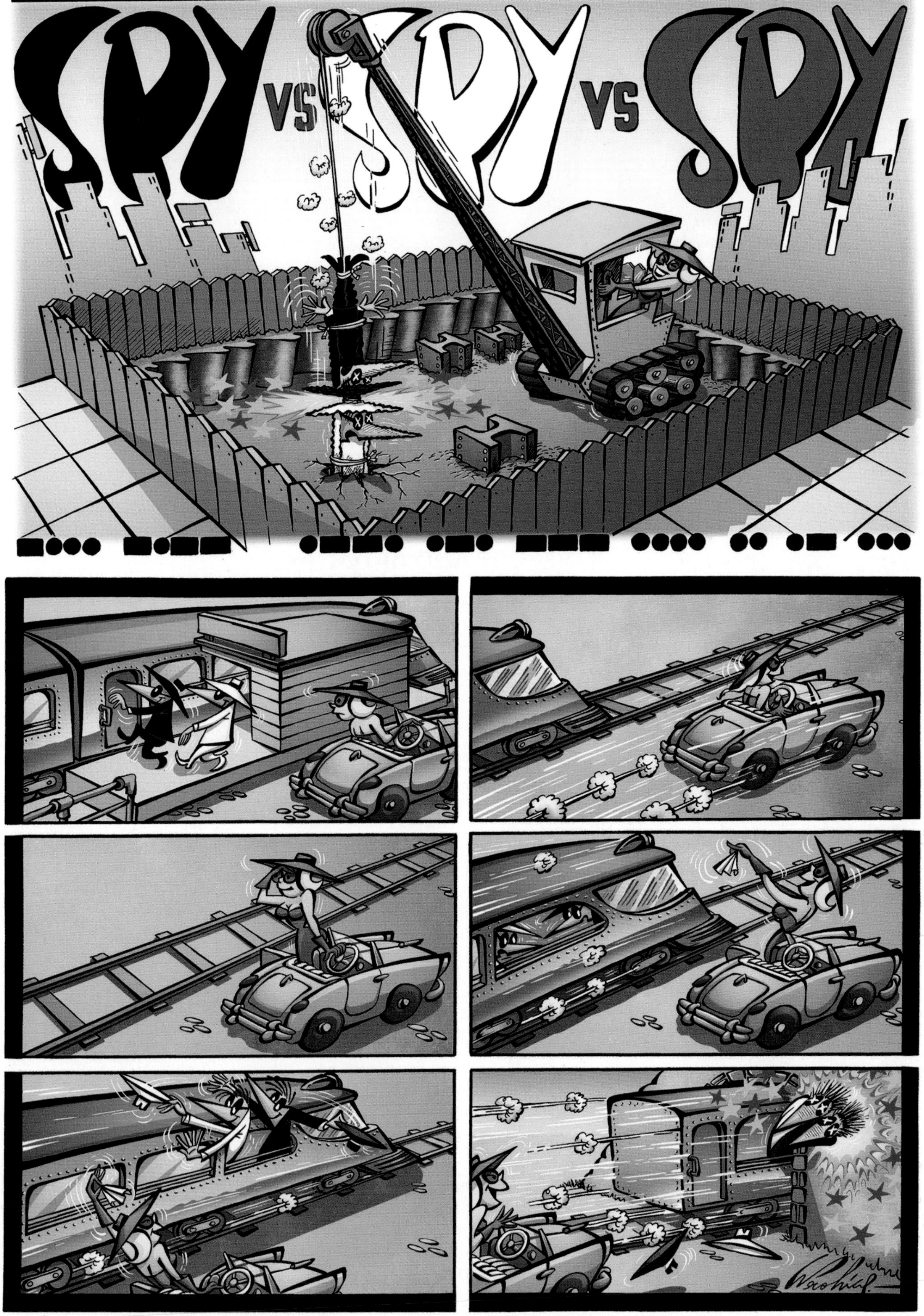
SPY VS SPY VS SPY

WRITER AND ARTIST: ANTONIO PROHIAS COLORIST: CARRIE STRACHAN

MAD's Brain Drool PART TWO

FREE WILLY MEETS AIR BUD
IN SNACK TIME FOR WILLY

NEW on DVD

THEIR FIRST (AND LAST) MOVIE TOGETHER!

Questions and answers your parents and teachers think you should know!

5th grade LAME QUEST

QUESTIONS

Was writing invented in 5,000 B.C., 3,000 B.C. or 1,000 B.C.?

 In space, what do astronauts breathe?

What does the Roman Numeral XL mean?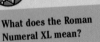

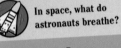 What do we call the scientists who study early civilizations?

What device uses the Sun's rays to tell the time?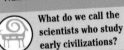

 True or False? When people ask a true or false question, they always say true before false.

What is found near the Polar Ice Cap?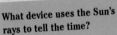

 Is Barack Obama a doctor, a butcher or the president?

Who enforced the rules at chariot races?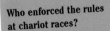

 What covered almost one-fourth of the Earth during the Ice Age?

BEFORE AND AFTER GROCERY PRODUCTS

Before there was...
There was...

all — some

Before there was...
There was...

CAP'N CRUNCH — FIRST MATE CRUNCH

Before there was...
There was...

GAIN — NO LOSS

WRITER: GREG BENSON
ARTIST: CHARLES AKINS

ANSWERS

We don't know — nobody wrote down the date. **?**

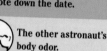 The other astronaut's body odor.

That it is an Extra-Large number. **XL**

 Very boring people.

A solar-powered wristwatch.

! True.

The Polar Ice Mittens and the Polar Ice Earmuffs.

 A butcher — he just happens to have the same name as the president.

Roman Umpires.

 Ice. DUH.

WRITER: CHARLIE KADAU

78

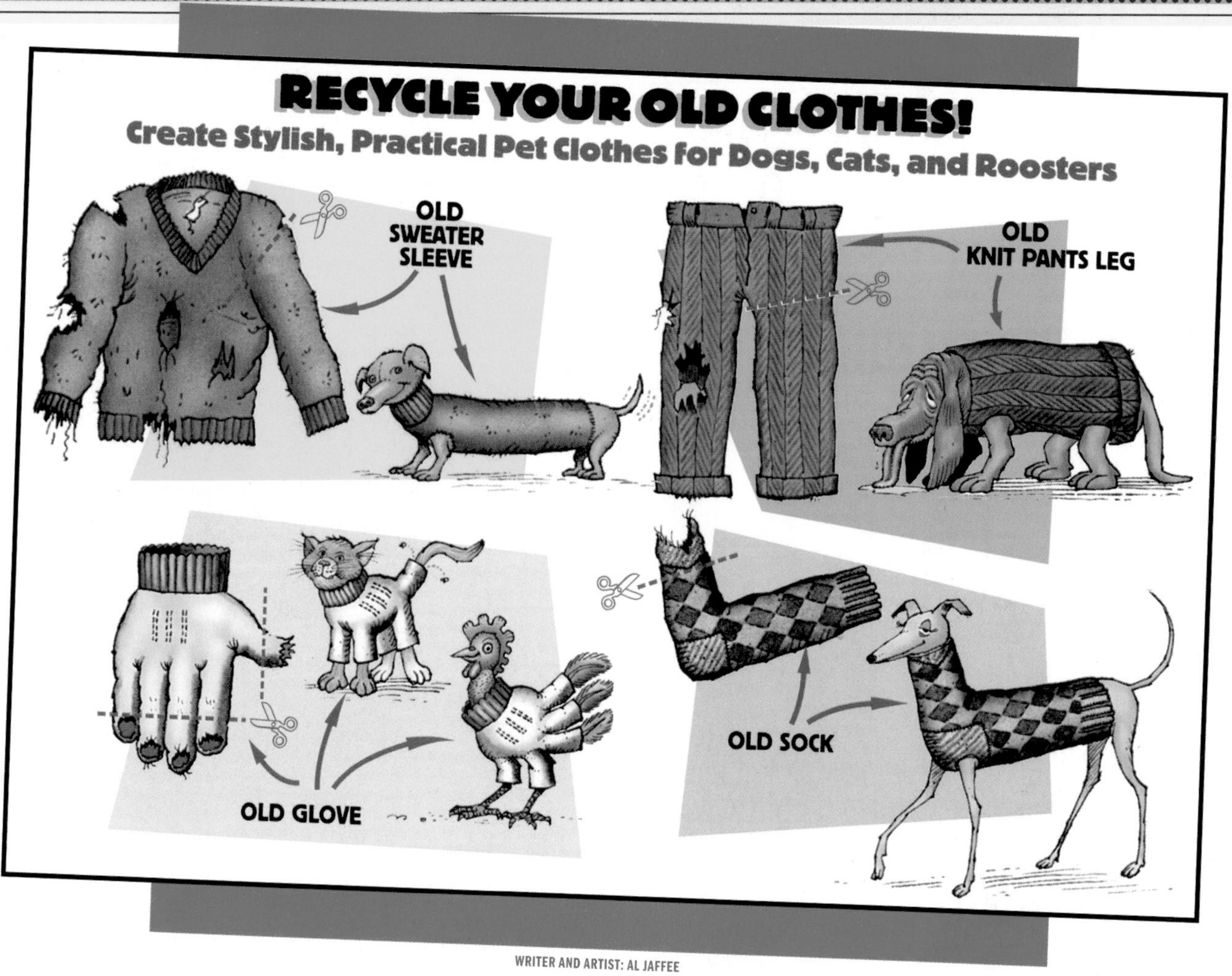
RECYCLE YOUR OLD CLOTHES!
Create Stylish, Practical Pet Clothes for Dogs, Cats, and Roosters
OLD SWEATER SLEEVE
OLD KNIT PANTS LEG
OLD GLOVE
OLD SOCK

WRITER AND ARTIST: AL JAFFEE

SWITCH CAME FIRST?

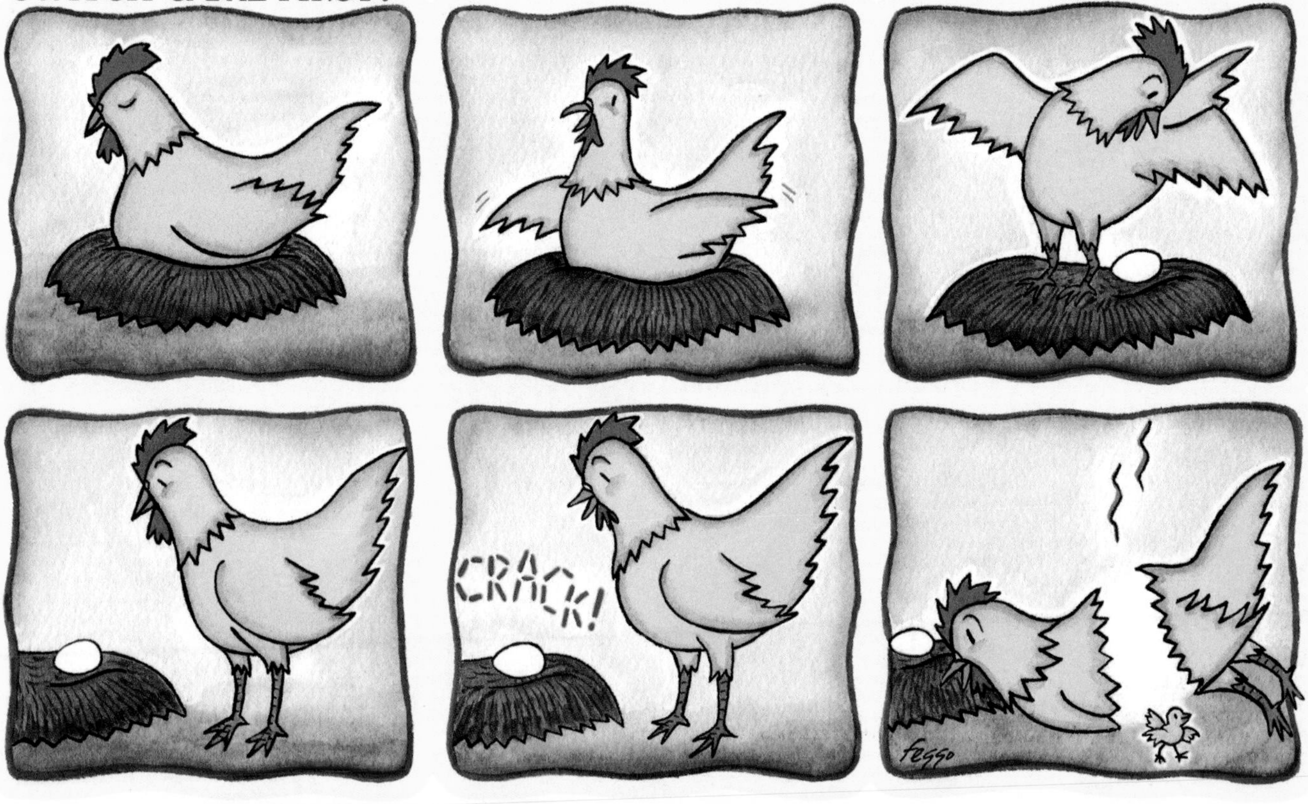
CRACK!
FEGGO

WRITER AND ARTIST: FELIPE GALINDO

MAD's Brain Drool Part Two

CLASS DISMISSED

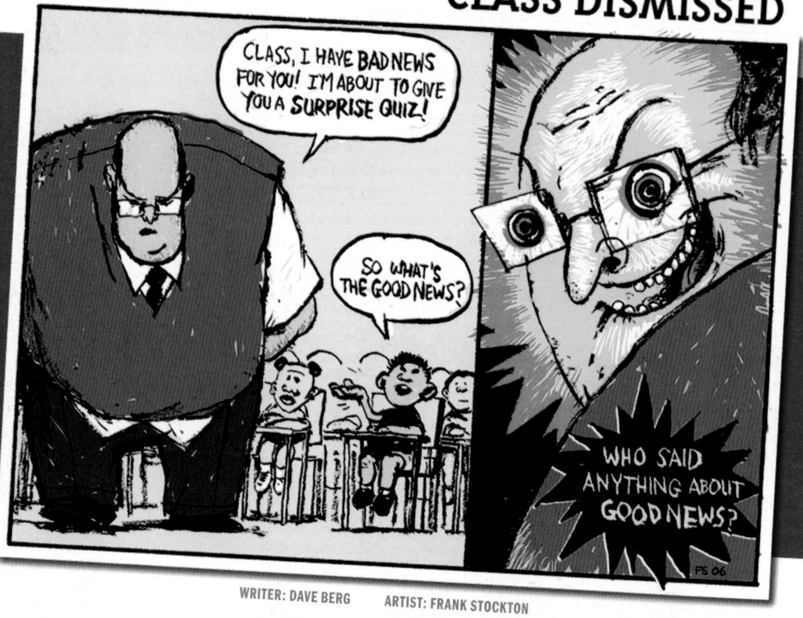

CLASS, I HAVE BAD NEWS FOR YOU! I'M ABOUT TO GIVE YOU A SURPRISE QUIZ!
SO WHAT'S THE GOOD NEWS?
WHO SAID ANYTHING ABOUT GOOD NEWS?
FS 06

WRITER: DAVE BERG ARTIST: FRANK STOCKTON

WHEN IS WEARING A BIKE HELMET MORE DANGEROUS THAN NOT WEARING ONE? WHEN YOU WEAR IT WRONG! BE SURE NOT TO WEAR YOURS IN ANY OF THESE DUMB WAYS!

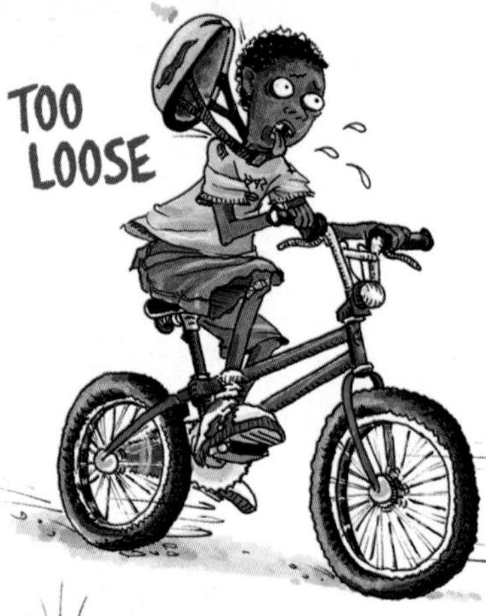

TOO LOOSE

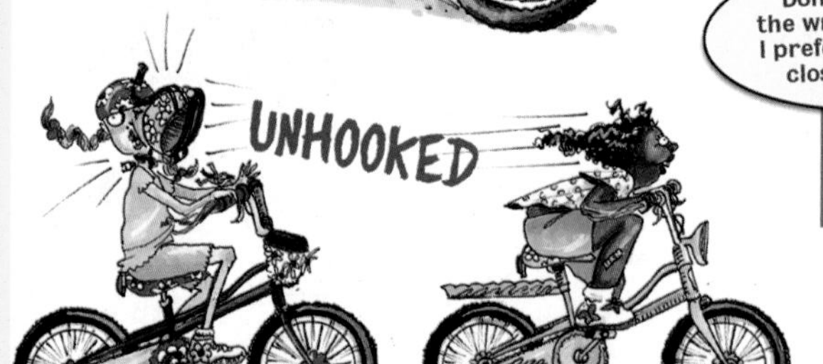

UNHOOKED

A TOY WE'RE SURPRISED THEY HAVEN'T MADE YET

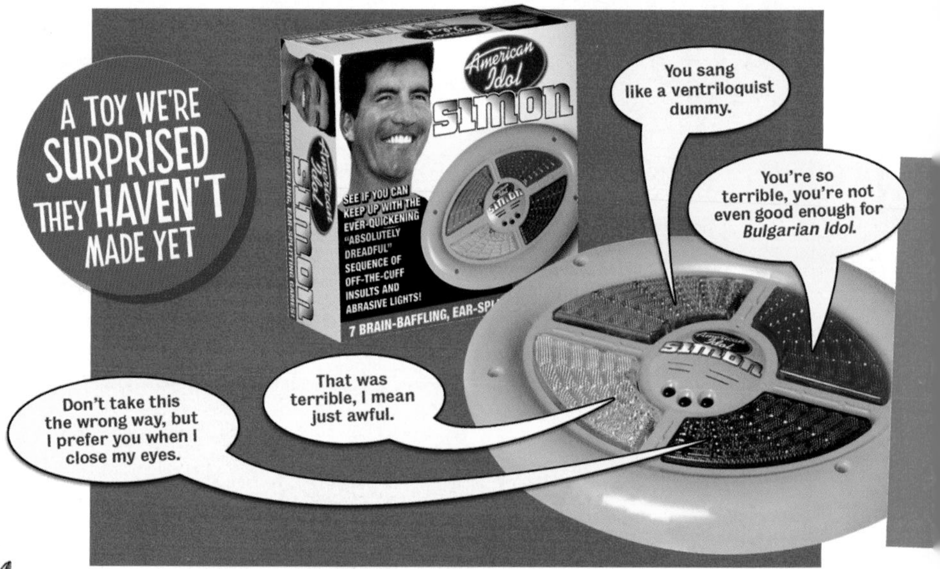

American Idol
SIMON
SEE IF YOU CAN KEEP UP WITH THE EVER-QUICKENING "ABSOLUTELY DREADFUL" SEQUENCE OF OFF-THE-CUFF INSULTS AND ABRASIVE LIGHTS!
7 BRAIN-BAFFLING, EAR-SPL
You sang like a ventriloquist dummy.
You're so terrible, you're not even good enough for *Bulgarian Idol*.
That was terrible, I mean just awful.
Don't take this the wrong way, but I prefer you when I close my eyes.

ARTIST: SCOTT BRICHER PHOTOGRAPHER: DARREN JOHNSON

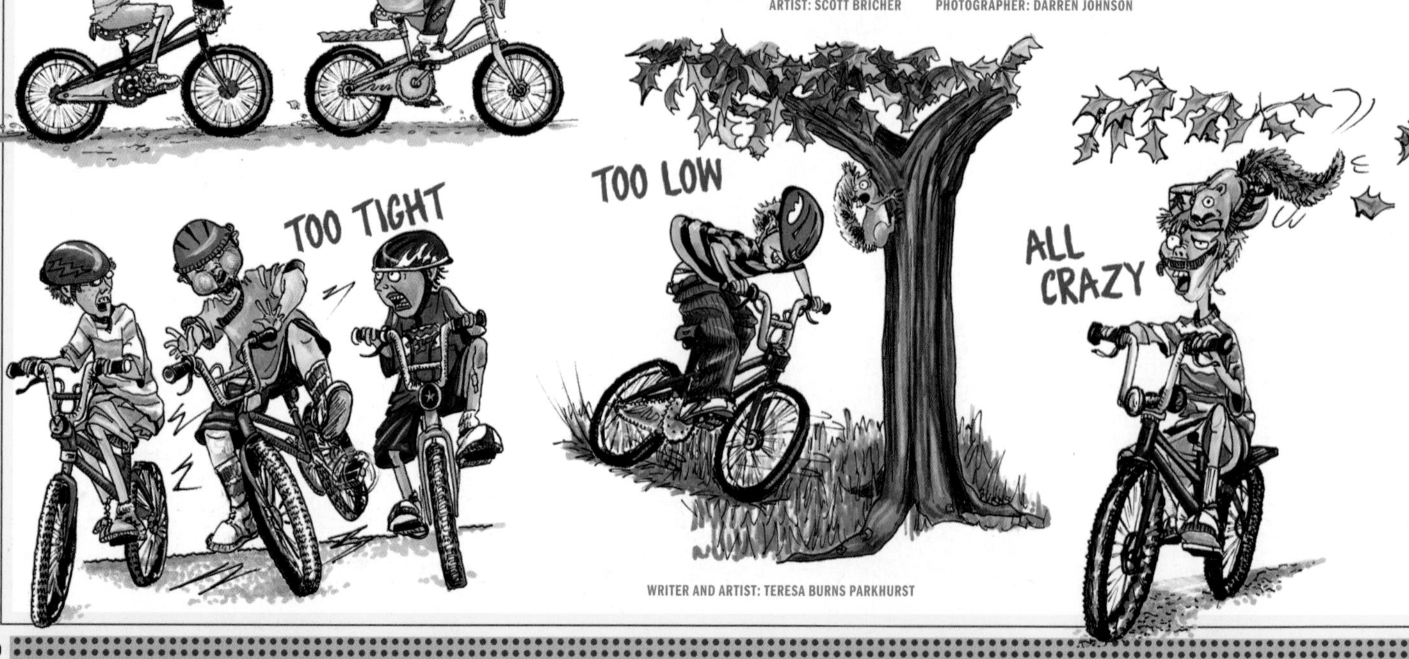

TOO TIGHT
TOO LOW
ALL CRAZY

WRITER AND ARTIST: TERESA BURNS PARKHURST

IMPORTANT DATES TO REMEMBER

APRIL 24, 1938:
Popularity of bowling soars when the bow and arrow is replaced by a heavy ball.

APRIL 29, 1984:
McDonald's scraps plan to offer on-track drive-thru window at Daytona 500.

MAY 8, 1966:
Park ranger accidentally turns wrong valve, shuts off Niagara Falls for two hours.

MAY 16, 1973:
Three Flags merges with One Flag and Two Flags to become Six Flags.

JUNE 9, 1957:
A sweaty man invents the sweatsuit.

JUNE 30, 2001:
Animal Rights Groups protest mistreatment of the computer mouse.

Here On Gilligan's Bile

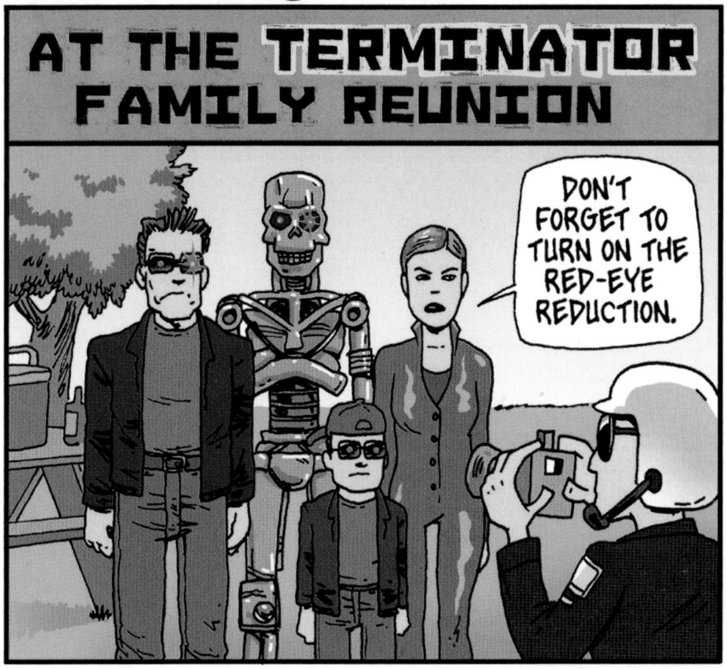

AT THE TERMINATOR FAMILY REUNION
DON'T FORGET TO TURN ON THE RED-EYE REDUCTION.

WRITER AND ARTIST: PAUL GILLIGAN

MOTOR MUTTS

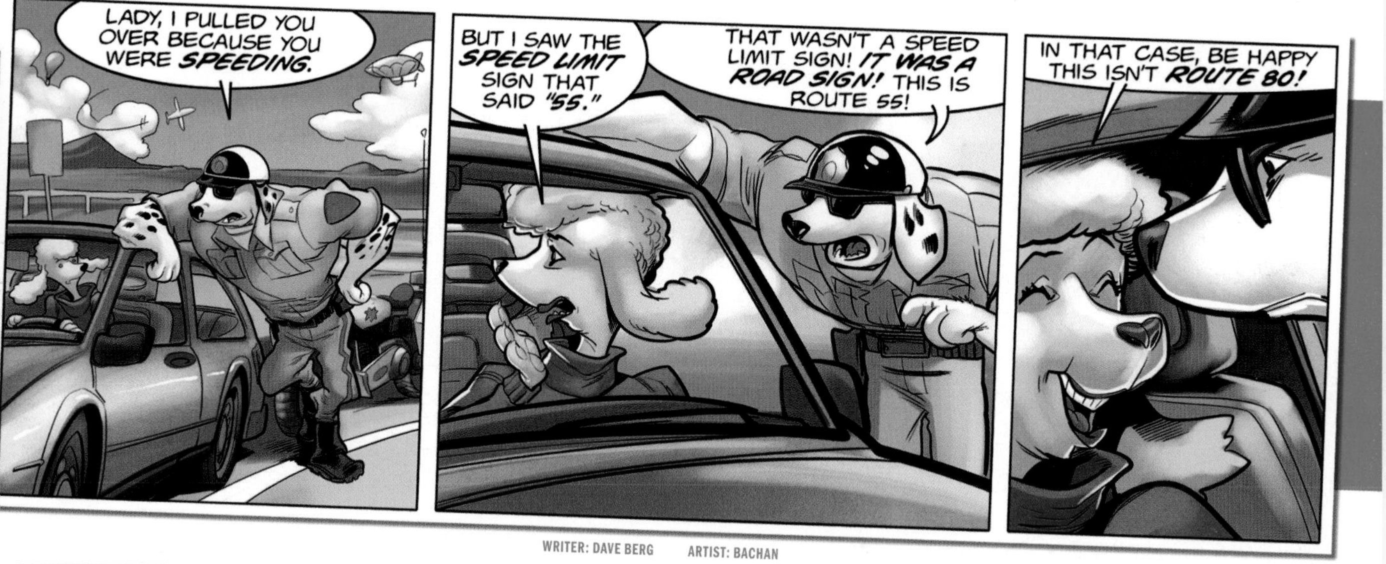

LADY, I PULLED YOU OVER BECAUSE YOU WERE *SPEEDING.*
BUT I SAW THE *SPEED LIMIT* SIGN THAT SAID *"55."*
THAT WASN'T A SPEED LIMIT SIGN! *IT WAS A ROAD SIGN!* THIS IS ROUTE 55!
IN THAT CASE, BE HAPPY THIS ISN'T *ROUTE 80!*

WRITER: DAVE BERG ARTIST: BACHAN

ALFRED

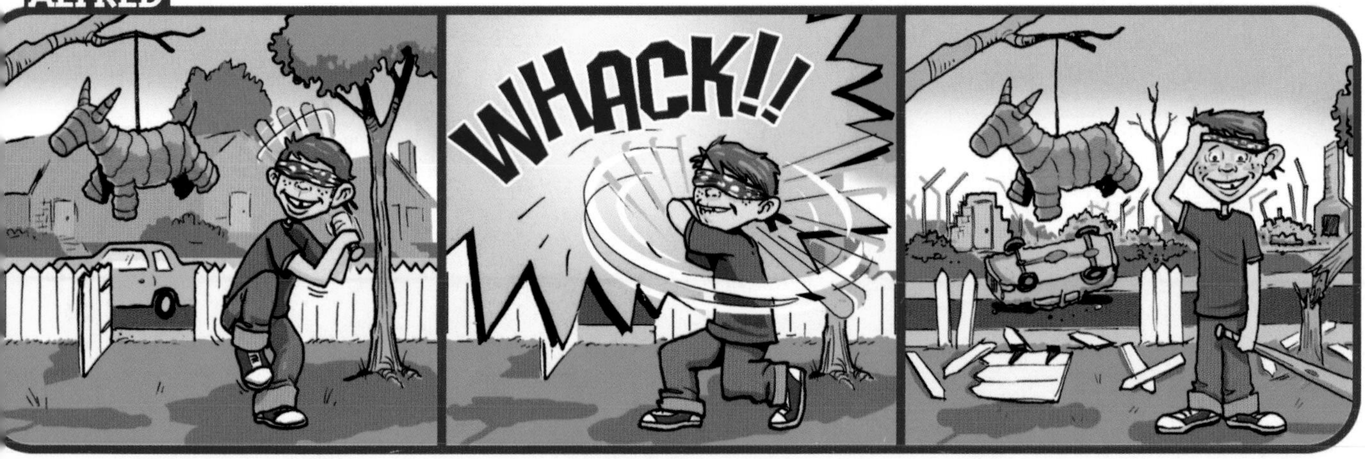

WHACK!!

ARTIST: CLAY MEYER

WARN IN THE U.S.A. DEPT.

In these socially responsible times, Americans are paying closer attention to the products they buy. Environmentally conscious merchandise labeling such as "Dolphin Safe" on tuna cans, "Ozone Friendly" on spray deodorant and "No Animal Testing"

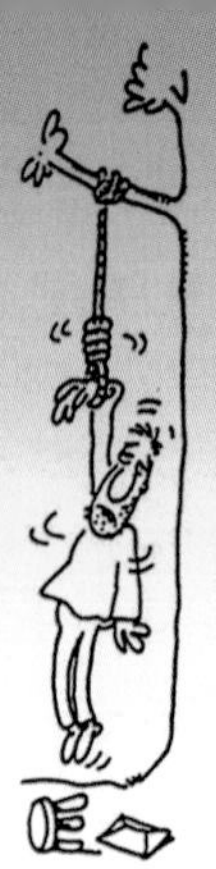

CONSUMER SA
WE'D LOV

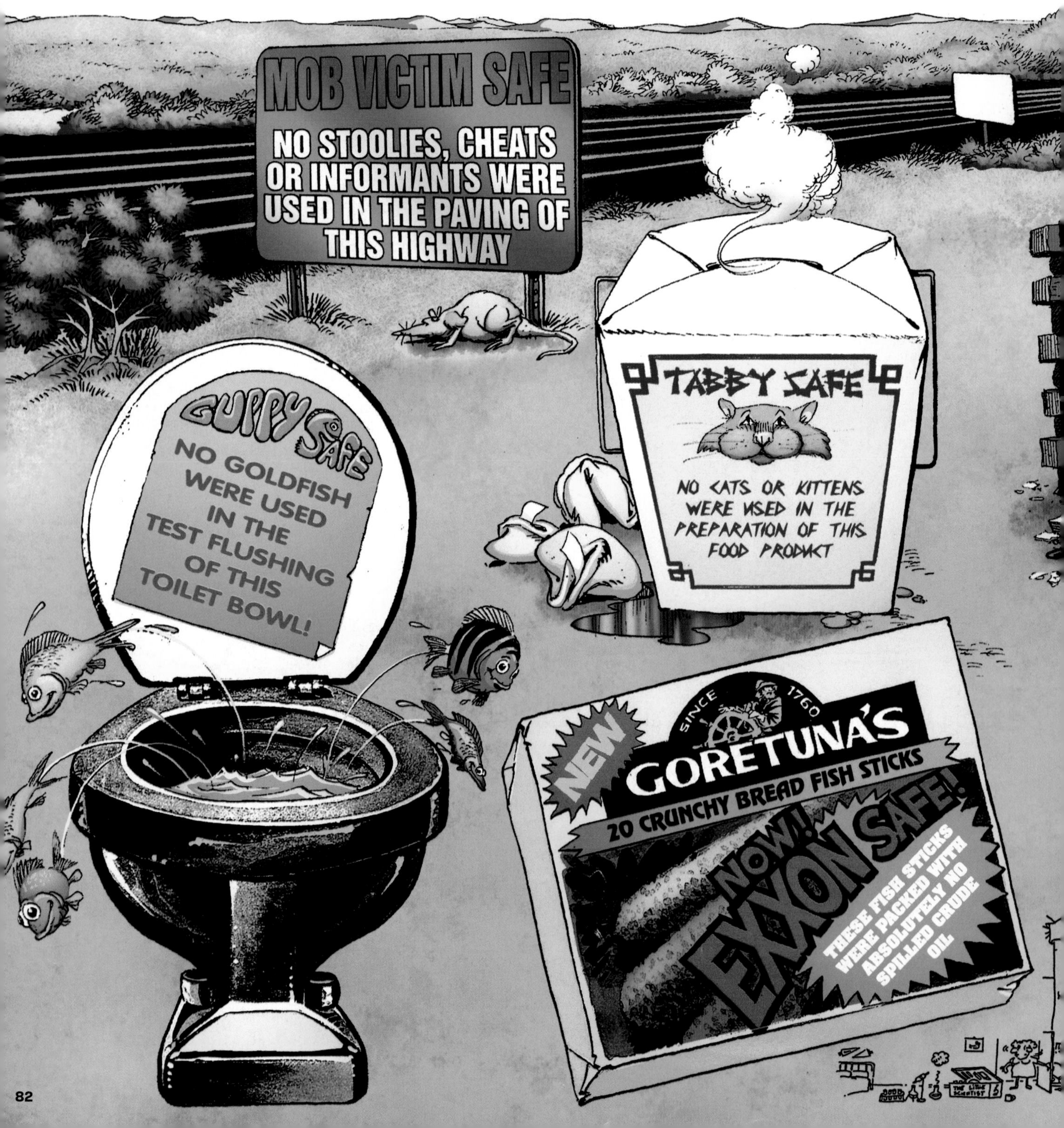
MOB VICTIM SAFE
NO STOOLIES, CHEATS OR INFORMANTS WERE USED IN THE PAVING OF THIS HIGHWAY
TABBY SAFE
NO CATS OR KITTENS WERE USED IN THE PREPARATION OF THIS FOOD PRODUCT
GUPPY SAFE
NO GOLDFISH WERE USED IN THE TEST FLUSHING OF THIS TOILET BOWL!
NEW
SINCE 1760
GORETUNA'S
20 CRUNCHY BREAD FISH STICKS
NOW! EXXON SAFE!
THESE FISH STICKS WERE PACKED WITH ABSOLUTELY NO SPILLED CRUDE OIL

on cosmetics have attempted to allay consumer concerns. We figure that in order to survive in the competitive marketplace, soon virtually every product will need to call attention to its own political correctness and it's with that in mind we present...

FETY LABELS E TO SEE

WRITER: FRANK SANTOPADRE ARTIST: GEORGE WOODBRIDGE
COLORIST: CARRIE STRACHAN

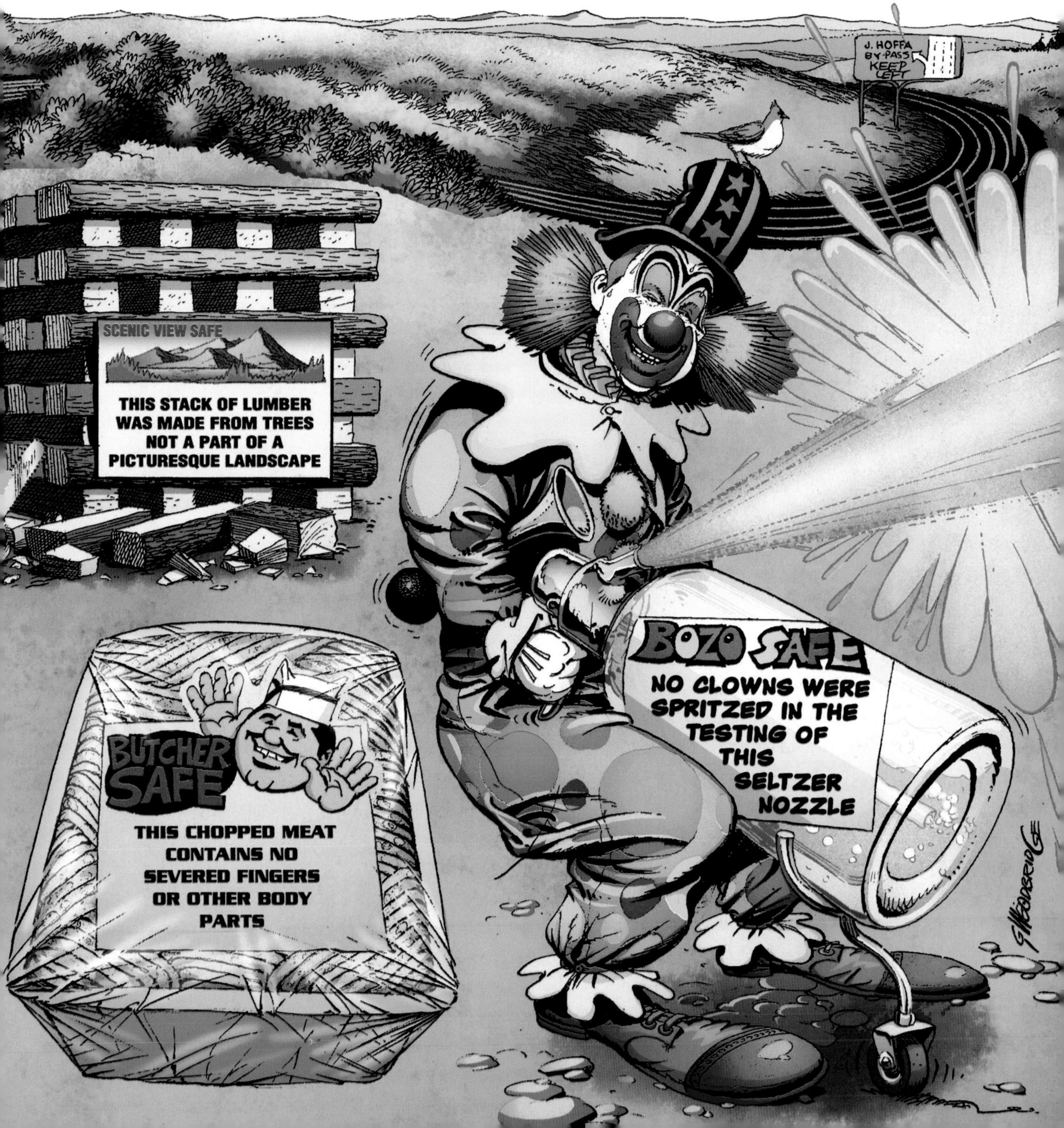

J. HOFFA BY-PASS KEEP LEFT
SCENIC VIEW SAFE
THIS STACK OF LUMBER WAS MADE FROM TREES NOT A PART OF A PICTURESQUE LANDSCAPE
BOZO SAFE
NO CLOWNS WERE SPRITZED IN THE TESTING OF THIS SELTZER NOZZLE
BUTCHER SAFE
THIS CHOPPED MEAT CONTAINS NO SEVERED FINGERS OR OTHER BODY PARTS
G. WOODBRIDGE

THE 25 LEAST POWERFUL PEOPLE IN SHOW BUSINESS

Every year, magazines like *Premiere* and *Entertainment Weekly* concoct their master lists of The 100 Most Powerful Figures in Show Biz. Which always makes us wonder, "Uhhh, what's the point?" Do we really need some hack staff writer's list to know that one phone call from Steven Spielberg would convince any studio to greenlight the label on the side of a jar of Ragu? Does Tom Hanks cry out in horror if he "slips" from #7 to #9? And considering that 90 of this year's 100 names are the same names as last year, who cares? Instead of informing us that Julia Roberts is the #1 actress, why can't they tell us something we don't know...like, who's the #200,001 actress? They'll never do it, though. It takes losers like us to tell losers like you about the Hollywood losers who are...

ARTIST: HERMANN MEJIA WRITER: DESMOND DEVLIN

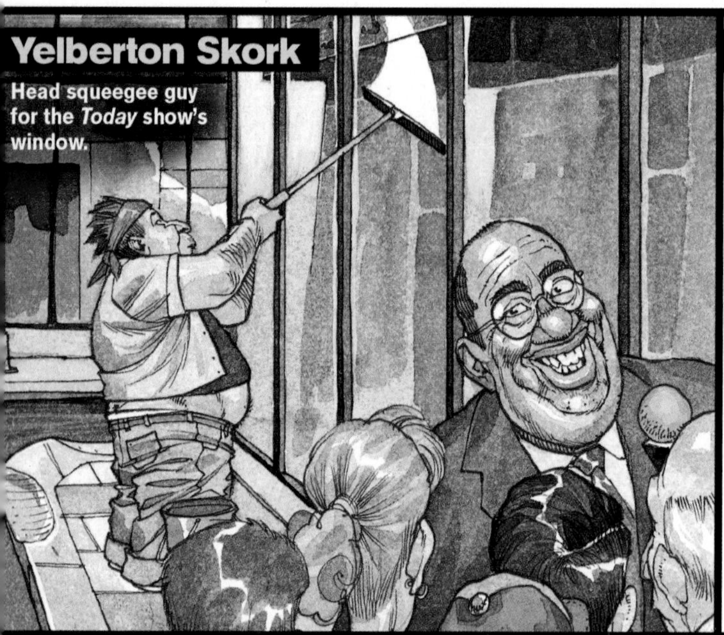

Yelberton Skork

Head squeegee guy for the *Today* show's window.

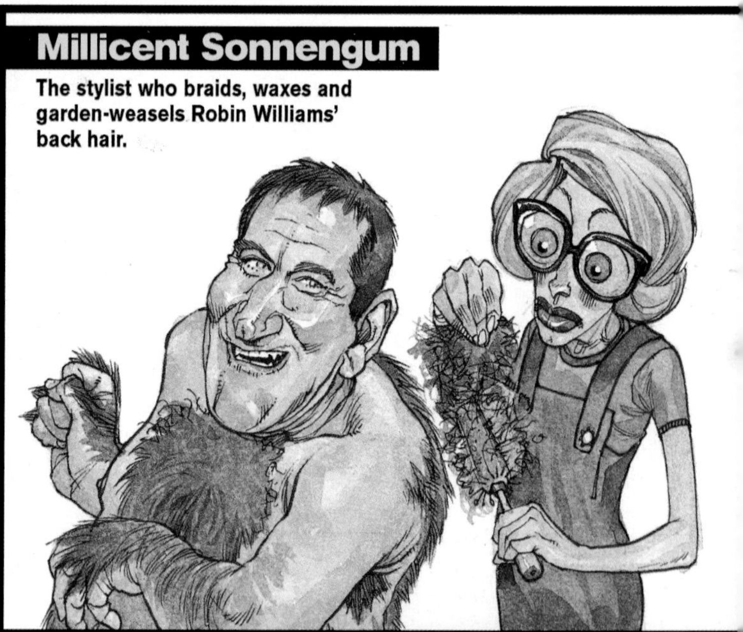

Millicent Sonnengum

The stylist who braids, waxes and garden-weasels Robin Williams' back hair.

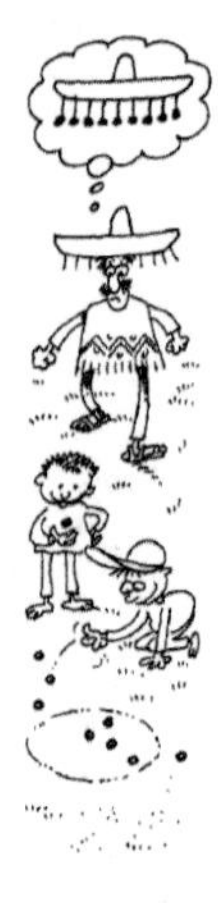

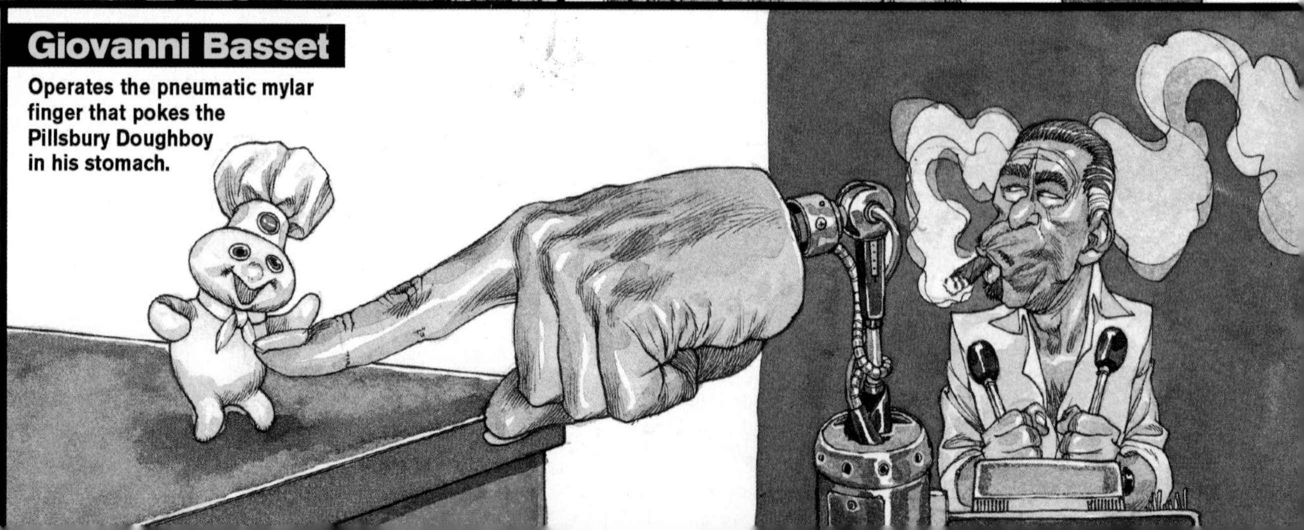

Giovanni Basset

Operates the pneumatic mylar finger that pokes the Pillsbury Doughboy in his stomach.

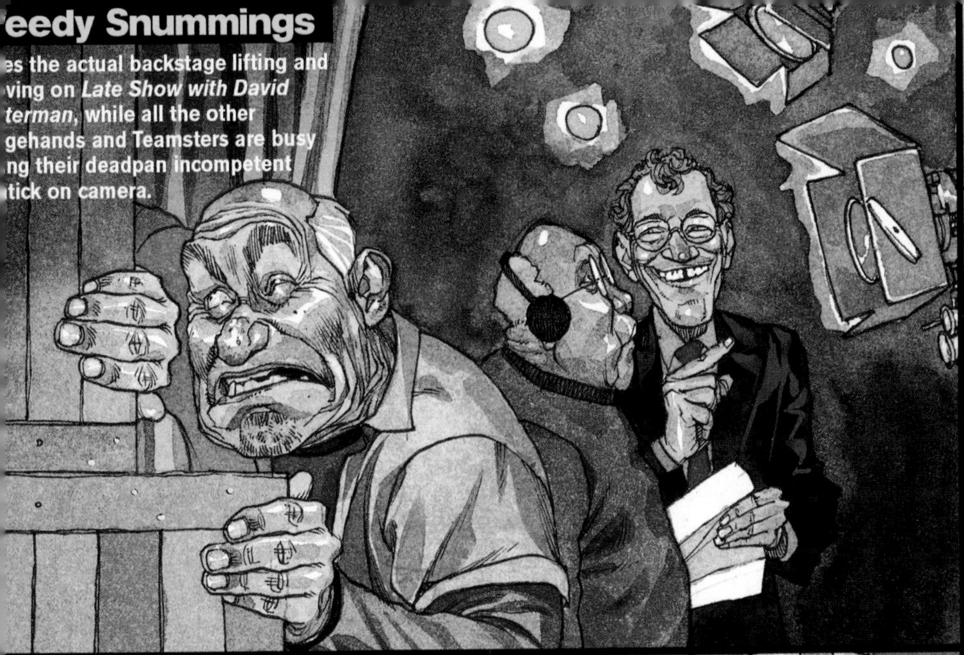

eedy Snummings

es the actual backstage lifting and ving on *Late Show with David terman*, while all the other gehands and Teamsters are busy ng their deadpan incompetent tick on camera.

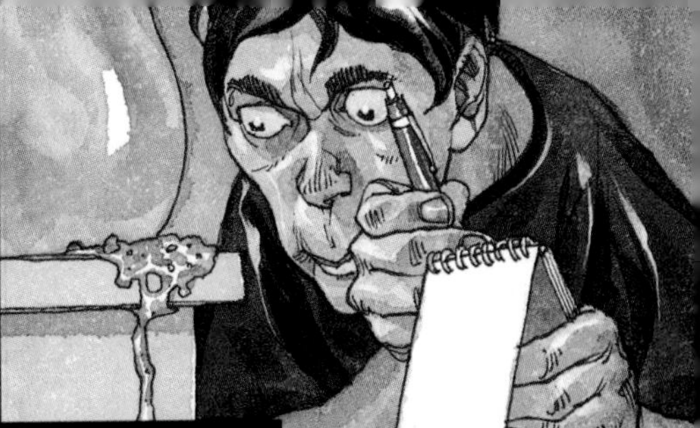

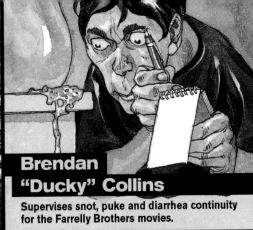

Brendan "Ducky" Collins

Supervises snot, puke and diarrhea continuity for the Farrelly Brothers movies.

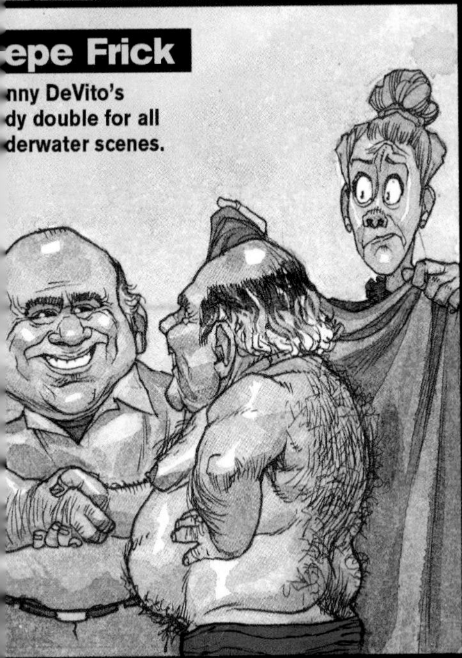

epe Frick

nny DeVito's dy double for all derwater scenes.

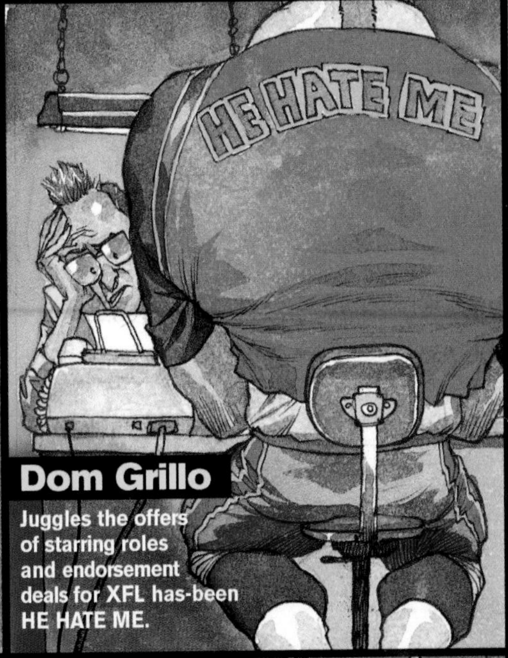
HE HATE ME

Dom Grillo

Juggles the offers of starring roles and endorsement deals for XFL has-been HE HATE ME.

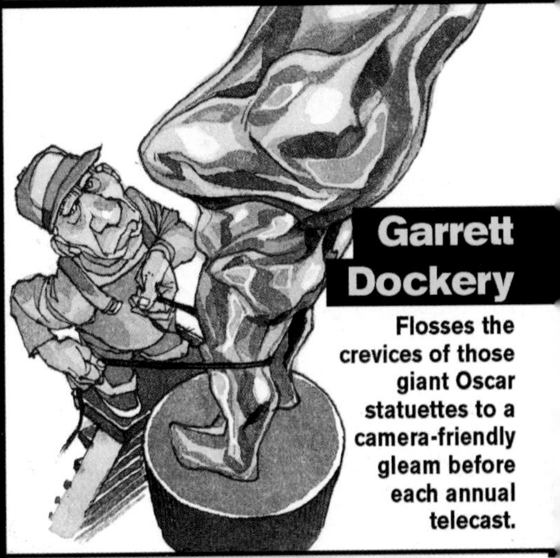

Garrett Dockery

Flosses the crevices of those giant Oscar statuettes to a camera-friendly gleam before each annual telecast.

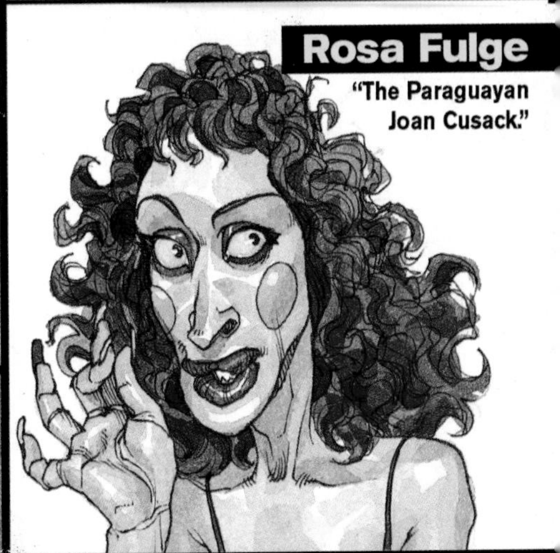

Rosa Fulge

"The Paraguayan Joan Cusack."

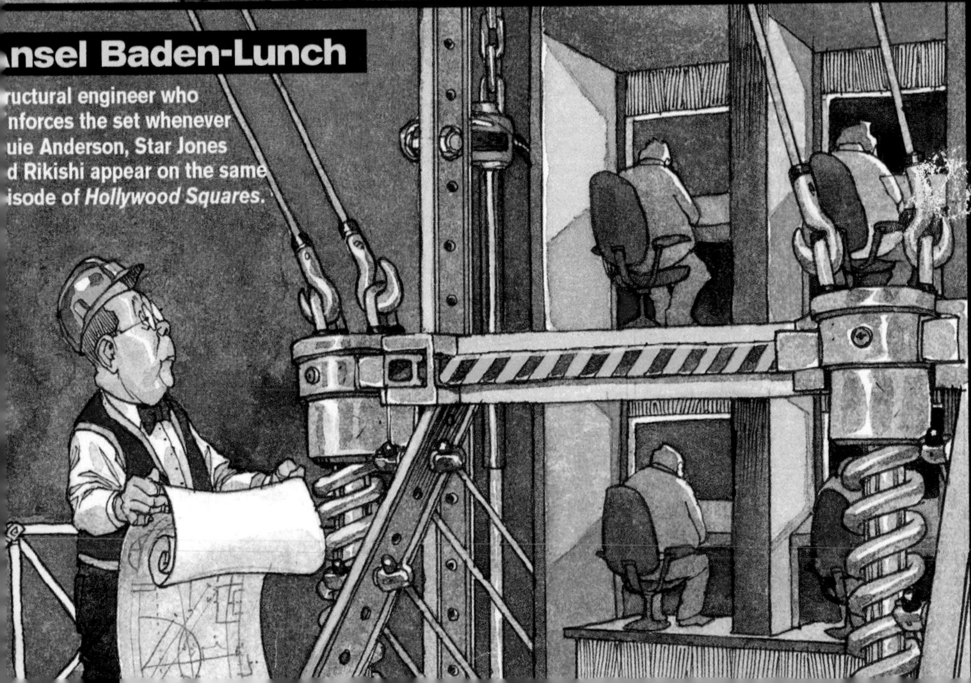

nsel Baden-Lunch

ructural engineer who nforces the set whenever uie Anderson, Star Jones d Rikishi appear on the same isode of *Hollywood Squares*.

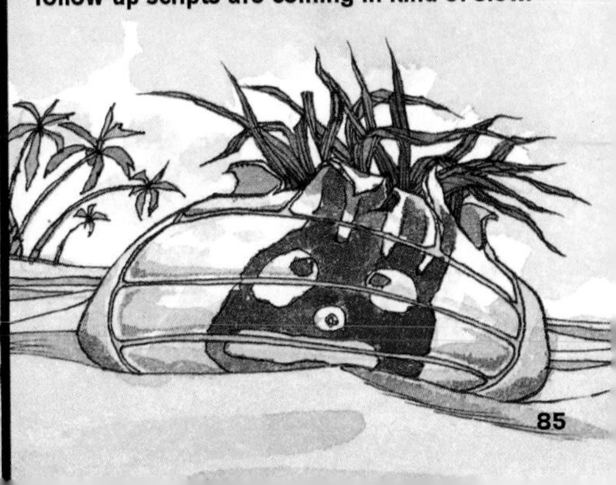

Wilson the Volleyball

Despite being in the #1 movie of 2000, this year, follow-up scripts are coming in kind of slow.

THE 25 LEAST POWERFUL PEOPLE IN SHOW BUSINESS

Ellen Speculum

Hoses out the Disney World bodysuits after each delightful 12-hour shift in 105-degree swampland.

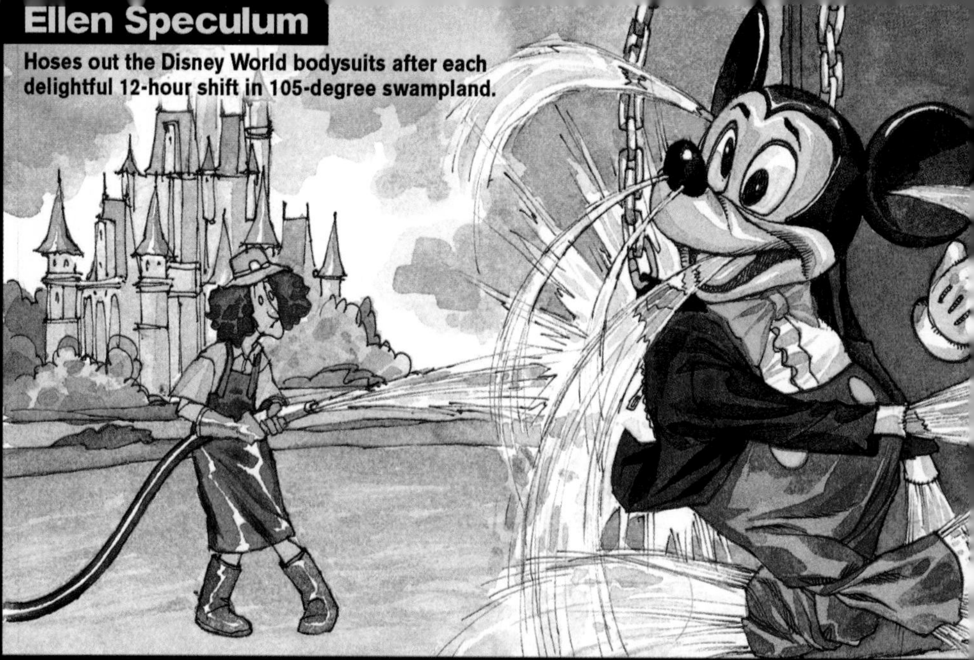

Kareem Skoom

Represented Hank the Angry Drunken Dwarf for everything *except The Howard Stern Show.* Hasn't worked since.

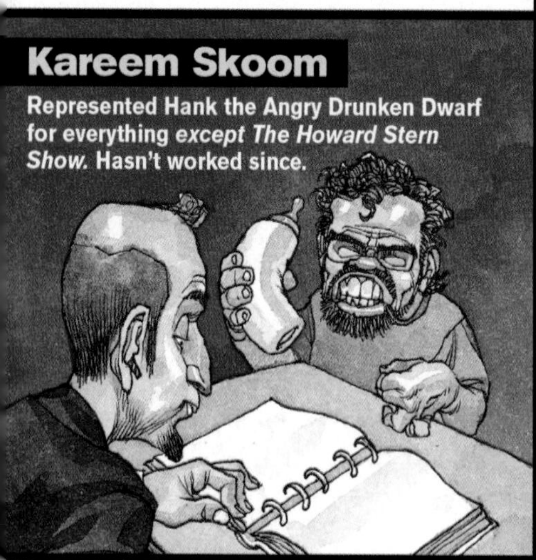

Emmett Smelly

The perennial 29th clown out of the car at the Ringlin Brothers Circus.

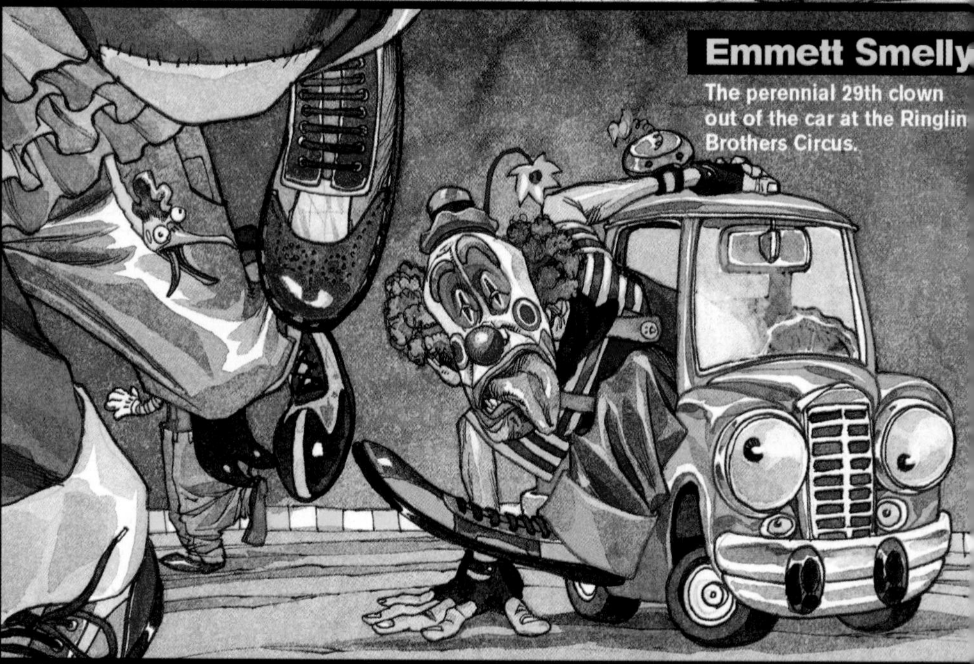

Ta'a'a'rffa F'a

Selected to belt out the Olympic anthem, if and when the tiny island nation of Tonga ever gets the games.

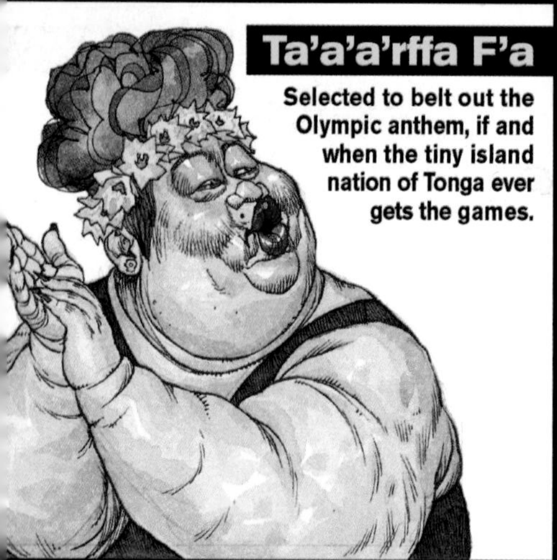

Carla Wocketty

Vaseline wrangler for actor/director/writer/producer Barbra Streisand's self-absorbed closeup shots.

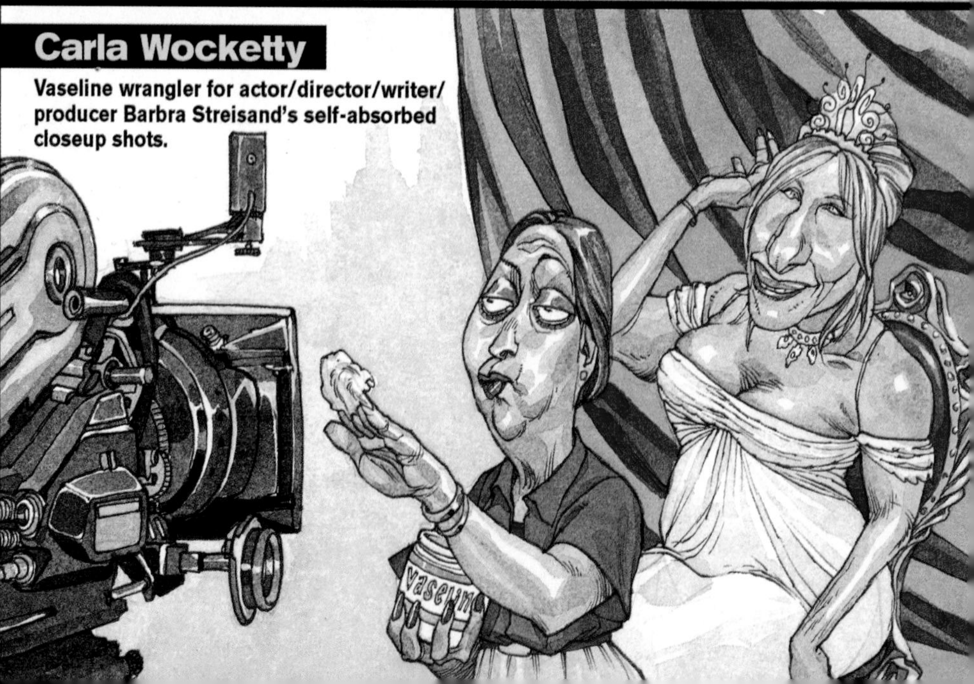
Vaseline

Duffy O'Sweat

If you want to get to Jamie Farr, you have to go through him!

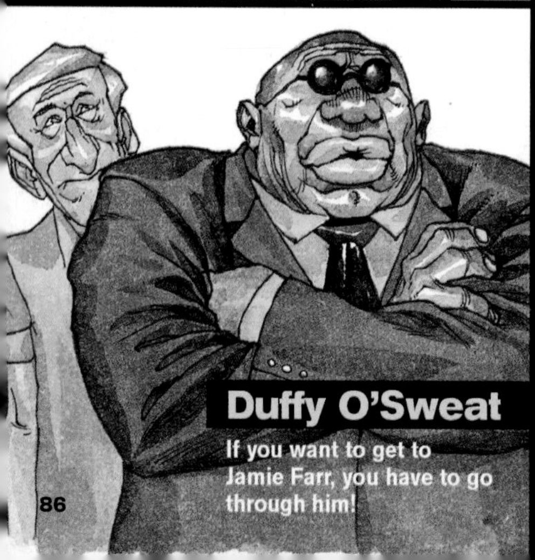

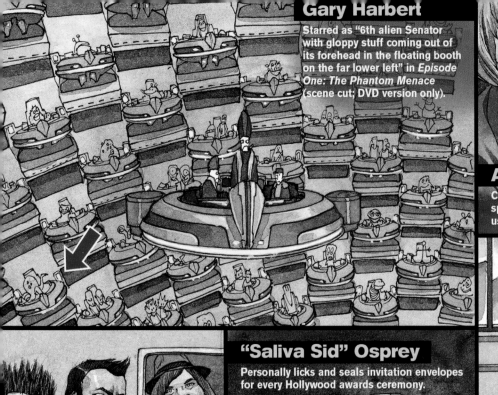

Gary Harbert

Starred as "6th alien Senator with gloppy stuff coming out of its forehead in the floating booth on the far lower left" in *Episode One: The Phantom Menace* (scene cut; DVD version only).

Amy Gugig

Cleans Larry King's old-man spittle out of his microphone, using only Windex and a toothpick.

Kimby Wadsworth

Lower East Side New York performance artist whose in-your-face "jello head" dance remains as piercing a critique of the 1985 Iran-Contra scandal as ever.

"Saliva Sid" Osprey

Personally licks and seals invitation envelopes for every Hollywood awards ceremony.

ethany Foozball nd Matilda Mulch

eling webmasters for w.paulapoundstone.org l www.paulapoundstone.org.uk.

run-Helga Olsen

e unacknowledged third Olsen triplet, believed e the talented one, whom Mary-Kate and ley keep locked up in the basement.

Jean-Luc Mustard

Portland's leading mime.

Stumpy Seepalot

Backup bailiff on *Judge Judy*.

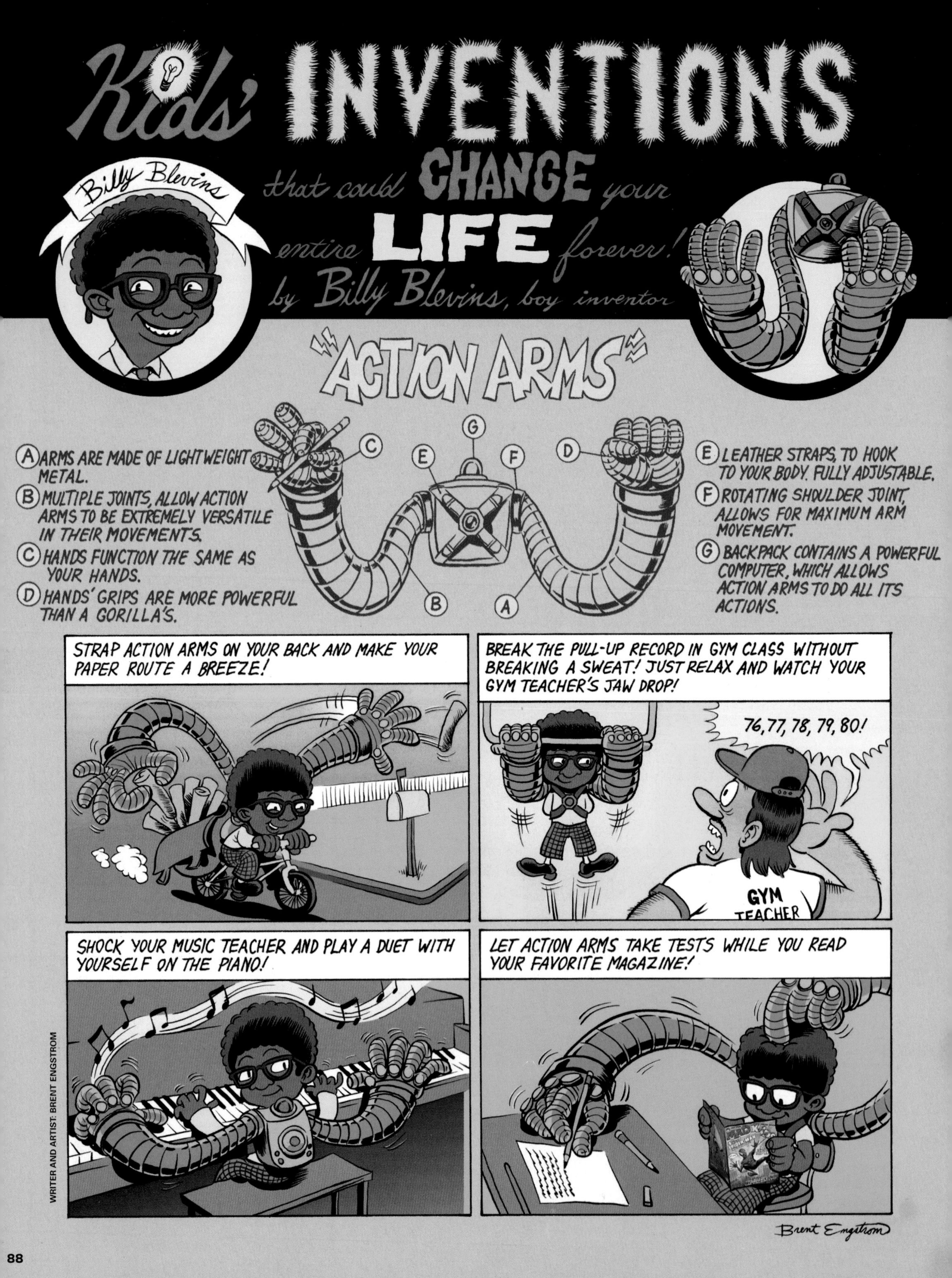
Kids' INVENTIONS
Billy Blevins
that could CHANGE your entire LIFE forever!
by Billy Blevins, boy inventor
"ACTION ARMS"
(A) ARMS ARE MADE OF LIGHTWEIGHT METAL.
(B) MULTIPLE JOINTS, ALLOW ACTION ARMS TO BE EXTREMELY VERSATILE IN THEIR MOVEMENTS.
(C) HANDS FUNCTION THE SAME AS YOUR HANDS.
(D) HANDS' GRIPS ARE MORE POWERFUL THAN A GORILLA'S.
(E) LEATHER STRAPS, TO HOOK TO YOUR BODY. FULLY ADJUSTABLE.
(F) ROTATING SHOULDER JOINT, ALLOWS FOR MAXIMUM ARM MOVEMENT.
(G) BACKPACK CONTAINS A POWERFUL COMPUTER, WHICH ALLOWS ACTION ARMS TO DO ALL ITS ACTIONS.
STRAP ACTION ARMS ON YOUR BACK AND MAKE YOUR PAPER ROUTE A BREEZE!
BREAK THE PULL-UP RECORD IN GYM CLASS WITHOUT BREAKING A SWEAT! JUST RELAX AND WATCH YOUR GYM TEACHER'S JAW DROP!
76, 77, 78, 79, 80!
GYM TEACHER
SHOCK YOUR MUSIC TEACHER AND PLAY A DUET WITH YOURSELF ON THE PIANO!
LET ACTION ARMS TAKE TESTS WHILE YOU READ YOUR FAVORITE MAGAZINE!
Brent Engstrom

WRITER AND ARTIST: BRENT ENGSTROM

PEN AND STINK DEPT.

The COMIC CLUB

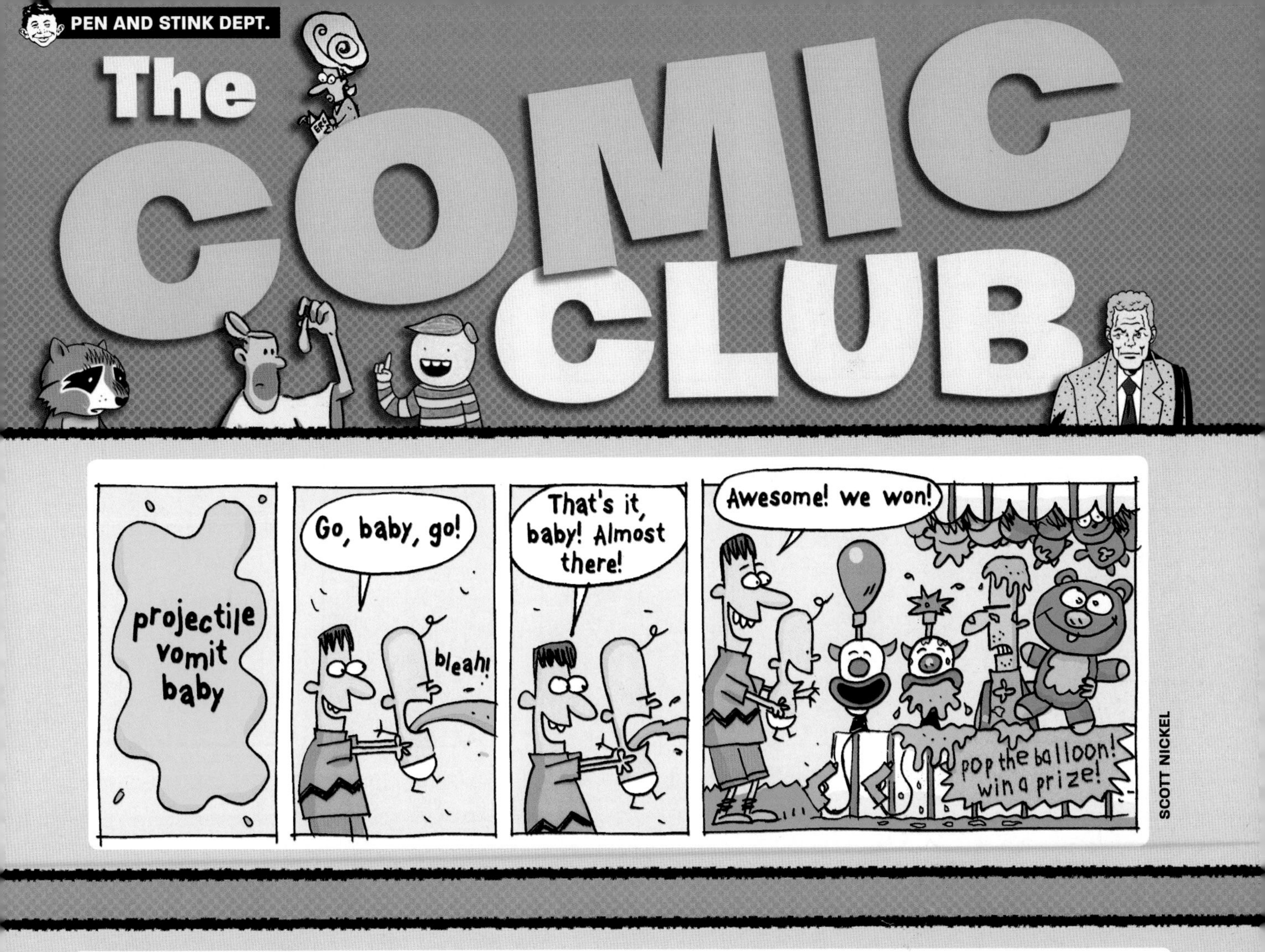
projectile vomit baby
Go, baby, go!
bleah!
That's it, baby! Almost there!
Awesome! we won!
pop the balloon! win a prize!

SCOTT NICKEL

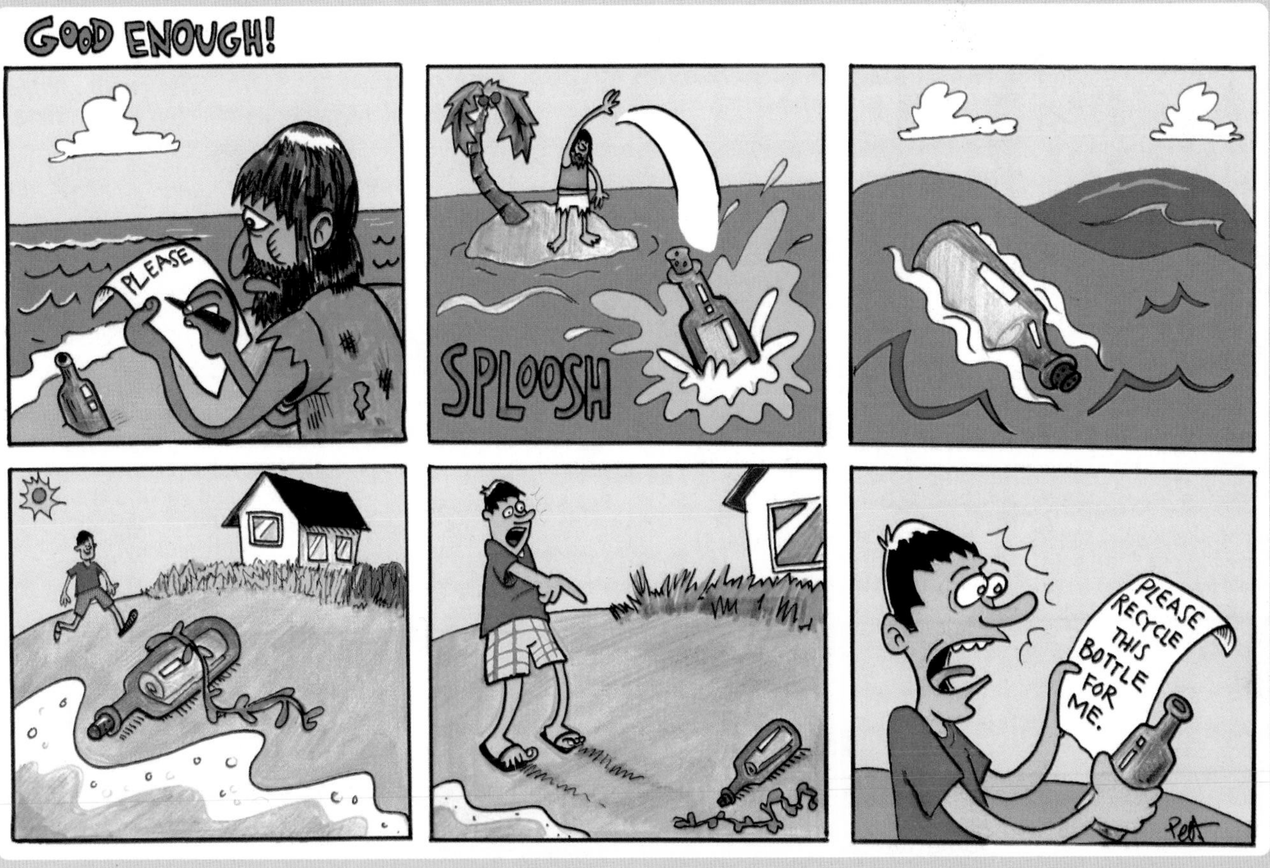
GOOD ENOUGH!
PLEASE
SPLOOSH
PLEASE RECYCLE THIS BOTTLE FOR ME.

PEET TAMBURINO

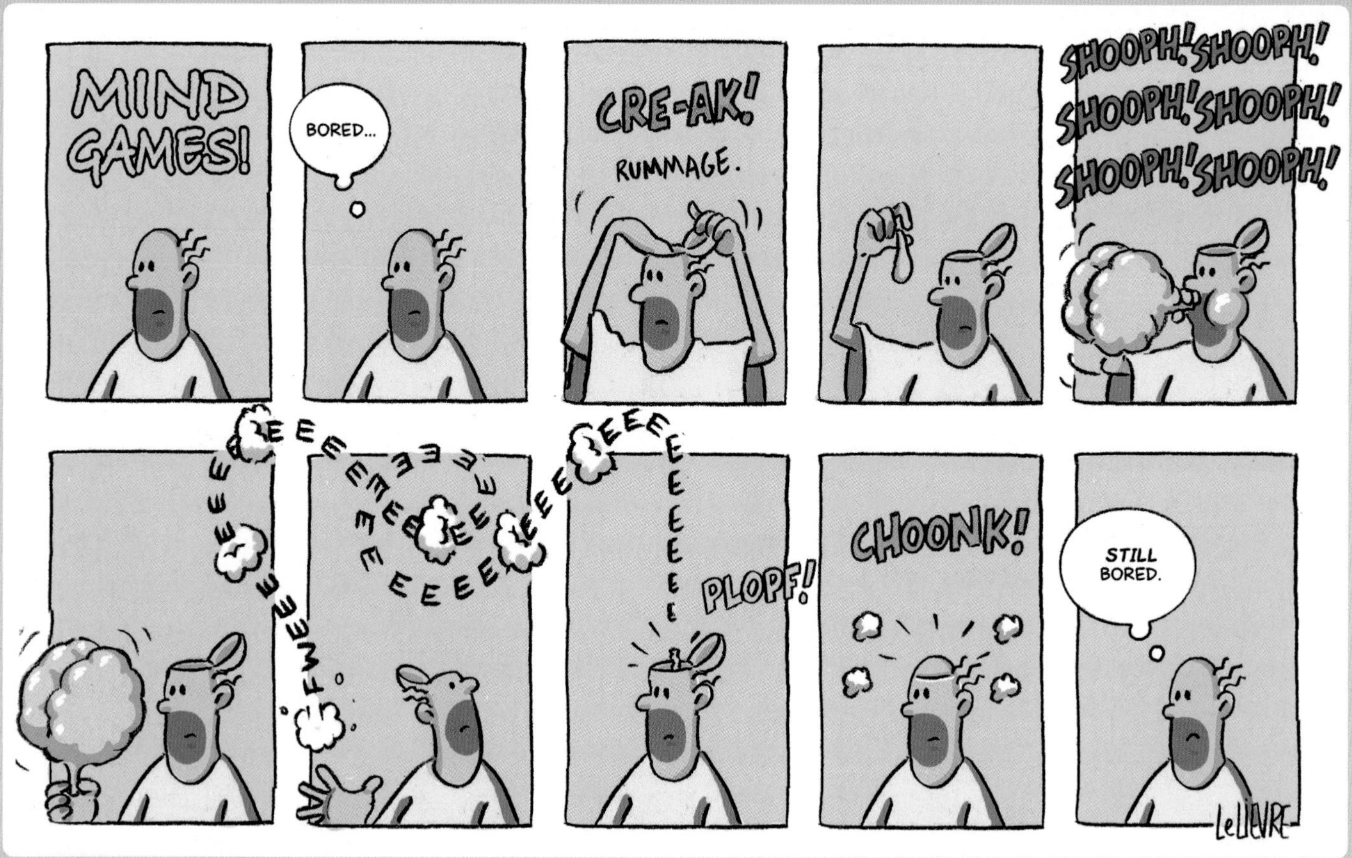
MIND GAMES!
BORED...
CRE-AK!
RUMMAGE.
SHOOPH! SHOOPH! SHOOPH! SHOOPH! SHOOPH! SHOOPH!
FWEEEEEEEEEEEEEEEEEEEEEEEEEEEEEEEEEEE
PLOPF!
CHOONK!
STILL BORED.
LeLIEVRE

GLEN LE LIEVRE

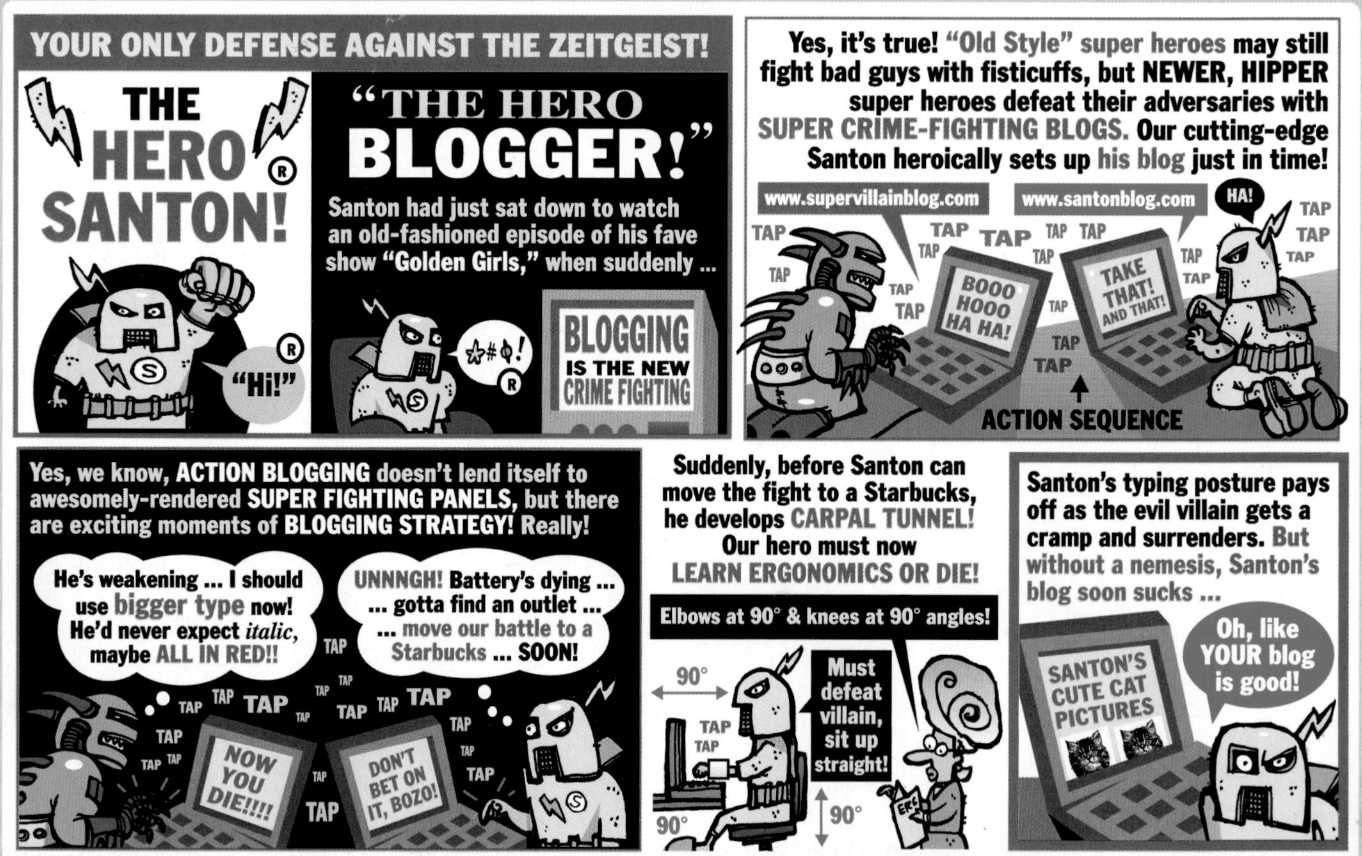
YOUR ONLY DEFENSE AGAINST THE ZEITGEIST!
THE HERO SANTON!®
"THE HERO BLOGGER!"
Santon had just sat down to watch an old-fashioned episode of his fave show "Golden Girls," when suddenly ...
"Hi!"®
BLOGGING IS THE NEW CRIME FIGHTING
Yes, it's true! "Old Style" super heroes may still fight bad guys with fisticuffs, but NEWER, HIPPER super heroes defeat their adversaries with SUPER CRIME-FIGHTING BLOGS. Our cutting-edge Santon heroically sets up his blog just in time!
www.supervillainblog.com
www.santonblog.com
HA!
TAP TAP TAP TAP TAP
BOOO HOOO HA HA!
TAKE THAT! AND THAT!
ACTION SEQUENCE
Yes, we know, ACTION BLOGGING doesn't lend itself to awesomely-rendered SUPER FIGHTING PANELS, but there are exciting moments of BLOGGING STRATEGY! Really!
He's weakening ... I should use bigger type now! He'd never expect *italic*, maybe ALL IN RED!!
UNNNGH! Battery's dying ... ... gotta find an outlet ... ... move our battle to a Starbucks ... SOON!
TAP TAP TAP TAP TAP
NOW YOU DIE!!!!
DON'T BET ON IT, BOZO!
Suddenly, before Santon can move the fight to a Starbucks, he develops CARPAL TUNNEL! Our hero must now LEARN ERGONOMICS OR DIE!
Elbows at 90° & knees at 90° angles!
90°
Must defeat villain, sit up straight!
90°
90°
Santon's typing posture pays off as the evil villain gets a cramp and surrenders. But without a nemesis, Santon's blog soon sucks ...
SANTON'S CUTE CAT PICTURES
Oh, like YOUR blog is good!

DON ASMUSSEN

GOT YOUR NOSE

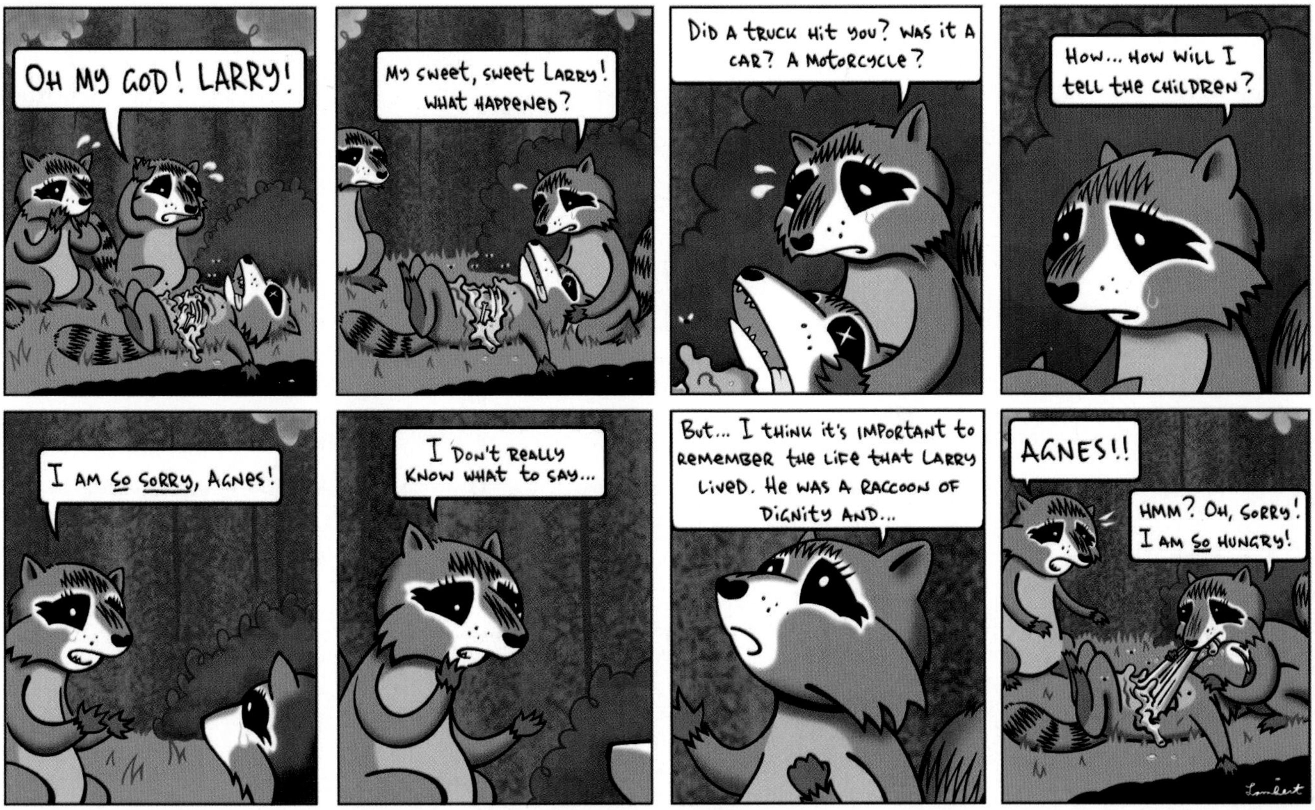

OH MY GOD! LARRY!
My sweet, sweet Larry! What happened?
Did a truck hit you? Was it a car? A motorcycle?
How... how will I tell the children?
I am so sorry, Agnes!
I don't really know what to say...
But... I think it's important to remember the life that Larry lived. He was a raccoon of dignity and...
AGNES!!
HMM? Oh, sorry! I am so hungry!

JACOB LAMBERT

38 DEGREES of SEPARATION

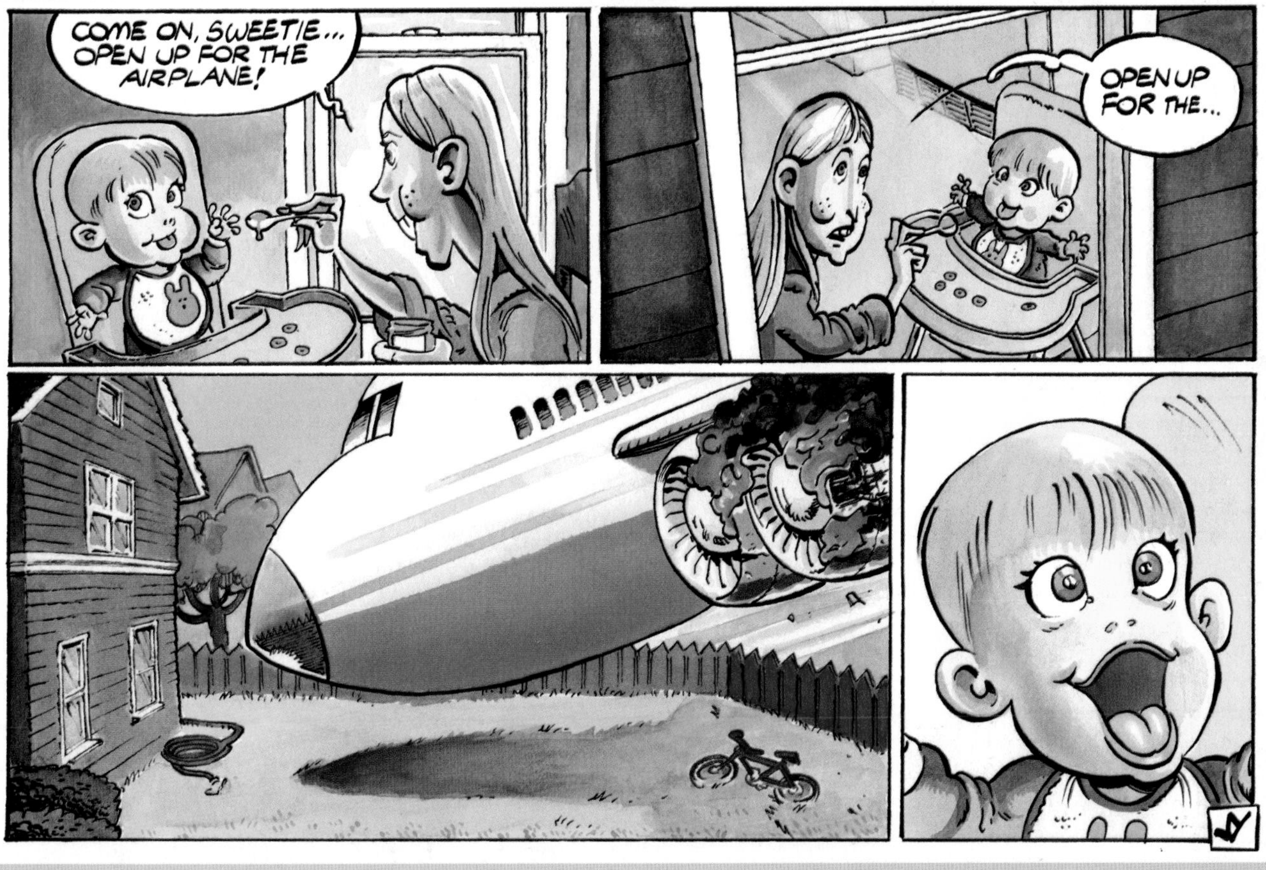

COME ON, SWEETIE... OPEN UP FOR THE AIRPLANE!
OPEN UP FOR THE...

JASON YUNGBLUTH

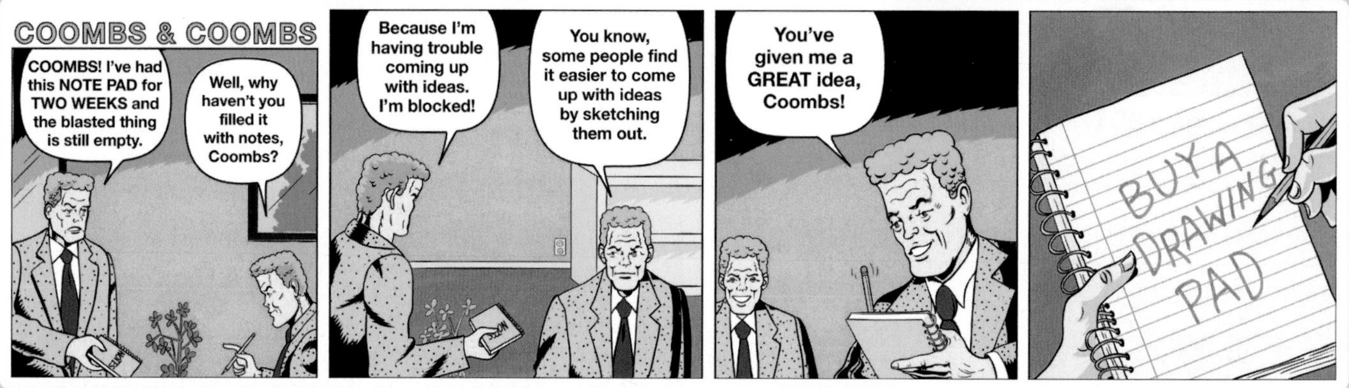
COOMBS & COOMBS
COOMBS! I've had this NOTE PAD for TWO WEEKS and the blasted thing is still empty.
Well, why haven't you filled it with notes, Coombs?
Because I'm having trouble coming up with ideas. I'm blocked!
You know, some people find it easier to come up with ideas by sketching them out.
You've given me a GREAT idea, Coombs!
BUY A DRAWING PAD
JASON COATES

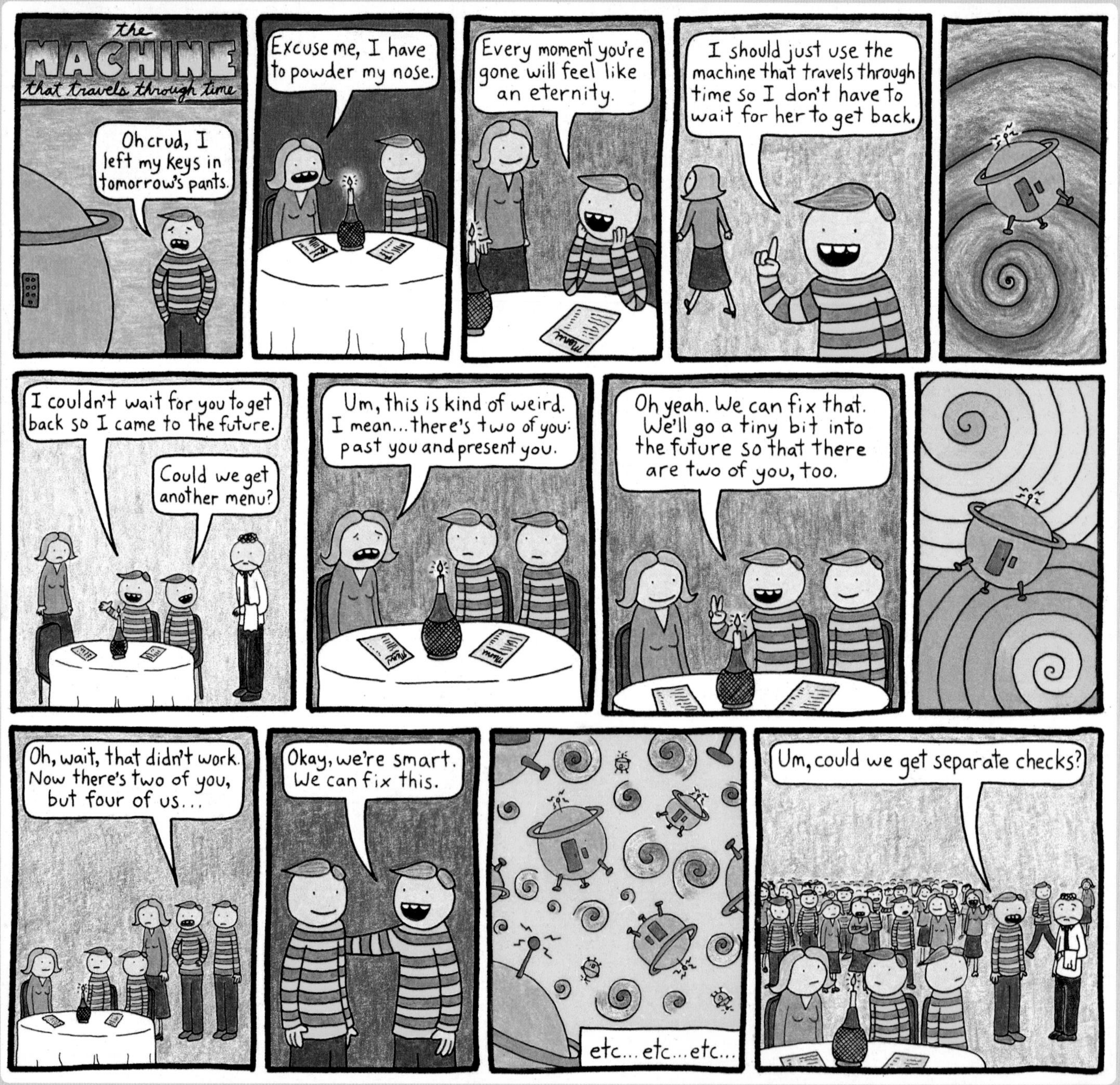
the MACHINE that travels through time
Oh crud, I left my keys in tomorrow's pants.
Excuse me, I have to powder my nose.
Every moment you're gone will feel like an eternity.
I should just use the machine that travels through time so I don't have to wait for her to get back.
I couldn't wait for you to get back so I came to the future.
Could we get another menu?
Um, this is kind of weird. I mean... there's two of you: past you and present you.
Oh yeah. We can fix that. We'll go a tiny bit into the future so that there are two of you, too.
Oh, wait, that didn't work. Now there's two of you, but four of us...
Okay, we're smart. We can fix this.
etc... etc... etc...
Um, could we get separate checks?
JOEY ALISON SAYERS

THE LITTLE WOODEN PUPPET

A Scene We'd Like to See

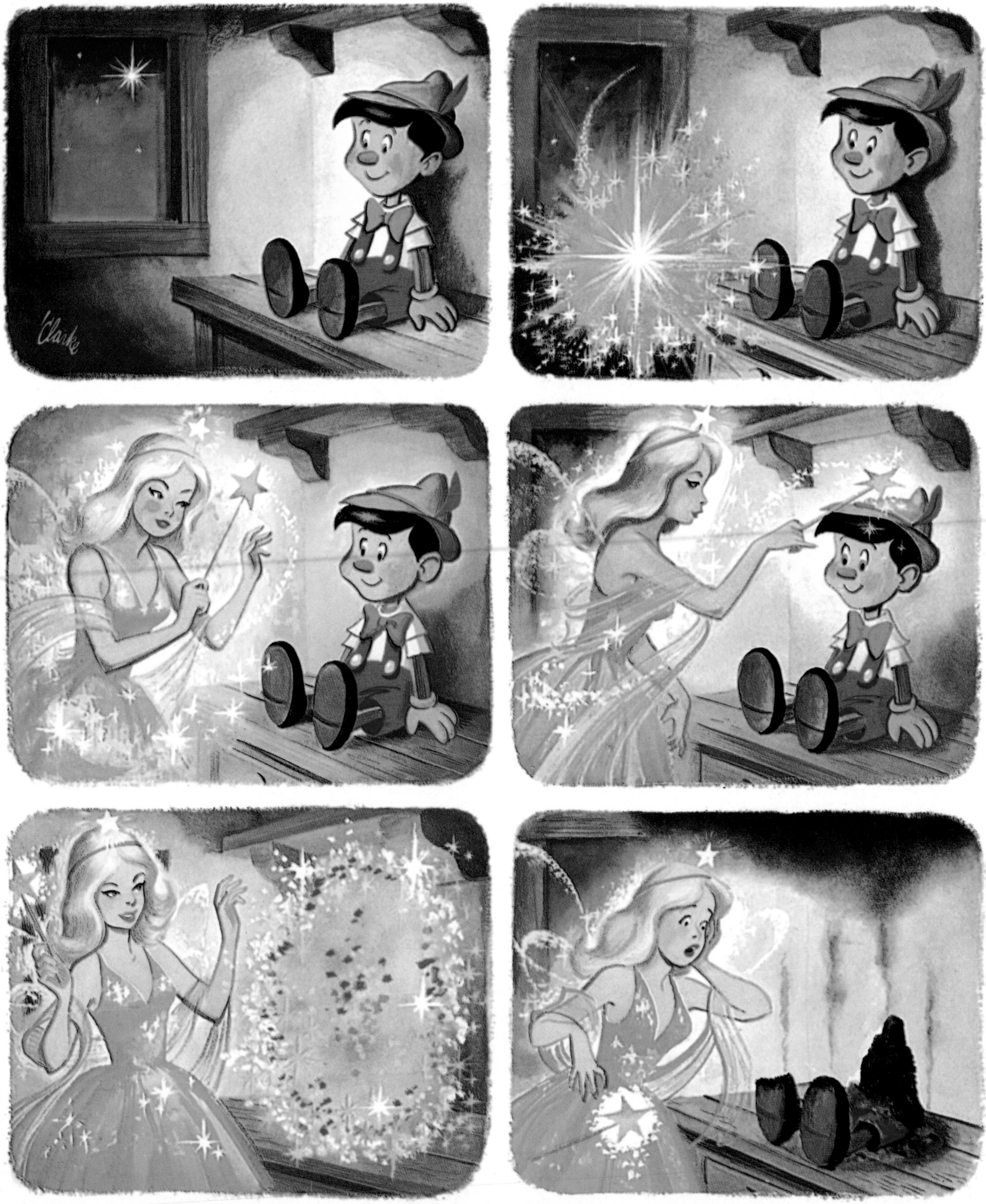
Clarke

ARTIST: BOB CLARKE

SERGIO ARAGONES MARGINALS XL

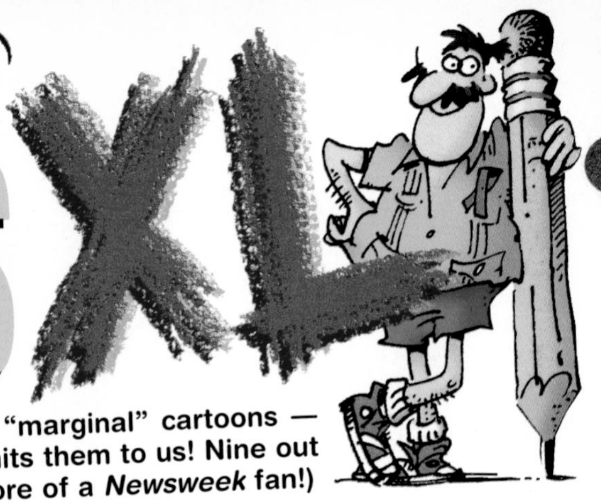

Enjoy this extra-large collection of Sergio Aragones' "marginal" cartoons — printed here in the same eye-pampering size he submits them to us! Nine out of ten ophthalmologists approve! (The tenth one is more of a *Newsweek* fan!)

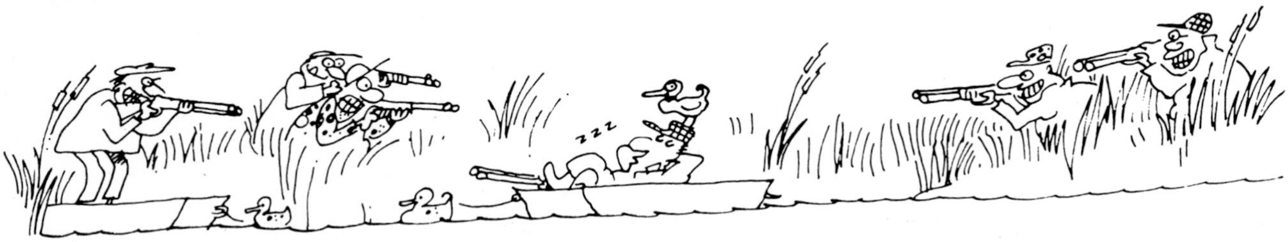
zzz

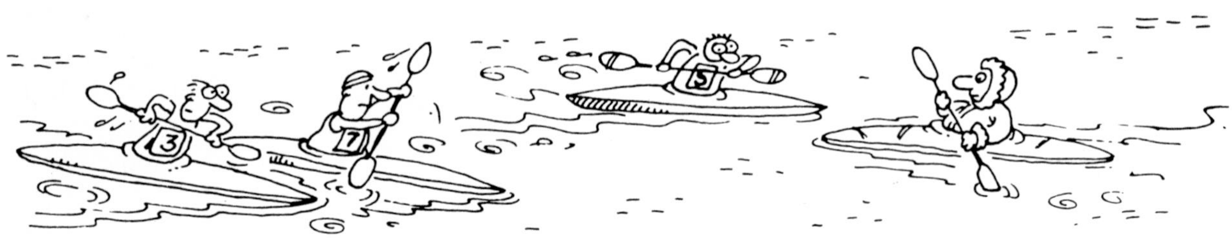
3
7
5

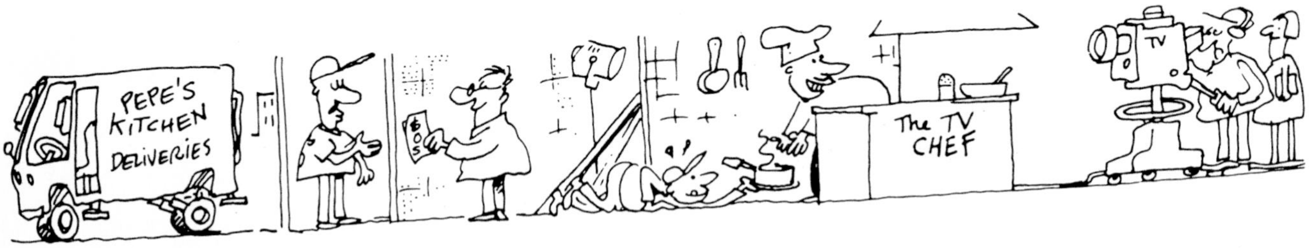
PEPE'S KITCHEN DELIVERIES
The TV CHEF
TV

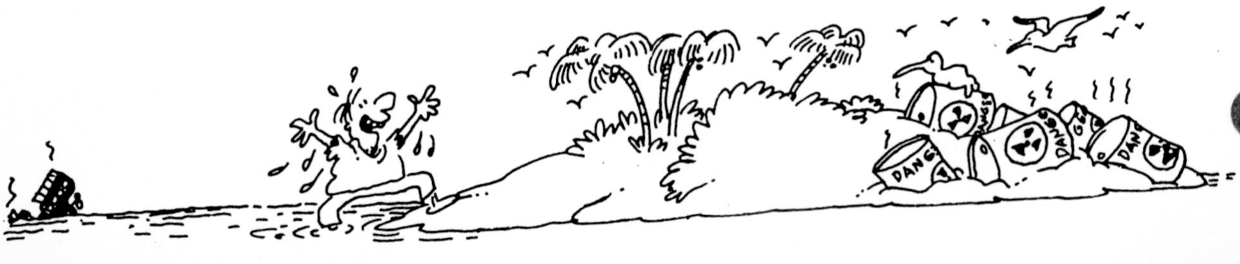

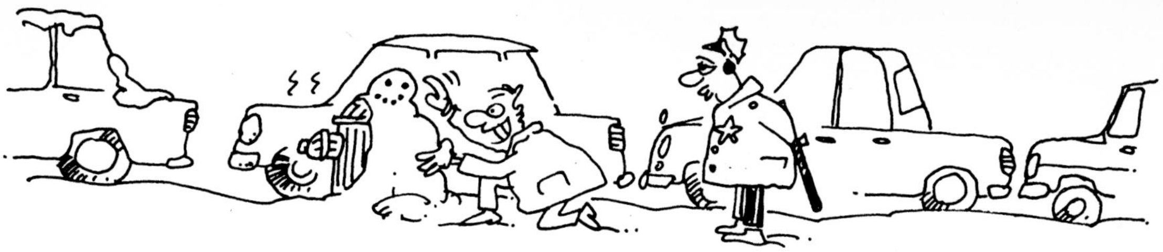

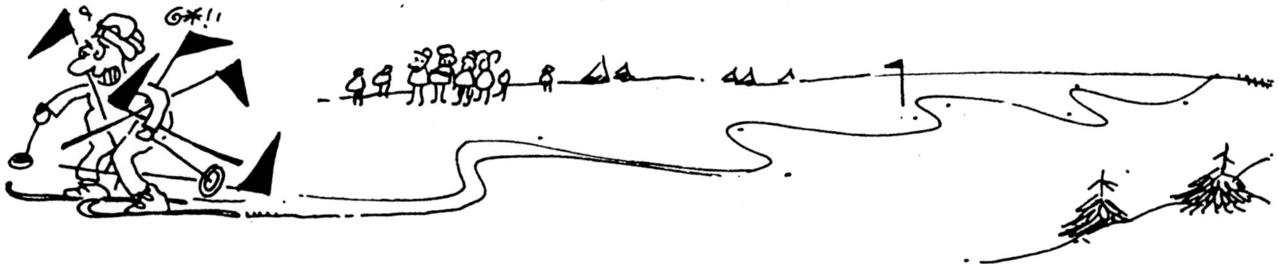
G*!!

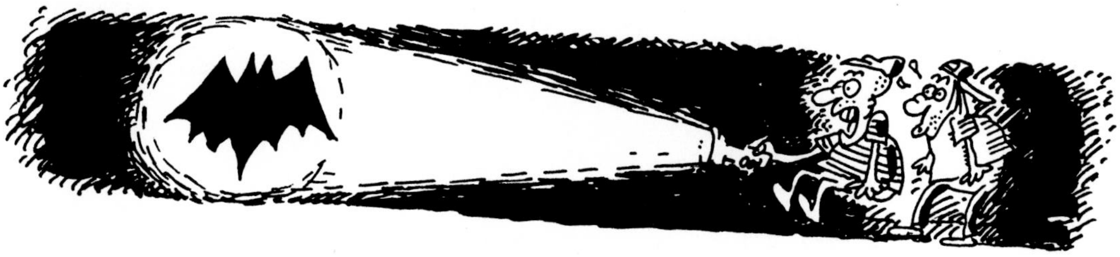

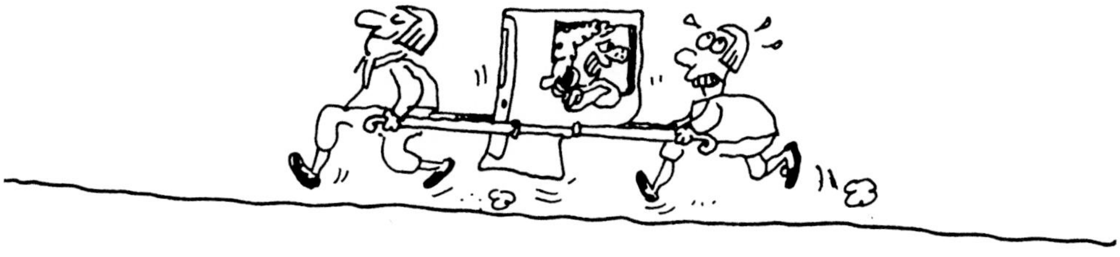

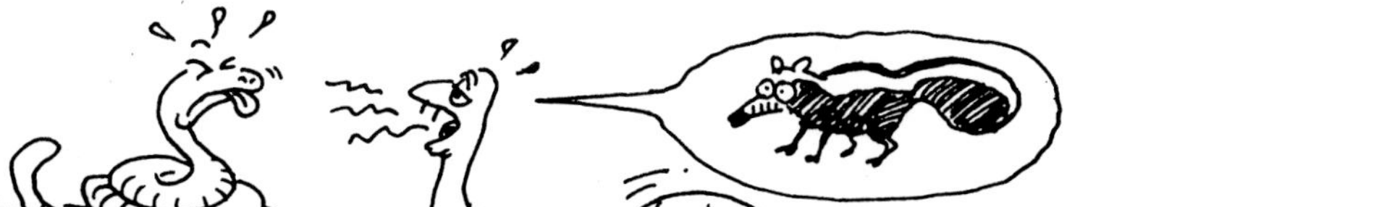

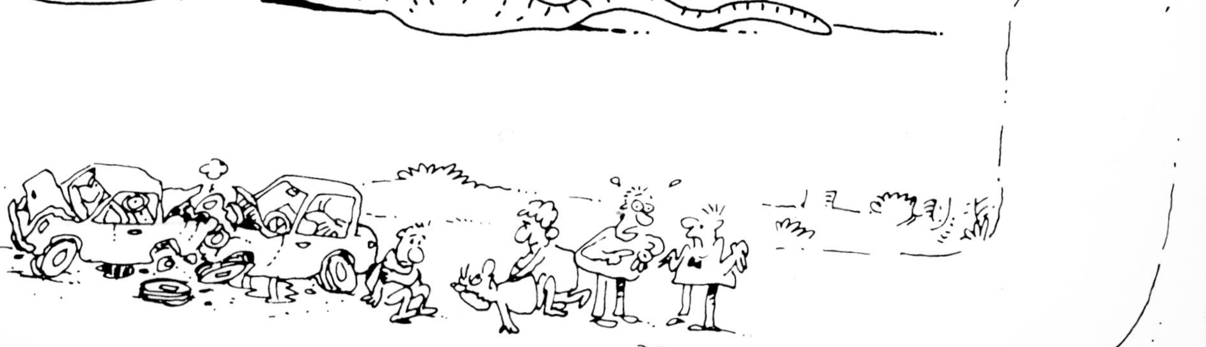

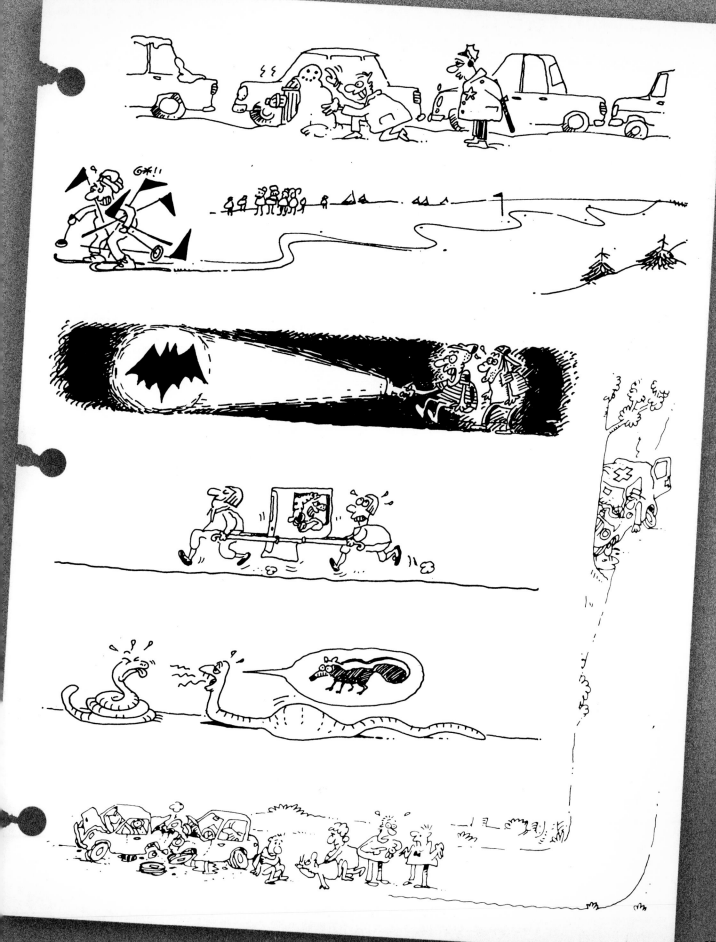

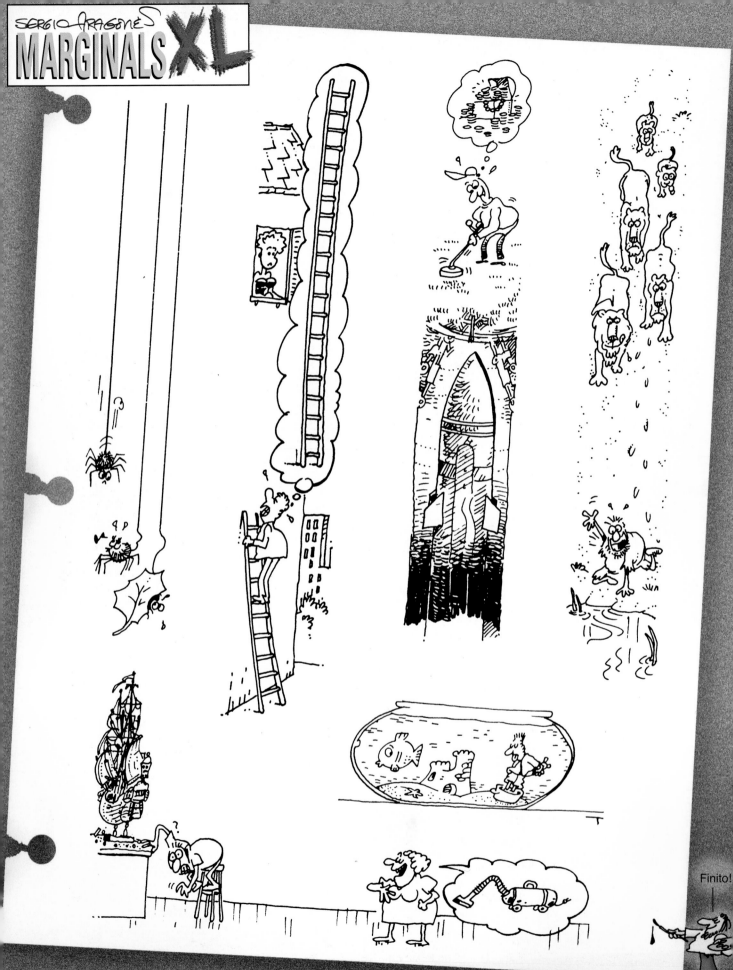

Finito!

JOKE-AND-DAGGER DEPT.

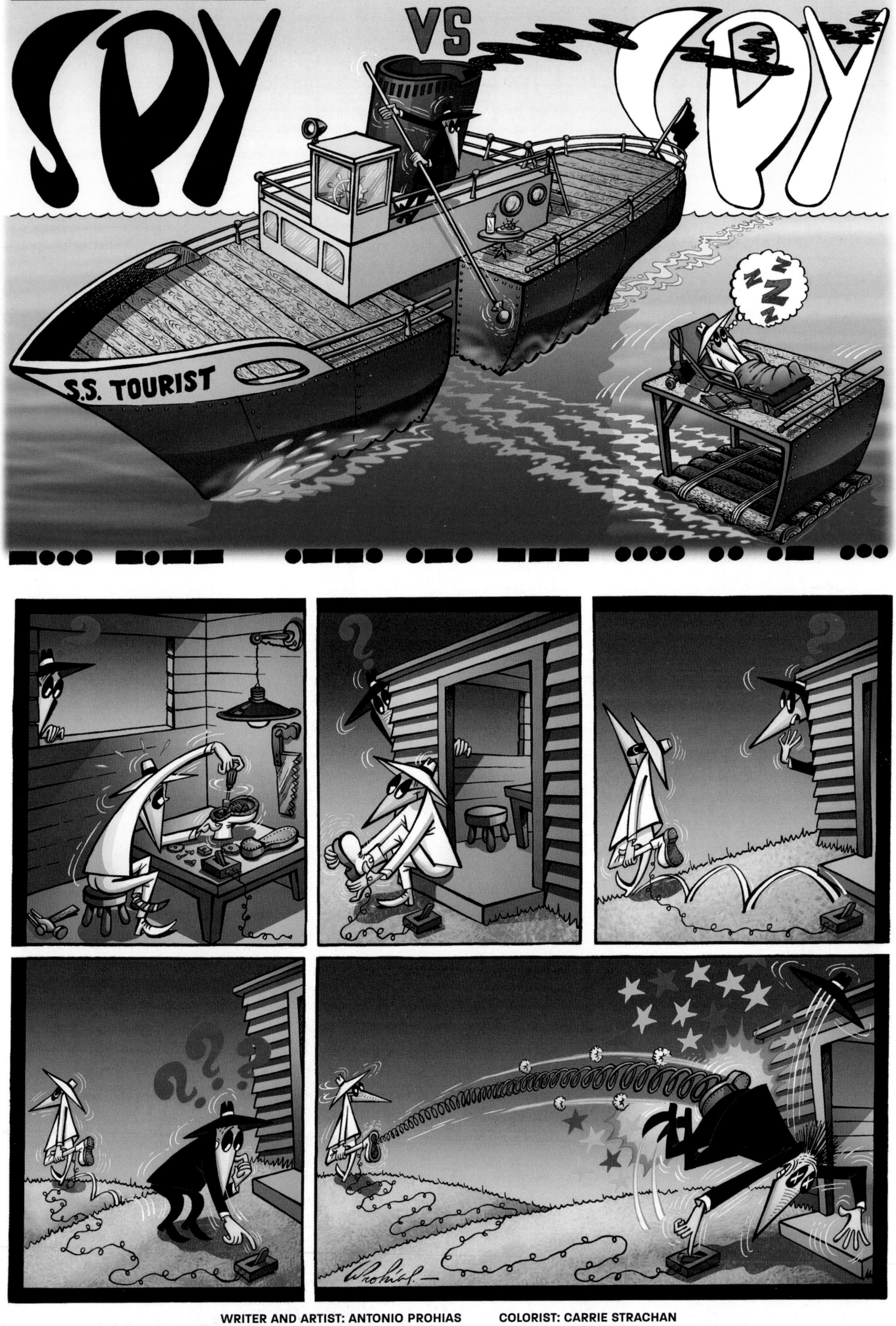

SPY VS SPY
S.S. TOURIST

WRITER AND ARTIST: ANTONIO PROHIAS COLORIST: CARRIE STRACHAN

Next time your parents complain about crime, tell them about these...

NEW CRIME-STOP

THE PHONY FRONT

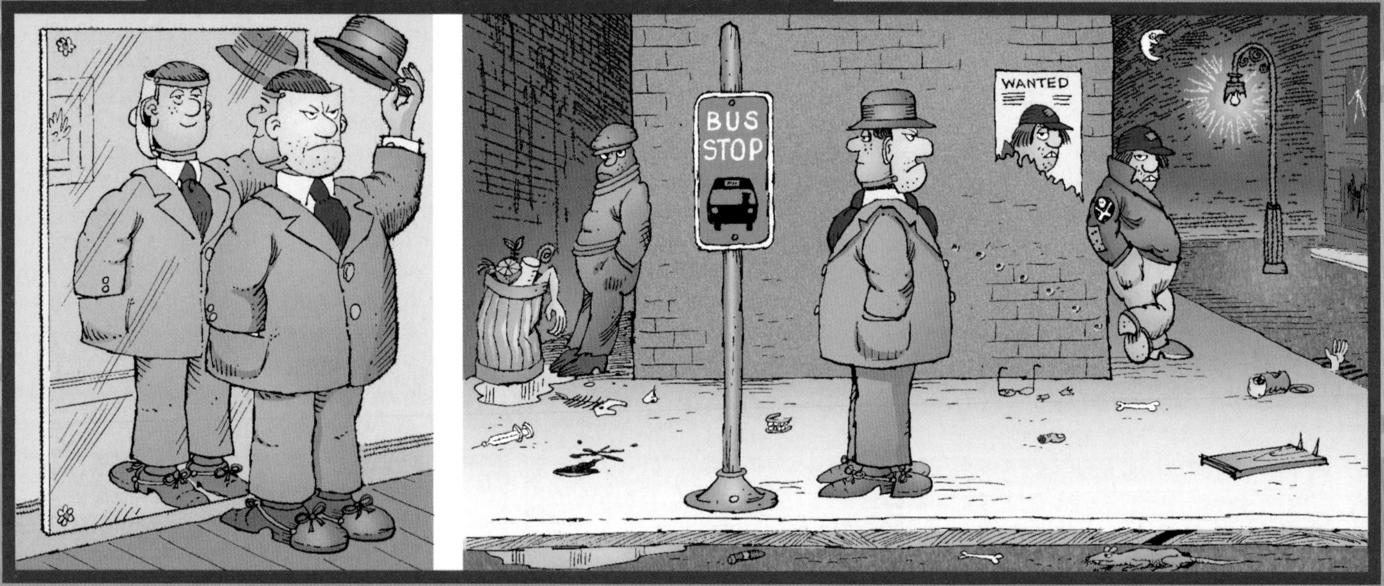
BUS STOP
WANTED

Almost all muggers attack from behind. This invention prevents that. A two-way shirt and jacket, a back-of-head mask and phony shoe fronts are easy to wear. Now, a mugger thinks you're always facing and watching him, so he stays away!

THE SMOKESCREEN BRIEFCASE

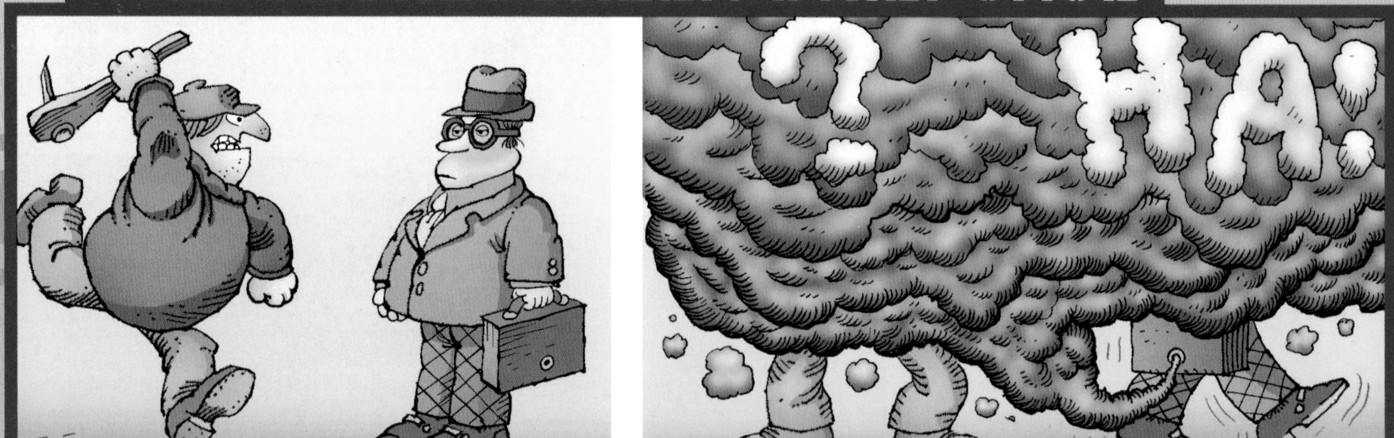
?
HA!

When threatened by a street thug, squeezing the briefcase handle releases a huge smoke cloud. Special eyeglasses permit clear vision for the wearer, who can take off without fear of bumping into the confused crook!

PING INVENTIONS!

WRITER AND ARTIST: AL JAFFEE

THE MARBLE MUGGER MASHER

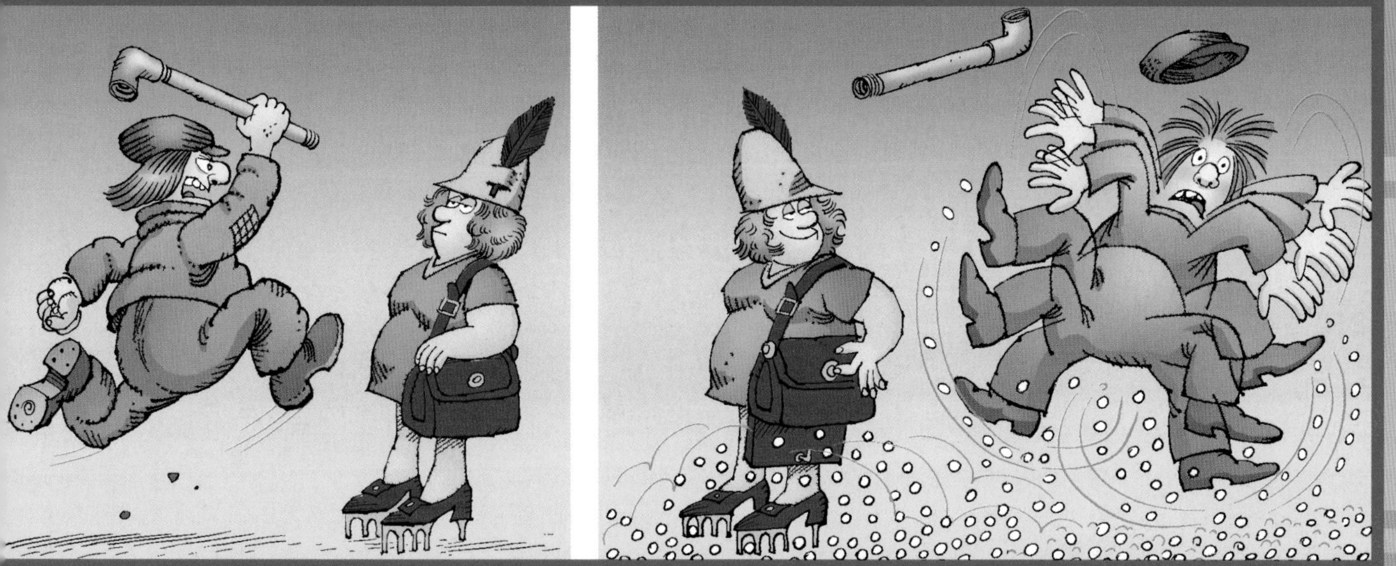

As an attacker approaches, pocketbook holder pushes a hidden button and hundreds of marbles are released. The attacker slips and slides while his target safely walks away with the aid of specially-designed spiked shoes!

THE AIRBAG OUTFIT

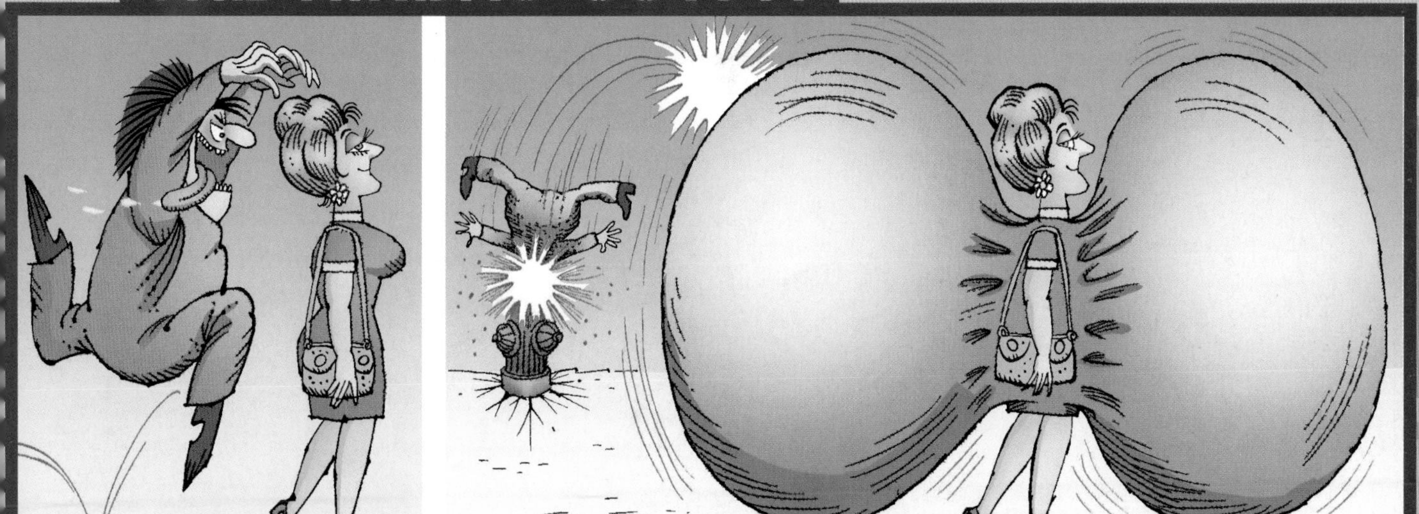

This invention uses the same idea behind automobile airbags. When a mugger attacks, airbags immediately inflate to fling the criminal away and protect the wearer. Just be careful it doesn't go off when embraced by loved ones!

THE WELCOME MAT TRAP

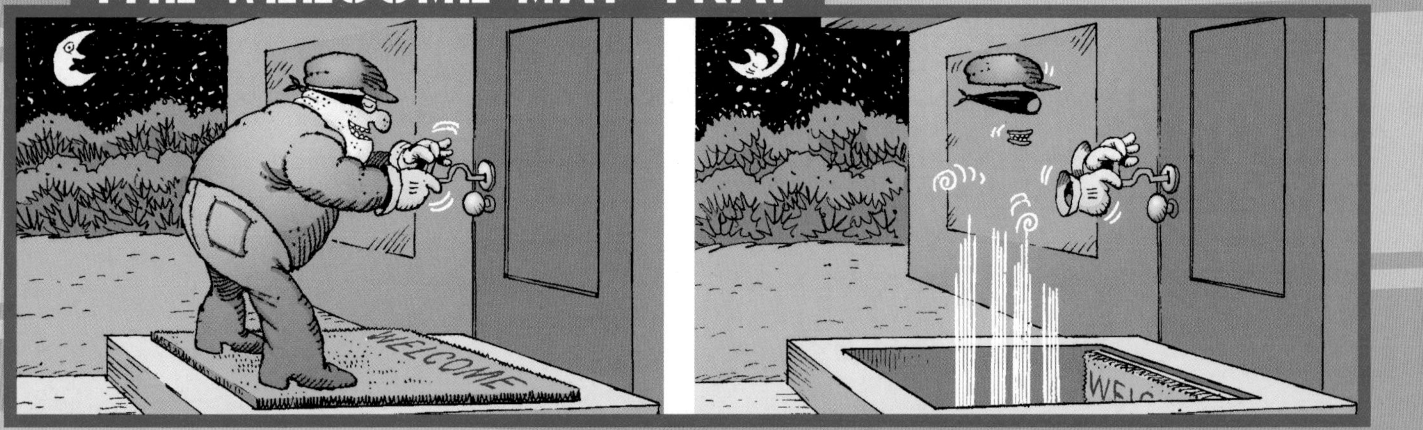
WELCOME

A special sensor in the door lock detects when something other than a key is inserted into it, causing a trap door to spring open. The intruder plunges into a pit 20 feet deep. If you're going away on vacation, make sure there's food and water in the pit or you'll return to a disgusting sight!

THE OILY DEFENSE SYSTEM

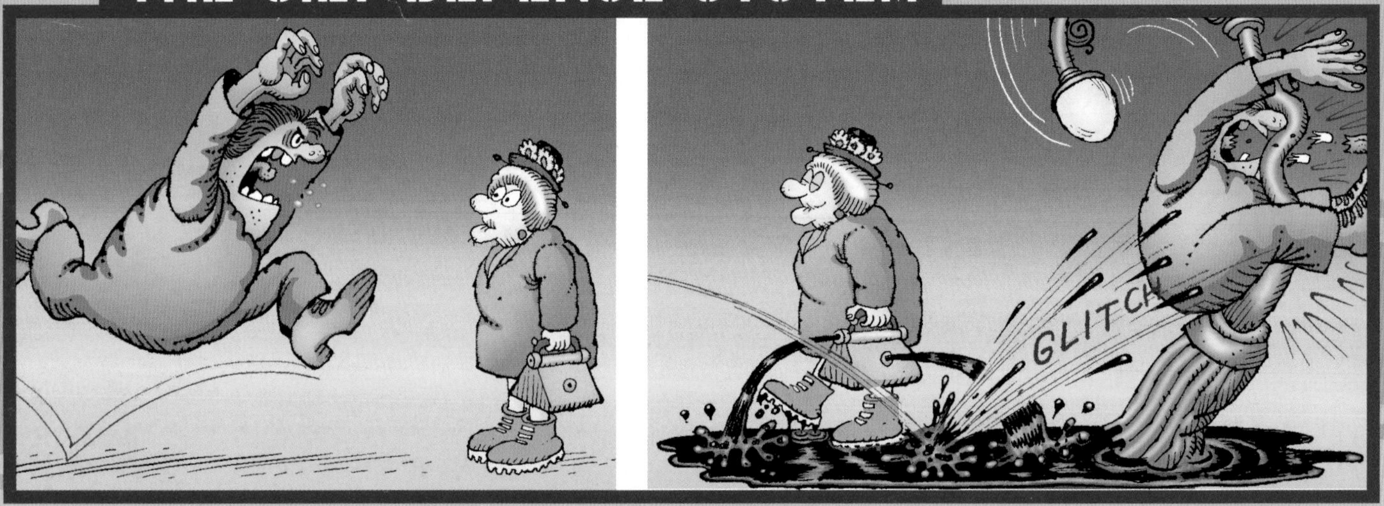
GLITCH

As danger approaches, the threatened person activates and releases a concealed supply of super-slippery goo. Special oil-proof shoes don't affect the wearer, while the attacker goes flying!

THE PURSE-SNATCHER CATCHER

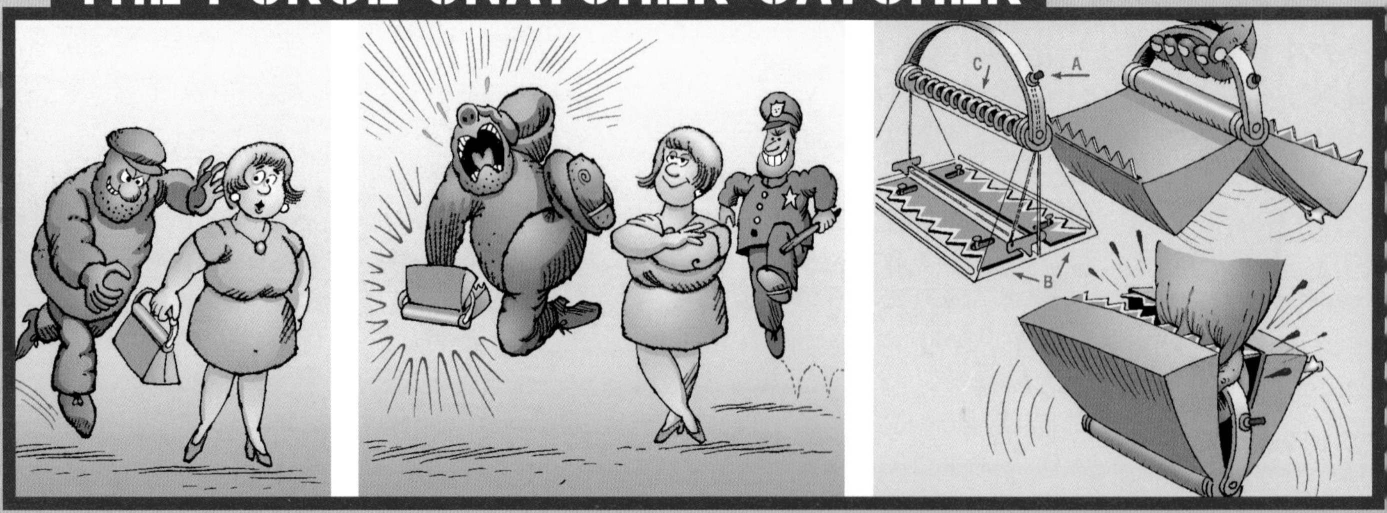
C
A
B

As law-breaking goon grabs the purse, handle button (A) is released and trigger (B) unlocks the two separate bag sections. The powerful bear trap spring mechanism (C) gives the thief the message that he should find something better to do with his time!

THE EXPLODING HAT NET

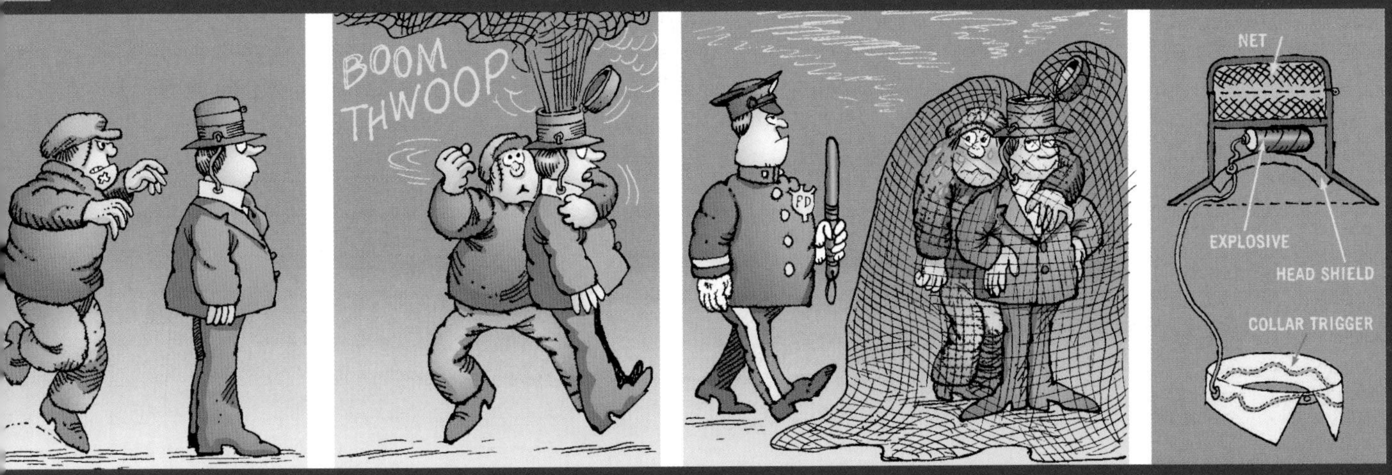
BOOM
THWOOP
NET
EXPLOSIVE
HEAD SHIELD
COLLAR TRIGGER

A strong, lightweight net is carefully packed into an ordinary-looking hat. When the wearer is grabbed by a mugger, a specially-wired shirt collar triggers an explosive charge, causing the net to cover both attacker and his target. Since they are both trapped until police arrive, the attacker will not harm the victim, fearing more serious punishment!

THE SLAMMING SHUTTER STOPPER

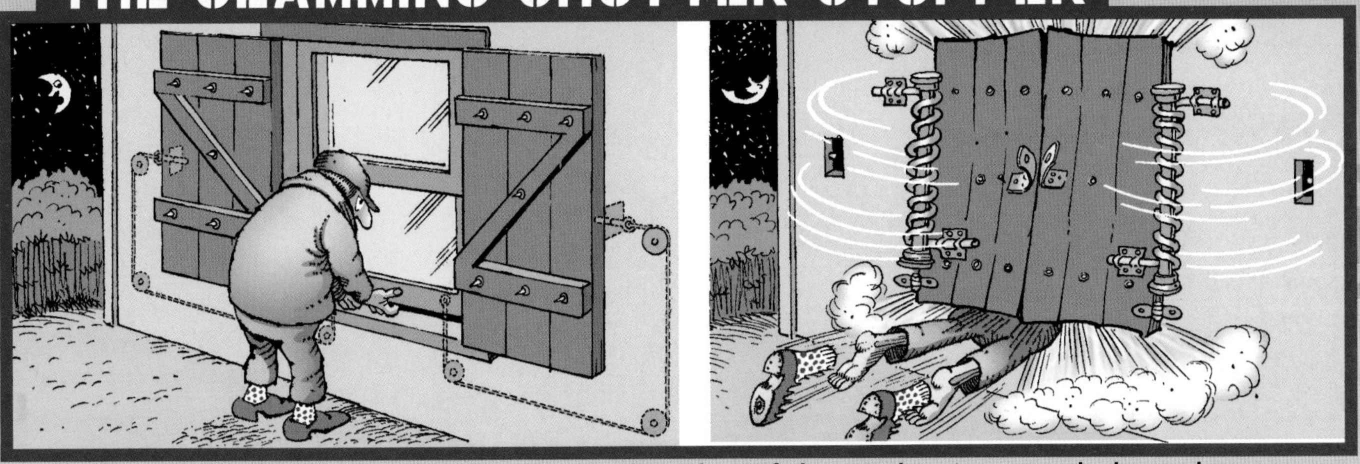

These innocent-looking shutters are anything but! If the window is opened, they release super-strong spring hinges that keep any burglar trapped like a bug until police can arrive!

THE BACKPACK SMACKER

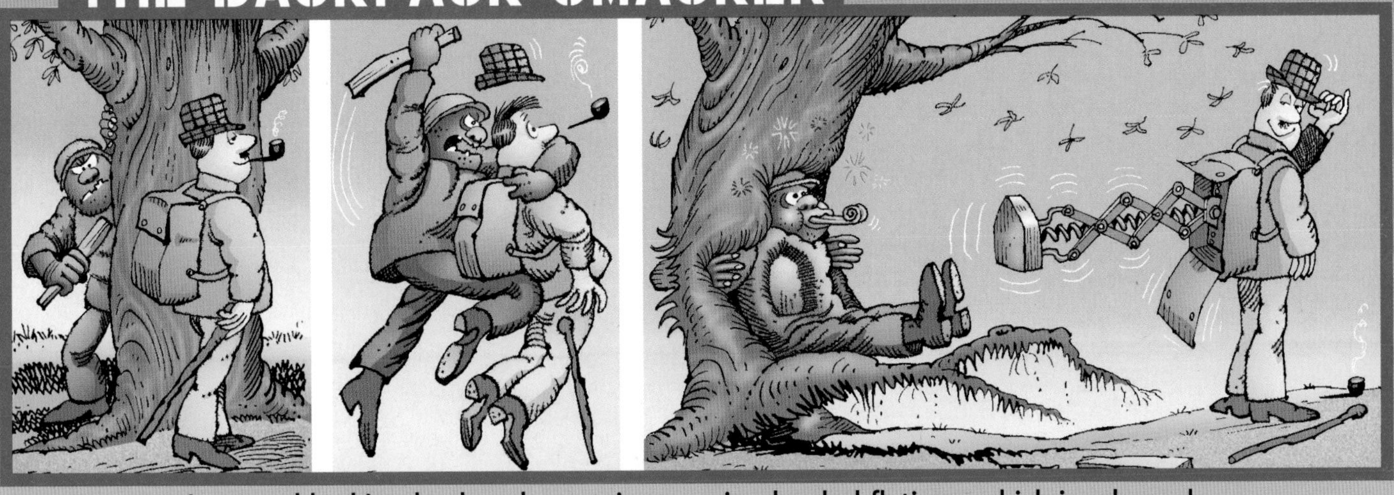

A normal-looking backpack contains a spring-loaded flatiron, which is released upon any attack from the rear. Its force delivers a blow equal to being hit by a five pound weight dropped from the top of the Empire State Building!

CELEBRITY ROCK, PAPER, SCISSORS

WRITER: DAVE CROATTO

Will.i.am throws...

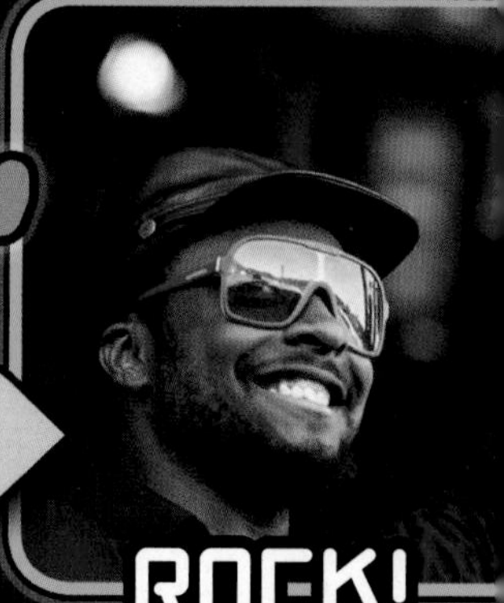

ROCK!

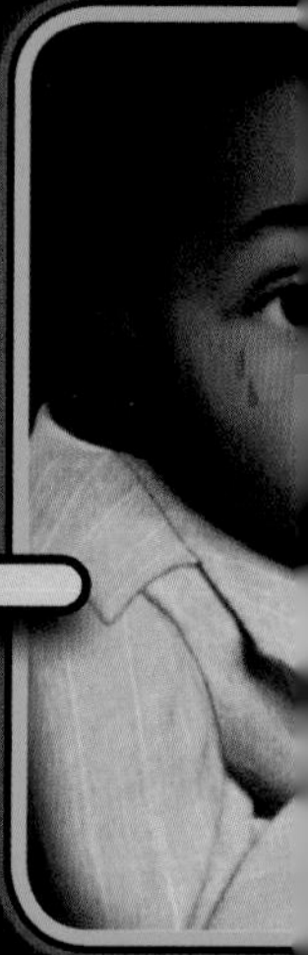

Which gets covered by LeBron James'...

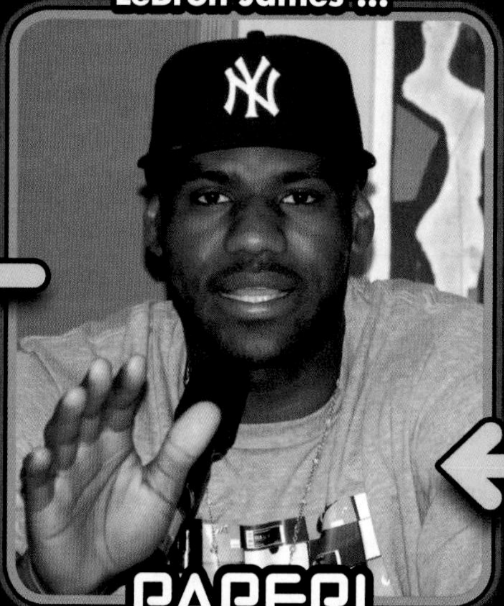

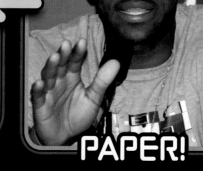

PAPER!

But The Situation slices through it with his...

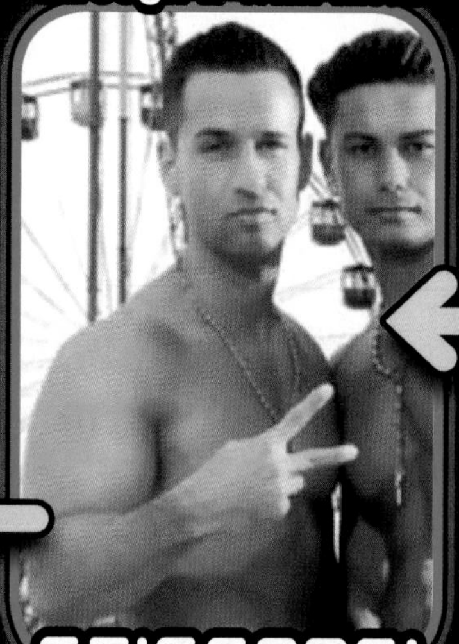

SCISSORS!

But Pauly D smashes them with...

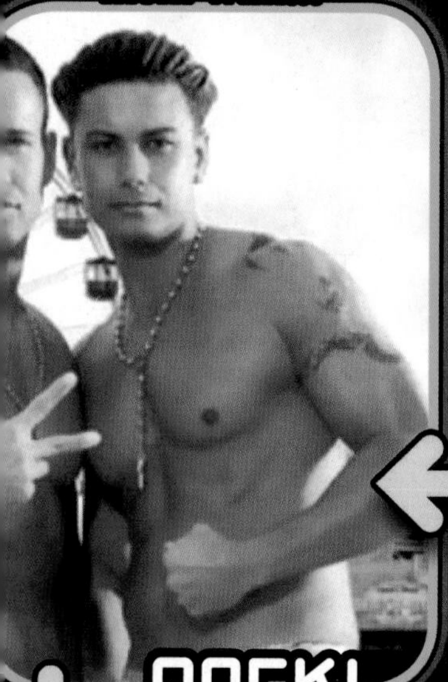

ROCK!
(Not cool, bro!)

Which gets covered by Hitler's...

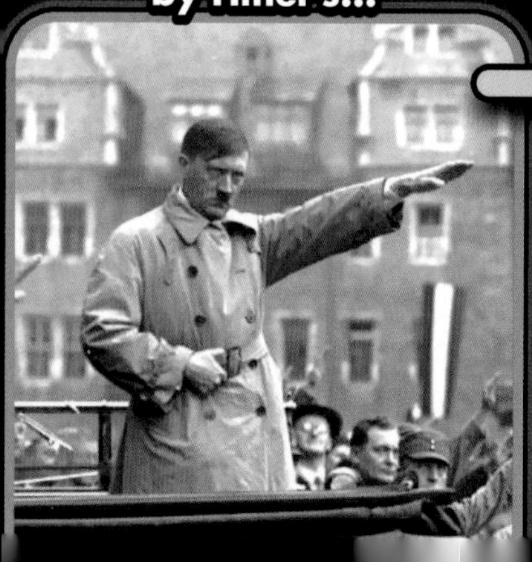

Which is defeated by Churchill's...

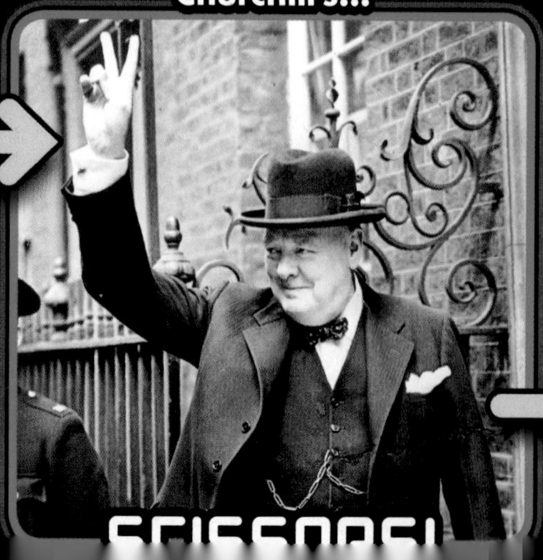

But those get smashed by Katy Perry's...

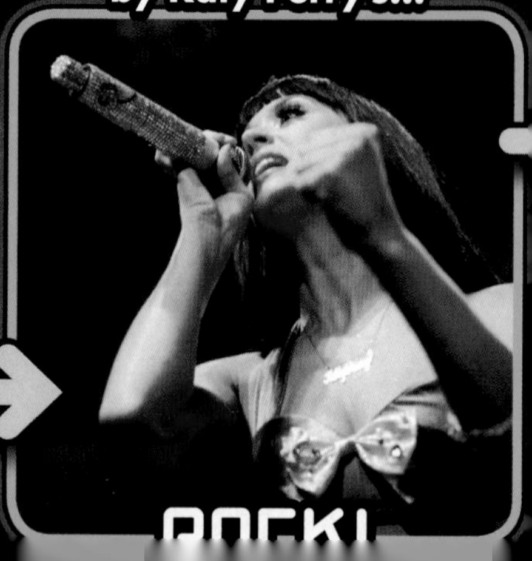

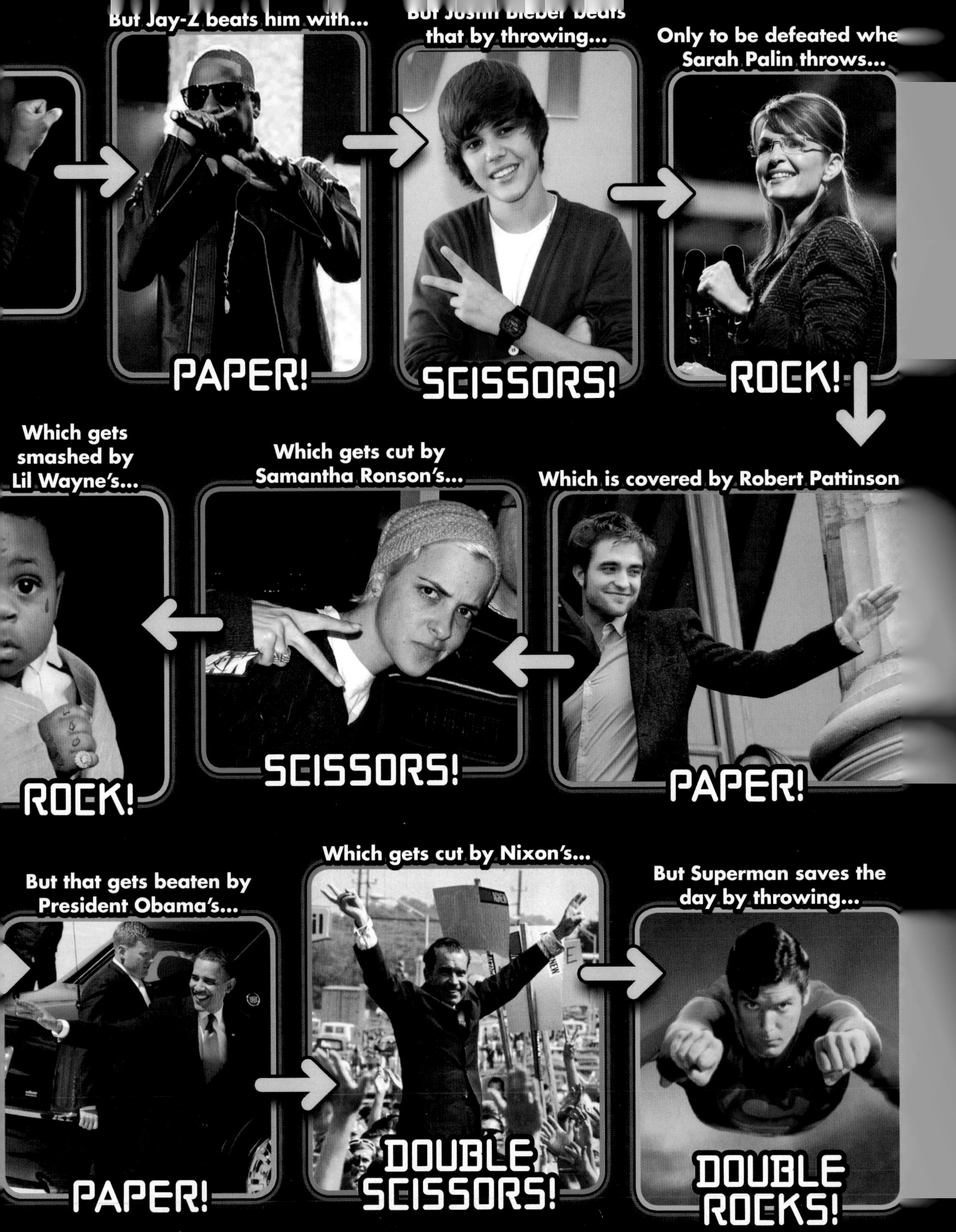
But Jay-Z beats him with...
PAPER!
But Justin Bieber beats that by throwing...
SCISSORS!
Only to be defeated whe
Sarah Palin throws...
ROCK!
Which is covered by Robert Pattinson
PAPER!
Which gets cut by Samantha Ronson's...
SCISSORS!
Which gets smashed by Lil Wayne's...
ROCK!
But that gets beaten by President Obama's...
PAPER!
Which gets cut by Nixon's...
DOUBLE SCISSORS!
But Superman saves the day by throwing...
DOUBLE ROCKS!

LeBron James: David Shankbone; Samantha Ronson: Roman Pinzon-Soto; Robert Pattinson: Nicolas Genin; Adolf Hitler: Bundesarchiv; Katy Perry: José Goulão

A MAD LOOK AT

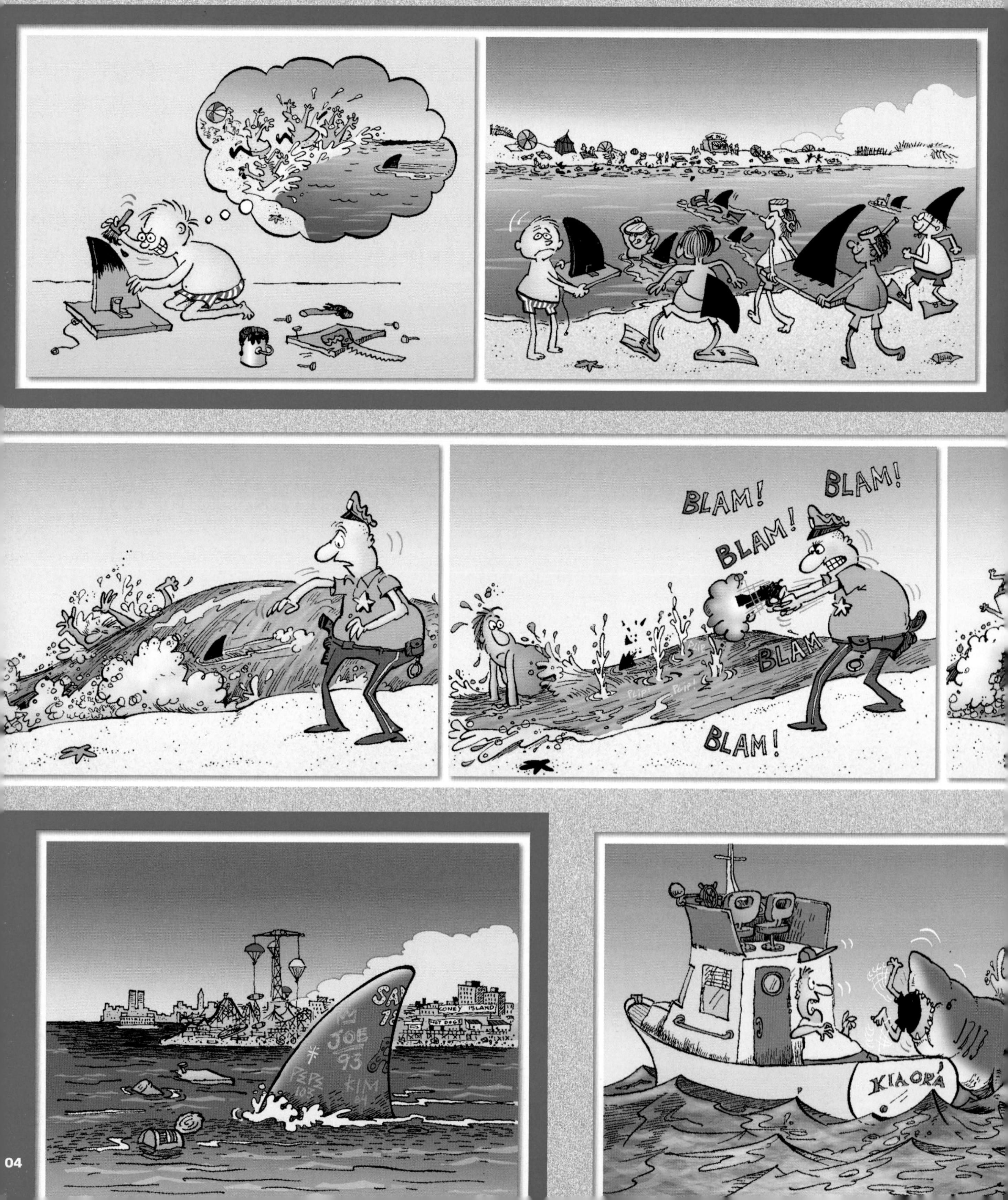
BLAM!
BLAM!
BLAM!
BLAM
BLAM!
JOE
93
KIM
PEPE
CONEY ISLAND
HOT DOGS
KIA ORA

SHARKS

WRITER AND ARTIST: SERGIO ARAGONES

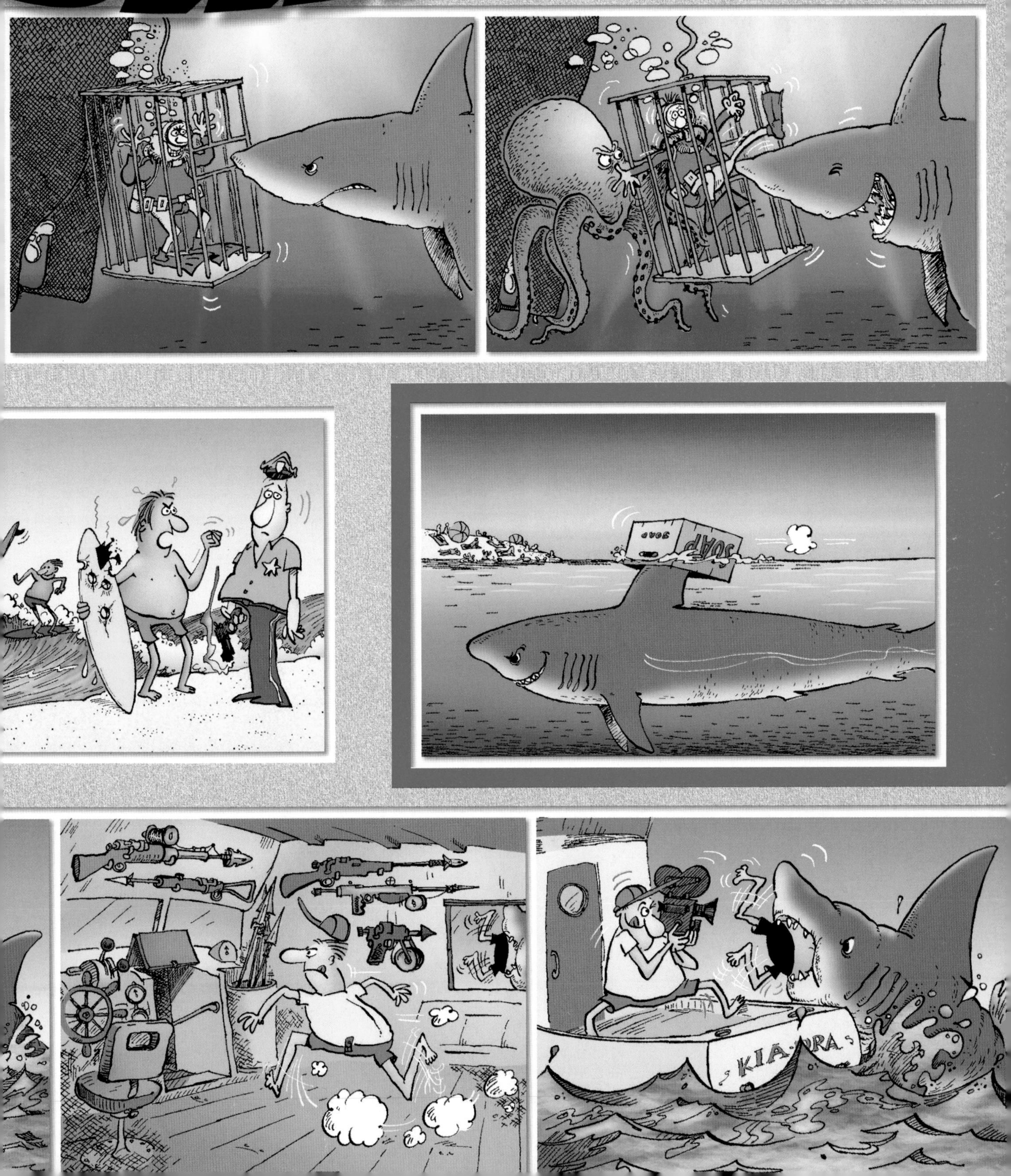
SOAP
SOAP
KIA-ORA

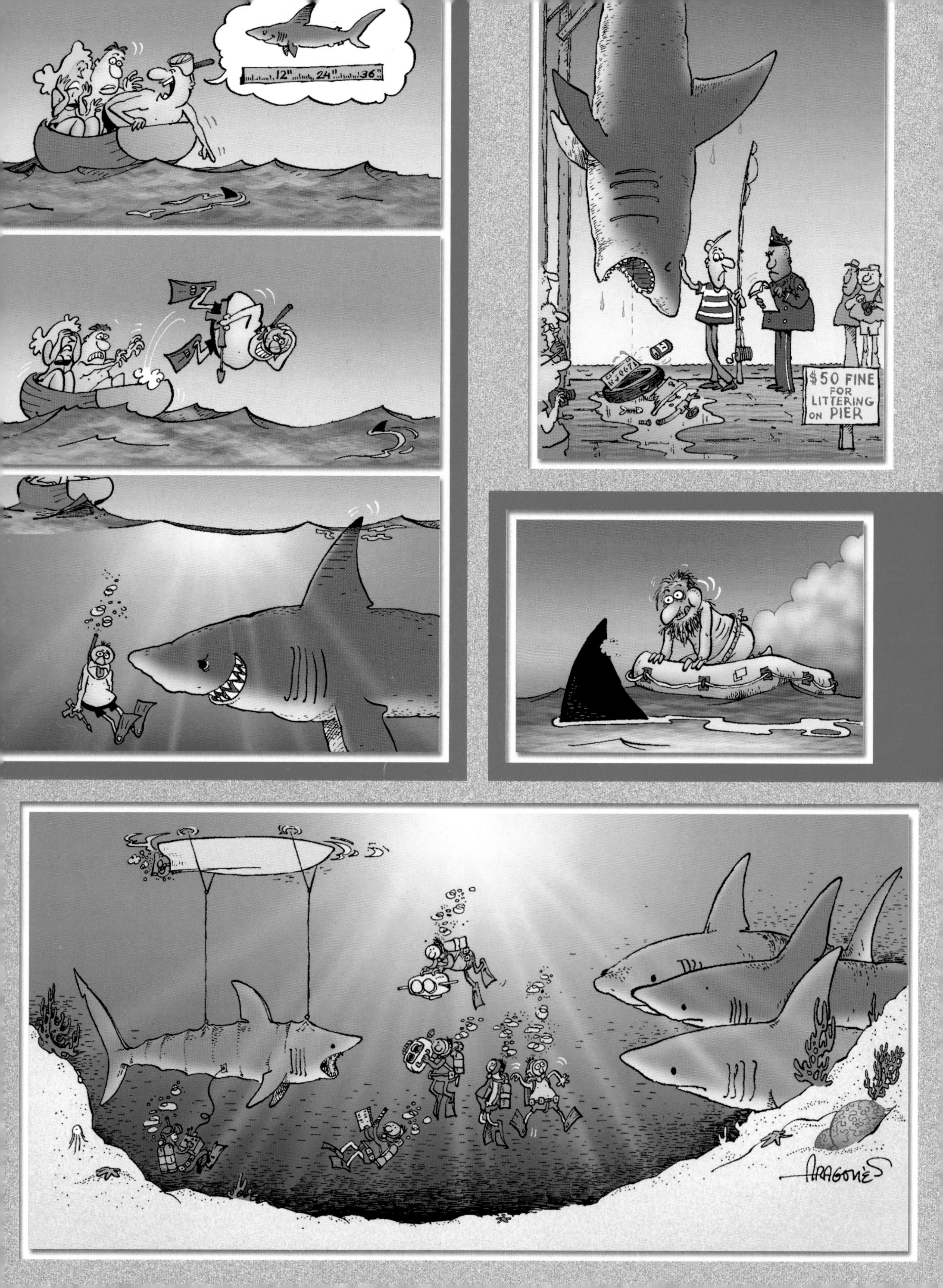

12" 24" 36"
$50 FINE FOR LITTERING ON PIER
ARAGONÉS

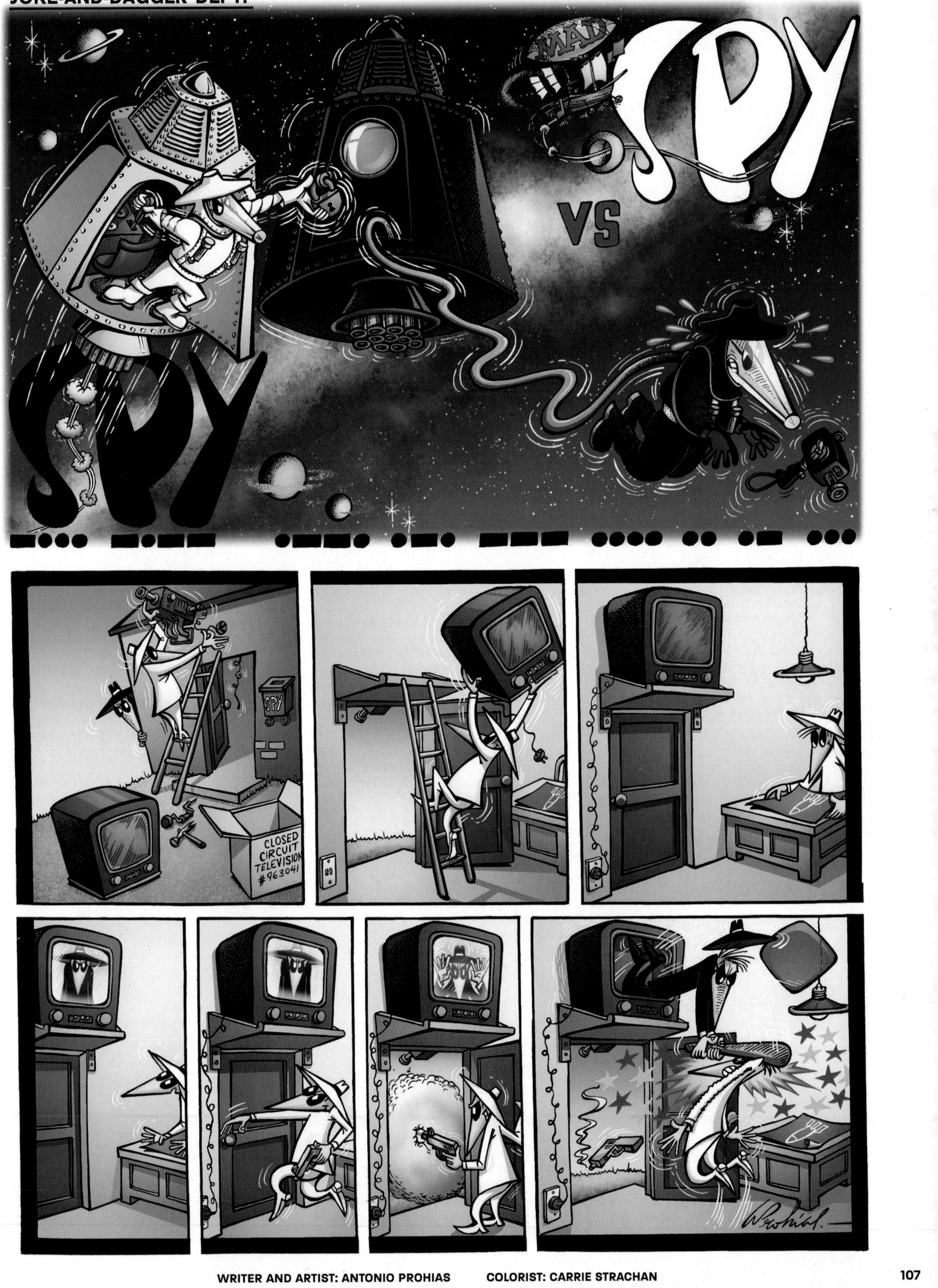
MAD
SPY
VS
SPY
SPY
CLOSED
CIRCUIT
TELEVISION
#963041
Prohias

WRITER AND ARTIST: ANTONIO PROHIAS COLORIST: CARRIE STRACHAN

BREAKING A NASTY HOBBIT DEPT.

BORED OF THE RINGS

How do you turn a dumb kiddie story into an "epic quest"? Make it big, make it long, and make it three times. Frantically cut back and forth between storylines, so nobody notices how drawn-out and repetitive each one is. Use made-up languages and subtitles to hide how boring the dialogue would be in English. Create a love story out of thin air. Every moment of alleged suspense should end with another character and his army showing up out of nowhere and saving the day. And whatever you do, make sure you buy the extra-large tub of popcorn. You'll need it before you're done! Because there are NO bathroom breaks during...

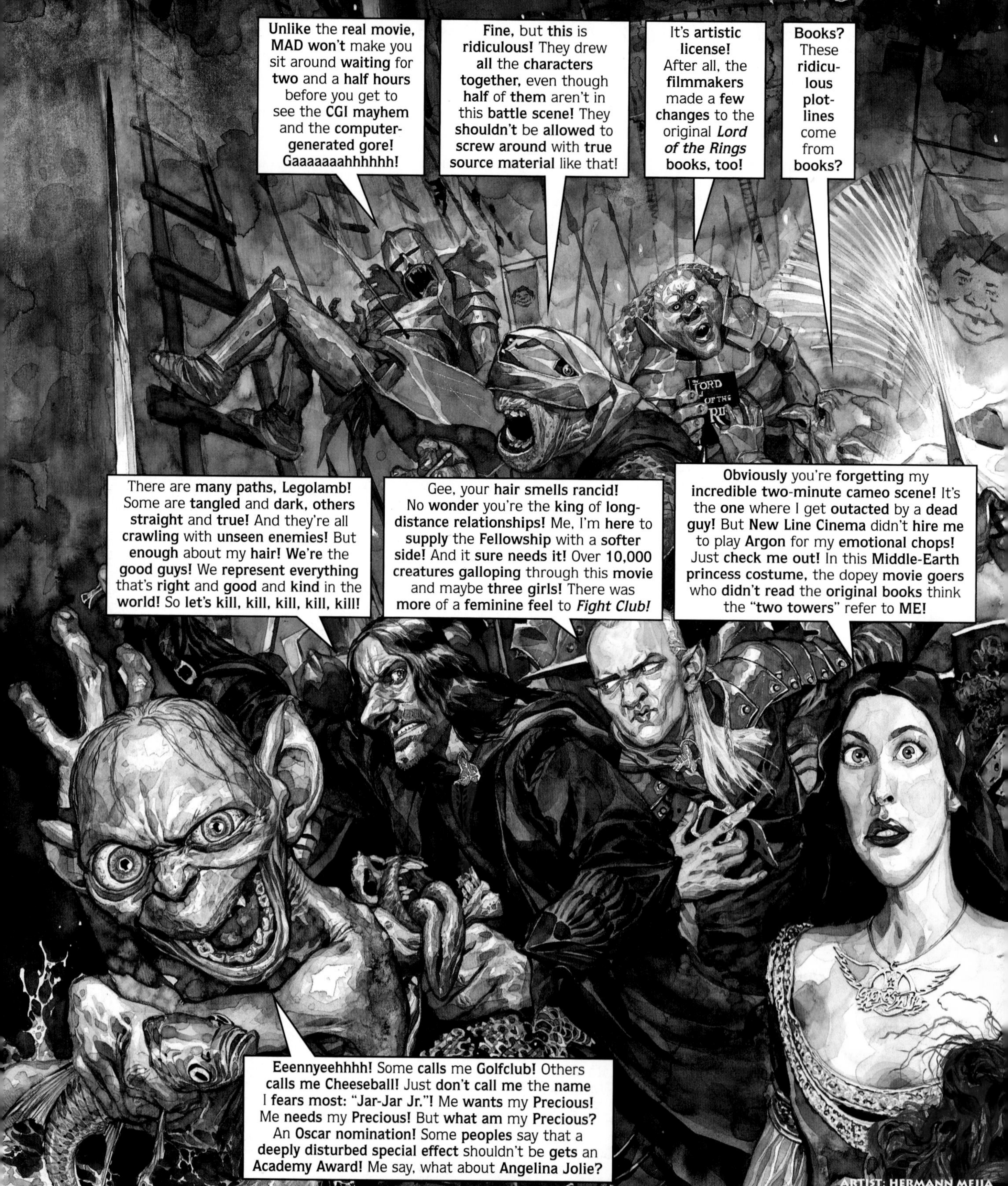
Unlike the real movie, MAD won't make you sit around waiting for two and a half hours before you get to see the CGI mayhem and the computer-generated gore! Gaaaaaaahhhhhh!
Fine, but this is ridiculous! They drew all the characters together, even though half of them aren't in this battle scene! They shouldn't be allowed to screw around with true source material like that!
It's artistic license! After all, the filmmakers made a few changes to the original *Lord of the Rings* books, too!
Books? These ridiculous plot-lines come from books?
LORD OF THE RINGS
There are many paths, Legolamb! Some are tangled and dark, others straight and true! And they're all crawling with unseen enemies! But enough about my hair! We're the good guys! We represent everything that's right and good and kind in the world! So let's kill, kill, kill, kill, kill!
Gee, your hair smells rancid! No wonder you're the king of long-distance relationships! Me, I'm here to supply the Fellowship with a softer side! And it sure needs it! Over 10,000 creatures galloping through this movie and maybe three girls! There was more of a feminine feel to *Fight Club!*
Obviously you're forgetting my incredible two-minute cameo scene! It's the one where I get outacted by a dead guy! But New Line Cinema didn't hire me to play Argon for my emotional chops! Just check me out! In this Middle-Earth princess costume, the dopey movie goers who didn't read the original books think the "two towers" refer to ME!
Eeennyeehhhh! Some calls me Golfclub! Others calls me Cheeseball! Just don't call me the name I fears most: "Jar-Jar Jr."! Me wants my Precious! Me needs my Precious! But what am my Precious? An Oscar nomination! Some peoples say that a deeply disturbed special effect shouldn't be gets an Academy Award! Me say, what about Angelina Jolie?
AEROSMITH

ARTIST: HERMANN MEJIA

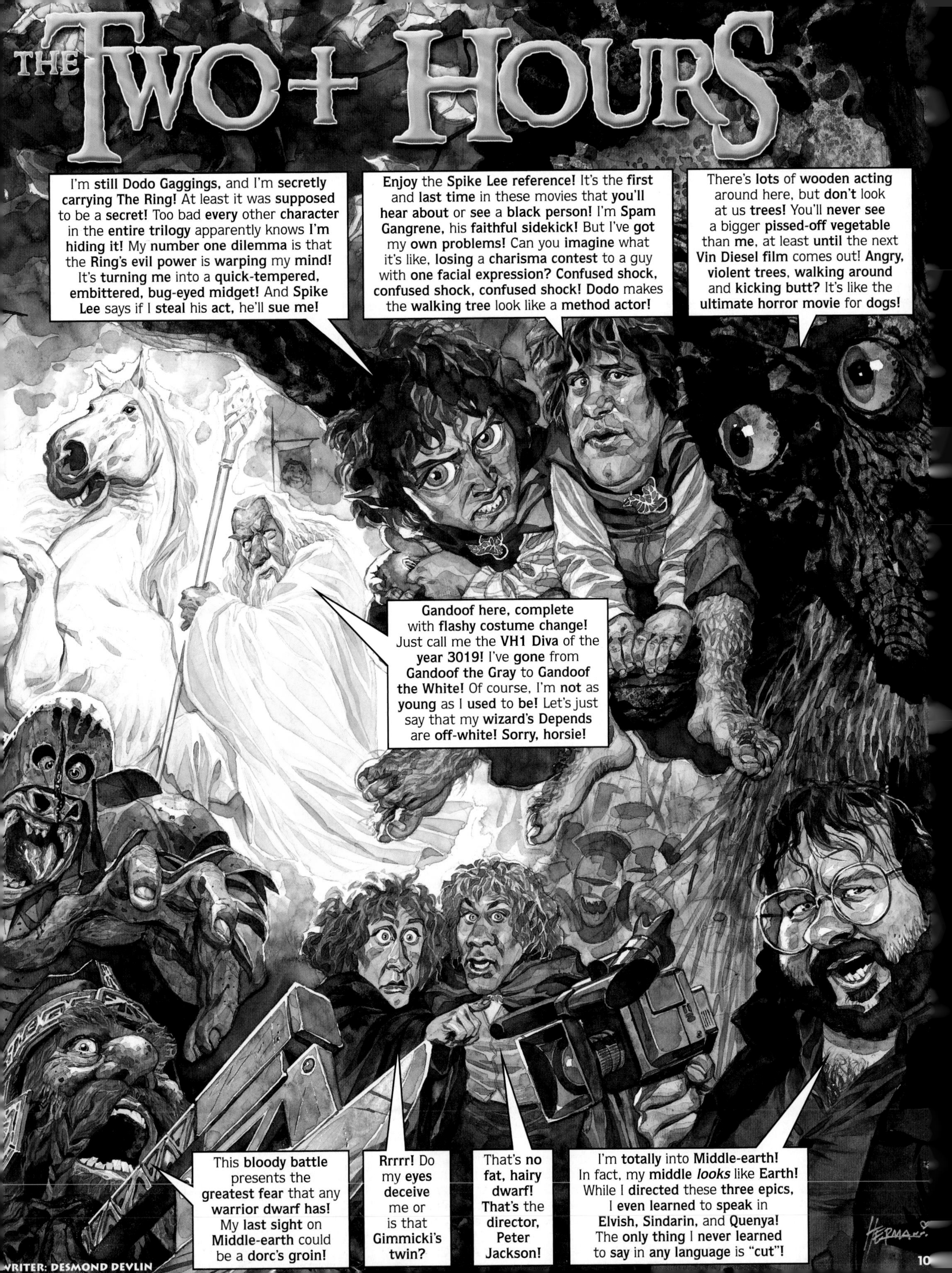
THE TWO+ HOURS
I'm still Dodo Gaggings, and I'm secretly carrying The Ring! At least it was supposed to be a secret! Too bad every other character in the entire trilogy apparently knows I'm hiding it! My number one dilemma is that the Ring's evil power is warping my mind! It's turning me into a quick-tempered, embittered, bug-eyed midget! And Spike Lee says if I steal his act, he'll sue me!
Enjoy the Spike Lee reference! It's the first and last time in these movies that you'll hear about or see a black person! I'm Spam Gangrene, his faithful sidekick! But I've got my own problems! Can you imagine what it's like, losing a charisma contest to a guy with one facial expression? Confused shock, confused shock, confused shock! Dodo makes the walking tree look like a method actor!
There's lots of wooden acting around here, but don't look at us trees! You'll never see a bigger pissed-off vegetable than me, at least until the next Vin Diesel film comes out! Angry, violent trees, walking around and kicking butt? It's like the ultimate horror movie for dogs!
Gandoof here, complete with flashy costume change! Just call me the VH1 Diva of the year 3019! I've gone from Gandoof the Gray to Gandoof the White! Of course, I'm not as young as I used to be! Let's just say that my wizard's Depends are off-white! Sorry, horsie!
This bloody battle presents the greatest fear that any warrior dwarf has! My last sight on Middle-earth could be a dorc's groin!
Rrrrr! Do my eyes deceive me or is that Gimmicki's twin?
That's no fat, hairy dwarf! That's the director, Peter Jackson!
I'm totally into Middle-earth! In fact, my middle *looks* like Earth! While I directed these three epics, I even learned to speak in Elvish, Sindarin, and Quenya! The only thing I never learned to say in any language is "cut"!

VRITER: DESMOND DEVLIN

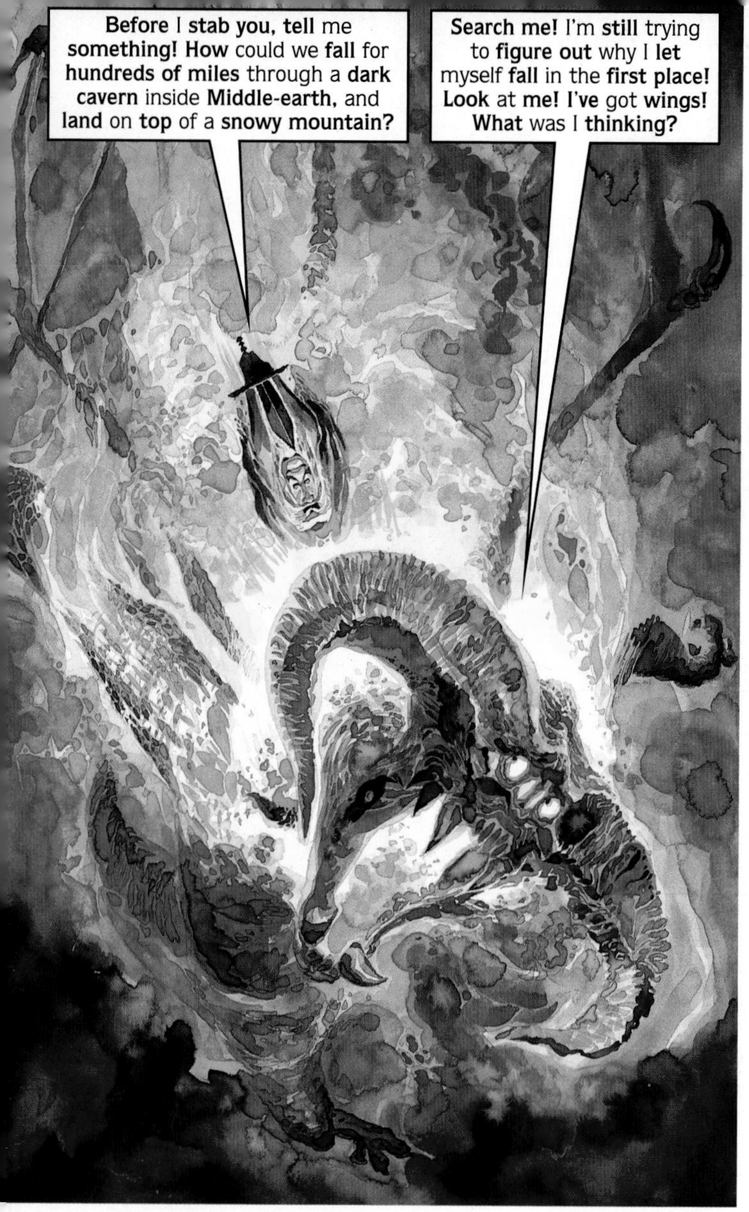
Before I stab you, tell me something! How could we fall for hundreds of miles through a dark cavern inside Middle-earth, and land on top of a snowy mountain?
Search me! I'm still trying to figure out why I let myself fall in the first place! Look at me! I've got wings! What was I thinking?

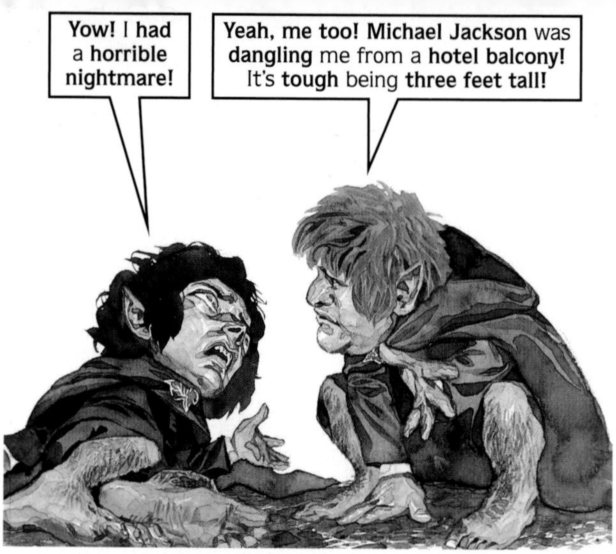
Yow! I had a horrible nightmare!
Yeah, me too! Michael Jackson was dangling me from a hotel balcony! It's tough being three feet tall!

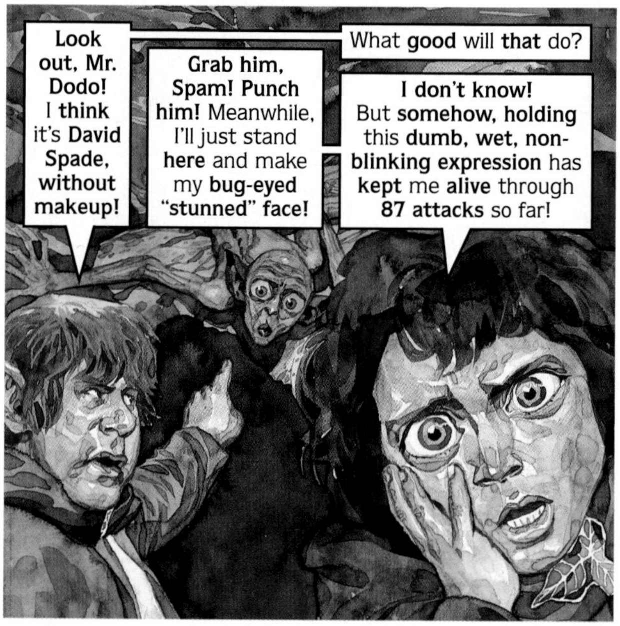
Look out, Mr. Dodo! I think it's David Spade, without makeup!
Grab him, Spam! Punch him! Meanwhile, I'll just stand here and make my bug-eyed "stunned" face!
What good will that do?
I don't know! But somehow, holding this dumb, wet, non-blinking expression has kept me alive through 87 attacks so far!

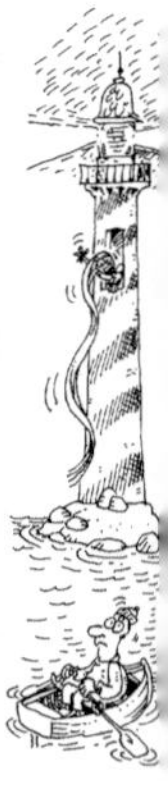

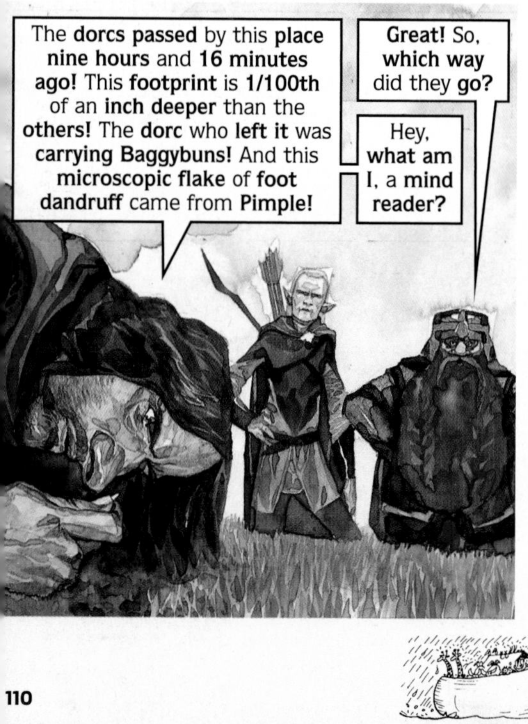
The dorcs passed by this place nine hours and 16 minutes ago! This footprint is 1/100th of an inch deeper than the others! The dorc who left it was carrying Baggybuns! And this microscopic flake of foot dandruff came from Pimple!
Great! So, which way did they go?
Hey, what am I, a mind reader?

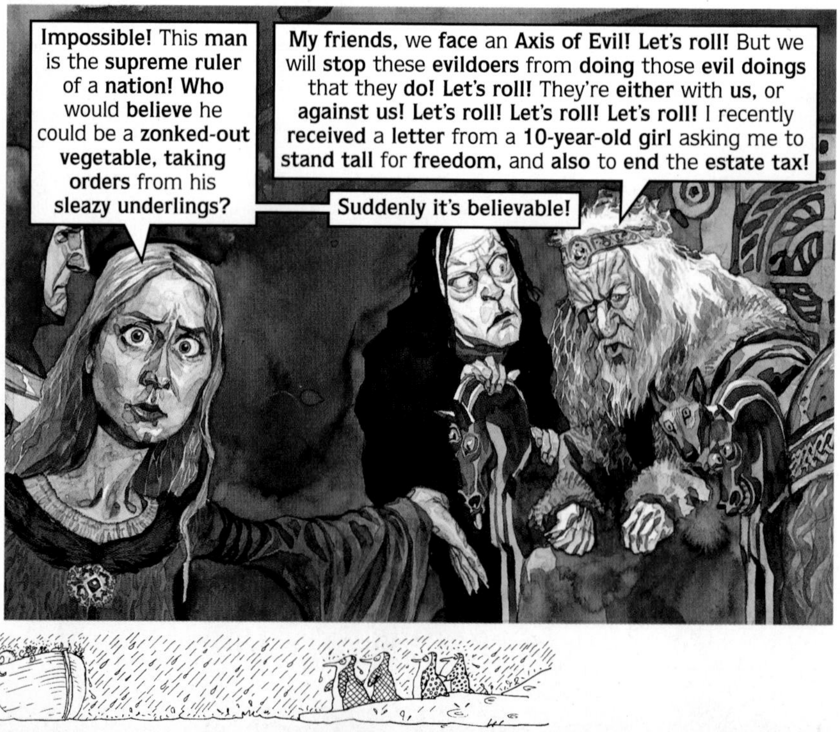
Impossible! This man is the supreme ruler of a nation! Who would believe he could be a zonked-out vegetable, taking orders from his sleazy underlings?
Suddenly it's believable!
My friends, we face an Axis of Evil! Let's roll! But we will stop these evildoers from doing those evil doings that they do! Let's roll! They're either with us, or against us! Let's roll! Let's roll! Let's roll! I recently received a letter from a 10-year-old girl asking me to stand tall for freedom, and also to end the estate tax!

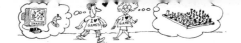

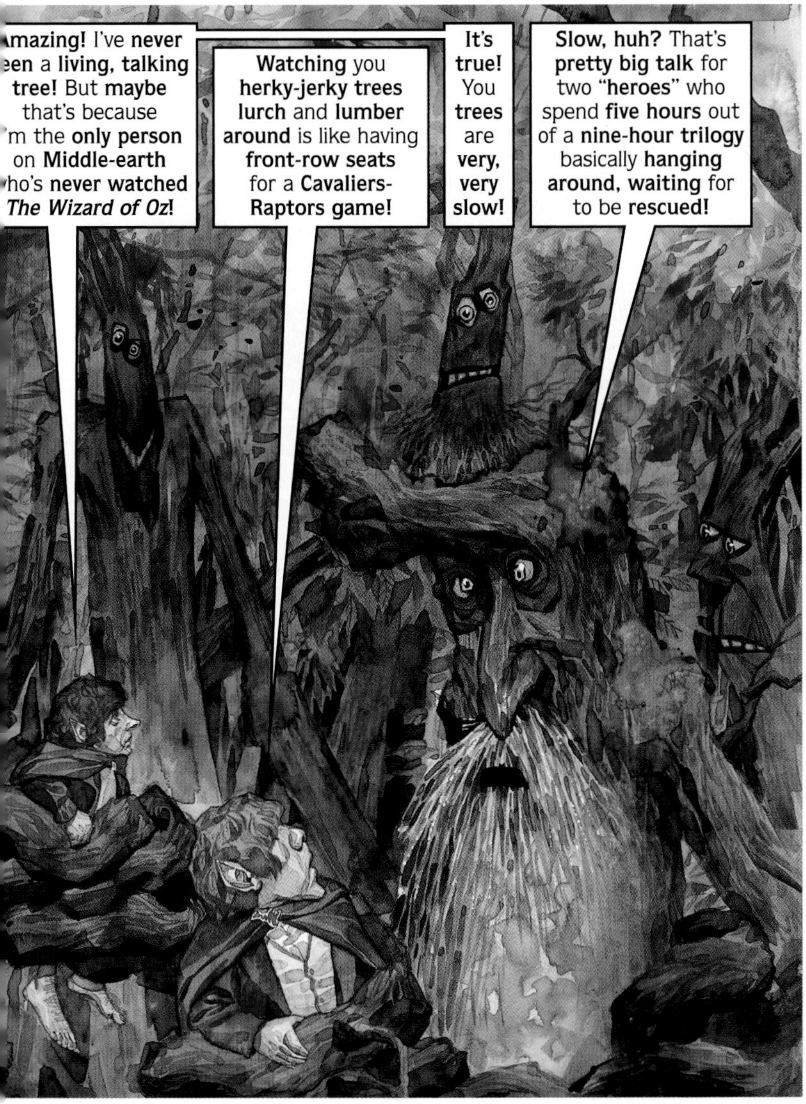
mazing! I've never een a living, talking tree! But maybe that's because 'm the only person on Middle-earth ho's never watched *The Wizard of Oz*!
Watching you herky-jerky trees lurch and lumber around is like having front-row seats for a Cavaliers-Raptors game!
It's true! You trees are very, very slow!
Slow, huh? That's pretty big talk for two "heroes" who spend five hours out of a nine-hour trilogy basically hanging around, waiting for to be rescued!

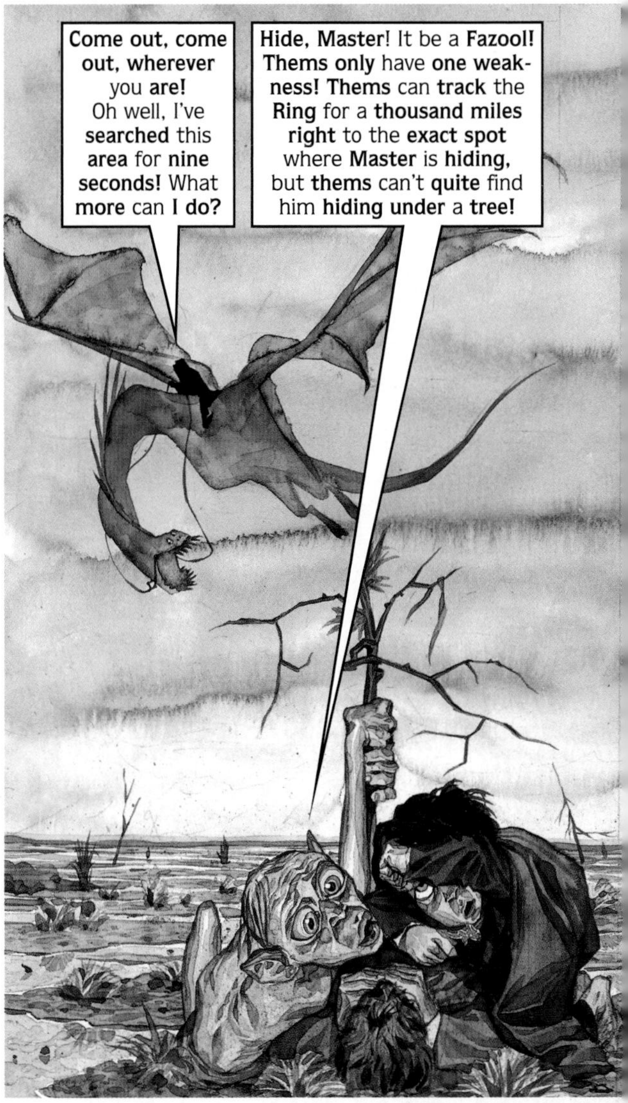
Come out, come out, wherever you are! Oh well, I've searched this area for nine seconds! What more can I do?
Hide, Master! It be a Fazool! Thems only have one weakness! Thems can track the Ring for a thousand miles right to the exact spot where Master is hiding, but thems can't quite find him hiding under a tree!

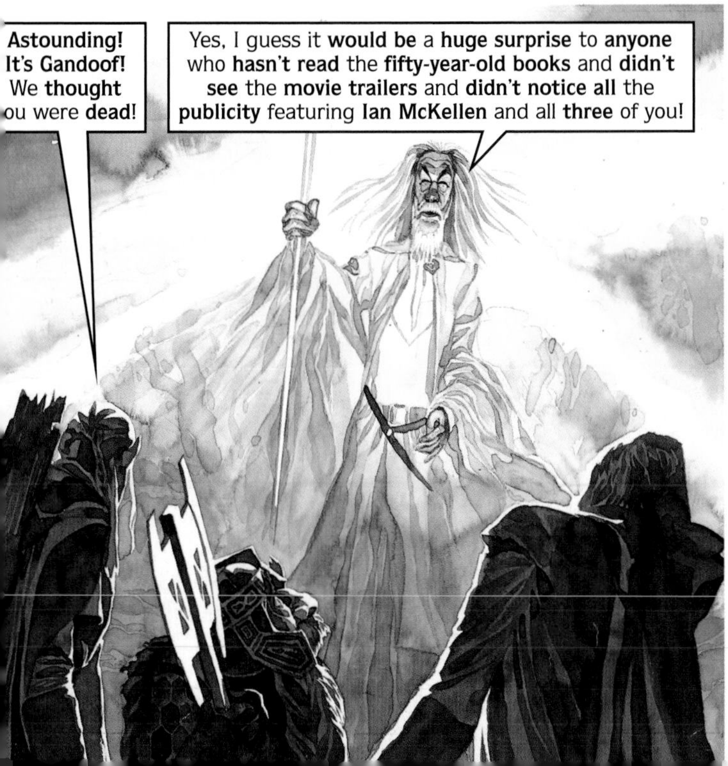
Astounding! It's Gandoof! We thought ou were dead!
Yes, I guess it would be a huge surprise to anyone who hasn't read the fifty-year-old books and didn't see the movie trailers and didn't notice all the publicity featuring Ian McKellen and all three of you!

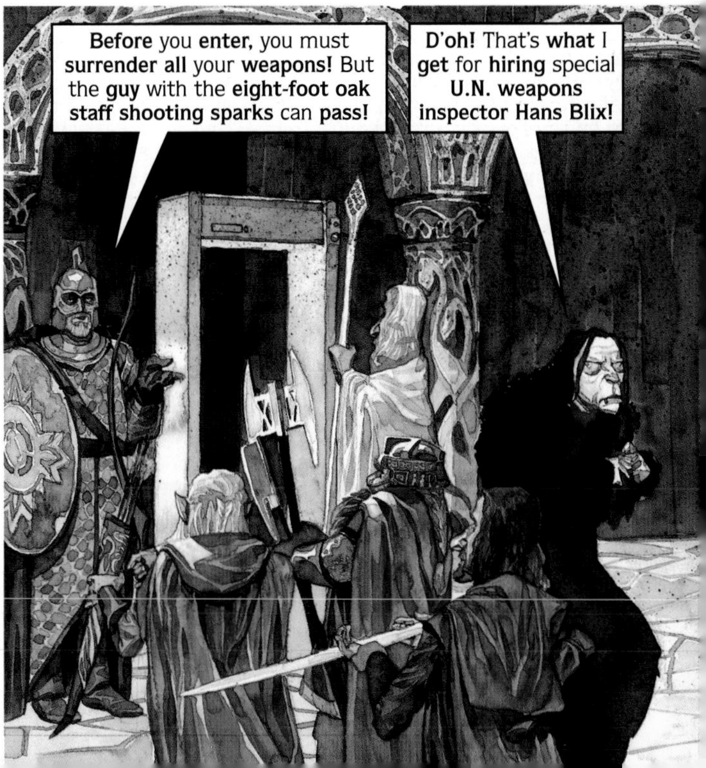
Before you enter, you must surrender all your weapons! But the guy with the eight-foot oak staff shooting sparks can pass!
D'oh! That's what I get for hiring special U.N. weapons inspector Hans Blix!

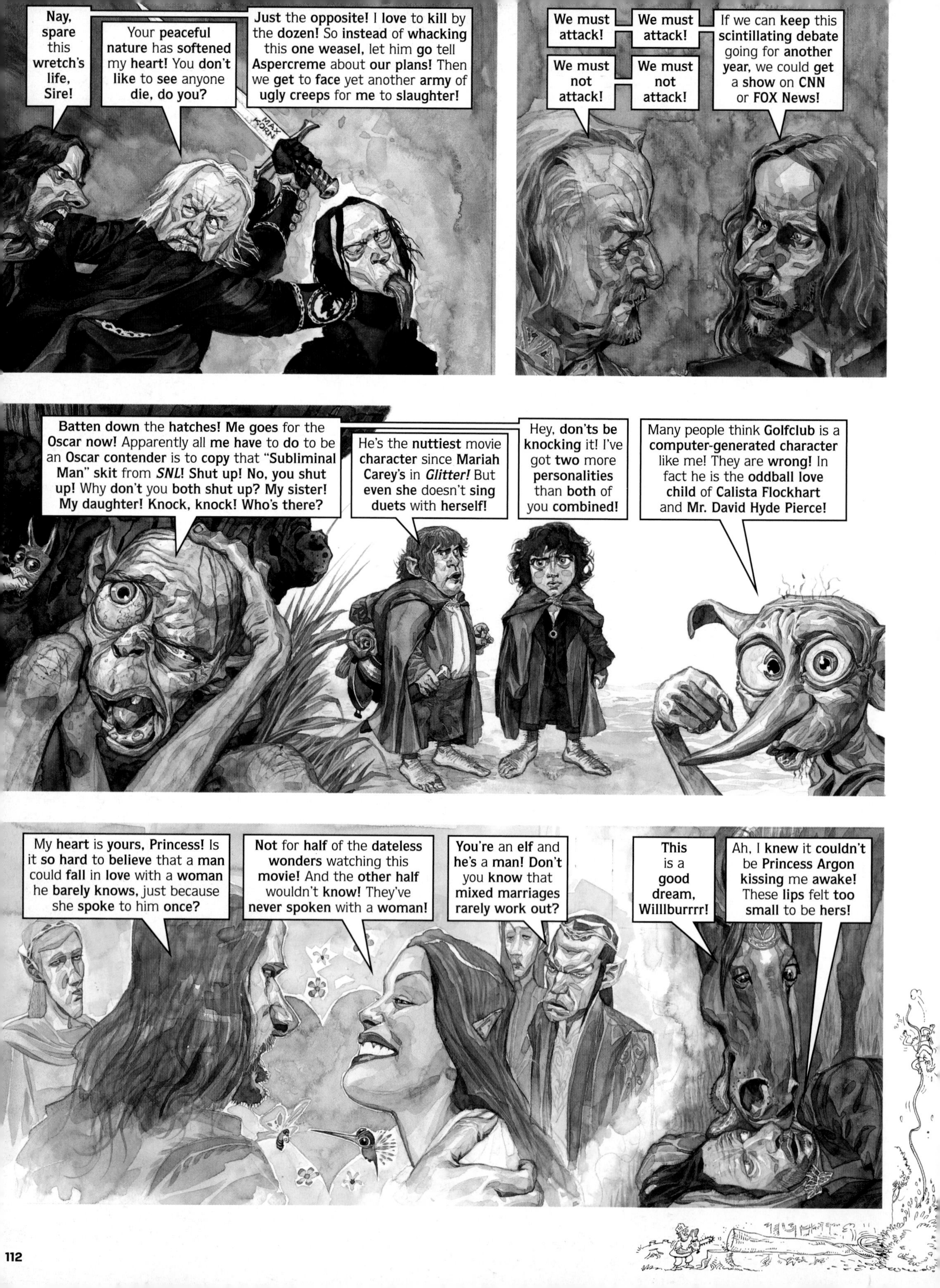

Nay, spare this wretch's life, Sire!
Your peaceful nature has softened my heart! You don't like to see anyone die, do you?
Just the opposite! I love to kill by the dozen! So instead of whacking this one weasel, let him go tell Aspercreme about our plans! Then we get to face yet another army of ugly creeps for me to slaughter!
We must attack!
We must attack!
We must not attack!
We must not attack!
If we can keep this scintillating debate going for another year, we could get a show on CNN or FOX News!
Batten down the hatches! Me goes for the Oscar now! Apparently all me have to do to be an Oscar contender is to copy that "Subliminal Man" skit from SNL! Shut up! No, you shut up! Why don't you both shut up? My sister! My daughter! Knock, knock! Who's there?
He's the nuttiest movie character since Mariah Carey's in Glitter! But even she doesn't sing duets with herself!
Hey, don'ts be knocking it! I've got two more personalities than both of you combined!
Many people think Golfclub is a computer-generated character like me! They are wrong! In fact he is the oddball love child of Calista Flockhart and Mr. David Hyde Pierce!
My heart is yours, Princess! Is it so hard to believe that a man could fall in love with a woman he barely knows, just because she spoke to him once?
Not for half of the dateless wonders watching this movie! And the other half wouldn't know! They've never spoken with a woman!
You're an elf and he's a man! Don't you know that mixed marriages rarely work out?
This is a good dream, Willlburrrr!
Ah, I knew it couldn't be Princess Argon kissing me awake! These lips felt too small to be hers!

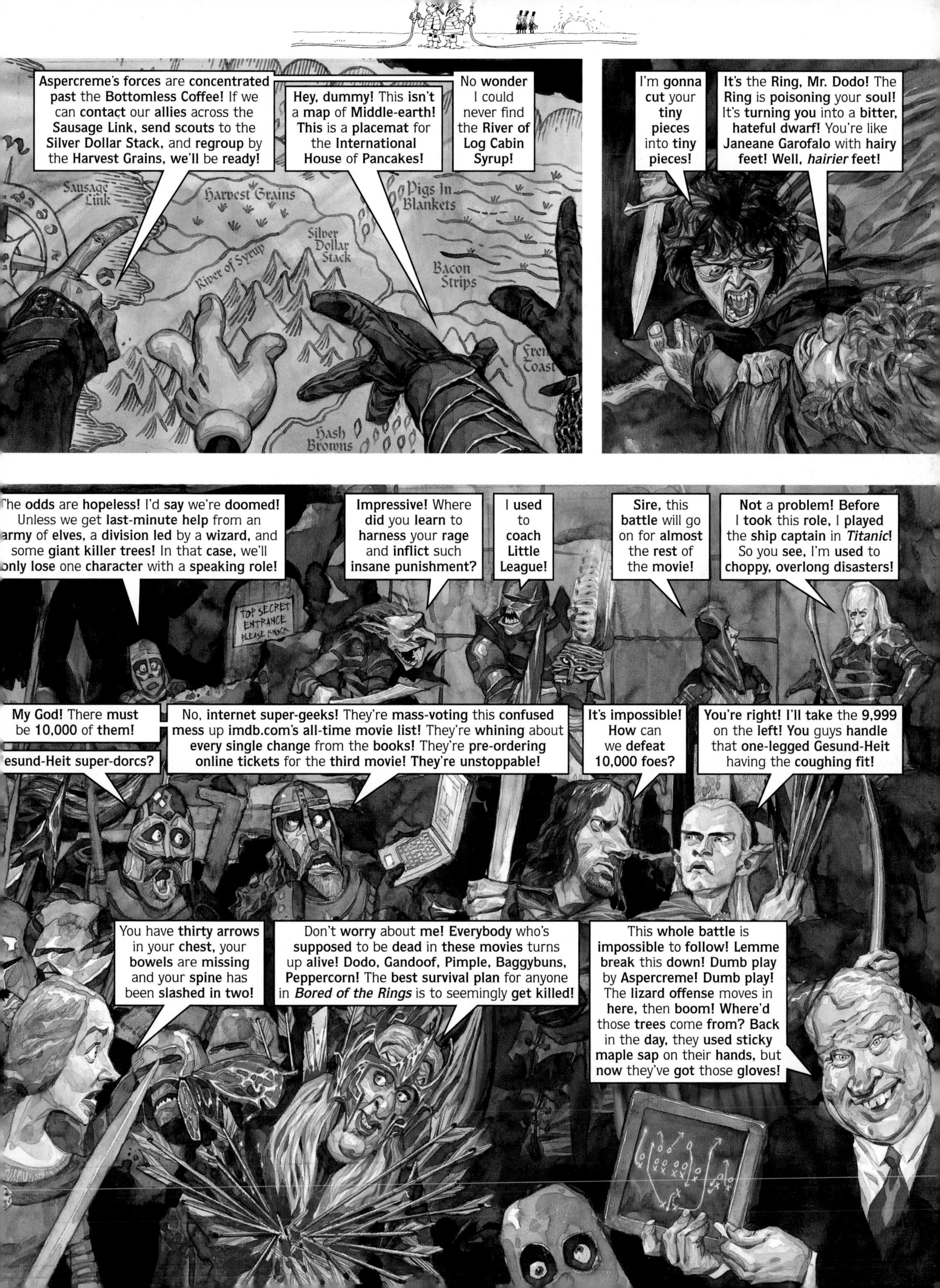

Aspercreme's forces are concentrated past the Bottomless Coffee! If we can contact our allies across the Sausage Link, send scouts to the Silver Dollar Stack, and regroup by the Harvest Grains, we'll be ready!
Hey, dummy! This isn't a map of Middle-earth! This is a placemat for the International House of Pancakes!
No wonder I could never find the River of Log Cabin Syrup!
Sausage Link
Harvest Grains
Pigs In Blankets
Silver Dollar Stack
River of Syrup
Bacon Strips
Hash Browns
I'm gonna cut your tiny pieces into tiny pieces!
It's the Ring, Mr. Dodo! The Ring is poisoning your soul! It's turning you into a bitter, hateful dwarf! You're like Janeane Garofalo with hairy feet! Well, *hairier* feet!
he odds are hopeless! I'd say we're doomed! Unless we get last-minute help from an rmy of elves, a division led by a wizard, and some giant killer trees! In that case, we'll nly lose one character with a speaking role!
Impressive! Where did you learn to harness your rage and inflict such insane punishment?
I used to coach Little League!
Sire, this battle will go on for almost the rest of the movie!
Not a problem! Before I took this role, I played the ship captain in *Titanic*! So you see, I'm used to choppy, overlong disasters!
TOP SECRET ENTRANCE PLEASE KNOCK
My God! There must be 10,000 of them! esund-Heit super-dorcs?
No, internet super-geeks! They're mass-voting this confused mess up imdb.com's all-time movie list! They're whining about every single change from the books! They're pre-ordering online tickets for the third movie! They're unstoppable!
It's impossible! How can we defeat 10,000 foes?
You're right! I'll take the 9,999 on the left! You guys handle that one-legged Gesund-Heit having the coughing fit!
You have thirty arrows in your chest, your bowels are missing and your spine has been slashed in two!
Don't worry about me! Everybody who's supposed to be dead in these movies turns up alive! Dodo, Gandoof, Pimple, Baggybuns, Peppercorn! The best survival plan for anyone in *Bored of the Rings* is to seemingly get killed!
This whole battle is impossible to follow! Lemme break this down! Dumb play by Aspercreme! Dumb play! The lizard offense moves in here, then boom! Where'd those trees come from? Back in the day, they used sticky maple sap on their hands, but now they've got those gloves!

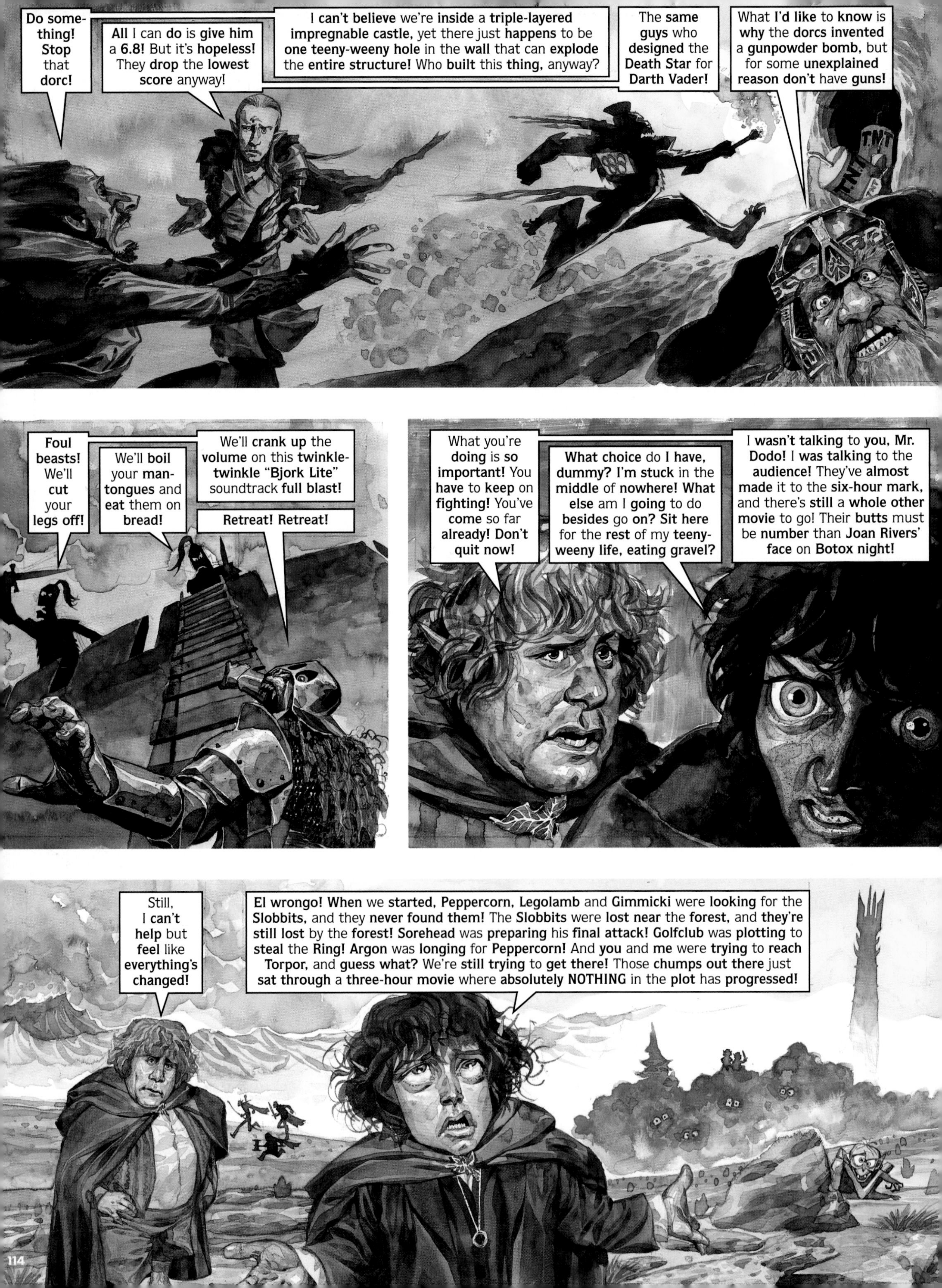
Do something! Stop that dorc!
All I can do is give him a 6.8! But it's hopeless! They drop the lowest score anyway!
I can't believe we're inside a triple-layered impregnable castle, yet there just happens to be one teeny-weeny hole in the wall that can explode the entire structure! Who built this thing, anyway?
The same guys who designed the Death Star for Darth Vader!
What I'd like to know is why the dorcs invented a gunpowder bomb, but for some unexplained reason don't have guns!
TNT
Foul beasts! We'll cut your legs off!
We'll boil your man-tongues and eat them on bread!
We'll crank up the volume on this twinkle-twinkle "Bjork Lite" soundtrack full blast!
Retreat! Retreat!
What you're doing is so important! You have to keep on fighting! You've come so far already! Don't quit now!
What choice do I have, dummy? I'm stuck in the middle of nowhere! What else am I going to do besides go on? Sit here for the rest of my teeny-weeny life, eating gravel?
I wasn't talking to you, Mr. Dodo! I was talking to the audience! They've almost made it to the six-hour mark, and there's still a whole other movie to go! Their butts must be number than Joan Rivers' face on Botox night!
Still, I can't help but feel like everything's changed!
El wrongo! When we started, Peppercorn, Legolamb and Gimmicki were looking for the Slobbits, and they never found them! The Slobbits were lost near the forest, and they're still lost by the forest! Sorehead was preparing his final attack! Golfclub was plotting to steal the Ring! Argon was longing for Peppercorn! And you and me were trying to reach Torpor, and guess what? We're still trying to get there! Those chumps out there just sat through a three-hour movie where absolutely NOTHING in the plot has progressed!

STILL MORE

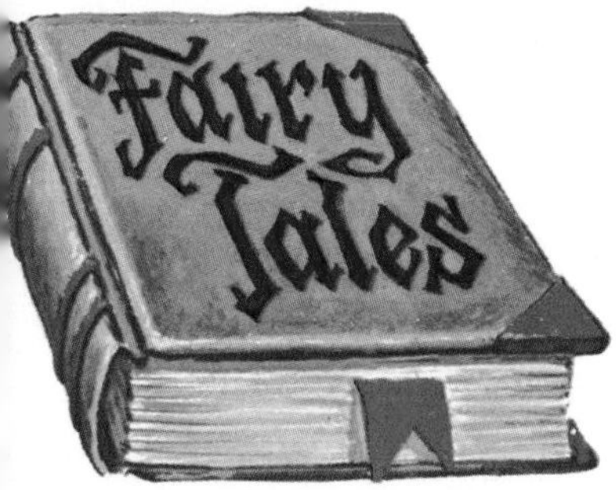
Fairy Tales

SCENES WE'D LIKE TO SEE

(RAPUNZEL)

ARTIST & WRITER:
DON MARTIN

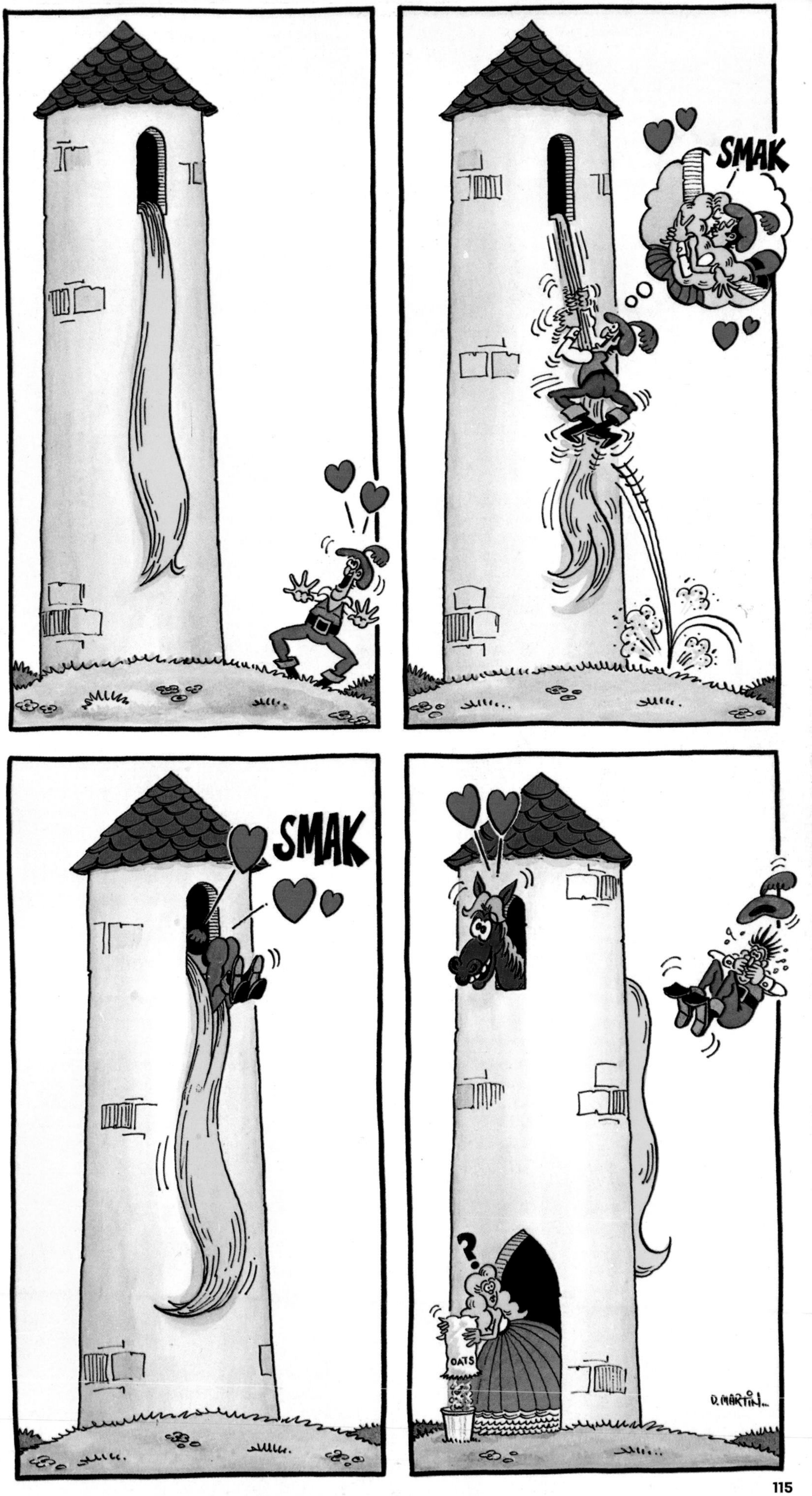
SMAK
SMAK
OATS

SCREAM GEMS DEPT.

The worst things about vacations is when **YOU** go on them . . . and then subject **US** to that most sadistic of all torture devices: **Your "HOME MOVIES" of them!** And so, not to be outdone, we now take sweet revenge by subjecting **YOU** to . . .

MAD'S

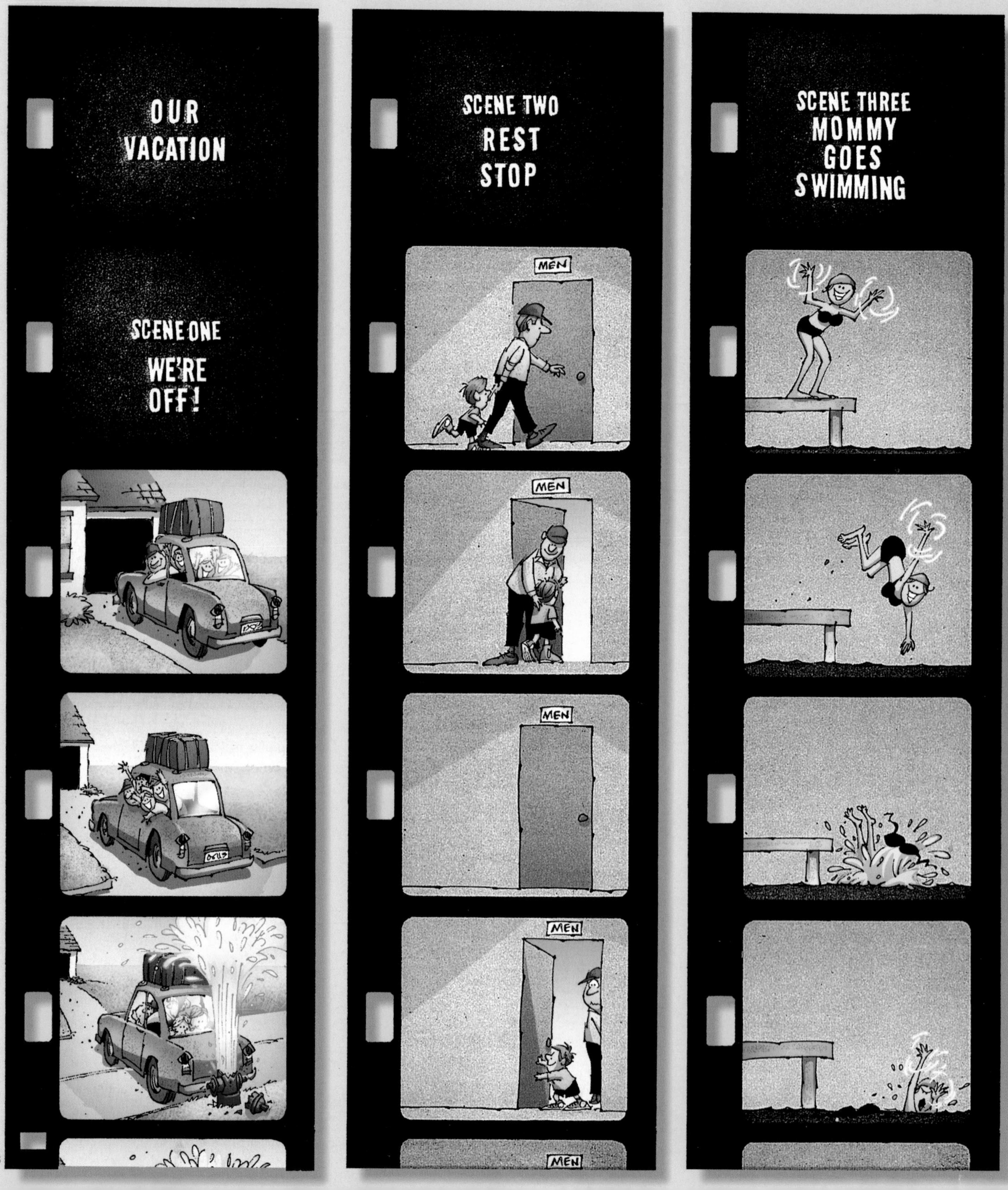

OUR VACATION
SCENE ONE
WE'RE OFF!
SCENE TWO
REST STOP
MEN
MEN
MEN
MEN
MEN
SCENE THREE
MOMMY GOES SWIMMING

HOME MOVIES

WRITER: DEAN NORMAN ARTIST: PAUL COKER, JR. COLORIST: CARRIE STRACHAN

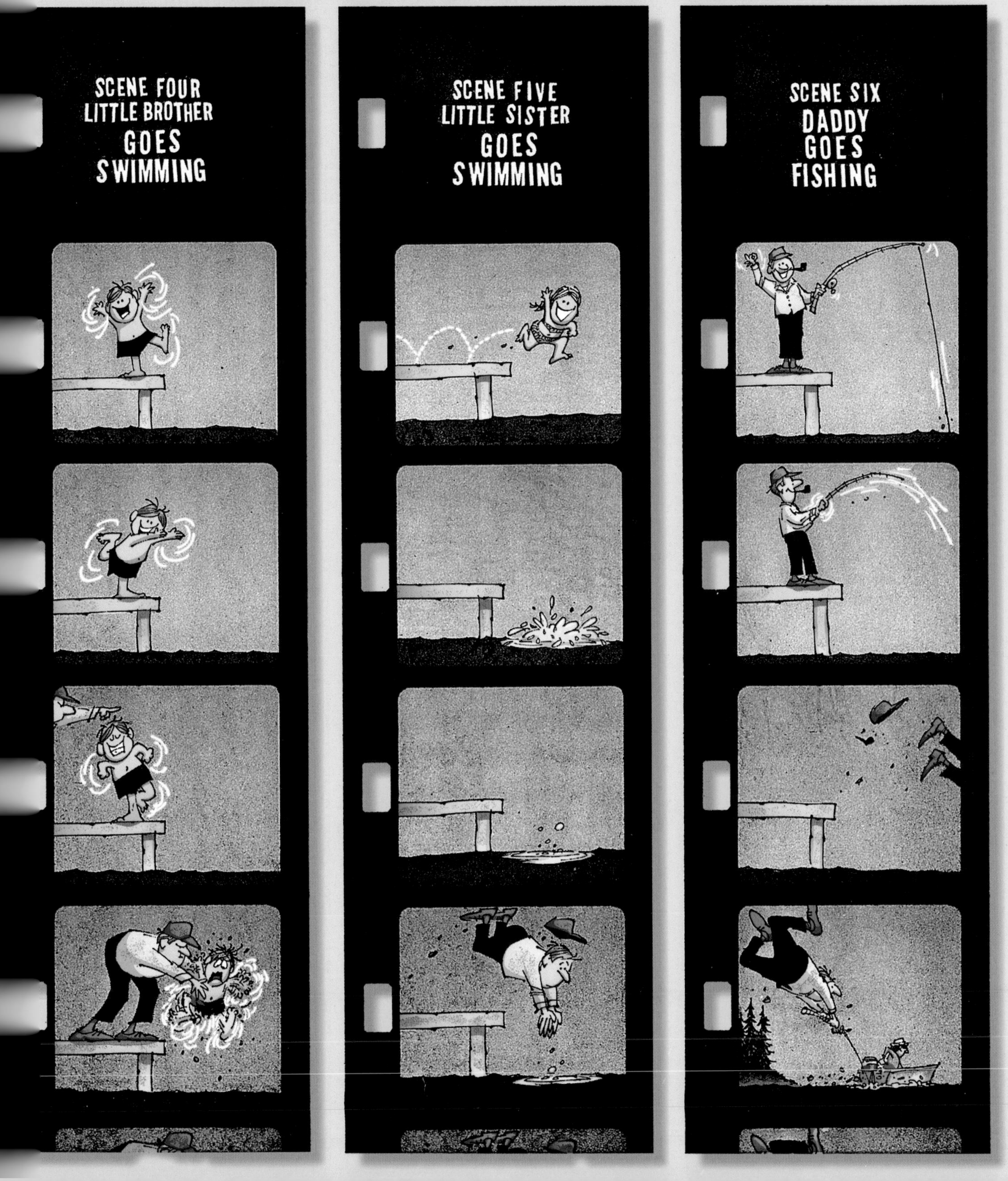
SCENE FOUR LITTLE BROTHER GOES SWIMMING
SCENE FIVE LITTLE SISTER GOES SWIMMING
SCENE SIX DADDY GOES FISHING

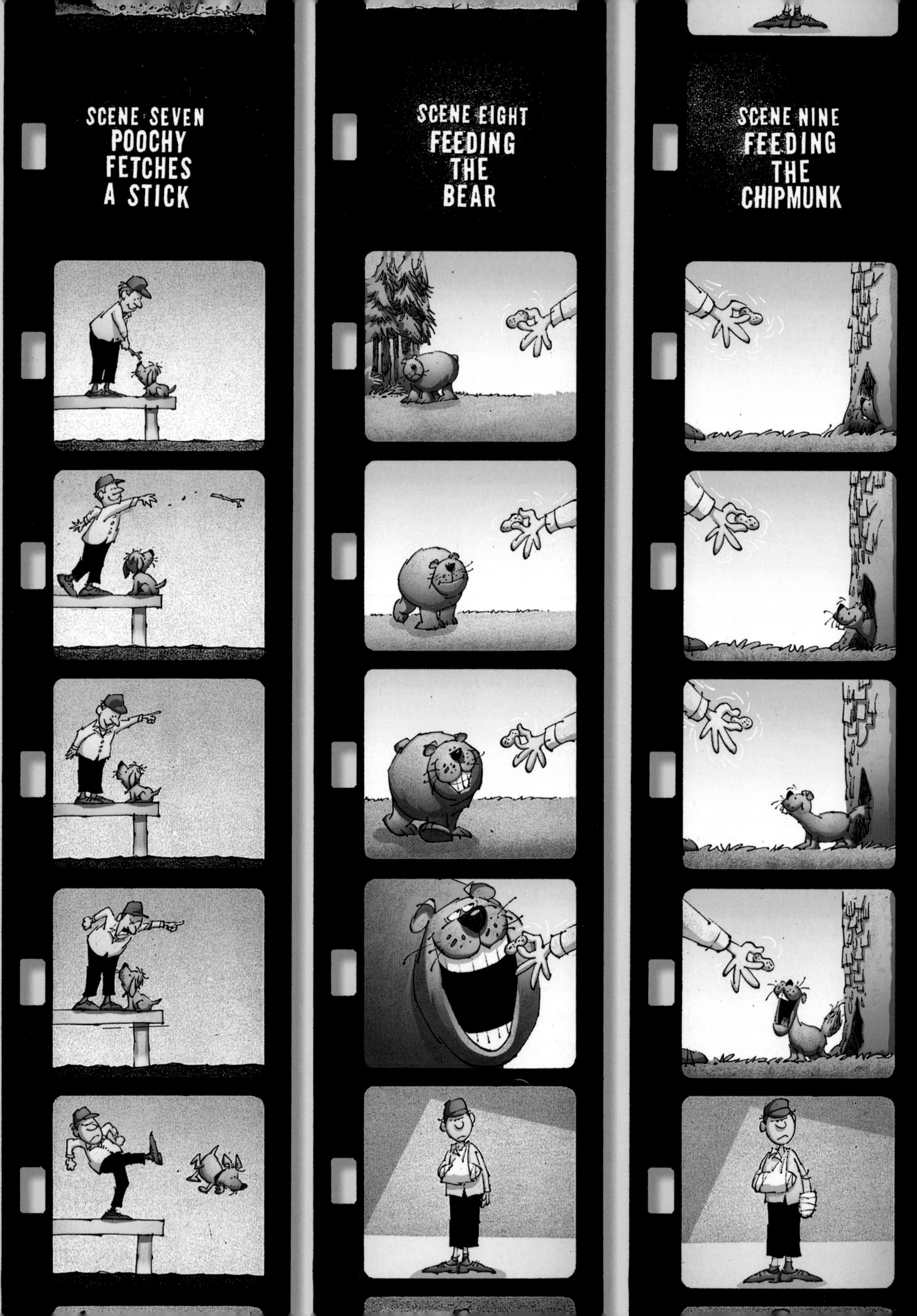
SCENE SEVEN
POOCHY FETCHES A STICK
SCENE EIGHT
FEEDING THE BEAR
SCENE NINE
FEEDING THE CHIPMUNK

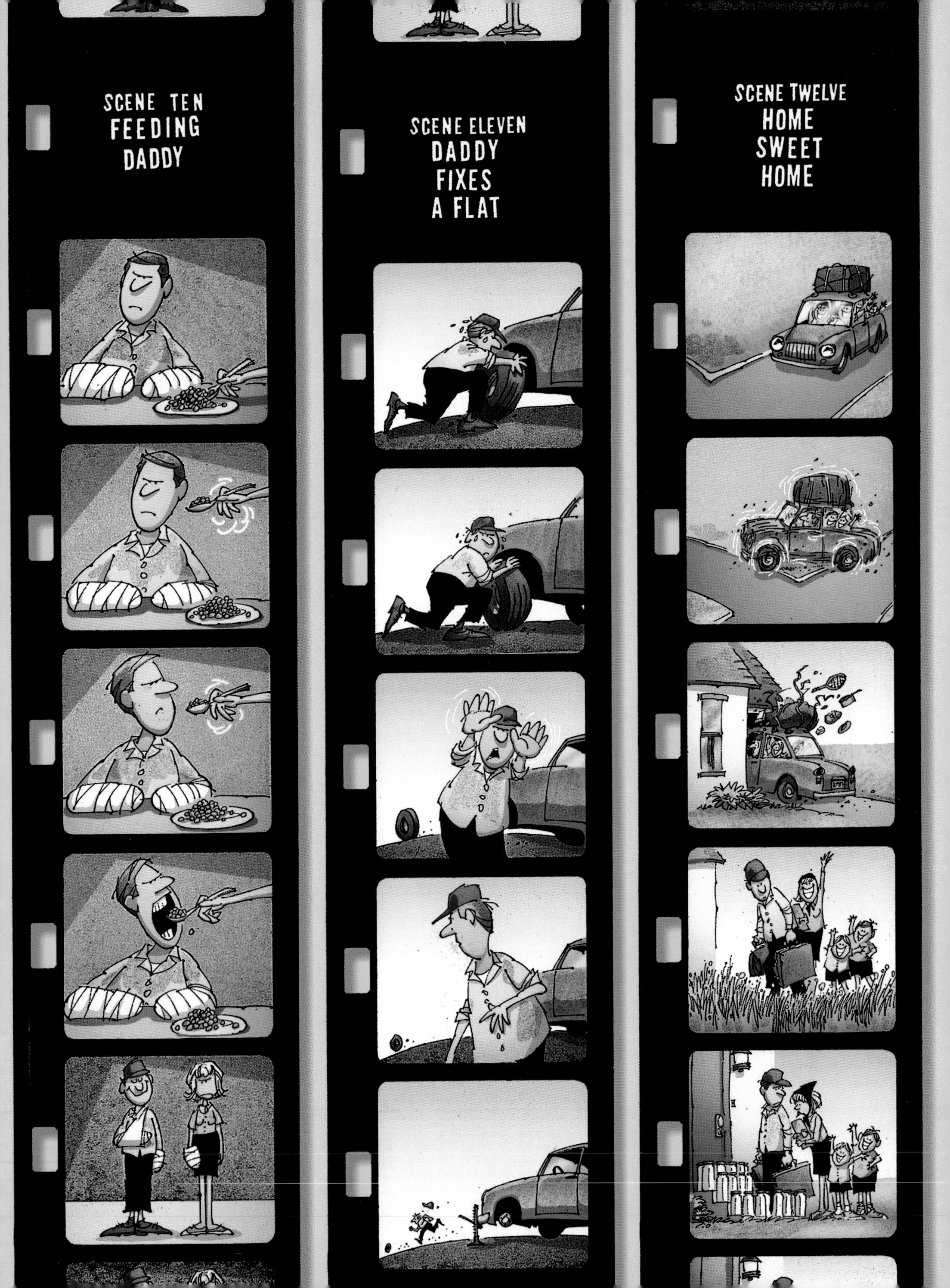
SCENE TEN
FEEDING DADDY
SCENE ELEVEN
DADDY FIXES A FLAT
SCENE TWELVE
HOME SWEET HOME

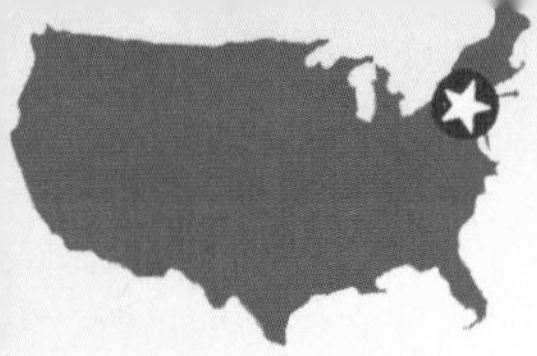

PHILADELPHIA, PA. — August 9

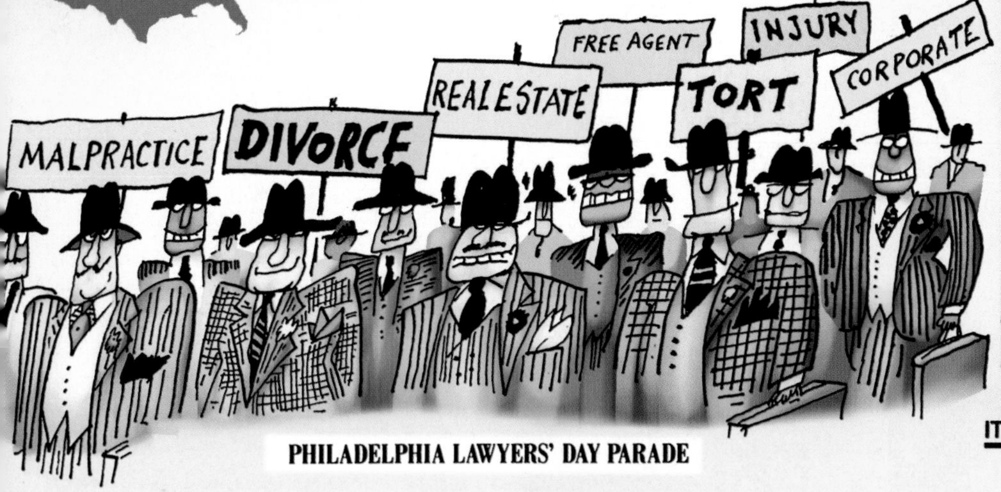
MALPRACTICE
DIVORCE
REAL ESTATE
FREE AGENT
TORT
INJURY
CORPORATE

PHILADELPHIA LAWYERS' DAY PARADE

SUN CITY, ARIZONA—Second Sund

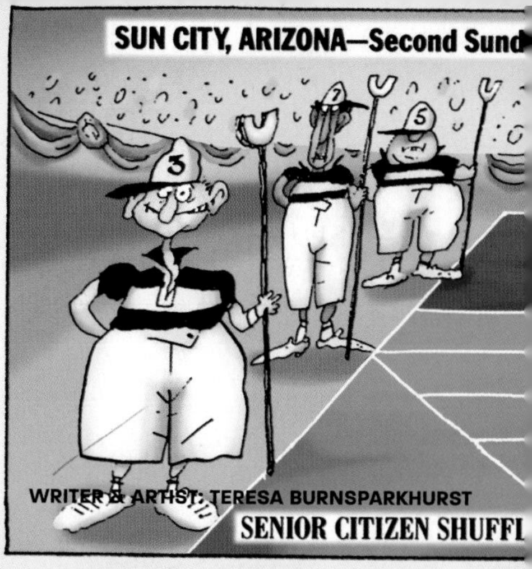

WRITER & ARTIST: TERESA BURNSPARKHURST

SENIOR CITIZEN SHUFFL

IT WAS THE FESTIVE TIMES...DEPT.

REGI CELEBR

YOU R HEAR

WRITER AND ARTIST: PAUL PETER PORGES

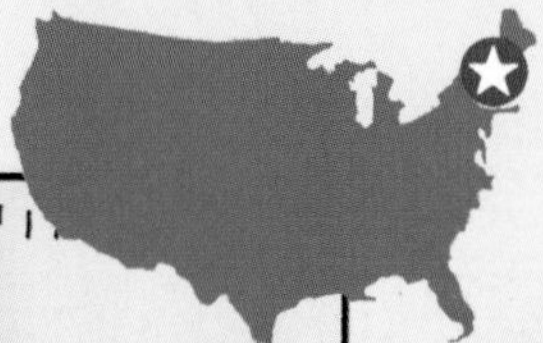

ANDOVER, MASS—April 15

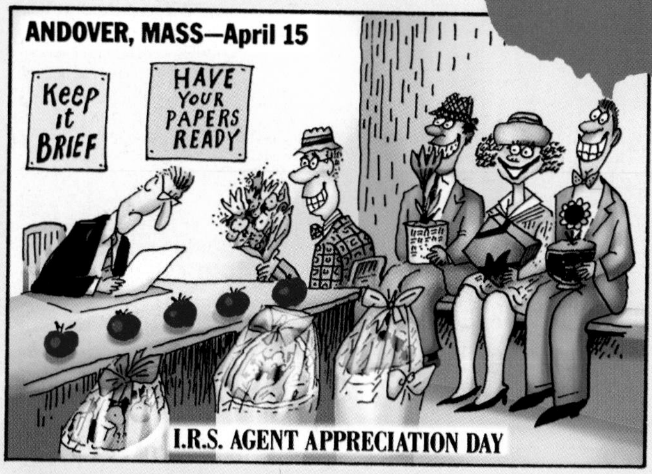
Keep it BRIEF
HAVE YOUR PAPERS READY

I.R.S. AGENT APPRECIATION DAY

BUFFALO, NEW YORK—December 13

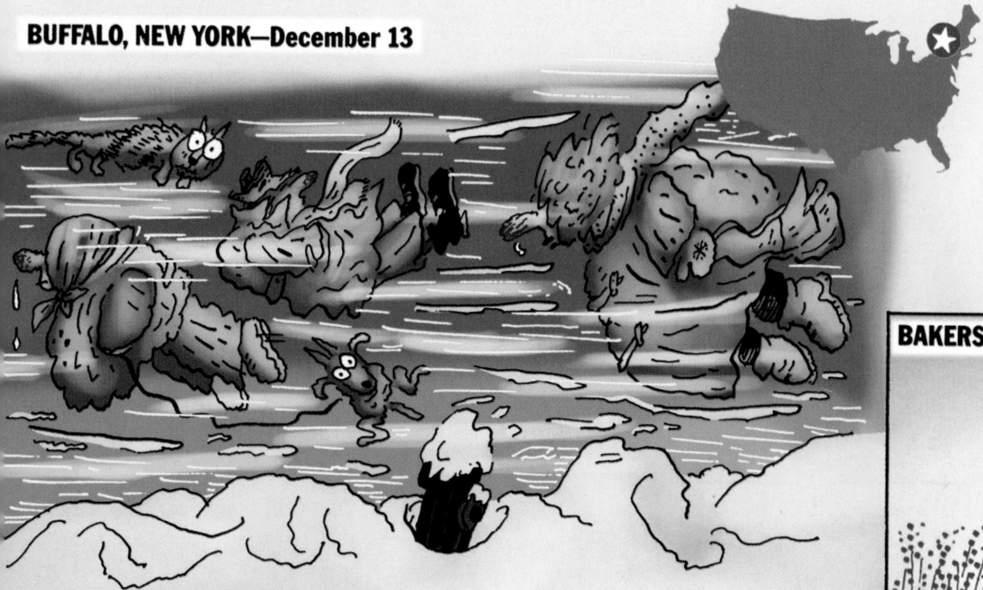

WIND CHILL FACTOR NIGHT

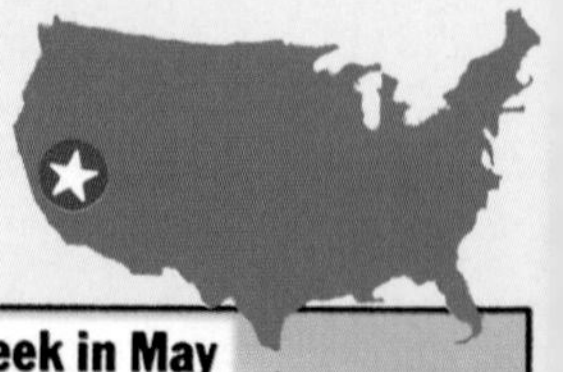

BAKERSFIELD, CA.—First week in May

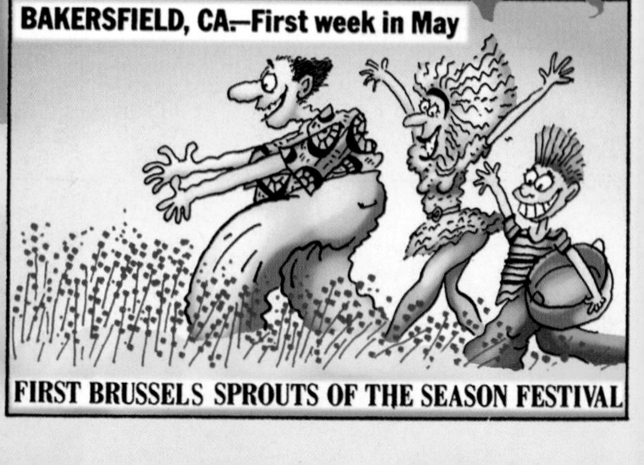

FIRST BRUSSELS SPROUTS OF THE SEASON FESTIVAL

ovember

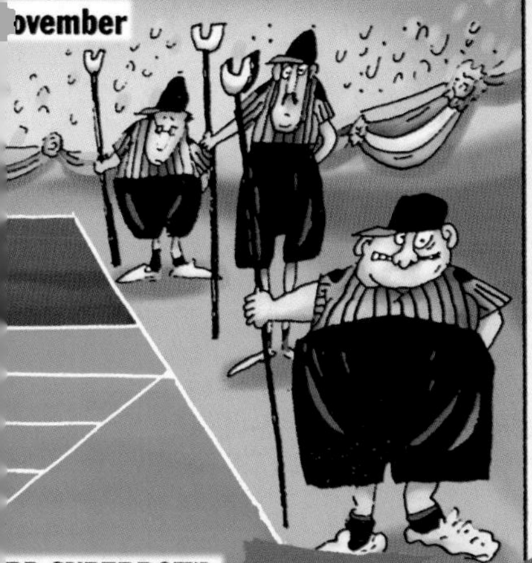

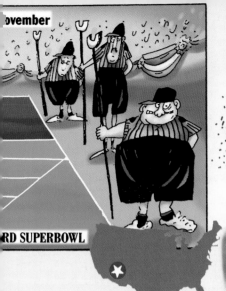

RD SUPERBOWL

EAST RUTHERFORD, NEW JERSEY—July 30

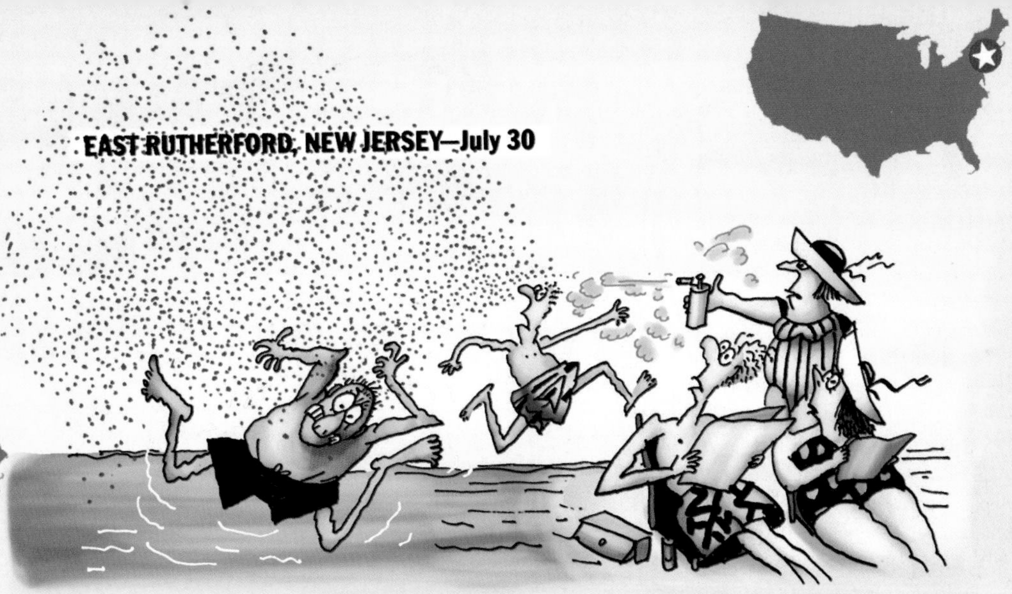

ANNUAL RETURN OF THE SECAUCUS MOSQUITO HORDES

ONAL
ATIONS
ARELY
ABOUT

SAN FRANCISCO, CALIFORNIA—September 27

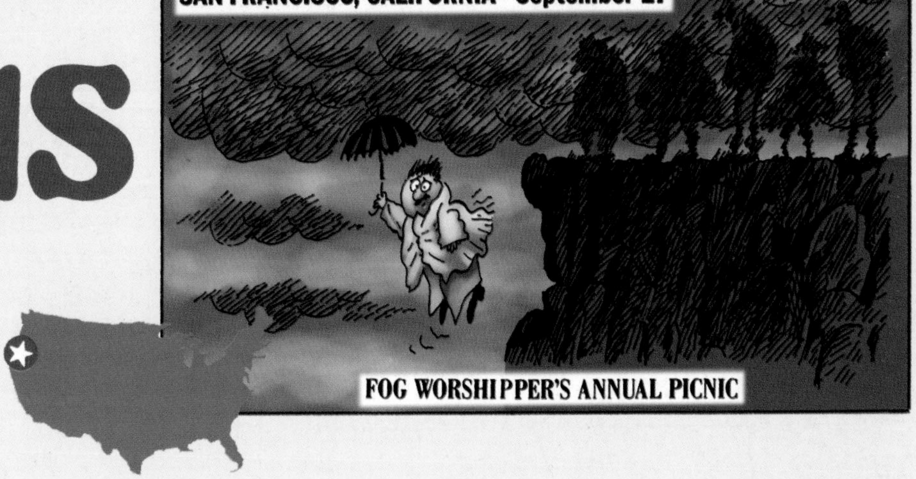

FOG WORSHIPPER'S ANNUAL PICNIC

LORIST: CARRIE STRACHAN

NEW YORK CITY—Date varies

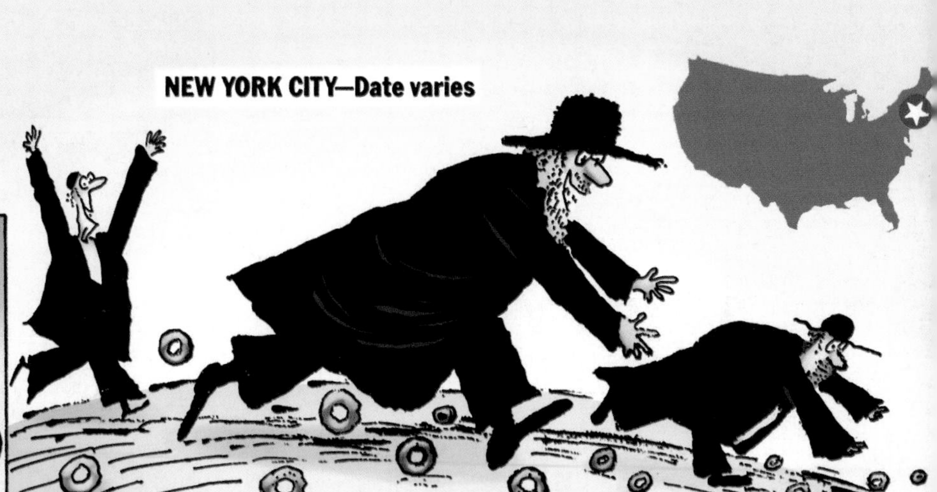
PORGES

CENTRAL PARK PRE-PASSOVER BAGEL ROLL

ALBUQUERQUE, NEW MEXICO—June 7-14th

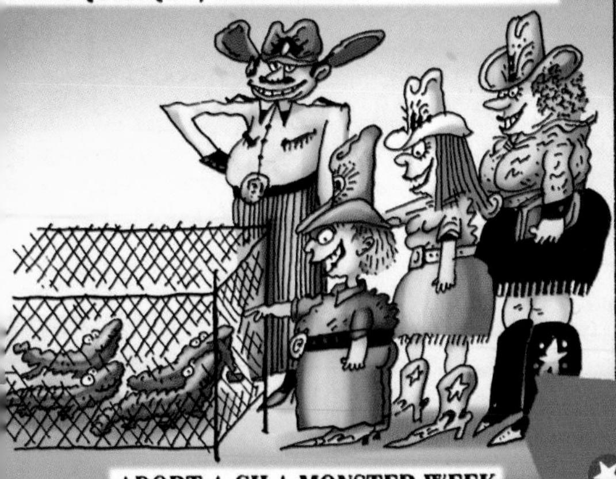

ADOPT A GILA MONSTER WEEK

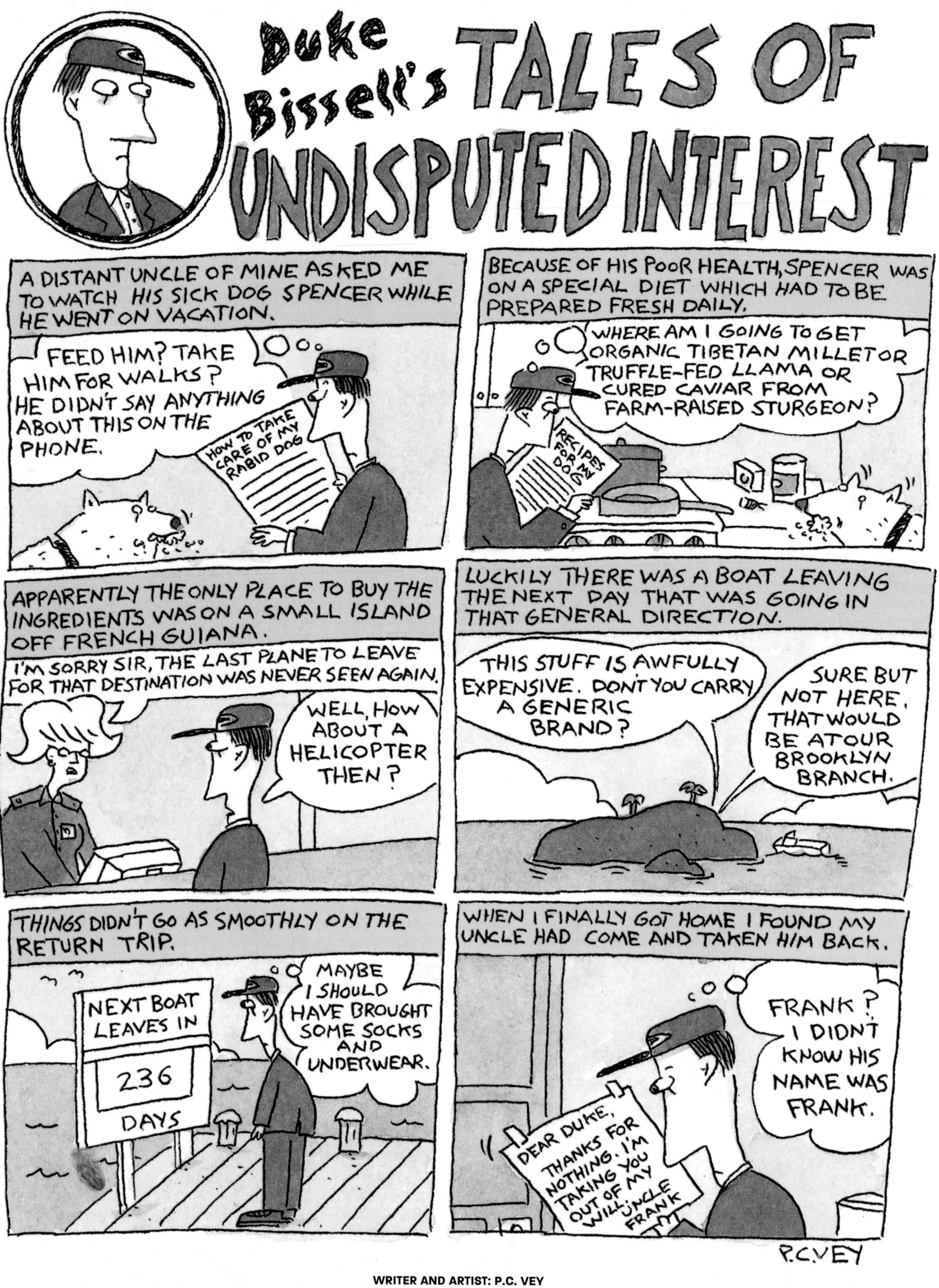
Duke Bissell's TALES OF UNDISPUTED INTEREST
A DISTANT UNCLE OF MINE ASKED ME TO WATCH HIS SICK DOG SPENCER WHILE HE WENT ON VACATION.
FEED HIM? TAKE HIM FOR WALKS? HE DIDN'T SAY ANYTHING ABOUT THIS ON THE PHONE.
HOW TO TAKE CARE OF MY RABID DOG
BECAUSE OF HIS POOR HEALTH, SPENCER WAS ON A SPECIAL DIET WHICH HAD TO BE PREPARED FRESH DAILY.
WHERE AM I GOING TO GET ORGANIC TIBETAN MILLET OR TRUFFLE-FED LLAMA OR CURED CAVIAR FROM FARM-RAISED STURGEON?
RECIPES FOR MY DOG
APPARENTLY THE ONLY PLACE TO BUY THE INGREDIENTS WAS ON A SMALL ISLAND OFF FRENCH GUIANA.
I'M SORRY SIR, THE LAST PLANE TO LEAVE FOR THAT DESTINATION WAS NEVER SEEN AGAIN.
WELL, HOW ABOUT A HELICOPTER THEN?
LUCKILY THERE WAS A BOAT LEAVING THE NEXT DAY THAT WAS GOING IN THAT GENERAL DIRECTION.
THIS STUFF IS AWFULLY EXPENSIVE. DON'T YOU CARRY A GENERIC BRAND?
SURE BUT NOT HERE. THAT WOULD BE AT OUR BROOKLYN BRANCH.
THINGS DIDN'T GO AS SMOOTHLY ON THE RETURN TRIP.
NEXT BOAT LEAVES IN 236 DAYS
MAYBE I SHOULD HAVE BROUGHT SOME SOCKS AND UNDERWEAR.
WHEN I FINALLY GOT HOME I FOUND MY UNCLE HAD COME AND TAKEN HIM BACK.
DEAR DUKE, THANKS FOR NOTHING. I'M TAKING YOU OUT OF MY WILL. UNCLE FRANK
FRANK? I DIDN'T KNOW HIS NAME WAS FRANK.
P.C. VEY

WRITER AND ARTIST: P.C. VEY

WHAT KIND OF BODY SCANNING IS CAUSING PEOPLE TO WASTE COUNTLESS HOURS?

HERE WE GO WITH ANOTHER RIDICULOUS

MAD FOLD-IN

There's a disturbing new movement that's caught the public's attention. A new innovation like this may seem like a good idea, but it's forcing people to endure awkward — even embarrassing — new activities, and it's a change that comes with a hefty price! So far, there's been an active response, as more and more people stand up for themselves.

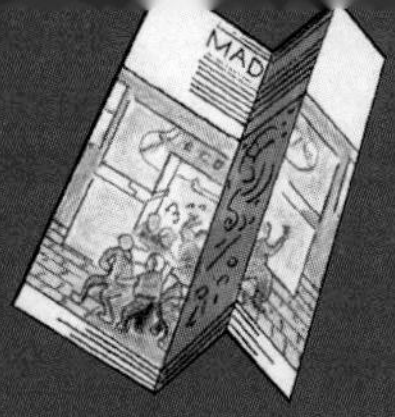

MAD

FOLD PAGE OVER LIKE THIS!

A ▶ FOLD PAGE OVER LEFT ◀ B FOLD BACK SO THAT "A" MEETS "B"

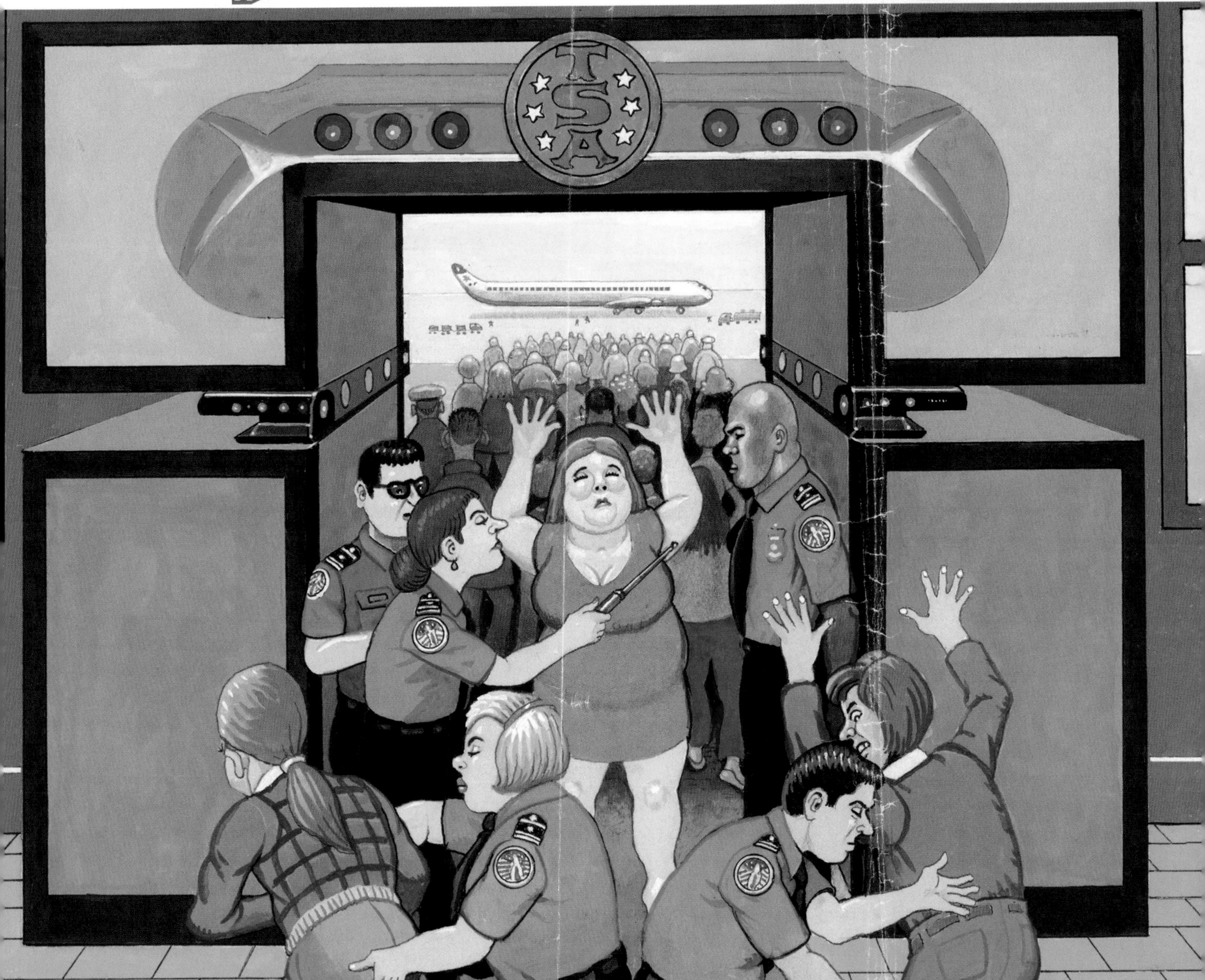

T
S
A

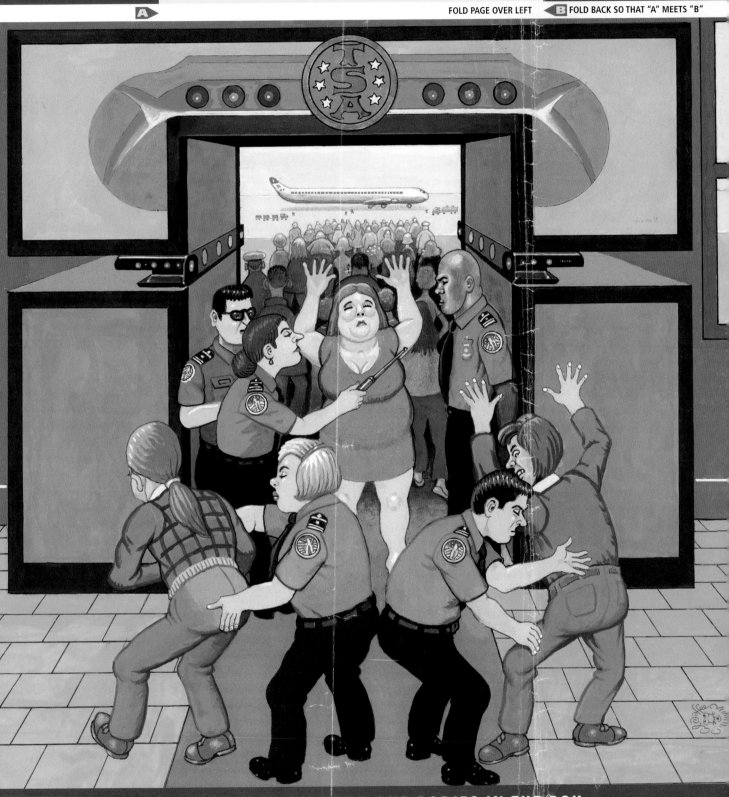

X-RAYS SURGE THROUGH OUR BODIES IN THE BOX -LIKE SCANNING DEVICES. WE'RE ASKED TO KINDLY COOPERATE SINCE IT IS US THEY PROTECT

A ▶ ◀ B

WRITER AND ARTIST: AL JAFFEE

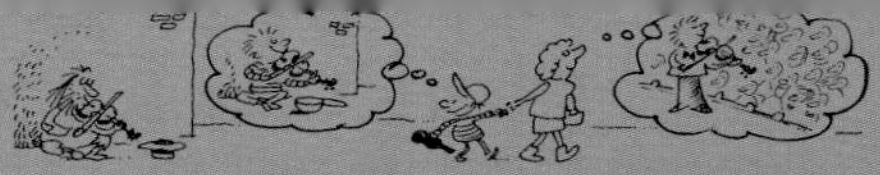

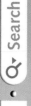

Planet TAD!!!!!

http://www.galaxyo'blogs.com/planettad

Search

Planet TAD!!!!!

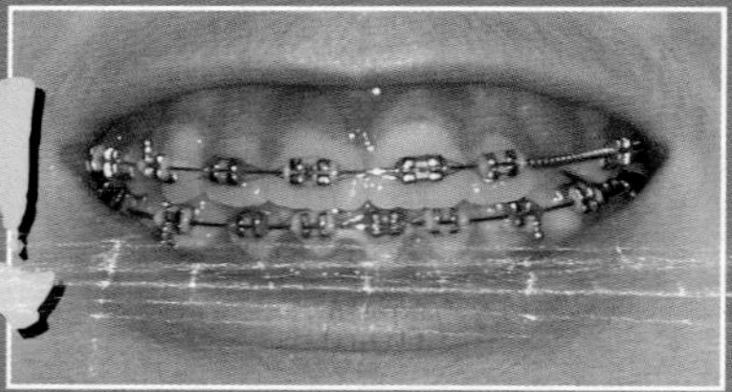

[**About Me**]

[**Name**|Tad]
[**Age**|Old enough to get a job, apparently]
[**Allergies**|Penicillin, Geometry]

[1 July|**12:17pm**]

[**mood**| miserable]

Summer sucks. Most of my friends have left town, and I waited too long to apply for summer jobs and now there aren't any left. Which means that not only don't I have any money to go do anything, but also that my parents keep coming up with chores for me to do when they're at work, "since you're not doing anything."

Still, it could be worse. My little sister Sophie is at math camp. I can't imagine anything could be worse than math camp. I think anytime you're required to show up with a calculator, it shouldn't even be called "camp" anymore.

[2 July|**02:44pm**]

I feel kind of sorry for Shia LaBeouf, because I bet that even now, a day doesn't go by when he doesn't have to go, "No, it's L-A-B-E-O-U-F."

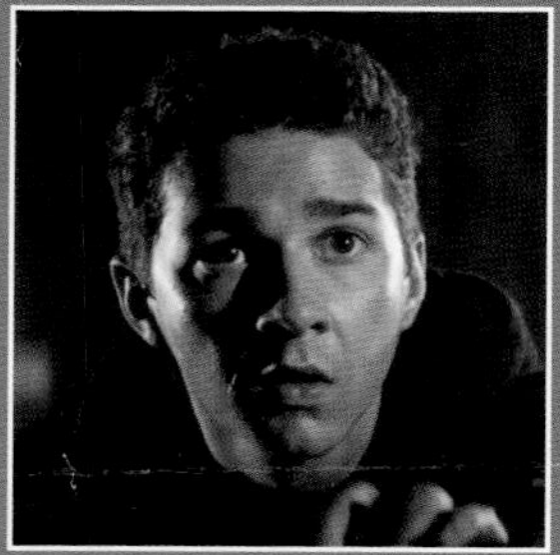

[4 July|**06:12pm**]

[**mood**| annoyed]

My parents made me clean all the gutters on the house today. I tried pointing out to them that today's Independence Day, and isn't that the day when we celebrate our independence from having to do stuff we don't want to do? And my dad said no, it's the day when Americans celebrate our independence from having leaves in our gutters, so I'd better get to it. And then my parents both laughed.

[6 July|**03:37pm**]

[**mood**| happy]

Hurray! I was out mowing our lawn today, and some woman was driving by and asked me how much I charge per lawn. I guess she thought I was some sort of lawn-mowing service. I tried to think fast, and told her $15. She said, "Wow! $15? That's so cheap!" And then she hired me to mow her lawn.

So, the good news is, someone's going to pay me for the chores my parents have been making me do for free.

Although the bad news is, I really, really wish I'd said $25.

[8 July|**08:50pm**]

I mowed that lady's lawn today, and she seemed pretty happy with it. She said she had some other friends who need yardwork done, and she asked if she could give them my number. I told her yes. Then I started thinking that I could turn this into an actual business, so I decided to make some signs to advertise my service. It took a few tries.

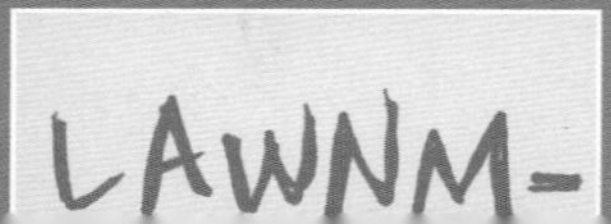
LAWNM-

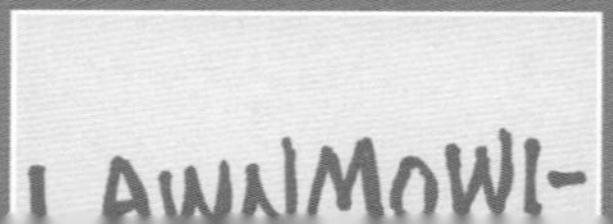
LAWNMOWI-

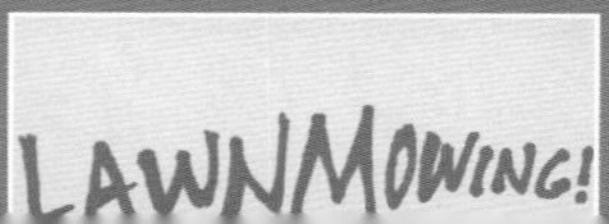
LAWNMOWING!

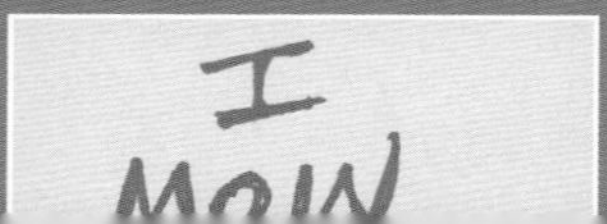
I

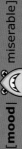

$15
CALL TAD!
TAD! ($15!)

"Lawnmowing" is really a much longer word than you would think it is. Anyway, I took the money she paid me, went to Kinko's, and made a bunch of copies.

[15 July|**11:06am**]

[**mood**| sore]

Here's what I've learned in a week of mowing lawns:

1. Mosquito repellent doesn't work.
2. If you're applying sunscreen, it's really important to do it evenly. Otherwise, you'll wind up with a big red splotch on your face, and your mom and dad will spend a whole dinner trying to figure out what country it's shaped like, no matter how many times you ask them to stop.
3. After you've been doing it for a week, mowing lawns makes your back super-sore.
4. Some people have much bigger lawns than others, so it's really, really stupid to charge a flat rate.
5. Aspirin, sunscreen, mosquito repellent and gasoline all cost a lot of money, which eat into your profits.

[16 July|**02:31pm**]

[**mood**| cranky]

I just got back from putting up some more of my flyers at the supermarket. While I was there, I bought a Snickers, and nearly puked when I bit into it, because the filling was all green — like, bread-mold green. Then I looked closer and realized it was a leftover "Shrek the Third" tie-in Snickers. I don't know whose idea it was to make the inside of a Snickers look like snot, but it was a lousy way to advertise their movie.

SNICKERS
WITH GREEN SHREK FILLING BAR
NET WT 2.07 OZ
SHREK THE THIRD

[19 July|**7:22pm**]

[**mood**| sore-er!]

Argh. I was supposed to go to Six Flags with Chet today, but this morning I woke up too sore to even move. So instead, I stayed home and sat on the couch all day, taking aspirin and watching TV. At one point I dropped the remote behind the couch and it hurt too much to get up and reach for it, so I wound up having to sit there, watching all of "The Lake House" and half of "The Sisterhood of the Traveling Pants," before my parents came home. Now I know what Hell is like.

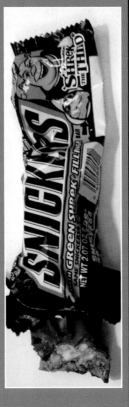

[22 July|**4:42pm**]

[**mood**| relieved]

So, today I went down to the supermarket to put up some of my flyers, and just as I got there, I saw a guy pulling down the ones I put up yesterday. I told him to stop, and he seemed sort of embarrassed, and said he was sorry, but he runs a lawn-mowing service, and I was really killing his business. I guess I charge only, like, one-third of what he does, so a lot of his customers went over to me.

I felt kind of bad for him, and then I thought of an idea: I don't like mowing lawns, and he doesn't like losing customers. So I told him that I'd give up my lawnmowing business, if he'd agree to pay me $10 for every lawn I didn't mow. He said that sounded fair to him. So now I work for Frank's Lawn Care as a lawn non-mower.

I may have the best summer job EVER.

WRITER: TIM CARVELL

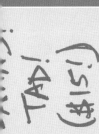

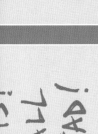

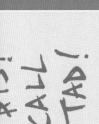

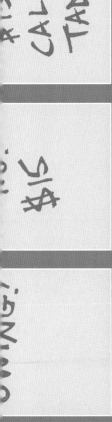

MAD'S GUIDE TO OUT-OF-BUSINESS Theme

The only theme we look for when eating out is fine dining in a relaxed atmosphere. But somewhere along the way somebody thought restaurant patrons would like to look at Rod Stewart's arch supports while chowing down, so The Hard Rock Cafe was born. Other theme restaurants followed, some going out of business faster than Ricki Lake going through an all-you-can-eat shrimp bar! The ones that tanked the fastest are catalogued in…

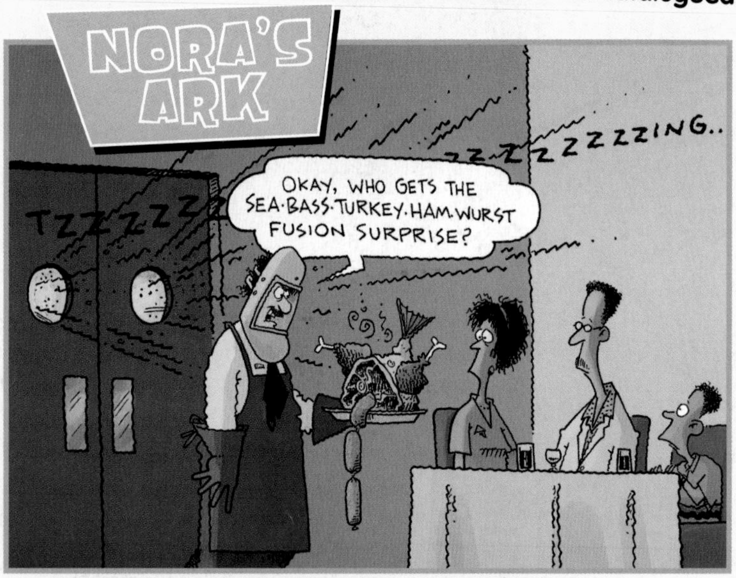
NORA'S ARK
TZZZZZ
ZZZZZZZZZING..
OKAY, WHO GETS THE SEA·BASS·TURKEY·HAM·WURST FUSION SURPRISE?

REASON FOR FAILURE…It turned out that welding is just not a theme conducive to fine dining

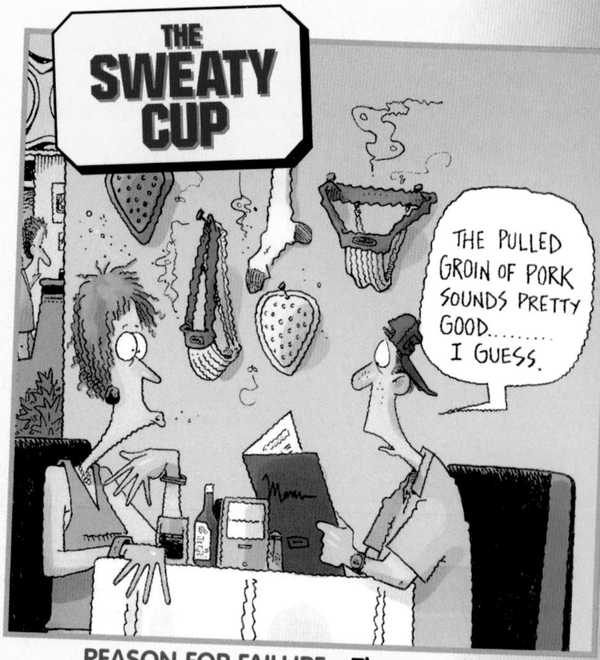
THE SWEATY CUP
THE PULLED GROIN OF PORK SOUNDS PRETTY GOOD........ I GUESS.

REASON FOR FAILURE…The so-called "Sports Memorabilia" adorning the walls left a lot to be desired

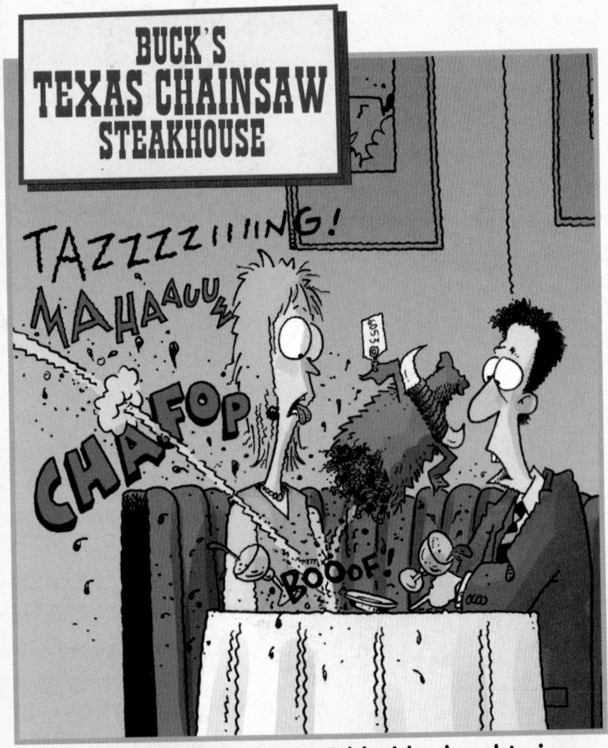
BUCK'S TEXAS CHAINSAW STEAKHOUSE
TAZZZZIIIING!
MAHAAUUW
CHAFOP
BOOOF!

REASON FOR FAILURE…Tableside slaughtering is not as romantic as it sounds

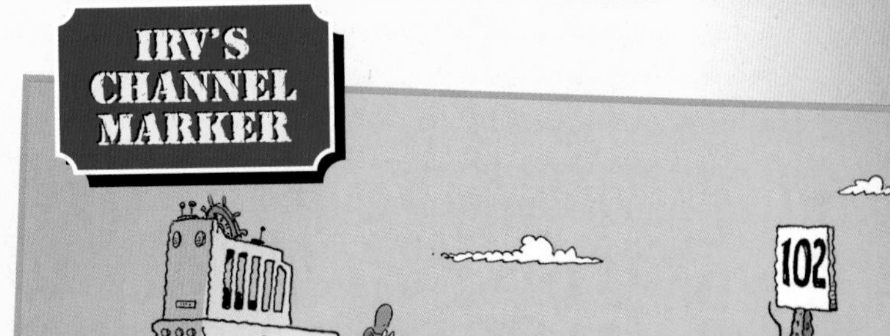
IRV'S CHANNEL MARKER
102
65039

REASON FOR FAILURE…Somehow, the innate charm of dining al fresco on a working buoy maintenance barge just never caught on

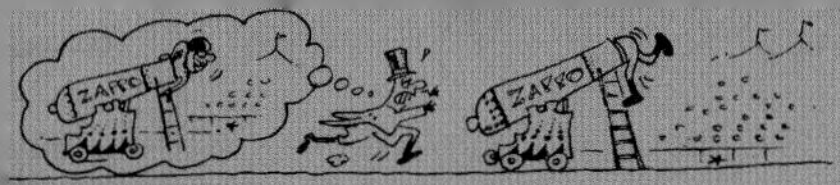

Restaurants ...AND THE REASON THEY WENT BELLY UP

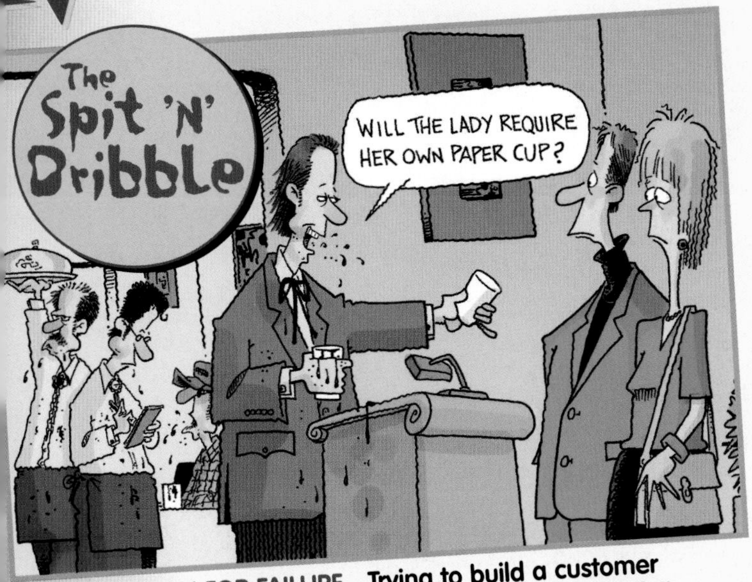
The Spit 'N' Dribble
WILL THE LADY REQUIRE HER OWN PAPER CUP?

REASON FOR FAILURE...Trying to build a customer base on the premise that they're a "Chaw Friendly" establishment was just a bad idea from the get-go

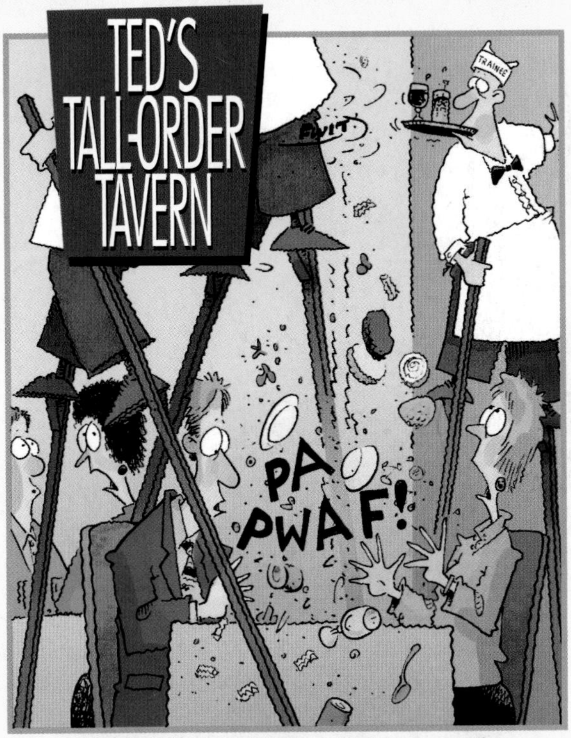
TED'S TALL-ORDER TAVERN
TRAINEE
PA
PWAF!

REASON FOR FAILURE...Waiters on stilts made some diners a bit uncomfortable

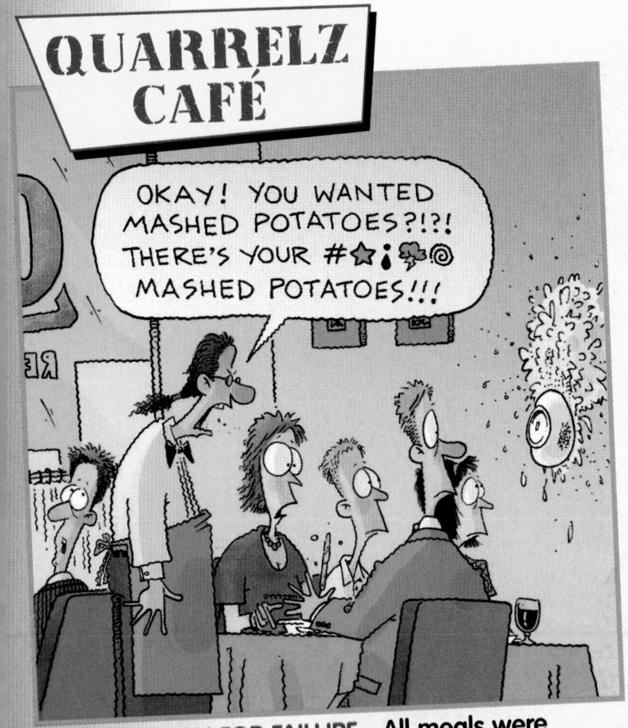
QUARRELZ CAFÉ
OKAY! YOU WANTED MASHED POTATOES?!?! THERE'S YOUR #✩¡✦◎ MASHED POTATOES!!!

REASON FOR FAILURE...All meals were served "Dysfunctional Family Style"

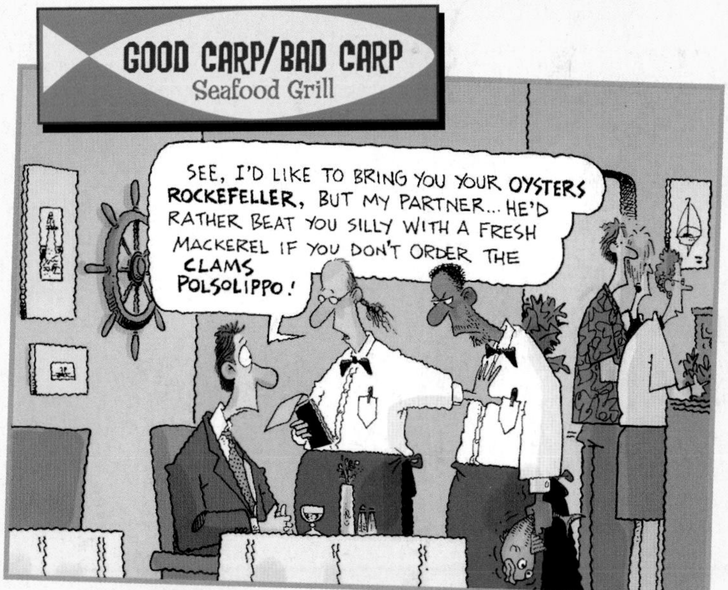
GOOD CARP/BAD CARP
Seafood Grill
SEE, I'D LIKE TO BRING YOU YOUR OYSTERS ROCKEFELLER, BUT MY PARTNER... HE'D RATHER BEAT YOU SILLY WITH A FRESH MACKEREL IF YOU DON'T ORDER THE CLAMS POLSOLIPPO!

REASON FOR FAILURE...The two-waiters-per-table experiment just didn't cut it

WRITER AND ARTIST: JOHN CALDWELL COLORIST: CARL PETERSON